McDougal Littell

**LITERATURE**

# ASSESSMENT FILE

## Unit and Benchmark Tests

ISBN-10: 0-618-90739-4

ISBN 978-0-618-90739-7



1 2 3 4 5 6 7 8 9 - MDO - 11 10 09 08 07

# Contents

## Unit Tests


Unit 1, A 3
Unit 1, B/C 15
Unit 2, A 27
Unit 2, B/C 39
Unit 3, A 51
Unit 3, B/C 63
Unit 4, A 75
Unit 4, B/C 87
Unit 5, A 99
Unit 5, B/C 111
Unit 6, A 123
Unit 6, B/C 135
Unit 7, A 147
Unit 7, B/C 159
Unit 8, A 171
Unit 8, B/C 183
Unit 9, A 195
Unit 9, B/C 207


## Benchmark Tests


Benchmark Test 1 221
Benchmark Test 2 246
Benchmark Test 3 271
Benchmark Test 4 296

# Contents

## Unit Tests


Unit 1, A 3
Unit 1, B/C 15
Unit 2, A 27
Unit 2, B/C 39
Unit 3, A 51
Unit 3, B/C 63
Unit 4, A 75
Unit 4, B/C 87
Unit 5, A 99
Unit 5, B/C 111
Unit 6, A 123
Unit 6, B/C 135
Unit 7, A 147
Unit 7, B/C 159
Unit 8, A 171
Unit 8, B/C 183
Unit 9, A 195
Unit 9, B/C 207

# Unit 1

TEST A

## Reading Comprehension

**Directions** Read the following selections. Then answer the questions that follow.

### *from* Banner in the Sky

**James Ramsey Ullman**

There was the sky. There was rock and ice. There was a mountain thrusting upward into blue emptiness—and at the foot of the mountain a tiny speck. This speck was the only thing that lived or moved in all that world of silent majesty.

Rudi climbed the white slope of the upper glacier. He did not hurry. He looked neither up at the peak nor down at the valley, but only at the ice flowing slowly past beneath his feet. In the ice were the marks of their boot nails from the previous day, and it was easy to follow the route. When the slope steepened, there were the steps cut by Winter and Saxo with their axes.

10 He had only to step up, balance briefly, step up again—and again.

With the step-cutting, it had required two hours to reach the *bergschrund.* Today it took him perhaps a third of that time. Coming out on the rim of the great crevasse, he approached the snow-bridge, tested it, and crossed without mishap. Then, still following the trail of the day before, he threaded his way through the steep maze of the icefall.

The seracs rose around him in frozen stillness. And Rudi's mind seemed frozen too. What he was doing was not a result of conscious choice or decision; it was simply what he *had* to do. He had not lost his senses. He knew that alone, and without food or a tent, there was no chance on earth of

20 his reaching the top of the Citadel. And it was not hope for the top that pushed him on. It was simply—well, he wasn't sure—perhaps simply the hope to set foot on the mountain. Or more than the hope. The need. The need of his body, his mind, his heart, to come at last to the place of which he had dreamed so long; to stand on the southeast ridge; to follow where his father had led; to climb, perhaps, even as high as the Fortress, which was as high as any man had gone. That was what he wanted; what he *had to have.* That much. Before it all ended. Before descending to the village; to his uncle's anger, his mother's tears, Klaus Wesselhoft's laughter; to the soap and mops and dishpans of the Beau Site Hotel.

30 He climbed on. The seracs slid past like tall hooded ghosts. And then they dropped away behind him and he came out at the base of the snowslope. Above him he could see a trail of zigzagging footprints, extending perhaps halfway to the ridge and disappearing into smooth drifts where the avalanche had erased them. The drifts were huge, billowing, dazzling in the sunlight; but he knew that they had frozen overnight and that the sun was not yet strong

enough to dislodge them. He shuffled his boots in the snow, and it was firm and dry. As Winter had said, the slope was safe in the morning.

Even so, he was cautious as he climbed upward, testing every step before trusting his weight to it. And when he came to the avalanche area he detoured
40 to the left and kept as close as possible to the bordering rock-wall, so that he would have something to cling to, just in case. . . . But nothing happened. The snow stayed as motionless as the rock. In all that spreading wilderness there was no movement except that of his own two legs plodding slowly on through the drifts.

And then—he stopped—then there *was* a movement. He felt it rather than saw it: the merest flicker or shadow, not on the slope, but on the cliff high above. He tensed, peering upward. . . . A stonefall? . . . No. There was no sound. And then again there was the flicker: a moving speck of reddish brown against the tall grayness of the rock. Suddenly it leapt into focus. It was
50 a chamois. For an instant it stood outlined on a crag, motionless, staring down at him; and Rudi, motionless too, stared back. Then the animal moved again—wheeled—vanished. It was as if the cliff had opened and swallowed it. And the stillness closed in again, even more absolute than before.

Rudi moved on. Through the stillness. Up the white slope. Kick—step, he went. Kick—step. Kick—step. And though the going through the deep drifts was slow, it was neither steep nor slippery, and his progress was steady. He looked back—and the icefall was far below; ahead—and the ridge loomed nearer. . . . Nearer. . . . And then at last the great moment came, and the slope was beneath him. There was no longer snow under his feet, but solid rock.
60 He took a step up—a second—a third . . . and stood on the southeast ridge of the Citadel.

## *from* To the Top of Everest

**Laurie Skreslet with Elizabeth MacLeod**

When I arrived back at Base Camp from Kunde, I was told the Icefall had been closed. I couldn't go through? Well, maybe—maybe not. I radioed Bill.

"Laurie, it's too dangerous. Stay in Base Camp!" Bill barked. "Do NOT—"

I flicked off the radio. That wasn't what I wanted to hear. After a year and a half of working on this expedition, I had too much energy invested to sit at the bottom of Everest. I'd gained a lot of experience in my years of climbing. I knew I could make an important contribution to the climbers struggling high on the mountain. It would all be wasted if I waited in Base Camp. So I took
10 the risk.

Next morning I shouldered my pack and set off. Base Camp had radioed Bill, and he did the only thing he could—he ordered that no one come with me. Bill also insisted that I radio Base Camp every time I crossed a crevasse. If I fell, I was still on my own—the radio call would just let them know where to find my body.

At first, the climb wasn't too bad—I'd done it many times before, and with a heavier pack. The route was in much worse shape than my last time there, three weeks before, but most ladders were usable. The Icefall was quiet and the wind light.

20 Then I came to a crevasse about 3.5 m (12 ft.) wide. There was a ladder across it, but the ice had shifted since it had been put in place. Now the bridge ended 1.5 m (5 ft.) from the far wall. On my side, the end of the ladder was frozen into the ice, but the other end hung 30 m (100 ft.) above the bottom of the crevasse.

No problem, I thought, I'll just find another place to cross.

For more than an hour, I searched desperately, but there was no other place. I had to admit defeat. Slowly, I started down to Base Camp.

Then I stopped. Did you give that your best? I asked myself.

Yes, I thought. But then I asked, Did you give it *more* than your best?

30 No, I had to answer. More than my best was to go back and jump from the ladder to the far side. I knew the impossible is often the untried. I couldn't leave without trying, so back I went.

I decided to use the handrail ropes that were still there, adding new anchors and Petzl ascenders pointing both forward and back. I figured I had a fifty—fifty chance of making it across.

The ladder bobbed up and down as I edged my way out. At the end of the ladder, I focused all my concentration—and jumped.

Thwack! My ice pick bit into the ice on the lip of the crevasse. It held. I

dug my crampons into the icy wall and used all my strength to pull myself
40 up.

As I lay gasping on the far side, I realized that something powerful had happened. I seemed to be seeing things differently—everything was clearer and colors more vivid. It was like a different world. In making that leap, I'd let go not only of the ladder, but of some of my fears, too. I knew then that things would work out for me as long as I kept giving more than my best.

As I climbed to Camp One and on toward Camp Two, I thought about Bill. What would happen when I had to explain face–to–face why I'd disobeyed his order to stay in Base Camp? Would he allow me to keep climbing?

50 He was right there when I arrived.

"Laurie!" Bill shouted. Then he smiled and said, "It's great you're here!"

"Huh?" I said, stunned by his good humor.

"Look," said Bill, "four people have died. If I'd asked you to come up and something had happened to you, I couldn't bear to have another death on my conscience. I had to tell you to stay put." Bill paused. "But I knew you'd come up no matter what. So, welcome. I need you here."

## COMPREHENSION

**Directions** Answer the following questions about the excerpt from *Banner in the Sky*.

**1.** The setting is a

**A.** cave **C.** river
**B.** desert **D.** mountain

**2.** Based on lines 01–04, you can make the inference that the *speck* is a

**A.** rock **C.** chamois
**B.** person **D.** snow drift

**3.** In lines 11–15, which words show chronological order?

**A.** Today, Then, day before
**B.** With, Today, day before
**C.** Today, following, way
**D.** Then, way, through

**4.** Rudi's conflict described in lines 16–29 is

**A.** rising **C.** external
**B.** internal **D.** falling

**5.** Based on lines 27–29, you can make the inference that Rudi works as a

**A.** repairman **C.** bellhop
**B.** hiking guide **D.** cleaner

**6.** The setting in lines 30–37 is a

**A.** snowslope **C.** rock-wall
**B.** crevasse **D.** ridge

**7.** Rudi stops climbing in lines 45–48 because he feels

**A.** a snow drift
**B.** something moving
**C.** an avalanche
**D.** the mountain top

**8.** The first event in lines 45–63 is that Rudi

**A.** reaches the Citadel
**B.** looks back at the icefall
**C.** takes a step up
**D.** sees the chamois

**9.** When Rudi reaches the Citadel, it is the story's

**A.** falling action **C.** exposition
**B.** conflict **D.** climax

## COMPREHENSION

**Directions** Answer the following questions about the excerpt from *To the Top of Everest.*

**10.** The first event in lines 01–05 of the excerpt is that Laurie

**A.** learns that the Icefall is closed
**B.** arrives back at Base Camp
**C.** radios Bill
**D.** climbs the mountain

**11.** The effect of the events in lines 01–02 is that Bill

**A.** tells Laurie to stay in Base Camp
**B.** offers advice for climbing
**C.** learns that Laurie is upset
**D.** reveals problems at Base Camp

**12.** Which of the following words from the excerpt are sequence clues?

**A.** "Next morning" **C.** "my pack"
**B.** "I shouldered" **D.** "set off"

**13.** According to the chronological order of events, Laurie had been on the same route

**A.** the morning before
**B.** three weeks earlier
**C.** last month
**D.** two years ago

**14.** The setting described in lines 20–24 is a

**A.** crevasse **C.** ledge
**B.** Base Camp **D.** ridge

**15.** Because he cannot cross the ladder bridge, Laurie

**A.** contacts Base Camp
**B.** sets up camp
**C.** looks for another crossing
**D.** makes a new bridge

**16.** The details in lines 46–49 are part of the story's

**A.** exposition **C.** climax
**B.** rising action **D.** falling action

## COMPREHENSION

**Directions** Answer these questions about both selections.

**17.** Based on the details in both selections, you can make the inference that Rudi and Laurie both feel that mountain climbing is

**A.** rewarding
**B.** easy
**C.** relaxing
**D.** graceful

**18.** How are the events of both selections organized?

**A.** compare and contrast
**B.** chronological order
**C.** cause and effect
**D.** main idea and details

**19.** Which of the following describes the conflict in both selections? "Man vs. Nature" describes which plot element of both selections?

**A.** animal vs. predator
**B.** human vs. nature
**C.** honesty vs. hard work
**D.** human vs. human

## Written Response

### SHORT RESPONSE

**Directions** Write two or three sentences to answer each question on a separate sheet of paper.

**20.** Identify the setting of *To the Top of Everest.* Provide two details from the text to support your answer.

**21.** Based on the information in both selections, you can make the inference that mountain climbers are determined. Provide one detail from each excerpt to support this inference.

### EXTENDED RESPONSE

**Directions** Answer the following question. Write two or more paragraphs on a separate sheet of paper.

**22.** Define the following plot stages: exposition, rising action, climax, falling action, and resolution. Then provide an example of each plot stage from *To the Top of Everest.*

## Vocabulary

**Directions** Use your knowledge of Latin word roots to answer the following questions.

**1.** The Latin word *appropiare* means "near." Which word in *Banner in the Sky* most likely comes from the word *appropiare*?

**A.** axes
**B.** approach
**C.** anger
**D.** avalanche

**2.** The Latin word *decidere* means "to decide." Which word in *Banner in the Sky* most likely comes from the word *decidere*?

**A.** descend
**B.** drifts
**C.** decision
**D.** dropped

**3.** The Latin word *experientia* means "act of trying." Which word in *To the Top of Everest* most likely comes from the word *experientia*?

**A.** experience
**B.** energy
**C.** Everest
**D.** edged

**Directions** Use your knowledge of prefixes and suffixes to answer the following questions. The line numbers will help you find the words in the excerpts.

**4.** The word *still* means "not moving." What is the most likely meaning of the suffix *-ness*, which is used to form *stillness* in line 16 of *Banner in the Sky*

**A.** skilled in
**B.** without
**C.** result
**D.** state of

**5.** The word *danger* means "exposure to harm or pain." What is the most likely meaning of the suffix *-ous*, which is used to form *dangerous* in line 3 of *To the Top of Everest*?

**A.** full of
**B.** the opposite of
**C.** result in
**D.** skilled in

**6.** The word *tried* means "attempted." What is the most likely meaning of the prefix *un-*, which is used to form *untried* in line 31 of *To the Top of Everest*?

**A.** with
**B.** again
**C.** not
**D.** apart

**Directions** Use your knowledge of analogies to complete each item.

**7.** Ditch is to canyon as hill is to

**A.** river
**B.** pile
**C.** sky
**D.** mountain

**8.** Dull is to bright as rough is to

**A.** smooth
**B.** hot
**C.** tall
**D.** bumpy

**9.** Safe is to dangerous as weak is to

**A.** clear
**B.** boring
**C.** silly
**D.** powerful

## Writing and Grammar

**Directions** Read the descriptive essay and answer the questions that follow.

(1) Located just 20 miles south of my hometown of Jamesville, Calton Canyon is one of the area's most beautiful features. (2) It is also my favorite place to go to escape from city life. (3) The canyon is not a desolate wilderness, though in fact, it is the most popular picnic spot around. (4) This is one of the reasons I love the canyon I like to see people enjoying nature as much as I enjoy it. (5) It is very relaxing to sit on the warm sandstone boulders and watch families and friends eat and play. (6) Children play tag and explore the canyon for interesting bugs or creatures. (7) Parents and grandparents place plastic silverware and cloth napkins on old, red picnic tables. (8) They take out juicy red apples, crisp carrot sticks, and crunchy potato chips for people to snack on.

(9) After the picnickers finish its fun, they often take walks. (10) Several scenic hiking trails snake through the canyons walls. (11) My favorite trail leads up onto a narrow ridge of the canyon. (12) On this trail, large boulders tower over hikers heads. (13) The trail loops through a wide, sweeping plain full of wild flowers. (14) Them are the most colorful flowers I have ever seen. (15) I am sure that each hiker on the trail wants to fill their pockets with the beautiful blooms! (16) I am just happy to look at the flowers and smell they, though. (17) Sometimes I lie down on the plain and take a nap. (18) The sweet smell of the flowers and the sound of the wind always relax me.

(19) After a great day of people-watching, hiking, and napping, I head home. (20) I tell my family about my adventures and any new people I meet. (21) My family agrees that no other place near Jamesville offers the same beauty and peace as Calton Canyon.

**1.** Sentence 1 identifies the essay's

**A.** conclusion
**B.** author
**C.** topic
**D.** organization

**2.** Which sentence explains why the topic is significant to the author?

**A.** sentence 2
**B.** sentence 5
**C.** sentence 8
**D.** sentence 12

**3.** What is the best way to correct sentence 3 so that it is no longer a run-on sentence?

**A.** The canyon is not a desolate wilderness, though. In fact, it is the most popular picnic spot in the area.
**B.** The canyon is not a desolate wilderness though in fact it is the most popular picnic spot in the area.
**C.** The canyon is not. A desolate wilderness. Though, in fact, it is the most popular picnic spot in the area.
**D.** The canyon, is not a desolate wilderness, though, in fact, it is the most popular, picnic spot in the area.

**4.** What is the best way to correct sentence 4 so that it is no longer a run-on sentence?

**A.** This, is one of the reasons, I love the canyon I like to see people, enjoying nature as much as I enjoy it.
**B.** This is one of the reasons I love the canyon. I like to see people enjoying nature as much as I enjoy it.
**C.** This is one of the reasons. I love the canyon I like to see people enjoying nature as much as I enjoy it.
**D.** This is one of the reasons, I love the canyon I like to see people. Enjoying nature as much as I enjoy it.

**5.** The words "warm sandstone boulders" in sentence 5 appeal to which of the following senses?

**A.** smell
**B.** hearing
**C.** touch
**D.** taste

**6.** To maintain pronoun-antecedent agreement in sentence 9, change "its" to

**A.** his
**B.** ours
**C.** their
**D.** her

**7.** Choose the correct way to write the possessive form of *canyons* in sentence 10.

**A.** canyons'
**B.** canyon's
**C.** canyon's'
**D.** canyons's

**8.** The words "narrow ridge" in sentence 11 appeal to which of the following senses?

**A.** hearing
**B.** taste
**C.** smell
**D.** sight

**9.** Choose the correct way to write the possessive form of *hikers* in sentence 12.

**A.** hiker's
**B.** hikers'
**C.** hiker's'
**D.** hikers's

**10.** To use the correct pronoun case in sentence 14, change "Them" to

**A.** They
**B.** Theirs
**C.** It
**D.** She

**11.** To maintain pronoun-antecedent agreement in sentence 15, change "their" to

**A.** us
**B.** my's
**C.** his or her
**D.** thems

**12.** To use the correct pronoun case in sentence 16, change "they" to

**A.** its
**B.** him's
**C.** them
**D.** we

## Writing

**Directions** Read the following quotation. Then read the prompt that follows and complete the writing activity.

> "[The writer] appeals through the senses, and you cannot appeal to the senses with abstractions."
>
> Flannery O'Connor

**Prompt:** Write a descriptive essay about a room in your home that is important to you. First, think about all of the things that make the room special. What sights, sounds, smells, tastes, and feelings do you experience in this room? Then, as the author of the quotation suggests, use specific sensory details to bring the room to life.

Now write your essay. Use the reminders that follow to help you write.

**Reminders**

- Be sure your writing does what the prompt asks.
- Identify why the room is significant.
- Use transitions to connect ideas.
- Use specific sensory details to bring the room to life.
- Check for correct grammar, spelling, and punctuation.

## Reading Comprehension

**Directions** Read the following selections. Then answer the questions that follow.

### *from* Banner in the Sky

**James Ramsey Ullman**

There was the sky. There was rock and ice. There was a mountain thrusting upward into blue emptiness—and at the foot of the mountain a tiny speck. This speck was the only thing that lived or moved in all that world of silent majesty.

Rudi climbed the white slope of the upper glacier. He did not hurry. He looked neither up at the peak nor down at the valley, but only at the ice flowing slowly past beneath his feet. In the ice were the marks of their boot nails from the previous day, and it was easy to follow the route. When the slope steepened, there were the steps cut by Winter and Saxo with their axes. 10 He had only to step up, balance briefly, step up again—and again.

With the step-cutting, it had required two hours to reach the *bergschrund*. Today it took him perhaps a third of that time. Coming out on the rim of the great crevasse, he approached the snow-bridge, tested it, and crossed without mishap. Then, still following the trail of the day before, he threaded his way through the steep maze of the icefall.

The seracs rose around him in frozen stillness. And Rudi's mind seemed frozen too. What he was doing was not a result of conscious choice or decision; it was simply what he *had* to do. He had not lost his senses. He knew that alone, and without food or a tent, there was no chance on earth of 20 his reaching the top of the Citadel. And it was not hope for the top that pushed him on. It was simply—well, he wasn't sure—perhaps simply the hope to set foot on the mountain. Or more than the hope. The need. The need of his body, his mind, his heart, to come at last to the place of which he had dreamed so long; to stand on the southeast ridge; to follow where his father had led; to climb, perhaps, even as high as the Fortress, which was as high as any man had gone. That was what he wanted; what he *had to have*. That much. Before it all ended. Before descending to the village; to his uncle's anger, his mother's tears, Klaus Wesselhoft's laughter; to the soap and mops and dishpans of the Beau Site Hotel.

30 He climbed on. The seracs slid past like tall hooded ghosts. And then they dropped away behind him and he came out at the base of the snowslope. Above him he could see a trail of zigzagging footprints, extending perhaps halfway to the ridge and disappearing into smooth drifts where the avalanche had erased them. The drifts were huge, billowing, dazzling in the sunlight; but he knew that they had frozen overnight and that the sun was not yet strong

enough to dislodge them. He shuffled his boots in the snow, and it was firm and dry. As Winter had said, the slope was safe in the morning.

Even so, he was cautious as he climbed upward, testing every step before trusting his weight to it. And when he came to the avalanche area he detoured 40 to the left and kept as close as possible to the bordering rock-wall, so that he would have something to cling to, just in case. . . . But nothing happened. The snow stayed as motionless as the rock. In all that spreading wilderness there was no movement except that of his own two legs plodding slowly on through the drifts.

And then—he stopped—then there *was* a movement. He felt it rather than saw it: the merest flicker or shadow, not on the slope, but on the cliff high above. He tensed, peering upward. . . . A stonefall? . . . No. There was no sound. And then again there was the flicker: a moving speck of reddish brown against the tall grayness of the rock. Suddenly it leapt into focus. It was 50 a chamois. For an instant it stood outlined on a crag, motionless, staring down at him; and Rudi, motionless too, stared back. Then the animal moved again—wheeled—vanished. It was as if the cliff had opened and swallowed it. And the stillness closed in again, even more absolute than before.

Rudi moved on. Through the stillness. Up the white slope. Kick—step, he went. Kick—step. Kick—step. And though the going through the deep drifts was slow, it was neither steep nor slippery, and his progress was steady. He looked back—and the icefall was far below; ahead—and the ridge loomed nearer. . . . Nearer. . . . And then at last the great moment came, and the slope was beneath him. There was no longer snow under his feet, but solid rock. 60 He took a step up—a second—a third . . . and stood on the southeast ridge of the Citadel.

## *from* To the Top of Everest

**Laurie Skreslet with Elizabeth MacLeod**

When I arrived back at Base Camp from Kunde, I was told the Icefall had been closed. I couldn't go through? Well, maybe—maybe not. I radioed Bill.

"Laurie, it's too dangerous. Stay in Base Camp!" Bill barked. "Do NOT—"

I flicked off the radio. That wasn't what I wanted to hear. After a year and a half of working on this expedition, I had too much energy invested to sit at the bottom of Everest. I'd gained a lot of experience in my years of climbing. I knew I could make an important contribution to the climbers struggling high on the mountain. It would all be wasted if I waited in Base Camp. So I took
10 the risk.

Next morning I shouldered my pack and set off. Base Camp had radioed Bill, and he did the only thing he could—he ordered that no one come with me. Bill also insisted that I radio Base Camp every time I crossed a crevasse. If I fell, I was still on my own—the radio call would just let them know where to find my body.

At first, the climb wasn't too bad—I'd done it many times before, and with a heavier pack. The route was in much worse shape than my last time there, three weeks before, but most ladders were usable. The Icefall was quiet and the wind light.

20 Then I came to a crevasse about 3.5 m (12 ft.) wide. There was a ladder across it, but the ice had shifted since it had been put in place. Now the bridge ended 1.5 m (5 ft.) from the far wall. On my side, the end of the ladder was frozen into the ice, but the other end hung 30 m (100 ft.) above the bottom of the crevasse.

No problem, I thought, I'll just find another place to cross.

For more than an hour, I searched desperately, but there was no other place. I had to admit defeat. Slowly, I started down to Base Camp.

Then I stopped. Did you give that your best? I asked myself.

Yes, I thought. But then I asked, Did you give it *more* than your best?

30 No, I had to answer. More than my best was to go back and jump from the ladder to the far side. I knew the impossible is often the untried. I couldn't leave without trying, so back I went.

I decided to use the handrail ropes that were still there, adding new anchors and Petzl ascenders pointing both forward and back. I figured I had a fifty–fifty chance of making it across.

The ladder bobbed up and down as I edged my way out. At the end of the ladder, I focused all my concentration—and jumped.

Thwack! My ice pick bit into the ice on the lip of the crevasse. It held. I

dug my crampons into the icy wall and used all my strength to pull myself
40 up.

As I lay gasping on the far side, I realized that something powerful had happened. I seemed to be seeing things differently—everything was clearer and colors more vivid. It was like a different world. In making that leap, I'd let go not only of the ladder, but of some of my fears, too. I knew then that things would work out for me as long as I kept giving more than my best.

As I climbed to Camp One and on toward Camp Two, I thought about Bill. What would happen when I had to explain face–to–face why I'd disobeyed his order to stay in Base Camp? Would he allow me to keep climbing?

50 He was right there when I arrived.

"Laurie!" Bill shouted. Then he smiled and said, "It's great you're here!"

"Huh?" I said, stunned by his good humor.

"Look," said Bill, "four people have died. If I'd asked you to come up and something had happened to you, I couldn't bear to have another death on my conscience. I had to tell you to stay put." Bill paused. "But I knew you'd come up no matter what. So, welcome. I need you here."



## COMPREHENSION

**Directions** Answer the following questions about the excerpt from *Banner in the Sky*.

**1.** The main setting of the excerpt is a

**A.** windy seaside cliff
**B.** warm grassy meadow
**C.** peaceful river valley
**D.** rugged mountain slope

**2.** Based on lines 4–13, you can make the inference that Rudi

**A.** wishes Winter and Saxo were with him
**B.** is a patient mountain climber
**C.** climbs with great speed and strength
**D.** is extremely tired and wants to rest

**3.** According to the chronological order of the excerpt, when does Rudi cross the snow bridge?

**A.** before climbing the upper glacier
**B.** after entering the icefall maze
**C.** after coming out on the crevasse rim
**D.** before climbing the ice steps

**4.** Rudi experiences an external conflict with

**A.** the mountain
**B.** himself
**C.** Winter
**D.** the seracs

**5.** Based on lines 19–25, you can make the inference that Rudi

**A.** wishes that he had friends
**B.** misses his mother and his uncle
**C.** wants to leave his village
**D.** dislikes his job at the Beau Site Hotel

**6.** According to the chronological order of lines 26–32, the last thing that Rudi does is

**A.** shuffle his boots in the snow
**B.** look at the zigzagging footprints
**C.** move past the base of the snowslope
**D.** gaze at the passing seracs

**7.** Rudi stays close to the rock-wall as he climbs because he is afraid of

**A.** sliding down a snow drift
**B.** being swept away by an avalanche
**C.** slipping on the rocks
**D.** being hit by falling rocks

**8.** In lines 39–46, the first event that takes place is that Rudi

**A.** tenses with fear
**B.** stares at the chamois
**C.** peers upward
**D.** stops climbing

**9.** The climax occurs when Rudi

**A.** crosses the snow-bridge
**B.** clings to the rock-wall
**C.** sees the chamois
**D.** reaches the Citadel

## COMPREHENSION

**Directions** Answer the following questions about the excerpt from *To the Top of Everest.*

**10.** Laurie turns off the radio at the beginning of the excerpt because he

**A.** dislikes Bill's message
**B.** wishes Bill was in Base Camp
**C.** wants to talk to Bill in person
**D.** thinks that Bill is done speaking

**11.** Which sequence words tell you when Laurie leaves Base Camp?

**A.** "Next morning"
**B.** "At first"
**C.** "Then"
**D.** "After a year and a half"

**12.** According to the chronological order of events, Base Camp radios Bill

**A.** one day before Laurie fills his pack
**B.** before Laurie sets off
**C.** two hours after Laurie leaves
**D.** after Laurie reaches the first crevasse

**13.** The descriptions of setting in lines 16–19 are part of the story's

**A.** rising action
**B.** climax
**C.** falling action
**D.** resolution

**14.** What event causes Laurie to look for another place to cross the crevasse?

**A.** Bill tells him to find a new bridge.
**B.** The crevasse is too wide.
**C.** Laurie thinks the ice is too soft.
**D.** The ladder bridge is too short.

**15.** The first event in lines 31–44 is that Laurie

**A.** jumps across the crevasse
**B.** edges out onto the ladder
**C.** reaches Camp One and Camp Two
**D.** talks to Bill face-to-face

**16.** The effect of Laurie's leap across the crevasse is that he

**A.** realizes that good things will happen if he gives more than his best
**B.** learns to take chances because sometimes you get lucky
**C.** decides that he wants to teach others how to climb Mt. Everest
**D.** wishes Bill were there to share the moment with him

## COMPREHENSION

**Directions** Answer these questions about both selections.

**17.** The exposition in both selections hints at a conflict between a person and

**A.** an authority figure
**B.** a mountain
**C.** his family members
**D.** himself

**18.** The setting of both selections is a

**A.** snow drift
**B.** crevasse
**C.** mountain
**D.** ridge

**19.** You can make the inference that Rudi from *Banner in the Sky* and Laurie from *To the Top of Everest* both

**A.** think that mountain climbing is a rewarding experience
**B.** think that Mt. Everest is the hardest mountain to climb
**C.** wish they had company while mountain climbing
**D.** respect the wishes of family members and friends

## Written Response

### SHORT RESPONSE

**Directions** Write two or three sentences to answer each question on a separate sheet of paper.

**20.** What internal conflict is shared by Rudi in *Banner in the Sky* and Laurie in *To the Top of Everest*? Provide a detail from each selection to support your answer.

**21.** Identify the falling action and the resolution of *To the Top of Everest.* Support each answer with one example from the selection.

### EXTENDED RESPONSE

**Directions** Answer one of the following questions. Write two or more paragraphs on a separate sheet of paper.

**22.** How does the setting contribute to the plot in *Banner in the Sky* and *To the Top of Everest*? Use details from the selections to support your answer.

**23. Challenge** *To the Top of Everest* contains an external conflict and an internal conflict. Which conflict is more important to the plot? Use details from the selection to support your answer.

## Vocabulary

**Directions** Use your knowledge of Latin word roots to answer the following questions.

**1.** The Latin word *prae* means "in front of" or "before." Which word in *Banner in the Sky* most likely comes from the word *prae*?

**A.** speck **C.** upper
**B.** mountain **D.** previous

**2.** The Latin word *scire* means "to know." Which word in *Banner in the Sky* most likely comes from the word *scire*?

**A.** conscious **C.** detoured
**B.** mind **D.** simply

**3.** The Latin word *insistere* means "to persist." Which word in *To the Top of Everest* most likely comes from the word *insistere*?

**A.** heavier **C.** insisted
**B.** crevasse **D.** arrived

**Directions** Use your knowledge of prefixes and suffixes to answer the following questions. The line numbers will help you find the words in the excerpts.

**4.** The word *brief* means "short." What is the most likely meaning of the suffix *-ly*, which is used to form *briefly* in line 10 of *Banner in the Sky*?

**A.** capable of **C.** concrete result
**B.** in a certain way **D.** skilled in

**5.** The word *obeyed* means "followed commands." What is the most likely meaning of the prefix *dis-*, which is used to form *disobeyed* in line 48 of *To the Top of Everest*?

**A.** under **C.** not
**B.** again **D.** without

**6.** Which suffix can be added to the noun *humor* in line 52 of *To the Top of Everest* to form an adjective that means "not having humor"?

**A.** -less **C.** -ness
**B.** -ly **D.** -able

**Directions** Use your knowledge of analogies to complete each item.

**7.** Destruction is to creation as despair is to

**A.** dreamed **C.** wanted
**B.** hope **D.** majesty

**8.** Friendly is to reserved as movement is to

**A.** stillness **C.** statue
**B.** dance **D.** quietly

**9.** Slow is to sluggish as bright is to

**A.** peaceful **C.** hilarious
**B.** calm **D.** vivid

## Writing and Grammar

**Directions** Read the descriptive essay and answer the questions that follow.

(1) Located just 20 miles south of my hometown of Jamesville, Calton Canyon is one of the area's most beautiful features. (2) It is also my favorite place to go to escape from city life. (3) The canyon is not a desolate wilderness, though in fact, it is the most popular picnic spot around. (4) This is one of the reasons I love the canyon I like to see people enjoying nature as much as I enjoy it. (5) It is very relaxing to sit on the warm sandstone boulders and watch families and friends eat and play. (6) Children play tag and explore the canyon for interesting bugs or creatures. (7) Parents and grandparents place plastic silverware and cloth napkins on old, red picnic tables. (8) They take out juicy red apples, crisp carrot sticks, and crunchy potato chips for people to snack on.

(9) After the picnickers finish its fun, they often take walks. (10) Several scenic hiking trails snake through the canyons walls. (11) My favorite trail leads up onto a narrow ridge of the canyon. (12) On this trail, large boulders tower over hikers heads. (13) The trail loops through a wide, sweeping plain full of wild flowers. (14) Them are the most colorful flowers I have ever seen. (15) I am sure that each hiker on the trail wants to fill their pockets with the beautiful blooms! (16) I am just happy to look at the flowers and smell they, though. (17) Sometimes I lie down on the plain and take a nap. (18) The sweet smell of the flowers and the sound of the wind always relax me.

(19) After a great day of people-watching, hiking, and napping, I head home. (20) I tell my family about my adventures and any new people I meet. (21) My family agrees that no other place near Jamesville offers the same beauty and peace as Calton Canyon.

**1.** In sentence 1, the author identifies the topic as

**A.** Calton Canyon
**B.** beauty in nature
**C.** Jamesville
**D.** hometown cities

**2.** Why is the topic of the essay significant to the author?

**A.** The author believes that everyone should appreciate the beauty of nature.
**B.** Calton Canyon is the author's favorite place to go to escape from the city.
**C.** Jamesville is more important to the author than anywhere else in the world.
**D.** The author must decide whether to stay in Jamesville or move to Calton Canyon.

**3.** Choose the correct way to rewrite sentence 3 so that it is no longer a run-on sentence.

**A.** The canyon is not a desolate wilderness, though in fact: It is the most popular picnic spot in the area.
**B.** The canyon is not a desolate wilderness; though, in fact, it is the most popular picnic spot in the area.
**C.** The canyon is not a desolate wilderness, though. In fact, it is the most popular picnic spot in the area.
**D.** The canyon is not a desolate wilderness, though, in fact it is the most popular picnic spot in the area.

**4.** Choose the correct way to rewrite sentence 4 so that it is no longer a run-on sentence.

**A.** This is one of the reasons I love the canyon. I like to see people enjoying nature as much as I enjoy it.
**B.** This is one of the reasons I love the canyon, I like to see people enjoying nature as much as I enjoy it.
**C.** This is one of the reasons. I love the canyon I like to see people enjoying nature as much as I enjoy it.
**D.** This is one of the reasons, I love the canyon I like to see people enjoying nature as much as I enjoy it.

**5.** Which of the following sentences contains the most sensory details?

**A.** sentence 2
**B.** sentence 8
**C.** sentence 16
**D.** sentence 19

**6.** Choose the correct way to maintain pronoun-antecedent agreement in sentence 9.

**A.** After the picnickers finish our fun, they often take walks.
**B.** After the picnickers finish its fun, them often take walks.
**C.** After the picnickers finish their fun, they often take walks.
**D.** After the picnickers finish its fun, us often take walks.

**7.** Choose the correct way to write the possessive form of *canyons* in sentence 10.

**A.** canyons'
**B.** canyon's
**C.** canyon's'
**D.** canyons's

**8.** Which words in sentence 11 contain sensory details?

**A.** favorite trail
**B.** onto a
**C.** narrow ridge
**D.** the canyon

**9.** Choose the correct way to write the possessive form of *hikers* in sentence 12.

**A.** hiker's
**B.** hikers'
**C.** hiker's'
**D.** hikers's

**10.** Choose the correct way to correct the pronoun case in sentence 14.

**A.** Their are the most colorful flowers I have ever seen.
**B.** Them are the most colorful flowers me have ever seen.
**C.** They are the most colorful flowers I have ever seen.
**D.** Them are the most colorful flowers me have ever seen.

**11.** To maintain pronoun-antecedent agreement in sentence 15, change "their" to

**A.** us
**B.** my
**C.** them
**D.** his or her

**12.** To use the correct pronoun case in sentence 16, change "they" to

**A.** it
**B.** him
**C.** them
**D.** we

## Writing

**Directions** Read the following quotation. Then read the prompts that follow and complete one of the writing activities.

> "[The writer] appeals through the senses, and you cannot appeal to the senses with abstractions."
>
> Flannery O'Connor

**Prompt:** Write a descriptive essay about a place in your home that is important to you. Bring the place to life, as O'Connor suggests, by appealing to the reader with sensory details. What sights, sounds, smells, tastes, and feelings do you experience in this special place? Why are these details significant?

Now write your essay. Use the reminders that follow to help you write.

**Challenge Prompt:** Write a descriptive essay that explores the ways in which our senses help determine our favorite places. Begin by choosing a place in your home of which you are especially fond. As suggested in O'Connor's quotation, use vivid sensory details to engage your readers. Analyze why the appeal to your senses makes the place more important to you than other places are.

Now write your essay. Use the reminders that follow to help you write.

**Reminders**

- Be sure your writing does what the prompt asks.
- Identify why the place is significant.
- Use transitions to connect ideas.
- Use specific sensory details to bring the room to life.
- Check for correct grammar, spelling, and punctuation.

# Unit 2

**TEST A**

## Reading Comprehension

**Directions** Read the following selections. Then answer the questions that follow.

### *from* Break a Leg

**Joel Schwartz**

I wouldn't have gone to the "Getting to Know You" dance at school if it hadn't been for my father. He wouldn't have talked to me about it if it hadn't been for my mother. She wouldn't have talked to him about it if it hadn't been for my best friend Myron's mother. My best friend's mother wouldn't have talked to my mother about it if it hadn't been for my best friend. Myron wouldn't have talked to his mother about it if I hadn't talked to him about it, so I guess I'm to blame for everything.

It's not that I don't like dances and it's certainly not that I don't like girls. It's just that, well, all the twelve-year-old girls in the world are much taller than all 10 the twelve-year-old boys. I wouldn't mind having to look at them straight in the eye, but having to look up all the time is embarrassing and it hurts my neck too. When you dance with a girl, they are supposed to be able to put their head on your shoulder, not their chin on your head.

So when Myron asked me at lunch, "Are you going to the 'Getting to Know You' dance?"

I said, "Are you kidding? Nobody's going to that dance."

Myron took a giant bite of his sandwich and said, "Emrymoday ish gowig."

"Every Monday, what did you say?" I asked.

20 Myron wiped a large glob of mustard off his chin with his sleeve. "I said, everybody I know is going." Myron looked at the glob of mustard that now decorated his sleeve and without hesitation ground it into his pants. "Everybody, that is, except you."

I stared down at the spot on Myron's pants and then up at a new glob on his chin. At this rate, by the end of lunch, he would be wearing palomino-colored pants and a white shirt with gold cuffs. "Name one person who's going."

"Me!"

"Besides you."

"Todd Murray."

30 "Mr. Murray, our math teacher?" Myron nodded. "He has to go. He's the chaperon. Besides, teachers don't count."

"Come on, go." I shook my head no. "For me?" I shook my head no again. "Why not?" This time the mustard had migrated up both cheeks.

"Why do you use so much mustard on your sandwich?" I asked, purposely changing the subject.

"Because I hate the taste of the meat," replied Myron.

"If you hate the taste of the meat so much, why don't you put a different kind of meat on your sandwich?"

"If I put on the meat that I liked, I wouldn't put on any mustard, and I like
40 mustard on my sandwich." I stood up to go. "Not so fast. Why won't you go to the dance? Are you too chicken to go?"

"I don't want to talk about it anymore," I replied. "Finish eating your mustard sandwich and have a good time at the dance. You can tell me about it on Monday."

I thought I had heard the last of it, but after dinner that night my father asked me to go into the den because he wanted to talk to me about something. This usually means I've done something wrong and my mother has delegated my father to handle it.

"I've cleaned up my room," I said. "I did all my homework. I'll read a
50 book for half an hour before I go to sleep, and I took out the trash."

My father smiled."Why aren't you going to the 'Getting to Know You' dance?"

"How do you know that?" I asked.

"Your mother was talking to Myron's mother and—"

"I don't want to go, that's all. What's the big deal?"

My father lit his pipe and leaned back in his chair. This usually meant he was going to tell me a story about himself when he was my age. "When I was your age and just starting seventh grade like you, my school had a 'Getting to Know You' dance too, and I didn't want to go either. My dad sat me down, just
60 like this, and said to me, 'I'll bet you're a little afraid to go to the dance.' 'Afraid?' I replied. 'I'm not afraid of any school dance.' 'Not of the dance,' he continued, 'but of the girls. Girls can be scary at your age. They act like they feel more comfortable in social situations than boys, but they're just as scared as you are. Go to the dance, act like you know what you're doing, and I'll bet you'll have a good time.' I didn't want to admit it then, but what your grandfather said to me that day made sense and I decided to go to the dance. The night of the dance my father drove me to the school and as I got out of the car he said 'Break a leg.' That's an expression actors use when they want to wish another actor good luck on the night of a performance. I think he did that purposely because he knew I'd
70 have to be a good actor that night to hide my nervousness. I was nervous that night, but I covered it well and I ended up having a great time. Think about it."

I sat by myself in the den for a long time after Dad left and thought about what he just said. Usually what Dad says is either dumb or old-fashioned. This time he surprised me with something right on. Was he getting smarter?

After I called Myron and told him I had decided to go to the dance I spent half of the next twenty-four hours in and out of the bathroom. It was certainly a local record and probably a national and international one too. I could see myself in the Guinness Book of World Records for Most Trips in One Day to the Bathroom Without Actually Doing Anything.

80 I hardly ate dinner. After showering I smoothed on a manly hair gel, splashed on a mentholly after-shave, and sprayed on a musky deodorant. I smelled muskmantholly magnificent. I almost got out of the house with my old sneakers, but my mom made me go back and put on my new slippery loafers.

My father drove Myron and me to the dance. "Break a leg," he yelled as I got out of the car.

"What's that all about?" asked Myron.

"Who knows," I replied. "Probably some weird expression he picked up when he was my age."

## *from* Come a Stranger

**Cynthia Voigt**

Mina's heart was beating so fast, and so hard, she thought for sure it must show, thumping away under her blouse. Her father was driving slowly through the city of New London and then, slowly, up the river road. They had been riding for hours, without talking much, and Mina had made herself be patient. But now they were so close, and the car was going so slowly, waiting to turn and enter between the stone pillars and creeping up the road to the quadrangle.

When the car finally stopped, Mina burst out and took her suitcase from the back seat. Her father greeted Miss Maddinton. They talked about nothing in particular. Mina looked at her sneakers and felt her heart, beating.

10 It all soaked into her skin, and that was enough for now. If she looked around, at the stone buildings and trees, at all the familiar remembered places, she would start running around to touch everything, and her father would know-he'd know for sure what he'd only guessed, that she was gladder to be back at camp than anywhere else, that she could barely wait for him to leave so she could be by herself and be her own self again. She didn't want to hurt her father's feelings by letting him know that, so she stood there with her eyes closed, being there.

At last, he started to leave."Have a good time, Mina." He hugged her close and she hugged him back, her head almost up to his shoulder now. "Behave yourself."

"I will. Have a good summer, Dad."

20 She made herself stand and wave while the car drove away, a dusty black sedan with the Maryland license plate a little white square. Then she turned slowly around, and smiled.

"You're in room three-o-seven," Miss Maddinton said to her, consulting a list she had on her clipboard. She was wearing a silvery gray suit; her hair was in dark braids that she'd wound around her head like a corona. She looked busy, she looked distant and calm, she looked beautiful.

Mina was back where there was music around everywhere, every day. She was back where if you said Prokofiev, nobody said, "Who?"

"You've grown," Miss Maddinton said, sounding doubtful, looking doubtful.

30 What did she expect Mina to do? Not grow? Mina laughed out loud. "I guess. My mom says I've been shooting up and shooting out."

"You can find your own way, can't you? I've got to greet the new girls."

"Three-o-seven?" Mina asked, not that she didn't remember, but just to savor this first minute a little longer. "Is Tansy here yet?"

"She's up there," Miss Maddinton said.

At that, Mina couldn't wait another minute. She grabbed her suitcase and hurrying as fast as she could with the heavy case banging against her leg went into the dormitory, went home.

Room 307 was on the third floor. The second floor was for the littlest girls, the
40 top floor for the fourteen year olds. Mina climbed two flights of stairs and pushed through the heavy door onto the corridor. She heard voices, she heard music. Looking at the numbers painted on the doors, she went on down the hall. Her feet wanted to jump and run, her heart wanted to stop it all from going by so fast already. Room 307 was down toward the far end of the corridor. The door was open, but no music came out. Mina guessed Tansy was probably in somebody else's room, visiting.

But the room had only one bed in it. The room was too small for two beds anyway. The room was a single room.

Mina put her suitcase down on the floor and sat on the bed. For a long minute
50 her mind was empty-blank and silent, a cold white emptiness. Then she understood.

They were seeing the outside of her.

Because nobody, not even Tansy, had wanted to be her roommate. So the adults had put her into a single room too.

Mina got up and set her suitcase on the bed. She unpacked her clothes into the dresser, then made up the bed and thought. She just hadn't understood, she guessed; but as soon as she thought that she knew she was wrong. They had all been friends, they had all gotten along just fine. It was what her father had said, though, what he had noticed right away when he picked her up: She was
60 the only little black girl there.



## COMPREHENSION

**Directions** Answer the following questions about the excerpt from "Break a Leg."

**1.** Which of the following words best describes the narrator?

**A.** quiet **C.** orgetful
**B.** funny **D.** orgetful

**2.** Which of the following words from lines 1–6 shows that the excerpt is told from the first-person point of view?

**A.** I **C.** father
**B.** it **D.** Myron

**3.** Which of the following lines helps you visualize the conversation between the narrator and Myron?

**A.** line 15 **C.** line 27
**B.** line 21 **D.** line 33

**4.** Reread lines 41–49. Which detail helps you predict that the narrator will not get in trouble?

**A.** He has done all his homework.
**B.** His father wants to talk to him.
**C.** His father smiles at him.
**D.** He eats dinner with his family.

**5.** Based on the narrator's comments in lines 41–49, you can infer that he

**A.** rarely goes to bed on time
**B.** is lying about the trash
**C.** is on the honor roll
**D.** often gets in trouble

**6.** Based on the father's words in lines 50–64, you can infer that the father wants the narrator to

**A.** stay home so they can talk further
**B.** make his own decision
**C.** do what everyone else is doing
**D.** go to the dance for Myron

**7.** You can predict that the narrator will go to the dance because the

**A.** narrator thinks his dad has gotten smarter
**B.** narrator says he does not want to go
**C.** father leans back in his chair
**D.** father once hid his own nervousness

**8.** The narrator's character is shown in lines 65–67 by

**A.** the words of others
**B.** his own actions
**C.** his physical appearance
**D.** his own thoughts

**9.** Which of the following words best describes the narrator in lines 68–72?

**A.** nervous
**B.** bored
**C.** mischievous
**D.** tired

**10.** You know that the excerpt is told from the first-person point of view because the narrator

**A.** has a good sense of humor
**B.** is the father
**C.** is a character in the story
**D.** has anxiety

**COMPREHENSION**

**Directions** Answer the following questions about the excerpt from *Come a Stranger*.

**11.** You know that the excerpt is told from the third-person limited point of view because the narrator is

**A.** one of the kids at camp
**B.** the camp counselor
**C.** not in the story
**D.** at a place that she loves

**12.** Which detail in lines 1–6 helps you infer that Mina is excited?

**A.** Mina's heart is beating fast.
**B.** Mina's father drives slowly.
**C.** They drive through New London.
**D.** The car passes through two pillars.

**13.** Lines 15–16 reveal Mina's

**A.** playfulness
**B.** bravery
**C.** consideration
**D.** open-mindedness

**14.** The details in lines 24–26 help you visualize Miss Maddinton's

**A.** family
**B.** friends
**C.** surroundings
**D.** appearance

**15.** Lines 36–38 show that Mina is excited by describing her

**A.** actions
**B.** dreams
**C.** speech
**D.** appearance

**16.** Line 50 helps you predict that there is something different about the way Mina

**A.** talks
**B.** looks
**C.** laughs
**D.** runs

**17.** At the end of the excerpt, which of the following conclusions can you draw?

**A.** Mina's father wanted her to stay in her own room.
**B.** Mina's feelings about the camp have changed.
**C.** Tansy is upset because Mina did not write to her.
**D.** Mina is excited that she gets her own room.

**18.** At the end of the excerpt, what conclusion can you draw about Tansy?

**A.** Music is important to Tansy.
**B.** Tansy did not go to camp this year.
**C.** Miss Maddinton is Tansy's mother.
**D.** Tansy is not a good friend to Mina.

## COMPREHENSION

**Directions** Answer the following questions about both selections.

**19.** Which of the following words best describes the fathers in both excerpts?

**A.** courageous
**B.** lively
**C.** caring
**D.** talkative

**20.** You can draw the conclusion that the narrator of "Break a Leg" and Mina from *Come a Stranger* both

**A.** want the acceptance of other children
**B.** have a great sense of humor
**C.** have much knowledge about music
**D.** want to get away from home for awhile

## Written Response

### SHORT RESPONSE

**Directions** Write two or three sentences to answer each question on a separate sheet of paper.

**21.** Give two details that help you visualize Mina at the beginning of the excerpt from *Come a Stranger*.

**22.** Give one detail that supports the conclusion that the narrator and his father have a good relationship in the excerpt from "Break a Leg."

### EXTENDED RESPONSE

**Directions** Answer the following question. Write two or more paragraphs on a separate sheet of paper.

**23.** In the excerpt from "Break a Leg," what do you learn about the narrator's personality from his thoughts, speech, and actions? Support your answer with three details from the text.

## Vocabulary

**Directions** Use context clues and your knowledge of idioms to answer the following questions. The line numbers will help you find the words in the excerpt from "Break a Leg."

**1.** In line 28, the narrator says that "teachers don't count." The idiom *don't count* means that something is not

**A.** happy
**B.** read
**C.** taught
**D.** included

**2.** In line 38, Myron asks whether the narrator is "too chicken" to go to the dance. This idiom refers to someone who is

**A.** short
**B.** scared
**C.** fast
**D.** old

**3.** In line 49, the narrator asks "What's the big deal?" The idiom *big deal* means that something is

**A.** a fun experience
**B.** an annoying question
**C.** a bad influence
**D.** an important issue

**4.** In line 77, the father tells the narrator to "break a leg." This idiom means to

**A.** dance gracefully
**B.** avoid falling
**C.** have good luck
**D.** act friendly

**Directions** Use context clues and your knowledge of similes to answer the following questions.

**5.** Which of the following sentences contains a simile?

**A.** She is much taller than he is.
**B.** The girl towers above him like a tree.
**C.** The narrator feels short next to the girl.
**D.** The tall girl dances with the narrator.

**6.** Which of the following sentences contains a simile?

**A.** Like a firefighter putting out a fire, the narrator drenches himself with after-shave.
**B.** The narrator wants to smell good at the school dance.
**C.** The narrator takes special care with his appearance the night of the dance.
**D.** The after-shave the narrator wears smells similar to menthol.

**7.** Which of the following sentences contains a simile?

**A.** Mina expects to see her own heartbeat.
**B.** Mina's heart will not stop beating.
**C.** Who can hear Mina's heart?
**D.** Mina's heart thuds in her chest like a drum.

**8.** Which of the following sentences contains a simile?

**A.** When Mina sees the camp, she smiles.
**B.** Mina hears music playing all over camp.
**C.** Mina feels as content as a cat napping in the sun.
**D.** Being at camp makes Mina happy!

## Writing and Grammar

**Directions** Read the comparison-contrast essay and answer the questions that follow.

(1) I have lived in a small town, and I have lived in a city. (2) Most people in each place cannot imagine living in the other. (3) However, even though small towns and cities differ in people and activities, I have enjoyed living in both.

(4) The people in small towns are some of the friendliest I have ever met. (5) They want to know who your parents are, what sports you play, and where you come from. (6) They will give you directions and then tell you from their own lives a story. (7) People in cities, on the other hand, seem to take a little longer to open up. (8) They may not be as openly friendly, but they are most fun to watch. (9) I've seen true individuals in cities—people who do not blend into a crowd and who are happy about that.

(10) Small towns and cities also differed in the activities they offer. (11) Some small towns have festivals and community picnics. (12) In the summer, kids go to the pool and rode their bikes. (13) Cities in the summer are very different, they are just as fun. (14) There are museums and parks and outdoor concerts to attend. (15) Kids in old parking lots play hockey and basketball. (16) Most of all, there is nothing like leaving the hot sun to spend a cool day in the city library.

(17) I still know people who live in small towns and in big cities. (18) They may act a little different from each other. (19) They may do different activities after school or in the summer. (20) There is one thing, though, that small towns and cities have in common: I have made lifelong friends in each place, and they are the most greatest people in the world to me!

**1.** What subjects are being compared and contrasted in the passage?

**A.** swimming and bike-riding
**B.** small towns and cities
**C.** museums and parks
**D.** sun and shade

**2.** What does sentence 3 contain?

**A.** the writer's first point
**B.** a misplaced modifier
**C.** the thesis statement
**D.** a supporting detail

**3.** Choose the best way to rewrite sentence 6 to avoid a misplaced modifier.

**A.** They will give you directions and then tell you a story from their own lives.
**B.** From their own lives, they will give you directions and then tell you a story.
**C.** They will tell you a story and then give you directions from their own lives.
**D.** They will give you directions from their own lives and then tell you a story.

**4.** What transition is used in sentence 7?

**A.** people in cities
**B.** on the other hand
**C.** a little longer
**D.** to open up

**5.** Choose the correct comparative to replace the words "most fun" in sentence 8.

**A.** more fun
**B.** funner
**C.** more funner
**D.** most funnest

**6.** Choose the correct verb tense to replace the word "differed" in sentence 10.

**A.** differs
**B.** would differ
**C.** have differed
**D.** differ

**7.** Choose the correct verb tense to replace the word "rode" in sentence 12.

**A.** will be riding
**B.** ride
**C.** have ridden
**D.** rides

**8.** Choose the best transition to add to the beginning of sentence 13.

**A.** Although
**B.** Similarly
**C.** Because
**D.** Nevertheless

**9.** Choose the best way to rewrite sentence 15 to avoid a misplaced modifier.

**A.** Kids play hockey in old parking lots and basketball.
**B.** Hockey and basketball kids play in old parking lots.
**C.** Kids play hockey and basketball in old parking lots.
**D.** Kids play in old parking lots hockey and basketball.

**10.** Choose the correct superlative to replace the words "most greatest" in sentence 20.

**A.** greater
**B.** greatest
**C.** more greater
**D.** great

**11.** Which organizational method does this passage use?

**A.** cause-and-effect
**B.** chronological order
**C.** subject-by-subject
**D.** point-by-point

**12.** The passage's conclusion is satisfying because it

**A.** contains only four sentences
**B.** ends with an exclamation point
**C.** summarizes the writer's main points
**D.** uses the first-person point of view

## Writing

**Directions** Read the following quotation. Then read the prompt that follows and complete the writing activity.

> "We are sometimes as different from ourselves as we are from others."
>
> François, duc de La Rochefoucauld, French writer

**Prompt:** Write an essay that compares yourself with another person. The quote suggests that you are often very different from others. Explain two or three ways that you are different from that person.

Now write your essay. The following reminders will help you

**Reminders**

- Be sure your writing does what the prompt asks.
- Clearly state the activities being compared and contrasted.
- Include a focused thesis statement.
- Support your points with explanations and details.
- Use transitions to connect ideas.
- Use transitions to connect ideas.

## Reading Comprehension

**Directions** Read the following selections. Then answer the questions that follow.

### *from* Break a Leg

**Joel Schwartz**

I wouldn't have gone to the "Getting to Know You" dance at school if it hadn't been for my father. He wouldn't have talked to me about it if it hadn't been for my mother. She wouldn't have talked to him about it if it hadn't been for my best friend Myron's mother. My best friend's mother wouldn't have talked to my mother about it if it hadn't been for my best friend. Myron wouldn't have talked to his mother about it if I hadn't talked to him about it, so I guess I'm to blame for everything.

It's not that I don't like dances and it's certainly not that I don't like girls. It's just that, well, all the twelve-year-old girls in the world are much taller than all
10 the twelve-year-old boys. I wouldn't mind having to look at them straight in the eye, but having to look up all the time is embarrassing and it hurts my neck too. When you dance with a girl, they are supposed to be able to put their head on your shoulder, not their chin on your head.

So when Myron asked me at lunch, "Are you going to the 'Getting to Know You' dance?"

I said, "Are you kidding? Nobody's going to that dance."

Myron took a giant bite of his sandwich and said, "Emrymoday ish gowig."

"Every Monday, what did you say?" I asked.

20 Myron wiped a large glob of mustard off his chin with his sleeve. "I said, everybody I know is going." Myron looked at the glob of mustard that now decorated his sleeve and without hesitation ground it into his pants. "Everybody, that is, except you."

I stared down at the spot on Myron's pants and then up at a new glob on his chin. At this rate, by the end of lunch, he would be wearing palomino-colored pants and a white shirt with gold cuffs. "Name one person who's going."

"Me!"

"Besides you."

"Todd Murray."

30 "Mr. Murray, our math teacher?" Myron nodded. "He has to go. He's the chaperon. Besides, teachers don't count."

"Come on, go." I shook my head no. "For me?" I shook my head no again. "Why not?" This time the mustard had migrated up both cheeks.

"Why do you use so much mustard on your sandwich?" I asked, purposely changing the subject.

"Because I hate the taste of the meat," replied Myron.

"If you hate the taste of the meat so much, why don't you put a different kind of meat on your sandwich?"

"If I put on the meat that I liked, I wouldn't put on any mustard, and I like 40 mustard on my sandwich." I stood up to go. "Not so fast. Why won't you go to the dance? Are you too chicken to go?"

"I don't want to talk about it anymore," I replied. "Finish eating your mustard sandwich and have a good time at the dance. You can tell me about it on Monday."

I thought I had heard the last of it, but after dinner that night my father asked me to go into the den because he wanted to talk to me about something. This usually means I've done something wrong and my mother has delegated my father to handle it.

"I've cleaned up my room," I said. "I did all my homework. I'll read a 50 book for half an hour before I go to sleep, and I took out the trash."

My father smiled."Why aren't you going to the 'Getting to Know You' dance?"

"How do you know that?" I asked.

"Your mother was talking to Myron's mother and—"

"I don't want to go, that's all. What's the big deal?"

My father lit his pipe and leaned back in his chair. This usually meant he was going to tell me a story about himself when he was my age. "When I was your age and just starting seventh grade like you, my school had a 'Getting to Know You' dance too, and I didn't want to go either. My dad sat me down, just 60 like this, and said to me, 'I'll bet you're a little afraid to go to the dance.' 'Afraid?' I replied. 'I'm not afraid of any school dance.' 'Not of the dance,' he continued, 'but of the girls. Girls can be scary at your age. They act like they feel more comfortable in social situations than boys, but they're just as scared as you are. Go to the dance, act like you know what you're doing, and I'll bet you'll have a good time.' I didn't want to admit it then, but what your grandfather said to me that day made sense and I decided to go to the dance. The night of the dance my father drove me to the school and as I got out of the car he said 'Break a leg.' That's an expression actors use when they want to wish another actor good luck on the night of a performance. I think he did that purposely because he knew I'd 70 have to be a good actor that night to hide my nervousness. I was nervous that night, but I covered it well and I ended up having a great time. Think about it."

I sat by myself in the den for a long time after Dad left and thought about what he just said. Usually what Dad says is either dumb or old-fashioned. This time he surprised me with something right on. Was he getting smarter?

After I called Myron and told him I had decided to go to the dance I spent half of the next twenty-four hours in and out of the bathroom. It was certainly a local record and probably a national and international one too. I could see myself in the Guinness Book of World Records for Most Trips in One Day to the Bathroom Without Actually Doing Anything.

80 I hardly ate dinner. After showering I smoothed on a manly hair gel, splashed on a mentholly after-shave, and sprayed on a musky deodorant. I smelled muskmantholly magnificent. I almost got out of the house with my old sneakers, but my mom made me go back and put on my new slippery loafers.

My father drove Myron and me to the dance. "Break a leg," he yelled as I got out of the car.

"What's that all about?" asked Myron.

"Who knows," I replied. "Probably some weird expression he picked up when he was my age."

## *from* Come a Stranger

**Cynthia Voigt**

Mina's heart was beating so fast, and so hard, she thought for sure it must show, thumping away under her blouse. Her father was driving slowly through the city of New London and then, slowly, up the river road. They had been riding for hours, without talking much, and Mina had made herself be patient. But now they were so close, and the car was going so slowly, waiting to turn and enter between the stone pillars and creeping up the road to the quadrangle.

When the car finally stopped, Mina burst out and took her suitcase from the back seat. Her father greeted Miss Maddinton. They talked about nothing in particular. Mina looked at her sneakers and felt her heart, beating.

It all soaked into her skin, and that was enough for now. If she looked around, at the stone buildings and trees, at all the familiar remembered places, she would start running around to touch everything, and her father would know-he'd know for sure what he'd only guessed, that she was gladder to be back at camp than anywhere else, that she could barely wait for him to leave so she could be by herself and be her own self again. She didn't want to hurt her father's feelings by letting him know that, so she stood there with her eyes closed, being there.

At last, he started to leave."Have a good time, Mina." He hugged her close and she hugged him back, her head almost up to his shoulder now. "Behave yourself."

"I will. Have a good summer, Dad."

She made herself stand and wave while the car drove away, a dusty black sedan with the Maryland license plate a little white square. Then she turned slowly around, and smiled.

"You're in room three-o-seven," Miss Maddinton said to her, consulting a list she had on her clipboard. She was wearing a silvery gray suit; her hair was in dark braids that she'd wound around her head like a corona. She looked busy, she looked distant and calm, she looked beautiful.

Mina was back where there was music around everywhere, every day. She was back where if you said Prokofiev, nobody said, "Who?"

"You've grown," Miss Maddinton said, sounding doubtful, looking doubtful.

What did she expect Mina to do? Not grow? Mina laughed out loud. "I guess. My mom says I've been shooting up and shooting out."

"You can find your own way, can't you? I've got to greet the new girls."

"Three-o-seven?" Mina asked, not that she didn't remember, but just to savor this first minute a little longer. "Is Tansy here yet?"

"She's up there," Miss Maddinton said.

At that, Mina couldn't wait another minute. She grabbed her suitcase and hurrying as fast as she could with the heavy case banging against her leg went into the dormitory, went home.

Room 307 was on the third floor. The second floor was for the littlest girls, the 40 top floor for the fourteen year olds. Mina climbed two flights of stairs and pushed through the heavy door onto the corridor. She heard voices, she heard music. Looking at the numbers painted on the doors, she went on down the hall. Her feet wanted to jump and run, her heart wanted to stop it all from going by so fast already. Room 307 was down toward the far end of the corridor. The door was open, but no music came out. Mina guessed Tansy was probably in somebody else's room, visiting.

But the room had only one bed in it. The room was too small for two beds anyway. The room was a single room.

Mina put her suitcase down on the floor and sat on the bed. For a long minute 50 her mind was empty-blank and silent, a cold white emptiness. Then she understood.

They were seeing the outside of her.

Because nobody, not even Tansy, had wanted to be her roommate. So the adults had put her into a single room too.

Mina got up and set her suitcase on the bed. She unpacked her clothes into the dresser, then made up the bed and thought. She just hadn't understood, she guessed; but as soon as she thought that she knew she was wrong. They had all been friends, they had all gotten along just fine. It was what her father had said, though, what he had noticed right away when he picked her up: She was 60 the only little black girl there.



## COMPREHENSION

**Directions** Answer the following questions about the excerpt from "Break a Leg."

**1.** Which of the following phrases best describes the narrator?

**A.** quiet, but comfortable with friends
**B.** funny, but self-conscious
**C.** obedient, but uninterested
**D.** uptight, but relaxed at home

**2.** You know that the excerpt is told from the first-person point of view because the narrator

**A.** describes his own thoughts and feelings
**B.** is not a character in the story
**C.** reveals the thoughts of his father
**D.** knows everything that Myron is thinking

**3.** Based on the narrator's thoughts in lines 7–12, you can make the inference that he

**A.** suffers from constant neck pain
**B.** is a skilled dancer
**C.** is uncomfortable around girls
**D.** wants to go to the dance alone

**4.** The details in lines 13–40 most help you visualize the

**A.** inside of the school cafeteria at a busy lunch time
**B.** mustard smeared on Myron's face as well as his shirt and pants
**C.** narrator dancing with a tall girl who is much taller than he is
**D.** different kinds of lunch meat in Myron's sandwiches

**5.** Which of the following sentences shows you that this excerpt is told in the first person?

**A.** "Myron took a big bite of his sandwich and said, 'Emrymoday ish gowig.'" (line 16)
**B.** "Myron wiped a large glob of mustard off his chin with his sleeve." (line 18)
**C.** "I stared down at the spot on Myron's pants and then up at a new glob on his chin." (line 21)
**D.** "'Because I hate the taste of the meat,' replied Myron." " (line 33)

**6.** Lines 41–43 help you predict that the

**A.** father will talk to the narrator about going to the dance
**B.** narrator will spend too much time in the bathroom getting ready
**C.** father will give the narrator and Myron a ride to the dance
**D.** narrator will try to wear his old sneakers to the dance

**7.** In lines 41–45, the author characterizes the narrator as a good son by using the

**A.** narrator's gestures and facial expressions
**B.** father's opinion of the narrator
**C.** narrator's physical appearance
**D.** narrator's own thoughts and speech

**8.** In line 46, the father's smile helps you predict that the

**A.** father will not scold the narrator
**B.** father will tell a story about his childhood
**C.** narrator will go to the dance
**D.** narrator will not eat much of his dinner

**9.** You can make the inference that the narrator is nervous because he

**A.** attentively listens to his father's story
**B.** suspects that his father is getting smarter
**C.** calls Myron to say he is going to the dance
**D.** hardly eats dinner before the dance

**10.** What conclusion can you draw about the relationship between the narrator and his father?

**A.** The father prefers talking to the narrator after work.
**B.** The narrator never finds his father's stories helpful.
**C.** The narrator and his father are comfortable talking and sharing ideas.
**D.** The father thinks it is important to make life easy for the narrator.

**COMPREHENSION**

**Directions** Answer the following questions about the excerpt from *Come a Stranger*.

**11.** You can tell that this excerpt is told from a third-person limited point of view because the narrator

**A.** reveals only Mina's thoughts
**B.** is the main character
**C.** reveals the father's thoughts
**D.** is a fellow camper

**12.** The details in lines 1–16 help you visualize that Mina is so excited she

**A.** looks around, taking in every detail
**B.** has to force herself to stand still
**C.** runs up and hugs Miss Maddinton
**D.** can't stop smiling and laughing

**13.** Which sentence from the excerpt shows that Mina is considerate?

**A.** "They had been riding for hours, without talking much." (lines 3–4)
**B.** B "It all soaked into her skin, and that was enough for now." (line 10)
**C.** "She made herself stand and wave while the car drove away." (lines 15–16)
**D.** "Then she turned slowly around, and smiled." (lines 21–22)

**14.** You can draw the conclusion that Mina enjoyed the camp so much the year before because she could

**A.** relax and be who she is, without fear of rejection
**B.** get into trouble and mischief without her parents finding out
**C.** enjoy some alone time, away from all of her good friends
**D.** spend time in a place that doesn't have loud music

**15.** The details in lines 24–35 help you visualize Miss Maddinton as a woman who

**A.** does not take her job seriously
**B.** wants to make sure Mina is comfortable
**C.** takes great care in her appearance
**D.** greets every camper cheerfully

**16.** Mina's actions in lines 36–38 tell you that she is

**A.** happy to be at camp
**B.** nervous about finding Tansy
**C.** scared about being alone
**D.** glad to see Miss Maddinton

**17.** Lines 50–52 help you predict that Mina probably will

**A.** go find Tansy so that she can tell her how much she missed her
**B.** feel uncomfortable around Tansy and the other children
**C.** laugh about the situation and excitedly unpack her things
**D.** assume that the adults made a mistake and go talk to them about it

**18.** At the end of the excerpt, which of the following conclusions can you draw?

**A.** Mina is alone because she needs to spend more time practicing.
**B.** Mina's father told Miss Maddinton to give Mina her own room.
**C.** Miss Maddinton forced Tansy to stay in a separate room.
**D.** Mina is being rejected because of the color of her skin.

## COMPREHENSION

**Directions** Answer the following questions about both selections.

**19.** The narrator from "Break a Leg" and Mina from *Come a Stranger* both

**A.** love to listen to music
**B.** get into trouble often
**C.** respect their fathers
**D.** dislike school functions

**20.** You can conclude that the narrator from "Break a Leg" and Mina from *Come a Stranger* would probably agree that

**A.** most children want to fit in with their peers
**B.** family members do not always know what's best
**C.** children always should show their feelings when they are excited
**D.** humor is the best way to make light of a difficult situation

# Written Response

## SHORT RESPONSE

**Directions** Write two or three sentences to answer each question on a separate sheet of paper.

**21.** Identify something you learn about Mina through her actions in lines 17–34 from *Come a Stranger*. Support your inference with details from the text.

**22.** Draw a conclusion about Mina and Tansy's friendship in the excerpt from *Come a Stranger*. Explain how you arrived at your conclusion.

## EXTENDED RESPONSE

**Directions** Answer one of the following questions. Write two or more paragraphs on a separate sheet of paper.

**23.** What methods of characterization does Schwartz use to describe the narrator in the excerpt from "Break a Leg"? Give examples of what you learn about the narrator from each method.

**24. Challenge** How would the excerpt from *Come a Stranger* be different if it were told from the third-person omniscient point of view? Do you think it would be more or less effective this way? Explain.

## Vocabulary

**Directions** Use context clues and your knowledge of idioms to answer the following questions. The line numbers will help you find the words in the excerpt from "Break a Leg."

**1.** In line 28, the narrator says that "teachers *don't count*." The idiom *don't count* means that something is not

**A.** missed
**B.** divided
**C.** asked
**D.** included

**2.** In line 38, Myron asks whether the narrator is "too chicken" to go to the dance. This idiom refers to someone who is

**A.** silly
**B.** scared
**C.** fast
**D.** small

**3.** In line 49, the narrator asks "What's the big deal?" The idiom *big deal* means that something is

**A.** an everyday event
**B.** a strange question
**C.** a large purchase
**D.** an important issue

**4.** In line 67, the narrator says that the father told him something that was "right on." This idiom refers to something that is

**A.** current
**B.** careful
**C.** accurate
**D.** friendly

**Directions** Use context clues and your knowledge of similes to answer the following questions.

**5.** Which of the following sentences contains a simile?

**A.** Myron likes mustard more than any other sandwich topping.
**B.** Mustard spreads over Myron's face like clouds covering the sun.
**C.** As Myron eats, mustard oozes out of his sandwich and onto his clothes.
**D.** The narrator watches with disgust as mustard falls onto Myron's pants.

**6.** The narrator and the girl dance like a pair of wooden boards. This simile means that the narrator and the girl dance

**A.** stiffly
**B.** quickly
**C.** resentfully
**D.** tiredly

**7.** Which of the following expressions contains a simile?

**A.** As the car creeps up the road, Mina's heart beats faster.
**B.** Mina waits impatiently for the journey to end.
**C.** Mina's father carefully drives along the winding road.
**D.** Watching Mina's father drive is like watching grass grow.

**8.** Mina climbs the stairs like a sprinting cougar. This simile means that Mina climbs

**A.** clumsily
**B.** heavenly
**C.** quickly
**D.** shyly

## Writing and Grammar

**Directions** Read the comparison-contrast essay and answer the questions that follow.

(1) I have lived in a small town, and I have lived in a city. (2) Most people in each place cannot imagine living in the other. (3) However, even though small towns and cities differ in people and activities, I have enjoyed living in both.

(4) The people in small towns are some of the friendliest I have ever met. (5) They want to know who your parents are, what sports you play, and where you come from. (6) They will give you directions and then tell you from their own lives a story. (7) People in cities, on the other hand, seem to take a little longer to open up. (8) They may not be as openly friendly, but they are most fun to watch. (9) I've seen true individuals in cities—people who do not blend into a crowd and who are happy about that.

(10) Small towns and cities also differed in the activities they offer. (11) Some small towns have festivals and community picnics. (12) In the summer, kids go to the pool and rode their bikes. (13) Cities in the summer are very different, they are just as fun. (14) There are museums and parks and outdoor concerts to attend. (15) Kids in old parking lots play hockey and basketball. (16) Most of all, there is nothing like leaving the hot sun to spend a cool day in the city library.

(17) I still know people who live in small towns and in big cities. (18) They may act a little different from each other. (19) They may do different activities after school or in the summer. (20) There is one thing, though, that small towns and cities have in common: I have made lifelong friends in each place, and they are the most greatest people in the world to me!

**1.** What is the purpose of sentence 1?

**A.** It supports a key idea with a specific example.
**B.** It describes what the writer enjoys about each subject.
**C.** It presents the thesis statement of the passage.
**D.** It identifies the subjects being compared and contrasted.

**2.** Which sentence introduces the idea that cities and small towns are different?

**A.** sentence 1 **C.** sentence 3
**B.** sentence 2 **D.** sentence 4

**3.** Choose the best way to rewrite sentence 6 to avoid a misplaced modifier.

**A.** They will give you directions and then tell you a story from their own lives.
**B.** From their own lives, they will give you directions and then tell you a story.
**C.** They will tell you a story and then give you directions from their own lives.
**D.** They will give you directions from their own lives and then tell you a story.

**4.** Choose the correct comparative to replace the word "most fun" in sentence 8.

**A.** funner
**B.** more fun
**C.** more funner
**D.** funnest

**5.** Identify the transitions used in sentences 4–9.

**A.** some, do not, I've seen
**B.** who, what, where
**C.** then, on the other hand, but
**D.** ever, blend into a crowd

**6.** The writer uses point-by-point organization. The first point the writer covers is how small towns and cities have different

**A.** sports teams
**B.** people
**C.** lifelong friends
**D.** activities

**7.** Choose the correct verb tense to replace the word "differed" in sentence 10.

**A.** differs
**B.** have differed
**C.** differ
**D.** would differ

**8.** Choose the correct verb tense to replace the word "rode" in sentence 12.

**A.** will ride
**B.** ride
**C.** were riding
**D.** rides

**9.** Choose the best transition to add to the beginning of sentence 13.

**A.** Likewise
**B.** Because
**C.** Although
**D.** Nevertheless

**10.** Choose the best way to rewrite sentence 15 to avoid a misplaced modifier.

**A.** Kids play hockey in old parking lots and basketball.
**B.** Hockey and basketball kids play in old parking lots.
**C.** Kids play in old parking lots hockey and basketball.
**D.** Kids play hockey and basketball in old parking lots.

**11.** Choose the correct superlative to replace the words "most greatest" in sentence 20.

**A.** greatest
**B.** greater
**C.** more greater
**D.** great

**12.** The passage's conclusion might be improved by

**A.** deleting the final paragraph and adding another point of comparison
**B.** including a story about a friend who still lives in a big city
**C.** adding a thoughtful comment about the subjects being compared
**D.** shortening the final paragraph to one sentence

## Writing

**Directions** Read the following quotation. Then read the prompts that follow and complete one of the writing activities.

> "We are sometimes as different from ourselves as we are from others."
>
> François, duc de La Rochefoucauld, French writer

**Prompt:** Write an essay that compares and contrasts two of your friends or family members. As the author of the quote suggests, one person can behave in many different ways. Think about the characteristics you have seen each person show. Focus your essay on the most interesting similarities or differences.

Now write your essay. The following reminders will help you.

**Challenge Prompt:** Write an essay that compares and contrasts yourself at different periods in your life. As the author of the quote suggests, you have probably acted differently throughout your life, even though you have remained the same person. Explore ways you behaved similarly and ways you behaved differently.

Now write your essay. The following reminders will help you.

**Reminders**

- Be sure your writing does what the prompt asks.
- Clearly state the topics being compared and contrasted.
- Include a focused thesis statement.
- Support your points with explanations and details.
- Use transitions to connect ideas.
- Check for correct grammar, spelling, and punctuation.

## Reading Comprehension

**Directions** Read the following selections. Then answer the questions that follow.

### The Cat Who Thought She Was a Dog and the Dog Who Thought He Was a Cat

**Isaac Bashevis Singer**

Once there was a poor peasant, Jan Skiba by name. He lived with his wife and three daughters in a one-room hut with a straw roof, far from the village. The house had a bed, a bench bed, and a stove, but no mirror. A mirror was a luxury for a poor peasant. And why would a peasant need a mirror? Peasants aren't curious about their appearance.

But this peasant did have a dog and a cat in his hut. The dog was named Burek and the cat Kot. They had both been born within the same week. As little food as the peasant had for himself and his family, he still wouldn't let his dog and cat go hungry. Since the dog had never seen another dog and the cat had 10 never seen another cat and they only saw each other, the dog thought he was a cat and the cat thought she was a dog. True, they were far from being alike by nature. The dog barked and the cat meowed. The dog chased rabbits and the cat lurked after mice. But must all creatures be exactly like their own kind? The peasant's children weren't exactly alike either. Burek and Kot lived on good terms, often ate from the same dish, and tried to mimic each other. When Burek barked, Kot tried to bark along, and when Kot meowed, Burek tried to meow too. Kot occasionally chased rabbits and Burek made an effort to catch a mouse.

The peddlers who bought goats, chickens, eggs, honey, calves, and whatever was available from the peasants in the village never came to Jan Skiba's 20 poor hut. They knew that Jan was so poor he had nothing to sell. But one day a peddler happened to stray there. When he came inside and began to lay out his wares, Jan Skiba's wife and daughters were bedazzled by all the pretty doodads. From his sack the peddler drew yellow beads, false pearls, tin earrings, rings, brooches, colored kerchiefs, garters, and other such trinkets. But what enthralled the women of the house most was a mirror set in a wooden frame. They asked the peddler its price and he said a half gulden, which was a lot of money for poor peasants. After a while, Jan Skiba's wife, Marianna, made a proposition to the peddler. She would pay him five groshen a month for the mirror. The peddler hesitated a moment. The mirror took up too much space in his sack and there 30 was always the danger it might break. He, therefore, decided to go along, took the first payment of five groshen from Marianna, and left the mirror with the family. He visited the region often and he knew the Skibas to be honest people. He would gradually get his money back and a profit besides.

The mirror created a commotion in the hut. Until then Marianna and the children had seldom seen themselves. Before they had the mirror, they had only seen their reflections in the barrel of water that stood by the door. Now they could see themselves clearly and they began to find defects in their faces, defects they had never noticed before. Marianna was pretty but she had a tooth missing in front and she felt that this made her ugly. One daughter discovered that her nose 40 was too snub and too broad; a second that her chin was too narrow and too long; a third that her face was sprinkled with freckles. Jan Skiba too caught a glimpse of himself in the mirror and grew displeased by his thick lips and his teeth, which protruded like a buck's. That day, the women of the house became so absorbed in the mirror they didn't cook supper, didn't make up the bed, and neglected all the other household tasks. Marianna had heard of a dentist in the big city who could replace a missing tooth, but such things were expensive. The girls tried to console each other that they were pretty enough and that they would find suitors, but they no longer felt as jolly as before. They had been afflicted with the vanity of city girls. The one with the broad nose kept trying to pinch it together with her 50 fingers to make it narrower; the one with the too-long chin pushed it up with her fist to make it shorter; the one with the freckles wondered if there was a salve in the city that could remove freckles. But where would the money come from for the fare to the city? And what about the money to buy this salve? For the first time the Skiba family deeply felt its poverty and envied the rich.

But the human members of the household were not the only ones affected. The dog and the cat also grew disturbed by the mirror. The hut was low and the mirror had been hung just above a bench. The first time the cat sprang up on the bench and saw her image in the mirror, she became terribly perplexed. She had never before seen such a creature. Kot's whiskers bristled, she began to meow at 60 her reflection and raised a paw to it, but the other creature meowed back and raised her paw too. Soon the dog jumped up on the bench, and when he saw the other dog he became wild with rage and shock. He barked at the other dog and showed him his teeth, but the other barked back and bared his fangs too. So great was the distress of Burek and Kot that for the first time in their lives they turned on each other. Burek took a bite out of Kot's throat and Kot hissed and spat at him and clawed his muzzle. They both started to bleed and the sight of blood aroused them so that they nearly killed or crippled each other. The members of the household barely managed to separate them. Because a dog is stronger than a cat, Burek had to be tied outside, and he howled all day and all night. In their 70 anguish, both the dog and the cat stopped eating.

When Jan Skiba saw the disruption the mirror had created in his household, he decided a mirror wasn't what his family needed. "Why look at yourself," he said, "when you can see and admire the sky, the sun, the moon, the stars, and the earth, with all its forests, meadows, rivers, and plants?" He took the mirror down

from the wall and put it away in the woodshed. When the peddler came for his monthly installment, Jan Skiba gave him back the mirror and in its stead, bought kerchiefs and slippers for the women. After the mirror disappeared, Burek and Kot returned to normal. Again Burek thought he was a cat and Kot was sure she was a dog. Despite all the defects the girls had found in themselves, they made
80 good marriages. The village priest heard what had happened at Jan Skiba's house and he said, "A glass mirror shows only the skin of the body. The real image of a person is in his willingness to help himself and his family and, as far as possible, all those he comes in contact with. This kind of mirror reveals the very soul of the person."

**On the Cat Walk**

**Wladyslaw Pleszczynski**

It started a few years ago when I worked at home. An hour or so before sunset the doggie would end her slumbers, stretch and wag her tail to request a walk. Out would come her collar and leash and within a minute or two we'd have worked our way to the end of the driveway. Whereupon she'd freeze, and cattle prods couldn't get her to take another step.

She's a mini-dachshund, you see, not eager to go out into the greater world unless she's carried. There are ways to get around this. If my wife or sons are with me, I hand one of them the leash and walk ahead up our quiet street. As her alpha male I know she'll come running after. There's another way to get her going: our cats need to be in the picture. They're the real walkers in the family, and the doggie can't stand it when they're the center of attention. Her herding instinct does the jump-starting.

Decades ago in Indiana I had a tortoise-shell longhair named Arthur, the only cat who ever went on walks with me. But he did so only out of loyalty and fear of loneliness. A hundred yards from the house he'd be begging me to turn back. Not so our current pair. They're Abyssinian half-brothers, one ruddy (and big and fat), the other blue (meaning silvery and cream, and half his half-brother's size). They live to be outdoors, as curious about their surroundings as the doggie is suspicious. For all their fierce independence (good luck keeping one on your lap for even a split second), they're happiest to follow us anywhere.

A pattern develops. The doggie is now moving. The skinny blue trots alongside, the heavy ruddy already playing straggler ten yards behind. Both cats are neutered, their little bellies rocking left and right as they jog. Here and there they check out favorite storm drains for chipmunks or mice, stops that allow the doggie to ask to be carried. In due course we'll have reached the end of our street, then a sharp left and soon we're on a path leading up hill to our destination: a 100 x 120 yard grassy school field, lined on three sides by tall trees, with the school itself stretching atop a ridge along the fourth side.

It's the animals' idea of a front lawn. Off goes the dog's leash and soon she's plying the grass like a torpedo in search of a destroyer cat. The fearless blue sidesteps her with aplomb. The fat ruddy, though, either runs away or lifts a paw in a halfhearted move to show his annoyance. He prefers the edge of the field, where the trees and brush below offer the security he'll need if a stranger or another dog shows up. He keeps his tail cautiously down. Not the blue, of course. The field is his parade ground, as with tail erect he prances along in perfect step. On wet days we'll retreat to the walkways and attractions next to the school. Here the cats explore the newly upgraded playground and check out the back side of bushes that line the school's brick walls.

The return home has its own routines. The doggie is always the first to
40 want to head back. If we're on the field, the blue will make sure to come racing off it and leap down the hill toward the path, but not before scurrying up a tree or two, just to earn the usual plaudits. Big ruddy can't match him here, but don't write him off. At the start of our walk a few months back, he was focused on something in the ivy and didn't join us. But when we reached the end of our street I looked back and saw him dash out of the driveway and head toward us, 150 yards away. We waited for him near the field. As he approached I could see he had something in his mouth. It was a small bird, a gift he'd hunted up for us and carried all this distance. Even the doggie was touched.

## COMPREHENSION

**Directions** Answer the following questions about "The Cat Who Thought She Was a Dog and the Dog Who Thought He Was a Cat."

**1.** What do lines 1–4 reveal about the author's perspective?

**A.** Mirrors fascinate the author.
**B.** Villages frighten the author.
**C.** The author knows about poverty.
**D.** The author is a vain person.

**2.** Based on lines 5–7, you can infer that Jan

**A.** has plenty of food
**B.** loves animals
**C.** has a large hut
**D.** does not like food

**3.** How do Burek and Kot behave similarly?

**A.** Both animals like the mirror.
**B.** They both chase animals.
**C.** Both animals mimic rabbits.
**D.** They both refuse to eat.

**4.** What causes peddlers to avoid the Skiba hut?

**A.** The family has nothing to sell.
**B.** Burek and Kot threaten visitors.
**C.** Jan is very unfriendly.
**D.** The hut is hard to reach.

**5.** Seeing the peddler's merchandise causes Jan's wife and daughters to

**A.** beg the peddler for lower prices
**B.** grab the jewelry and try it on
**C.** admire the goods longingly
**D.** offer the peddler food in exchange

**6.** What do lines 23–25 reveal about the author's perspective?

**A.** Peddlers often visit the author's house and offer him deals.
**B.** The author does not understand what peasants can afford.
**C.** The high price of mirrors angers the author.
**D.** The author is familiar with a type of foreign money.

**7.** Based on lines 73–74, you can infer that the daughters' husbands

**A.** accept their defects
**B.** are rich
**C.** live in the city
**D.** are peddlers

**8.** The dog and cat are symbols for

**A.** peddlers
**B.** people
**C.** rabbits
**D.** money

**9.** Which quotation from the story best demonstrates the theme "Material possessions do not bring happiness"?

**A.** "Jan Skiba's wife and daughters were bedazzled by all the pretty doodads."
**B.** "He would gradually get his money back and a profit besides."
**C.** "But where would the money come from for the fare to the city?"
**D.** "For the first time the Skiba family deeply felt its poverty and envied the rich."

**10.** The mirror symbolizes

**A.** poverty
**B.** anger
**C.** vanity
**D.** jealousy

**11.** Which statement best describes a theme of the story?

**A.** A peddler should never be trusted.
**B.** Mirrors always bring trouble.
**C.** Village priests offer wise advice.
**D.** A simple, humble life is best.

**COMPREHENSION**

**Directions** Answer the following questions about "On the Cat Walk."

**12.** Based on lines 4–5, you can make the inference that the dog is

**A.** stubborn
**B.** territorial
**C.** sleepy
**D.** angry

**13.** According to lines 7–9, when the author walks ahead of the dog, the dog

**A.** begs to be carried
**B.** follows the author
**C.** takes the lead
**D.** runs away

**14.** According to lines 6–11, the cats like walking, but the dog prefers

**A.** playing games
**B.** lying outside
**C.** hunting birds
**D.** being carried

**15.** One of the author's cats is silvery, and the other cat is

**A.** long
**B.** short-haired
**C.** fat
**D.** black

**16.** Based on lines 27–28, you can make the inference that the dog

**A.** runs away from the cats
**B.** enjoys playing in the field
**C.** is afraid of the cats
**D.** will try to catch rabbits

**17.** According to lines 29–31, the fat ruddy stays near the edges of the field because the

**A.** shrubs provide a place to hide
**B.** other cat scares him
**C.** mice hide in the field
**D.** trees are good places to rest

**18.** The author's perspective on pets is that they are

**A.** cold
**B.** amusing
**C.** misunderstood
**D.** lazy

## COMPREHENSION

**Directions** Answer the following questions about both selections.

**19.** What subject do both selections describe?

**A.** past events
**B.** pet training
**C.** animal behavior
**D.** peasant life

**20.** How are the forms of the selections different?

**A.** Both selections are short stories, but one is longer than the other.
**B.** One selection is an essay, and the other selection is a short story.
**C.** The first selection is a short story, and the other selection is a poem.
**D.** Both selections are essays, but one is shorter than the other.

# Written Response

## SHORT RESPONSE

**Directions** Write two or three sentences to answer each question on a separate sheet of paper.

**21.** Compare and contrast the actions of the two Abyssinian cats in "On the Cat Walk." Provide two details from the selection.

**22.** What symbolizes true beauty in lines 66–69 of "The Cat Who Thought She Was a Dog and the Dog Who Thought He Was a Cat"?

## EXTENDED RESPONSE

**Directions** Answer the following question. Write two or more paragraphs on a separate sheet of paper.

**23.** Explain how the theme "Vanity is bad" is illustrated by the story "The Cat Who Thought She Was a Dog and the Dog Who Thought He Was a Cat." Give examples to support your answer.

## Vocabulary

**Directions** Use context clues and your knowledge of connotation and denotation to answer the following questions about vocabulary in "The Cat Who Thought She Was a Dog and the Dog Who Thought He Was a Cat."

**1.** In line 6, the word *peasant* has a connotation of

**A.** silliness
**B.** cleverness
**C.** cleanliness
**D.** plainness

**2.** In line 24, the word *trinkets* has a connotation of

**A.** thickness
**B.** cheapness
**C.** brightness
**D.** cleanliness

**3.** In lin 40, the word *broad* has a connotation of

**A.** ugliness
**B.** cruelty
**C.** mystery
**D.** toughness

**4.** In line 49, the word *city* has a connotation of

**A.** dirtiness
**B.** misery
**C.** shallowness
**D.** mischief

**Directions** Use context clues to answer the following questions.

**5.** Which is the most likely meaning of *enthralled* in line 24 of "The Cat Who Thought She Was a Dog and the Dog Who Thought He Was a Cat"?

**A.** helped
**B.** interested
**C.** numbed
**D.** confused

**6.** Which is the most likely meaning of *slumbers* in line 2 of "On the Cat Walk"?

**A.** nap
**B.** meal
**C.** guard
**D.** exercise

**7.** Which is the most likely meaning of *instinct* in line 12 of "On the Cat Walk"?

**A.** practiced skill
**B.** natural ability
**C.** good judgment
**D.** body shape

**8.** Which is the most likely meaning of *routines* in line 39 of "On the Cat Walk"?

**A.** regulations of parks
**B.** points of development
**C.** rules for leaving
**D.** patterns of activities

## Writing and Grammar

**Directions** Read the short story and answer the questions that follow.

(1) "Oddities Await You in Clariser's Curio Shop," the brightly colored banner read. (2) "The Urn Looks Empty But It Is Not." (3) Devon had simply turned into the damp alley as a shortcut, and now he was standing under this strange sign. (4) A door gaped open before him. (5) No light was visible. (6) He could hear only the far-off sound of water dripping somewhere in the blanketing darkness.

(7) "Should I enter"? Devon muttered to himself. (8) He pondered the banner's strange message again. (9) It was all so mysterious! (10) Devon drew a breath and stepped through the doorway and into the darkness.

(11) Immediately he smelled many things. (12) Not one was recognizable. (13) He moved through the darkness. (14) Until he saw a glow of light spreading toward him. (15) Soon he was standing before a fountain. (16) Beyond that, the passage opened up into a large room. (17) It was filled with objects of all kinds.

(18) "Is there something I can do for you? a voice rang out. (19) Devon could see no one in the room, just piles and piles of stuff.

(20) "I saw your sign," Devon answered. (21) "I was just . . .well, I'm not really sure. . . ." his voice trailed off. (22) Devon didn't know why he was standing in this strange place talking to this strange voice. (23) What had drawn him here? (24) He gazed up the length of a humongous wooden door. (25) While he ran his hand over its carved surface. (26) Suddenly, a hand gripped his shoulder. (27) Devon's eyes widened as he gasped loudly and spun around.

(28) "Ah!" A thin, hunched little man smiled up at Devon. (29) "We've been waiting so long, and finally you are here!

**1.** The first two sentences get the reader's attention by making the reader curious about

**A.** how the main character looks
**B.** what the banner means
**C.** how old the main character is
**D.** what color the banner is

**2.** Choose the correct coordinating conjunction to combine sentences 4 and 5.

**A.** but
**B.** so
**C.** or
**D.** nor

**3.** The sensory language in sentence 6 shows that the setting is

**A.** bright
**B.** disgusting
**C.** crowded
**D.** scary

**4.** Choose the correct way to punctuate the dialogue in sentence 7.

**A.** "Should I enter?" "Devon muttered to himself."
**B.** "Should I enter," Devon muttered to himself?
**C.** "Should I enter?" Devon muttered to himself.
**D.** Should I enter? Devon muttered to himself.

**5.** The conflict described in sentences 7–10 is between Devon and

**A.** his own fears
**B.** the shopkeeper
**C.** his reckless nature
**D.** the forces of nature

**6.** Choose the correct coordinating conjunction to combine sentences 11 and 12.

**A.** so
**B.** but
**C.** or
**D.** for

**7.** Combine sentence 13 and fragment 14 to form one sentence with an independent clause and a dependent clause.

**A.** He moved through the darkness and until he saw a glow of light spreading toward him.
**B.** He moved through the darkness until he saw a glow of light spreading toward him.
**C.** He moved through the darkness; until he saw a glow of light spreading toward him.
**D.** He moved through the darkness so until he saw a glow of light spreading toward him.

**8.** He moved through the darkness so until he saw a glow of light spreading toward him.

**A.** until, soon
**B.** toward, before
**C.** spreading, soon
**D.** glow, before

**9.** Choose the best way to rewrite sentence 15 to better show the setting.

**A.** Devon's palms perspired as he approached a fountain.
**B.** Soon he was standing before a low, stout fountain.
**C.** "What a fantastic fountain!" Devon exclaimed.
**D.** Devon stood up straight and tall, afraid to touch anything.

**10.** Choose the best way to better show the setting by adding sensory language to sentence 17.

**A.** It was filled with several fascinating objects.
**B.** It was filled with objects that Devon had never seen before.
**C.** It was filled with objects of all kinds, such as gleaming stone figures and vases.
**D.** It was filled with objects of all kinds, which made Devon even more curious.

**11.** Choose the correct way to punctuate the dialogue in line 18.

**A.** "Is there something I can do for you?" a voice rang out.
**B.** "Is there something I can do for you?" a voice rang out."
**C.** Is there something I can do for you? a voice rang out.
**D.** "Is there something I can do for you?" "a voice rang out."

**12.** Combine sentence 24 and fragment 25 to form one sentence with an independent clause and a dependent clause.

**A.** While he ran his hand over its carved surface: he gazed up the length of a humongous wooden door.
**B.** He gazed up the length of a humongous wooden door yet while he ran his hand over its carved surface.
**C.** While he ran his hand over its carved surface; and he gazed up the length of a humongous wooden door.
**D.** He gazed up the length of a humongous wooden door while he ran his hand over its carved surface.

## Writing

**Directions** Read the following quotation. Then read the prompt that follows and complete the writing activity

> The short story is rather like a surgical operation. It has a beginning, middle, and an end.
>
> Richard Selzer, author and physician

**Prompt:** Write a short story based on a place that you like to visit. Think of something mysterious or wonderful that could happen at this place. As the quote suggests, make sure your short story follows a clear sequence of events.

Now write your short story. The following reminders will help you.

**Reminders**

- Be sure your writing does what the prompt asks.
- Include an interesting plot and at least one character.
- Develop and resolve a central conflict.
- Use descriptive details, sensory language, and dialogue to reveal the setting and characters.
- Check for correct grammar, spelling, and punctuation.

## Reading Comprehension

**Directions** Read the following selections. Then answer the questions that follow.

### The Cat Who Thought She Was a Dog and the Dog Who Thought He Was a Cat

**Isaac Bashevis Singer**

Once there was a poor peasant, Jan Skiba by name. He lived with his wife and three daughters in a one-room hut with a straw roof, far from the village. The house had a bed, a bench bed, and a stove, but no mirror. A mirror was a luxury for a poor peasant. And why would a peasant need a mirror? Peasants aren't curious about their appearance.

But this peasant did have a dog and a cat in his hut. The dog was named Burek and the cat Kot. They had both been born within the same week. As little food as the peasant had for himself and his family, he still wouldn't let his dog and cat go hungry. Since the dog had never seen another dog and the cat had never seen another cat and they only saw each other, the dog thought he was a cat and the cat thought she was a dog. True, they were far from being alike by nature. The dog barked and the cat meowed. The dog chased rabbits and the cat lurked after mice. But must all creatures be exactly like their own kind? The peasant's children weren't exactly alike either. Burek and Kot lived on good terms, often ate from the same dish, and tried to mimic each other. When Burek barked, Kot tried to bark along, and when Kot meowed, Burek tried to meow too. Kot occasionally chased rabbits and Burek made an effort to catch a mouse.

The peddlers who bought goats, chickens, eggs, honey, calves, and whatever was available from the peasants in the village never came to Jan Skiba's poor hut. They knew that Jan was so poor he had nothing to sell. But one day a peddler happened to stray there. When he came inside and began to lay out his wares, Jan Skiba's wife and daughters were bedazzled by all the pretty doodads. From his sack the peddler drew yellow beads, false pearls, tin earrings, rings, brooches, colored kerchiefs, garters, and other such trinkets. But what enthralled the women of the house most was a mirror set in a wooden frame. They asked the peddler its price and he said a half gulden, which was a lot of money for poor peasants. After a while, Jan Skiba's wife, Marianna, made a proposition to the peddler. She would pay him five groshen a month for the mirror. The peddler hesitated a moment. The mirror took up too much space in his sack and there was always the danger it might break. He, therefore, decided to go along, took the first payment of five groshen from Marianna, and left the mirror with the family. He visited the region often and he knew the Skibas to be honest people. He would gradually get his money back and a profit besides.

The mirror created a commotion in the hut. Until then Marianna and the children had seldom seen themselves. Before they had the mirror, they had only seen their reflections in the barrel of water that stood by the door. Now they could see themselves clearly and they began to find defects in their faces, defects they had never noticed before. Marianna was pretty but she had a tooth missing in front and she felt that this made her ugly. One daughter discovered that her nose
40 was too snub and too broad; a second that her chin was too narrow and too long; a third that her face was sprinkled with freckles. Jan Skiba too caught a glimpse of himself in the mirror and grew displeased by his thick lips and his teeth, which protruded like a buck's. That day, the women of the house became so absorbed in the mirror they didn't cook supper, didn't make up the bed, and neglected all the other household tasks. Marianna had heard of a dentist in the big city who could replace a missing tooth, but such things were expensive. The girls tried to console each other that they were pretty enough and that they would find suitors, but they no longer felt as jolly as before. They had been afflicted with the vanity of city girls. The one with the broad nose kept trying to pinch it together with her
50 fingers to make it narrower; the one with the too-long chin pushed it up with her fist to make it shorter; the one with the freckles wondered if there was a salve in the city that could remove freckles. But where would the money come from for the fare to the city? And what about the money to buy this salve? For the first time the Skiba family deeply felt its poverty and envied the rich.

But the human members of the household were not the only ones affected. The dog and the cat also grew disturbed by the mirror. The hut was low and the mirror had been hung just above a bench. The first time the cat sprang up on the bench and saw her image in the mirror, she became terribly perplexed. She had never before seen such a creature. Kot's whiskers bristled, she began to meow at
60 her reflection and raised a paw to it, but the other creature meowed back and raised her paw too. Soon the dog jumped up on the bench, and when he saw the other dog he became wild with rage and shock. He barked at the other dog and showed him his teeth, but the other barked back and bared his fangs too. So great was the distress of Burek and Kot that for the first time in their lives they turned on each other. Burek took a bite out of Kot's throat and Kot hissed and spat at him and clawed his muzzle. They both started to bleed and the sight of blood aroused them so that they nearly killed or crippled each other. The members of the household barely managed to separate them. Because a dog is stronger than a cat, Burek had to be tied outside, and he howled all day and all night. In their
70 anguish, both the dog and the cat stopped eating.

When Jan Skiba saw the disruption the mirror had created in his household, he decided a mirror wasn't what his family needed. "Why look at yourself," he said, "when you can see and admire the sky, the sun, the moon, the stars, and the earth, with all its forests, meadows, rivers, and plants?" He took the mirror down from the wall and put it away in the woodshed. When the peddler came for his monthly installment, Jan Skiba gave him back the mirror and in its stead, bought kerchiefs and slippers for the women. After the mirror disappeared, Burek and Kot returned to normal. Again Burek thought he was a cat and Kot was sure she was a dog. Despite all the defects the girls had found in themselves, they made

80 good marriages. The village priest heard what had happened at Jan Skiba's house and he said, "A glass mirror shows only the skin of the body. The real image of a person is in his willingness to help himself and his family and, as far as possible, all those he comes in contact with. This kind of mirror reveals the very soul of the person."



## On the Cat Walk

**Wladyslaw Pleszczynski**

It started a few years ago when I worked at home. An hour or so before sunset the doggie would end her slumbers, stretch and wag her tail to request a walk. Out would come her collar and leash and within a minute or two we'd have worked our way to the end of the driveway. Whereupon she'd freeze, and cattle prods couldn't get her to take another step.

She's a mini-dachshund, you see, not eager to go out into the greater world unless she's carried. There are ways to get around this. If my wife or sons are with me, I hand one of them the leash and walk ahead up our quiet street. As her alpha male I know she'll come running after. There's another way to get her

10 going: our cats need to be in the picture. They're the real walkers in the family, and the doggie can't stand it when they're the center of attention. Her herding instinct does the jump-starting.

Decades ago in Indiana I had a tortoise-shell longhair named Arthur, the only cat who ever went on walks with me. But he did so only out of loyalty and fear of loneliness. A hundred yards from the house he'd be begging me to turn back. Not so our current pair. They're Abyssinian half-brothers, one ruddy (and big and fat), the other blue (meaning silvery and cream, and half his half-brother's size). They live to be outdoors, as curious about their surroundings as the doggie is suspicious. For all their fierce independence (good luck keeping one

20 on your lap for even a split second), they're happiest to follow us anywhere.

A pattern develops. The doggie is now moving. The skinny blue trots alongside, the heavy ruddy already playing straggler ten yards behind. Both cats are neutered, their little bellies rocking left and right as they jog. Here and there they check out favorite storm drains for chipmunks or mice, stops that allow the doggie to ask to be carried. In due course we'll have reached the end of our street, then a sharp left and soon we're on a path leading up hill to our destination: a 100 x 120 yard grassy school field, lined on three sides by tall trees, with the school itself stretching atop a ridge along the fourth side.

It's the animals' idea of a front lawn. Off goes the dog's leash and soon 30 she's plying the grass like a torpedo in search of a destroyer cat. The fearless blue sidesteps her with aplomb. The fat ruddy, though, either runs away or lifts a paw in a halfhearted move to show his annoyance. He prefers the edge of the field, where the trees and brush below offer the security he'll need if a stranger or another dog shows up. He keeps his tail cautiously down. Not the blue, of course. The field is his parade ground, as with tail erect he prances along in perfect step. On wet days we'll retreat to the walkways and attractions next to the school. Here the cats explore the newly upgraded playground and check out the back side of bushes that line the school's brick walls.

The return home has its own routines. The doggie is always the first to 40 want to head back. If we're on the field, the blue will make sure to come racing off it and leap down the hill toward the path, but not before scurrying up a tree or two, just to earn the usual plaudits. Big ruddy can't match him here, but don't write him off. At the start of our walk a few months back, he was focused on something in the ivy and didn't join us. But when we reached the end of our street I looked back and saw him dash out of the driveway and head toward us, 150 yards away. We waited for him near the field. As he approached I could see he had something in his mouth. It was a small bird, a gift he'd hunted up for us and carried all this distance. Even the doggie was touched.



## COMPREHENSION

**Directions** Answer the following questions about "The Cat Who Thought She Was a Dog and the Dog Who Thought He Was a Cat."

**1.** Lines 1–4 show you that the author is

**A.** knowledgeable about poverty
**B.** ashamed of his unnecessary luxuries
**C.** concerned about his appearance
**D.** unfamiliar with large houses

**2.** Based on lines 6–7, you can infer that Jan Skiba is

**A.** forced to take food away from his pets so his children can eat
**B.** concerned about the welfare of those around him
**C.** trying to provide for every animal in the neighborhood
**D.** tired of having animals that eat all of his food

**3.** The peddler's trinkets symbolize

**A.** honesty
**B.** wealth
**C.** nature
**D.** loyalty

**4.** Lines 22–30 reveal that the author is familiar with

**A.** the many dangers peddlers face
**B.** various peddlers in the area
**C.** different types of mirrors
**D.** a type of foreign money

**5.** What causes the peddler to accept Marianna's offer for the mirror?

**A.** He knows the mirror is worthless.
**B.** Jan Skiba threatens him.
**C.** He feels sorry for Marianna.
**D.** The mirror is difficult to carry.

**6.** The daughters reveal which of the following themes through their actions in lines 31–50?

**A.** It is better to know one's flaws.
**B.** Housework is unimportant.
**C.** Vanity brings sorrow.
**D.** Living in the city is exciting.

**7.** Based on lines 51–62, you can infer that the animals turn on each other because they

**A.** realize that they are different
**B.** are tired of sharing a dish
**C.** want their owner's attention
**D.** are scared of the mirror

**8.** What causes Burek and Kot to return to normal?

**A.** Jan Skiba punishes them.
**B.** They grow tired of fighting.
**C.** Jan Skiba removes the mirror.
**D.** They avoid the mirror.

**9.** Which quotation from the story best demonstrates that the mirror is a symbol of vanity?

**A.** "The house had a bed, a bench bed, and a stove, but no mirror."
**B.** "In their anguish, both the dog and the cat stopped eating."
**C.** "After the mirror disappeared, Burek and Kot returned to normal."
**D.** "'A glass mirror shows only the skin of the body.'"

**10.** Which quotation from the story best demonstrates the story's theme?

**A.** "Since the dog had never seen another dog and the cat had never seen another cat and they only saw each other, the dog thought he was a cat and the cat thought she was a dog."
**B.** "The peddlers who bought goats, chickens, eggs, honey, calves, and whatever was available from the peasants in the village never came to Jan Skiba's poor hut."
**C.** "Kot's whiskers bristled, she began to meow at her reflection and raised a paw to it, but the other creature meowed back and raised her paw too."
**D.** "'The real image of a person is in his willingness to help himself and his family and, as far as possible, all those he comes in contact with.'"

## COMPREHENSION

**Directions** Answer the following questions about "On the Cat Walk."

**11.** What is the effect of the dog's wagging its tail?

**A.** The cats become the center of attention.
**B.** One of the author's sons goes on a walk.
**C.** The author gets out the collar and leash.
**D.** One of the cats wakes from a nap.

**12.** According to lines 9–12, what is the effect of the cats' presence on the walks?

**A.** The dog decides to move.
**B.** The dog runs away from the cats.
**C.** The cats and dog get into a fight.
**D.** The cats follow the dog's lead.

**13.** Based on lines 12–19, you can make the inference that the author is

**A.** lonely without several pets
**B.** knowledgeable about cats
**C.** excited about the state of Indiana
**D.** particular about the names of his cats

**14.** According to lines 12–19, what is the difference between Arthur and the author's current cats?

**A.** Arthur went for walks only because he was afraid to be alone.
**B.** The current cats are suspicious and afraid of the outdoors.
**C.** Arthur would walk only a few feet and then go home.
**D.** The current cats will walk only if the dog goes along.

**15.** According to lines 22–23, what is the effect of the cats' stopping to check the storm drains?

**A.** The dog chases mice in the streets.
**B.** The cats always catch chipmunks.
**C.** The dog has a chance to ask to be carried.
**D.** The cats stop and play in the water.

**16.** Based on lines 33–35, you can make the inference that the field is

**A.** located on a busy city street
**B.** a safe place for the pets to play
**C.** surrounded by two different schools
**D.** a favorite spot for people and their pets

**17.** According to lines 33–35, what causes the author and his pets to stay close to the school?

**A.** wet conditions
**B.** other animals
**C.** nearby children
**D.** bright sunlight

**18.** What does the selection best reveal about the author's perspective on pets?

**A.** He believes that pets ensure happiness.
**B.** The author thinks pets should be spoiled.
**C.** He appreciates every animal's personality.
**D.** The author respects dogs more than cats.

## COMPREHENSION

**Directions** Answer the following questions about both selections.

**19.** Both selections focus on which topic?

**A.** extreme poverty of peasants
**B.** pet behavior on family walks
**C.** destructive nature of vanity
**D.** different aspects of animal behavior

**20.** What is the best way to describe the difference between these two types of selections?

**A.** The first selection is nonfiction, and the other selection is a mystery.
**B.** One selection is fiction, and the other selection is nonfiction.
**C.** Both selections are nonfiction, but one selection is longer than the other.
**D.** The second selection is a poem, and the other selection is an essay.

# Written Response

## SHORT RESPONSE

**Directions** Write two or three sentences to answer each question on a separate sheet of paper.

**21.** Provide two examples that demonstrate the theme "Material possessions do not bring happiness" from "The Cat Who Thought She Was a Dog and the Dog Who Thought He Was a Cat."

**22.** Explain what the dog and cat symbolize in "The Cat Who Thought She Was a Dog and the Dog Who Thought He Was a Cat."

## EXTENDED RESPONSE

**Directions** Answer one of the following questions. Write two or more paragraphs on a separate sheet of paper.

**23.** Trace the chain of cause and effect in "The Cat Who Thought She Was a Dog and the Dog Who Thought He Was a Cat." Begin with the visit from the peddler.

**24. Challenge** Do the characters' actions from "The Cat Who Thought She Was a Dog and the Dog Who Thought He Was a Cat" effectively demonstrate the theme "Vanity is destructive"?

## Vocabulary

**Directions** Use context clues and your knowledge of connotation and denotation to answer the following questions about vocabulary in "The Cat Who Thought She Was a Dog and the Dog Who Thought He Was a Cat."

**1.** On line 2, the word *hut* has a connotation of

**A.** poor
**B.** empty
**C.** clean
**D.** large

**2.** In line 22, the word *doodads* has a connotation of

**A.** cheap
**B.** shiny
**C.** useless
**D.** expensive

**3.** In line 40, the word *snub* has a connotation of

**A.** big
**B.** ugly
**C.** plain
**D.** broken

**4.** In line 59, the word *creature* has a connotation of

**A.** miser
**B.** coward
**C.** fool
**D.** monster

**Directions** Use context clues to answer the following questions.

**5.** Which is the most likely meaning of *disruption* in line 71 of "The Cat Who Thought She Was a Dog and the Dog Who Thought He Was a Cat"?

**A.** disorder caused by an outside influence
**B.** a person's reflection in a mirror
**C.** beauty of a household decoration
**D.** a family's happiness at home

**6.** Which is the most likely meaning of *plying* in line 30 of "On the Cat Walk"?

**A.** performing in
**B.** crossing through
**C.** twisting together
**D.** carrying out

**7.** Which is the most likely meaning of *halfhearted* in line 32 of "On the Cat Walk"?

**A.** in distrust
**B.** with caution
**C.** in poor health
**D.** without interest

**8.** Which is the most likely meaning of *security* in line 33 of "On the Cat Walk"?

**A.** protection
**B.** self-consciousness
**C.** distraction
**D.** authority

## Writing and Grammar

**Directions** Read the short story and answer the questions that follow.

(1) "Oddities Await You in Clariser's Curio Shop," the brightly colored banner read. (2) "The Urn Looks Empty But It Is Not." (3) Devon had simply turned into the damp alley as a shortcut, and now he was standing under this strange sign. (4) A door gaped open before him. (5) No light was visible. (6) He could hear only the far-off sound of water dripping somewhere in the blanketing darkness.

(7) "Should I enter"? Devon muttered to himself. (8) He pondered the banner's strange message again. (9) It was all so mysterious! (10) Devon drew a breath and stepped through the doorway and into the darkness.

(11) Immediately he smelled many things. (12) Not one was recognizable. (13) He moved through the darkness. (14) Until he saw a glow of light spreading toward him. (15) Soon he was standing before a fountain. (16) Beyond that, the passage opened up into a large room. (17) It was filled with objects of all kinds.

(18) "Is there something I can do for you? a voice rang out. (19) Devon could see no one in the room, just piles and piles of stuff.

(20) "I saw your sign," Devon answered. (21) "I was just . . .well, I'm not really sure. . . ." his voice trailed off. (22) Devon didn't know why he was standing in this strange place talking to this strange voice. (23) What had drawn him here? (24) He gazed up the length of a humongous wooden door. (25) While he ran his hand over its carved surface. (26) Suddenly, a hand gripped his shoulder. (27) Devon's eyes widened as he gasped loudly and spun around.

(28) "Ah!" A thin, hunched little man smiled up at Devon. (29) "We've been waiting so long, and finally you are here!"

**1.** The first two sentences get the reader's attention by

**A.** including dialogue between Devon and the shopkeeper

**B.** making the reader curious about what the banner means

**C.** including a vivid description of the main character

**D.** making the reader curious about the color of the banner

**2.** Choose the correct coordinating conjunction to combine sentences 4 and 5.

**A.** yet

**B.** so

**C.** or

**D.** for

**3.** Choose the correct way to punctuate the dialogue in sentence 7.

**A.** "Should I enter? Devon muttered to himself."
**B.** "Should I enter," Devon muttered to himself.
**C.** "Should I enter?" Devon muttered to himself.
**D.** "Should I enter?" Devon muttered to himself."

**4.** Sentences 7–10 describe the conflict between

**A.** Devon and his own fears
**B.** the shopkeeper and forces of nature
**C.** the shopkeeper and forces of nature
**D.** the shopkeeper and his own fears

**5.** Choose the correct coordinating conjunction to combine sentences 11 and 12.

**A.** so
**B.** but
**C.** or
**D.** for

**6.** Which words in sentences 11 through 15 make the sequence of events clear?

**A.** immediately, until, soon
**B.** many, through, until
**C.** moved, toward, soon
**D.** through, toward, before

**7.** Combine sentence 13 and fragment 14 to form one sentence with an independent clause and a dependent clause.

**A.** He moved through the darkness and until he saw a glow of light spreading toward him.
**B.** He moved through the darkness—until he saw a glow of light spreading toward him.
**C.** He moved through the darkness; until he saw a glow of light spreading toward him.
**D.** He moved through the darkness until he saw a glow of light spreading toward him.

**8.** Choose the best way to rewrite sentence 15 to better show the setting.

**A.** Devon's palms perspired as he approached a fountain.
**B.** The sound of water grew louder, and soon he was standing before a low, stout fountain.
**C.** "What a fantastic fountain!" Devon exclaimed.
**D.** Devon stood up straight and tall, afraid to touch anything.

**9.** Choose the best way to better show the setting by adding sensory language to sentence 17.

**A.** It was filled with objects of all kinds, and Devon was fascinated with every one of them.

**B.** It was filled with objects of all kinds—most of which Devon had never seen before.

**C.** It was filled with objects of all kinds—enormous copper pots, gleaming stone figures, and detailed iron gates.

**D.** It was filled with objects of all kinds, which made Devon wonder how long it took the owner to collect so many things.

**10.** Choose the correct way to punctuate the dialogue in sentence 18.

**A.** "Is there something I can do for you?" "a voice rang out."

**B.** "Is there something I can do for you?" a voice rang out."

**C.** Is there something I can do for you? a voice rang out.

**D.** "Is there something I can do for you?" a voice rang out.

**11.** Combine sentence 24 and fragment 25 to form one sentence with an independent clause and a dependent clause.

**A.** He gazed up the length of a humongous wooden door while he ran his hand over its carved surface.

**B.** He gazed up the length of a humongous wooden door; while he ran his hand over its carved surface.

**C.** While he ran his hand over its carved surface; he gazed up the length of a humongous wooden door.

**D.** He gazed up the length of a humongous wooden door—while he ran his hand over its carved surface.

**12.** The sensory language in sentence 27 shows the reader that the main character is

**A.** disappointed

**B.** angry

**C.** lazy

**D.** frightened

## Writing

**Directions** Read the following quotation. Then read the prompts that follow and complete one of the writing activities.

> The short story is rather like a surgical operation. It has a beginning, middle, and an end.
>
> Richard Selzer, author and physician

**Prompt:** Write a short story about someone who makes a great discovery. For example, you might write about a character who uncovers a priceless treasure. As the quote suggests, make sure that readers can follow your story's sequence of events.

Now write your short story. The following reminders will help you.

**Challenge Prompt:** Write a short story based on a well-known saying, such as "All good things come to those who wait" or "Revenge is a dish best served cold." As the quote suggests, make sure that your short story follows a logical and recognizable sequence of events.

Now write your short story. The following reminders will help you.

**Reminders**

- Be sure your writing does what the prompt asks.
- Include an interesting plot and at least one character.
- Develop and resolve a central conflict.
- Use descriptive details, sensory language, and dialogue to reveal the setting and characters.
- Check for correct grammar, spelling, and punctuation.

## Reading Comprehension

**Directions** Read the following selection. Then answer the questions that follow

### After Twenty Years

**O. Henry**

The policeman on the beat moved up the avenue impressively. The impressiveness was habitual and not for show, for spectators were few. The time was barely 10 o'clock at night, but chilly gusts of wind with a taste of rain in them had well nigh depeopled the streets.

Trying doors as he went, twirling his club with many intricate and artful movements, turning now and then to cast his watchful eye down the pacific thoroughfare, the officer, with his stalwart form and slight swagger, made a fine picture of a guardian of the peace. The vicinity was one that kept early hours. Now and then you might see the lights of a cigar store or of an all-night lunch
10 counter; but the majority of the doors belonged to business places that had long since been closed.

When about midway of a certain block the policeman suddenly slowed his walk. In the doorway of a darkened hardware store a man leaned, with an unlighted cigar in his mouth. As the policeman walked up to him the man spoke up quickly.

"It's all right, officer "he said, reassuringly. "I'm just waiting for a friend. It's an appointment made twenty years ago. Sounds a little funny to you, doesn't it? Well, I'll explain if you'd like to make certain it's all straight. About that long ago there used to be a restaurant where this store stands - 'Big Joe' Brady's
20 restaurant."

"Until five years ago," said the policeman. "It was torn down then."

The man in the doorway struck a match and lit his cigar. The light showed a pale, square-jawed face with keen eyes, and a little white scar near his right eyebrow. His scarfpin was a large diamond, oddly set.

"Twenty years ago to-night,"said the man, "I dined here at 'Big Joe' Brady's with Jimmy Wells, my best chum, and the finest chap in the world. He and I were raised here in New York, just like two brothers, together. I was eighteen and Jimmy was twenty. The next morning I was to start for the West to make my fortune. You couldn't have dragged Jimmy out of New York; he
30 thought it was the only place on earth. Well, we agreed that night that we would meet here again exactly twenty years from that date and time, no matter what our conditions might be or from what distance we might have to come. We figured that in twenty years each of us ought to have our destiny worked out and our fortunes made, whatever they were going to be."

"It sounds pretty interesting," said the policeman. "Rather a long time between meets, though, it seems to me. Haven't you heard from your friend since you left?"

"Well, yes, for a time we corresponded," said the other. "But after a year or two we lost track of each other. You see, the West is a pretty big proposition, and 40 I kept hustling around over it pretty lively. But I know Jimmy will meet me here if he's alive, for he always was the truest, staunchest old chap in the world. He'll never forget. I came a thousand miles to stand in this door to-night, and it's worth it if my old partner turns up."

The waiting man pulled out a handsome watch, the lids of it set with small diamonds.

"Three minutes to ten," he announced. "It was exactly ten o'clock when we parted here at the restaurant door."

"Did pretty well out West, didn't you?" asked the policeman.

"You bet! I hope Jimmy has done half as well. He was a kind of plodder, 50 though, good fellow as he was. I've had to compete with some of the sharpest wits going to get my pile. A man gets in a groove in New York. It takes the West to put a razor-edge on him."

The policeman twirled his club and took a step or two.

"I'll be on my way. Hope your friend comes around all right. Going to call time on him sharp?"

"I should say not!" said the other. "I'll give him half an hour at least. If Jimmy is alive on earth he'll be here by that time. So long, officer."

"Good-night, sir," said the policeman, passing on along his beat, trying doors as he went.

60 There was now a fine, cold drizzle falling, and the wind had risen from its uncertain puffs into a steady blow. The few foot passengers astir in that quarter hurried dismally and silently along with coat collars turned high and pocketed hands. And in the door of the hardware store the man who had come a thousand miles to fill an appointment, uncertain almost to absurdity, with the friend of his youth, smoked his cigar and waited.

About twenty minutes he waited, and then a tall man in a long overcoat, with collar turned up to his ears, hurried across from the opposite side of the street. He went directly to the waiting man.

"Is that you, Bob?" he asked, doubtfully.

70 "Is that you, Jimmy Wells?" cried the man in the door.

"Bless my heart!" exclaimed the new arrival, grasping both the other's hands with his own. "It's Bob, sure as fate. I was certain I'd find you here if you were still in existence. Well, well, well! - twenty years is a long time. The old restaurant's gone, Bob; I wish it had lasted, so we could have had another dinner there. How has the West treated you, old man?"

"Bully; it has given me everything I asked it for. You've changed lots, Jimmy. I never thought you were so tall by two or three inches."

"Oh, I grew a bit after I was twenty."

"Doing well in New York, Jimmy?"

80 "Moderately. I have a position in one of the city departments. Come on, Bob; we'll go around to a place I know of, and have a good long talk about old times."

The two men started up the street, arm in arm. The man from the West, his egotism enlarged by success, was beginning to outline the history of his career. The other, submerged in his overcoat, listened with interest.

At the corner stood a drug store, brilliant with electric lights. When they came into this glare each of them turned simultaneously to gaze upon the other's face.

The man from the West stopped suddenly and released his arm.

90 "You're not Jimmy Wells," he snapped. "Twenty years is a long time, but not long enough to change a man's nose from a Roman to a pug."

"It sometimes changes a good man into a bad one," said the tall man. "You've been under arrest for ten minutes, 'Silky' Bob. Chicago thinks you may have dropped over our way and wires us she wants to have a chat with you. Going quietly, are you? That's sensible. Now, before we go to the station here's a note I was to hand to you. You may read it here at the window. It's from Patrolman Wells."

The man from the West unfolded the little piece of paper handed him. His hand was steady when he began to read, but it trembled a little by the time he had

100 finished. The note was rather short.

> Bob, I was at the appointed place on time. When you struck the match to light your cigar I saw it was the face of the man wanted in Chicago. Somehow I couldn't do it myself; so I went around and got a plain clothes man to do the job.
>
> Jimmy

**COMPREHENSION**

**Directions** Answer the following questions about "After Twenty Years."

**1.** The setting of the story is best summarized as a

**A.** street
**B.** trail
**C.** warehouse
**D.** home

**2.** What mood does the description in lines 1–4 create?

**A.** mysterious
**B.** anxious
**C.** depressing
**D.** stressful

**3.** Which words in lines 5–8 suggest a respectful tone?

**A.** turning, many
**B.** artful, watchful
**C.** form, slight
**D.** made, picture

**4.** Look at the dialogue in lines 40–41. Who is speaking?

**A.** "Silky" Bob
**B.** the plains clothes officer
**C.** Jimmy Wells
**D.** the policeman

**5.** Summarize the police officer's actions in lines 13–53. After he meets Bob he

**A.** gets something to eat
**B.** takes Bob to a restaurant
**C.** arrests Bob
**D.** continues patrolling

**6.** The dialogue in lines 63–66 changes the story's mood from anticipating to

**A.** thoughtful
**B.** excited
**C.** romantic
**D.** silly

**7.** Look at the dialogue in lines 84–88. The character speaking is

**A.** the restaurant owner
**B.** the plain clothes officer
**C.** "Silky" Bob
**D.** Jimmy Wells

**8.** What is the author's tone toward Bob in lines 84–95?

**A.** sarcastic
**B.** frightened
**C.** nervous
**D.** critical

## Written Response

**SHORT RESPONSE**

**Directions** Write two or three sentences to answer each question.

**9.** Identify one of Bob's character traits that the dialogue reveals. Give one example from "After Twenty Years" to support your response.

**10.** Clarify the ending of "After Twenty Years" by rephrasing the note that Jimmy wrote to Bob.

**EXTENDED RESPONSE**

**Directions** Answer the following question. Write two or more paragraphs.

**11.** Summarize "After Twenty Years." Include details about the setting, the conflict, and the characters in your summary.

## Reading Comprehension

**Directions** Read the following selection. Then answer the questions that follow.

### Getups *from* Wouldn't Take Nothing for My Journey Now

**Maya Angelou**

I was a twenty-one-year-old single parent with my son in kindergarten. Two jobs allowed me an apartment, food, and child care payment. Little money was left over for clothes, but I kept us nicely dressed in discoveries bought at the Salvation Army and other secondhand shops. Loving colors, I bought for myself beautiful reds and oranges, and greens and pinks, and teals and turquoise. I chose azure dresses and blouses and sweaters. And quite often I wore them in mixtures which brought surprise, to say the least, to the eyes of people who could not avoid noticing me. In fact, I concocted what southern black women used to call "getups."

10 Because I was very keen that my son not feel that he was neglected or different, I went frequently to his school. Sometimes between my jobs I would just go and stand outside the fenced play area. And he would, I am happy to say, always come and acknowledge me in the colorful regalia. I always wore beads. Lots of beads. The cheaper they were, the more I got, and sometimes I wore head wraps.

When my son was six and I twenty-two, he told me quite solemnly that he had to talk to me. We both sat down at the kitchen table, and he asked with an old man's eyes and a young boy's voice, "Mother, do you have any sweaters that match?" I was puzzled at first. I said, "No," and then I understood that he was
20 talking about the pullover and cardigan sets which were popular with white women. And I said, "No, I don't," maybe a little huffily. And he said, "Oh, I wish you did. So that you could wear them to school when you come to see me."

I was tickled, but I'm glad I didn't laugh because he continued, "Mother, could you please only come to school when they call you?" Then I realized that my attire, which delighted my heart and certainly activated my creativity, was an embarrassment to him.

When people are young, they desperately need to conform, and no one can embarrass a young person in public so much as an adult to whom he or she is related. Any outré action or wearing of "getups" can make a young person burn
30 with self-consciousness.

I learned to be a little more discreet to avoid causing him displeasure. As he grew older and more confident, I gradually returned to what friends thought of as my eccentric way of dressing. I was happier when I chose and created my own fashion.

I have lived in this body all my life and I know it much better than any fashion designer. I think I know what looks good on me, and I certainly know what feels good in me.

I appreciate the creativity which is employed in the design of fabric and the design of clothes, and when something does fit my body and personality, I rush 40 to it, buy it quickly, and wear it frequently. But I must not lie to myself for fashion's sake. I am only willing to purchase the item which becomes me and to wear that which enhances my image of myself to myself.

If I am comfortable inside my skin, I have the ability to make other people comfortable inside their skins although their feelings are not my primary reason for making my fashion choice. If I feel good inside my skin and clothes, I am thus free to allow my body its sway, its natural grace, its natural gesture. Then I am so comfortable that whatever I wear looks good on me even to the external fashion arbiters.

Dress is important to mention because many people are imprisoned by 50 powerful dictates on what is right and proper to wear. Those decisions made by others and sometimes at their convenience are not truly meant to make life better or finer or more graceful or more gracious. Many times they stem from greed, insensitivity, and the need for control.

I have been in company, not long to be sure, but in company where a purveyor of taste will look at a woman or a man who enters a room and will say with a sneer, "That was last year's jacket." As hastily as possible, I leave that company, but not before I record the snide attitude which has nothing to do with the beauty or effectiveness of the garment, but rather gives the speaker a moment's sense of superiority at, of course, someone else's expense.

60 Seek the fashion which truly fits and befits you. You will always be in fashion if you are true to yourself, and only if you are true to yourself. You might, of course, rightly wear that style which is emblazoned on the pages of the fashion magazines of the day, or you might not.

The statement, "Clothes make the man" should be looked at, reexamined, and in fact reevaluated. Clothes can make the man or woman look silly and foppish and foolish. Try rather to be so much yourself that the clothes you choose increase your naturalness and grace.

## COMPREHENSION

**Directions** Answer the following questions about "Getups."

**1.** Which of the following lines from the selection is a fact?

**A.** "I was a twenty-one-year-old single parent with my son in kindergarten."
**B.** "I kept us nicely dressed in discoveries bought at the Salvation Army."
**C.** "When people are young, they desperately need to conform."
**D.** "You will always be in fashion if you are true to yourself."

**2.** Monitor your understanding of lines 6–7. What does *them* refer to?

**A.** beads
**B.** clothes
**C.** head wraps
**D.** shoes

**3.** What type of style does the sentence structure in lines 9–13 reveal?

**A.** journalistic
**B.** conversational
**C.** objective
**D.** whimsical

**4.** What type of style does the word choice of "lots" and "got" in lines 12–13 reveal?

**A.** informal
**B.** persuasive
**C.** scientific
**D.** flowery

**5.** Which words in lines 19–24 best suggest a sincere tone?

**A.** wear, school
**B.** come, see
**C.** realized, embarrassment
**D.** continued, only

**6.** Clarify your understanding by rephrasing lines 29–31. The author

**A.** wore clothes that her friends liked
**B.** kept her clothes secret from her son
**C.** borrowed clothes from her friends
**D.** changed her style of dress for her son

**7.** Which words in lines 32–34 best show that the author is giving an opinion?

**A.** fashion designer
**B.** I think
**C.** this body
**D.** have lived

**8.** What is the author's tone in lines 56–59?

**A.** joking
**B.** confident
**C.** happy
**D.** gentle

## Written Response

### SHORT RESPONSE

**Directions** Write two or three sentences to answer each question on a separate sheet of paper.

**9.** What are two examples of the author's word choice in "Getups" that help create an upbeat mood?

**10.** Identify two opinions from "Getups."

### EXTENDED RESPONSE

**Directions** Answer the following question. Write two or more paragraphs on a separate sheet of paper.

**11.** What kind of style does the author use, based on the imagery and word choice in "Getups"? Give three examples from the selection to support your response.

## Vocabulary

**Directions** Use context clues and your knowledge of synonyms to answer the following questions.

**1.** Which word is a synonym for *vicinity* in line 8 of "After Twenty Years"?

**A.** building
**B.** neighborhood
**C.** department
**D.** state

**2.** Which word is a synonym for *keen* in line 20 of "After Twenty Years"?

**A.** eager
**B.** closed
**C.** blue
**D.** tired

**3.** Which word is a synonym for *solemnly* in line 14 of "Getups"?

**A.** tiredly
**B.** angrily
**C.** immediately
**D.** seriously

**4.** Which word is a synonym for *attire* in lines 22–23 of "Getups"?

**A.** clothing
**B.** vehicle
**C.** house
**D.** painting

**Directions** Use context clues and your knowledge of literal and figurative meanings to answer the following questions.

**5.** Which words are the most likely meaning of the words "It takes the west to put a razor edge on him" in lines 45–46 of "After Twenty Years"?

**A.** help a man be athletic
**B.** show a person's personality
**C.** give a man authority
**D.** make a person driven to success

**6.** Which words are the most likely meaning of the other submerged in his overcoat word in line 78 of "After Twenty Years"?

**A.** very warm
**B.** totally angry
**C.** fully enclosed
**D.** quite sad

**7.** Which word is the most likely meaning of the words "...you may have dropped over out way..." in lines 85–86 of "After Twenty Years"?

**A.** showed
**B.** called
**C.** looked
**D.** raveled

**8.** Which word is the most likely meaning of the words "...but not before I record the..." in lines 52–55 of "Getups"?

**A.** rehearse
**B.** remember
**C.** reveal
**D.** recognize

## Writing and Grammar

**Directions** Read the interpretive essay and answer the questions that follow.

(1) Consider a time when you faced a difficult situation. (2) Did you go through it on your own, or did someone help you? (3) In Virginia Hamilton's "The People Could Fly," Sarah, Toby, and other unnamed characters experience the hardships of slavery. (4) Through the characters' actions, the author reveals the importance of working together during hard times.

(5) Early in the story, the narrator explain that Sarah works in the field with her baby tied to her back. (6) When the baby cries, the Driver cracks his whip across the baby. (7) Sarah and the baby falls to the ground. (8) Toby goes over to help Sarah up. (9) Sarah and Toby decides that it is almost time for Sarah to fly away. (10) The Driver cracks his whip around Sarah's legs, and she falls to the ground a second time. (11) The narrator says, "Toby was there where there was no one to help her and the babe." (12) Toby helps Sarah a second time. (13) This time Toby says the magic words so Sarah can fly away. (14) Sarah would not have been able to escape without Toby's help.

(15) Later in the story, Toby helps other slaves escape from the field. (16) The narrator says that when slaves fell from the unpleasant heat "Toby was there." (17) He whispers the magic words to the slaves, and they fly away to freedom. (18) In the end of the story, Toby fly away with a large group of slaves. (19) The narrator says, "And the old man, old Toby, flew behind them, takin' care of them." (20) Toby works with the slaves to secure their freedom.

(21) The characters' actions in "The People Could Fly" reveal the importance of working together during hard times. (22) The characters' support for each other and their ability to work together allow them to escape the bonds of slavery. (23) The author's message of working together is an important message for anyone in an especially difficult situation. (24) It is important to have a group of people that support you when times get bad.

**1.** Which tone does the writer use to achieve his or her purpose?

**A.** serious
**B.** bitter
**C.** nervous
**D.** modest

**2.** Which sentence identifies the title and author of the story?

**A.** sentence 1
**B.** sentence 2
**C.** sentence 3
**D.** sentence 4

**3.** Which sentence contains the writer's thesis statement?

**A.** sentence 2
**B.** sentence 4
**C.** sentence 6
**D.** sentence 8

**4.** To maintain subject-verb agreement in sentence 5, change "the narrator explain" to

**A.** the narrator explain's
**B.** the narrator's explain
**C.** the narrator explains
**D.** the narrators explains

**5.** To maintain subject-verb agreement in sentence 7, change "Sarah and the baby falls" to

**A.** Sarah and the baby fall
**B.** Sarahs and the baby falls
**C.** Sarahs and the babys fall
**D.** Sarah and the babys falls

**6.** To maintain subject-verb agreement in sentence 9, change "Sarah and Toby decides" to

**A.** Sarah and Toby decide's
**B.** Sarah and Tobys decide
**C.** Sarahs' and Toby decides
**D.** Sarah and Toby decide

**7.** Which element does the writer use in sentence 11 to support the key idea of people working together during hard times?

**A.** conclusion
**B.** quotation
**C.** tone
**D.** metaphor

**8.** Which precise adjective would best replace the word *unpleasant* in sentence 16?

**A.** extreme
**B.** hot
**C.** bad
**D.** imperfect

**9.** Which sentence provides plot details that help you understand the interpretation of the story?

**A.** sentence 1
**B.** sentence 6
**C.** sentence 14
**D.** sentence 21

**10.** To maintain subject-verb agreement in sentence 18, change "Toby fly" to

**A.** Tobys fly
**B.** Toby flies
**C.** Tobys flies
**D.** Toby flying

**11.** Which precise adjective would best replace the word bad in sentence 24?

**A.** uninspiring
**B.** exhausting
**C.** difficult
**D.** strange

**12.** Which tone did the writer select because it is appropriate for the purpose of arguing a viewpoint?

**A.** gentle
**B.** formal
**C.** amused
**D.** silly

## Writing

**Directions** Read the following quotation. Then read the prompt that follows and complete the writing activity.

> "All meanings, we know, depend on the key of interpretation."
>
> George Eliot (Mary Ann Evans)

**Prompt:** Write an interpretive essay that examines the conflict that Patrolman Wells faces. As the quote suggests, use your interpretation to find meaning in the story. Use details from the story to support your interpretation.

Now write your interpretive essay. The following reminders will help you.

**Reminders**

- Be sure your writing does what the prompt asks.
- Include a thesis statement that identifies the key points of the essay.
- Summarize the interpretation in a conclusion and tell why the story is interesting or important.
- Use precise language to examine and explain the work.
- Check for correct grammar, spelling, and punctuation.

# Unit 4



## Reading Comprehension

**Directions** Read the following selection. Then answer the questions that follow.

### After Twenty Years

**O. Henry**

The policeman on the beat moved up the avenue impressively. The impressiveness was habitual and not for show, for spectators were few. The time was barely 10 o'clock at night, but chilly gusts of wind with a taste of rain in them had well nigh depeopled the streets.

Trying doors as he went, twirling his club with many intricate and artful movements, turning now and then to cast his watchful eye down the pacific thoroughfare, the officer, with his stalwart form and slight swagger, made a fine picture of a guardian of the peace. The vicinity was one that kept early hours. Now and then you might see the lights of a cigar store or of an all-night lunch
10 counter; but the majority of the doors belonged to business places that had long since been closed.

When about midway of a certain block the policeman suddenly slowed his walk. In the doorway of a darkened hardware store a man leaned, with an unlighted cigar in his mouth. As the policeman walked up to him the man spoke up quickly.

"It's all right, officer "he said, reassuringly. "I'm just waiting for a friend. It's an appointment made twenty years ago. Sounds a little funny to you, doesn't it? Well, I'll explain if you'd like to make certain it's all straight. About that long ago there used to be a restaurant where this store stands - 'Big Joe' Brady's
20 restaurant."

"Until five years ago," said the policeman. "It was torn down then."

The man in the doorway struck a match and lit his cigar. The light showed a pale, square-jawed face with keen eyes, and a little white scar near his right eyebrow. His scarfpin was a large diamond, oddly set.

"Twenty years ago to-night,"said the man, "I dined here at 'Big Joe' Brady's with Jimmy Wells, my best chum, and the finest chap in the world. He and I were raised here in New York, just like two brothers, together. I was eighteen and Jimmy was twenty. The next morning I was to start for the West to make my fortune. You couldn't have dragged Jimmy out of New York; he
30 thought it was the only place on earth. Well, we agreed that night that we would meet here again exactly twenty years from that date and time, no matter what our conditions might be or from what distance we might have to come. We figured that in twenty years each of us ought to have our destiny worked out and our fortunes made, whatever they were going to be."

"It sounds pretty interesting," said the policeman. "Rather a long time between meets, though, it seems to me. Haven't you heard from your friend since you left?"

"Well, yes, for a time we corresponded," said the other. "But after a year or two we lost track of each other. You see, the West is a pretty big proposition, and 40 I kept hustling around over it pretty lively. But I know Jimmy will meet me here if he's alive, for he always was the truest, staunchest old chap in the world. He'll never forget. I came a thousand miles to stand in this door to-night, and it's worth it if my old partner turns up."

The waiting man pulled out a handsome watch, the lids of it set with small diamonds.

"Three minutes to ten," he announced. "It was exactly ten o'clock when we parted here at the restaurant door."

"Did pretty well out West, didn't you?" asked the policeman.

"You bet! I hope Jimmy has done half as well. He was a kind of plodder, 50 though, good fellow as he was. I've had to compete with some of the sharpest wits going to get my pile. A man gets in a groove in New York. It takes the West to put a razor-edge on him."

The policeman twirled his club and took a step or two.

"I'll be on my way. Hope your friend comes around all right. Going to call time on him sharp?"

"I should say not!" said the other. "I'll give him half an hour at least. If Jimmy is alive on earth he'll be here by that time. So long, officer."

"Good-night, sir," said the policeman, passing on along his beat, trying doors as he went.

60 There was now a fine, cold drizzle falling, and the wind had risen from its uncertain puffs into a steady blow. The few foot passengers astir in that quarter hurried dismally and silently along with coat collars turned high and pocketed hands. And in the door of the hardware store the man who had come a thousand miles to fill an appointment, uncertain almost to absurdity, with the friend of his youth, smoked his cigar and waited.

About twenty minutes he waited, and then a tall man in a long overcoat, with collar turned up to his ears, hurried across from the opposite side of the street. He went directly to the waiting man.

"Is that you, Bob?" he asked, doubtfully.

70 "Is that you, Jimmy Wells?" cried the man in the door.

"Bless my heart!" exclaimed the new arrival, grasping both the other's hands with his own. "It's Bob, sure as fate. I was certain I'd find you here if you were still in existence. Well, well, well! - twenty years is a long time. The old restaurant's gone, Bob; I wish it had lasted, so we could have had another dinner there. How has the West treated you, old man?"

"Bully; it has given me everything I asked it for. You've changed lots, Jimmy. I never thought you were so tall by two or three inches."

"Oh, I grew a bit after I was twenty."

"Doing well in New York, Jimmy?"

80 "Moderately. I have a position in one of the city departments. Come on, Bob; we'll go around to a place I know of, and have a good long talk about old times."

The two men started up the street, arm in arm. The man from the West, his egotism enlarged by success, was beginning to outline the history of his career. The other, submerged in his overcoat, listened with interest.

At the corner stood a drug store, brilliant with electric lights. When they came into this glare each of them turned simultaneously to gaze upon the other's face.

The man from the West stopped suddenly and released his arm.

90 "You're not Jimmy Wells," he snapped. "Twenty years is a long time, but not long enough to change a man's nose from a Roman to a pug."

"It sometimes changes a good man into a bad one," said the tall man. "You've been under arrest for ten minutes, 'Silky' Bob. Chicago thinks you may have dropped over our way and wires us she wants to have a chat with you. Going quietly, are you? That's sensible. Now, before we go to the station here's a note I was to hand to you. You may read it here at the window. It's from Patrolman Wells."

The man from the West unfolded the little piece of paper handed him. His hand was steady when he began to read, but it trembled a little by the time he had

100 finished. The note was rather short.

Bob, I was at the appointed place on time. When you struck the match to light your cigar I saw it was the face of the man wanted in Chicago. Somehow I couldn't do it myself; so I went around and got a plain clothes man to do the job.

Jimmy

## COMPREHENSION

**Directions** Answer the following questions about "After Twenty Years."

**1.** The setting of the story can best be summarized as a

**A.** busy restaurant late at night
**B.** hardware store in early evening
**C.** police station in the evening
**D.** vacant street on a dark night

**2.** Which sentence best contributes to the mysterious mood of the story?

**A.** "In the doorway of a darkened hardware store a man leaned, with an unlighted cigar in his mouth."
**B.** "'Good-night, sir,' said the policeman, passing on along his beat, trying doors as he went."
**C.** "The man from the West, his egotism enlarged by success, was beginning to outline the history of his career."
**D.** "When they came into this glare each of them turned simultaneously to gaze upon the other's face."

**3.** You know that O. Henry's tone toward the police officer in lines 5–8 is respectful because O. Henry uses

**A.** words such as "watchful" and "fine"
**B.** complex and compound sentences
**C.** details about the neighborhood
**D.** imagery that appeals to the senses

**4.** The dialogue in lines 14–17 reveals that the speaker is

**A.** an intelligent businessman
**B.** a sensitive and caring individual
**C.** an outgoing and talkative person
**D.** a wealthy merchant from the West

**5.** The dialogue in lines 43–52

**A.** illustrates a flowery writing style
**B.** demonstrates the story's eerie mood
**C.** shows the police officer's courage
**D.** reveals the author's amused tone

**6.** In lines 64–65, the words "dismally" and "silently"

**A.** contribute to the gloomy mood of the story
**B.** reveal that Bob is impatient while waiting for his friend
**C.** help to vary the sentence structure of the story
**D.** provide details that explain the actions of the main characters

**7.** The speaker in line 64–65 is

**A.** the plain clothes officer
**B.** the restaurant owner
**C.** Jimmy Wells
**D.** "Silky" Bob

**8.** Which of the following best summarizes the characters' actions in lines 82–96?

**A.** Jimmy Wells reads a note concerning the reasons for Bob's arrest.
**B.** The plain clothes officer speaks to Bob and hands him a note from his friend.
**C.** The tall stranger turns out to be Bob's childhood friend, Jimmy Wells.
**D.** The tall stranger turns out to be Bob's childhood friend, Jimmy Wells.

## Written Response

### SHORT RESPONSE

**Directions** Write two or three sentences to answer each question on a separate sheet of paper.

**9.** What does the plain clothes officer's dialogue reveal about his personality? Give one example from the story to support your response.

**10.** Summarize the characters' actions in "After Twenty Years" by restating what Jimmy and Bob did between their two meetings.

### EXTENDED RESPONSE

**Directions** Answer one of the following questions. Write two or more paragraphs on a separate sheet of paper.

**11.** How would you describe the overall mood of "After Twenty Years"? Give examples of setting, characters, and dialogue to support your response.

**12.** What do the word choice, sentence structure, and tone in "After Twenty Years" reveal about O. Henry's style? Give examples from the story to support your response.

## Reading Comprehension

**Directions** Read the following selection. Then answer the questions that follow.

### Getups *from* Wouldn't Take Nothing for My Journey Now

I was a twenty-one-year-old single parent with my son in kindergarten. Two jobs allowed me an apartment, food, and child care payment. Little money was left over for clothes, but I kept us nicely dressed in discoveries bought at the Salvation Army and other secondhand shops. Loving colors, I bought for myself beautiful reds and oranges, and greens and pinks, and teals and turquoise. I chose azure dresses and blouses and sweaters. And quite often I wore them in mixtures which brought surprise, to say the least, to the eyes of people who could not avoid noticing me. In fact, I concocted what southern black women used to call "getups."

10 Because I was very keen that my son not feel that he was neglected or different, I went frequently to his school. Sometimes between my jobs I would just go and stand outside the fenced play area. And he would, I am happy to say, always come and acknowledge me in the colorful regalia. I always wore beads. Lots of beads. The cheaper they were, the more I got, and sometimes I wore head wraps.

When my son was six and I twenty-two, he told me quite solemnly that he had to talk to me. We both sat down at the kitchen table, and he asked with an old man's eyes and a young boy's voice, "Mother, do you have any sweaters that match?" I was puzzled at first. I said, "No," and then I understood that he was
20 talking about the pullover and cardigan sets which were popular with white women. And I said, "No, I don't," maybe a little huffily. And he said, "Oh, I wish you did. So that you could wear them to school when you come to see me."

I was tickled, but I'm glad I didn't laugh because he continued, "Mother, could you please only come to school when they call you?" Then I realized that my attire, which delighted my heart and certainly activated my creativity, was an embarrassment to him.

When people are young, they desperately need to conform, and no one can embarrass a young person in public so much as an adult to whom he or she is related. Any outré action or wearing of "getups" can make a young person burn
30 with self-consciousness.

I learned to be a little more discreet to avoid causing him displeasure. As he grew older and more confident, I gradually returned to what friends thought of as my eccentric way of dressing. I was happier when I chose and created my own fashion.

I have lived in this body all my life and I know it much better than any fashion designer. I think I know what looks good on me, and I certainly know what feels good in me.

I appreciate the creativity which is employed in the design of fabric and the design of clothes, and when something does fit my body and personality, I rush
40 to it, buy it quickly, and wear it frequently. But I must not lie to myself for fashion's sake. I am only willing to purchase the item which becomes me and to wear that which enhances my image of myself to myself.

If I am comfortable inside my skin, I have the ability to make other people comfortable inside their skins although their feelings are not my primary reason for making my fashion choice. If I feel good inside my skin and clothes, I am thus free to allow my body its sway, its natural grace, its natural gesture. Then I am so comfortable that whatever I wear looks good on me even to the external fashion arbiters.

Dress is important to mention because many people are imprisoned by
50 powerful dictates on what is right and proper to wear. Those decisions made by others and sometimes at their convenience are not truly meant to make life better or finer or more graceful or more gracious. Many times they stem from greed, insensitivity, and the need for control.

I have been in company, not long to be sure, but in company where a purveyor of taste will look at a woman or a man who enters a room and will say with a sneer, "That was last year's jacket." As hastily as possible, I leave that company, but not before I record the snide attitude which has nothing to do with the beauty or effectiveness of the garment, but rather gives the speaker a moment's sense of superiority at, of course, someone else's expense.

60 Seek the fashion which truly fits and befits you. You will always be in fashion if you are true to yourself, and only if you are true to yourself. You might, of course, rightly wear that style which is emblazoned on the pages of the fashion magazines of the day, or you might not.

The statement, "Clothes make the man" should be looked at, reexamined, and in fact reevaluated. Clothes can make the man or woman look silly and foppish and foolish. Try rather to be so much yourself that the clothes you choose increase your naturalness and grace.



## COMPREHENSION

**Directions** Answer the following questions about "Getups."

**1.** Monitor your understanding by rephrasing lines 1–8.

**A.** The author wore clothing that was considered fashionable at the time.

**B.** Maya Angelou purchased clothing from large department stores in town.

**C.** The author wore inexpensive, brightly colored outfits that she put together herself .

**D.** Maya Angelou purchased clothing that others thought looked good on her.

**2.** Which of the following sentences best shows an informal, conversational style?

**A.** "The cheaper they were, the more I got, and sometimes I wore head wraps."

**B.** "Many times they stem from greed, insensitivity, and the need for control."

**C.** "Seek the fashion which truly fits and befits you."

**D.** "Clothes can make the man or woman look silly and foppish and foolish."

**3.** You know that Angelou uses a sincere tone in lines 19–24 because she

**A.** uses a long, complex sentence

**B.** provides descriptive details

**C.** uses words such as "glad" and "realized"

**D.** provides dialogue to support her point

**4.** Which of the following statements is an opinion?

**A.** "Loving colors, I bought for myself beautiful reds and oranges, and greens and pinks, and teals and turquoise."

**B.** "Because I was very keen that my son not feel that he was neglected or different, I went frequently to his school."

**C.** "I am only willing to purchase the item which becomes me and to wear that which enhances my image of myself to myself."

**D.** "You will always be in fashion if you are true to yourself, and only if you are true to yourself."

**5.** Which sentence most helps create a mood of frustration?

**A.** "Two jobs allowed me an apartment, food, and child care payment."
**B.** "In fact, I concocted what southern black women used to call 'getups.'
**C.** "Sometimes between my jobs I would just go and stand outside the fenced play area."
**D.** "And I said, 'No, I don't,' maybe a little huffily."

**6.** Monitor your understanding. Which statement best rephrases lines 49–50?

**A.** Prisoners cannot choose their clothes.
**B.** It is best to follow fashion rules
**C.** Everyone looks better in good-fitting clothes.
**D.** People often let others influence how they dress.

**7.** Which statement in the selection is a fact?

**A.** "Two jobs allowed me an apartment, food, and child care payment."
**B.** "Many times they stem from greed, insensitivity, and the need for control."
**C.** "Seek the fashion which truly fits and befits you."
**D.** "Clothes can make the man or woman look silly and foppish and foolish."

**8.** Angelou's style in this selection could best be characterized as

**A.** an informal, conversational style
**B.** an objective, journalistic style
**C.** an informal, humorous style
**D.** a formal, flowery style

## Written Response

### SHORT RESPONSE

**Directions** Write two or three sentences to answer each question on a separate sheet of paper.

**9.** Identify one opinion from "Getups." Explain how you know that the statement is an opinion.

**10.** Clarify lines 14–24 by rephrasing the son's thoughts about Angelou's clothing.

### EXTENDED RESPONSE

**Directions** Answer one of the following questions. Write two or more paragraphs on a separate sheet of paper.

**11.** Explain Angelou's style by examining her word choice and sentence structure in "Getups." Support your response with examples from the selection.

**12. Challenge** Identify the changing tones in "Getups." Why do you think Angelou changes her tone throughout the selection? Support your response with examples from the selection.

## Vocabulary

**Directions** Use context clues and your knowledge of synonyms to answer the following questions.

**1.** Which word is a synonym for *spectators* in line 2 of "After Twenty Years"?

**A.** tourists
**B.** pedestrians
**C.** observers
**D.** customers

**2.** Which word is a synonym for *intricate* in line 5 of "After Twenty Years"?

**A.** complicated
**B.** efficient
**C.** dangerous
**D.** important

**3.** Which word is a synonym for *guardian* in line 8 of "After Twenty Years"?

**A.** maker
**B.** designer
**C.** leader
**D.** caretaker

**4.** Which word is a synonym for *dictates* in line 46 of "Getups"?

**A.** rules
**B.** models
**C.** factors
**D.** suggestions

**Directions** Use context clues and your knowledge of literal and figurative meanings to answer the following questions.

**5.** Which word is the most likely meaning of the to make certain iusall straight word in line 16 of "After Twenty Years"?

**A.** quick
**B.** planned
**C.** legal
**D.** convenient

**6.** Which word is the most likely meaning of the A man gets in a groove in New York. word in line 45 of "After Twenty Years"?

**A.** hole
**B.** path
**C.** daze
**D.** routine

**7.** Which word is the most likely meaning of the if I am comfortable inside my skin words in line 40 of "Getups"?

**A.** flexible
**B.** attractive
**C.** healthy
**D.** confident

**8.** Which word is the most likely meaning of the many people are imprisoned word in line 45of "Getups"?

**A.** jailed
**B.** restricted
**C.** locked
**D.** crushed

## Writing and Grammar

**Directions** Read the interpretive essay and answer the questions that follow.

(1) Consider a time when you faced a difficult situation. (2) Did you go through it on your own, or did someone help you? (3) In Virginia Hamilton's "The People Could Fly," Sarah, Toby, and other unnamed characters experience the hardships of slavery. (4) Through the characters' actions, the author reveals the importance of working together during hard times.

(5) Early in the story, the narrator explain that Sarah works in the field with her baby tied to her back. (6) When the baby cries, the Driver cracks his whip across the baby. (7) Sarah and the baby falls to the ground. (8) Toby goes over to help Sarah up. (9) Sarah and Toby decides that it is almost time for Sarah to fly away. (10) The Driver cracks his whip around Sarah's legs, and she falls to the ground a second time. (11) The narrator says, "Toby was there where there was no one to help her and the babe." (12) Toby helps Sarah a second time. (13) This time Toby says the magic words so Sarah can fly away. (14) Sarah would not have been able to escape without Toby's help.

(15) Later in the story, Toby helps other slaves escape from the field. (16) The narrator says that when slaves fell from the unpleasant heat "Toby was there." (17) He whispers the magic words to the slaves, and they fly away to freedom. (18) In the end of the story, Toby fly away with a large group of slaves. (19) The narrator says, "And the old man, old Toby, flew behind them, takin' care of them." (20) Toby works with the slaves to secure their freedom.

(21) The characters' actions in "The People Could Fly" reveal the importance of working together during hard times. (22) The characters' support for each other and their ability to work together allow them to escape the bonds of slavery. (23) The author's message of working together is an important message for anyone in an especially difficult situation. (24) It is important to have a group of people that support you when times get bad.

**1.** The writer's formal tone best reveals that his or her purpose is to

**A.** entertain readers
**B.** argue a viewpoint
**C.** describe a process
**D.** relay information

**2.** The main purpose of sentence 3 is to

**A.** identify the title and author of the story
**B.** support the writer's main point
**C.** grab the reader's attention
**D.** present the writer's message

**3.** The writer's thesis statement says that the

**A.** characters' actions show the importance of working together in tough times
**B.** story is about several characters that experience slavery
**C.** old man, Toby, helps many slaves escape to freedom
**D.** narrator uses descriptive language to reveal the meaning of the story

**4.** To maintain subject-verb agreement in sentence 5, change "explain" to

**A.** explaining
**B.** explained
**C.** explains
**D.** are explaining

**5.** To maintain subject-verb agreement in sentence 7, change "Sarah and the baby falls" to

**A.** Sarah and the baby fall
**B.** Sarah and the baby falls
**C.** Sarah and the baby are falling
**D.** Sarah and the babys fall

**6.** To maintain subject-verb agreement in sentence 9, change "Sarah and Toby decides" to

**A.** Sarah and Toby are deciding
**B.** Sarah and Tobys decide
**C.** Sarahs and Toby is decides
**D.** Sarah and Toby decide

**7.** The quotation in sentence 11 supports the key idea that

**A.** babies suffer most during times of struggle
**B.** Toby is like a grandfather to Sarah and the baby
**C.** it is important to work together during hard times
**D.** Toby and Sarah's friendship developed because of slavery

**8.** Which precise adjective would best replace the word *unpleasant* in sentence 16?

**A.** unbearable
**B.** intense
**C.** great
**D.** strong

**9.** Which sentence from the interpretive essay provides plot details that help you understand the interpretation?

**A.** Consider a time when you faced a difficult situation.
**B.** When the baby cries, the Driver cracks his whip across the baby.
**C.** Sarah would not have been able to escape without Toby's help.
**D.** It is important to have a group of people that support you when times get bad.

**10.** To maintain subject-verb agreement in sentence 18, change "Toby fly" to

**A.** Tobys are flying
**B.** Toby flies
**C.** Tobys flies
**D.** Toby flying

**11.** Which precise adjective would best replace the word bad in sentence 24?

**A.** challenging  
**B.** rough  
**C.** hard  
**D.** wild

**12.** The writer's formal tone in the essay is appropriate for the audience because readers will be most interested in

**A.** laughing at the story's characters  
**B.** visualizing Toby's appearance  
**C.** learning the art of storytelling  
**D.** reading a serious interpretation

## Writing

**Directions** Read the following quotation. Then read the prompts that follow and complete one of the writing activities.

> "All meanings, we know, depend on the key of interpretation."
>
> George Eliot (Mary Ann Evans)

**Prompt:** Write an interpretative essay about "After Twenty Years." Use the key of interpretation to unlock the deeper meaning of the story. For example, think about what the characters and dialogue reveal. Use details from the story to support your interpretation.

Now write your interpretive essay. The following reminders will help you.

**Challenge Prompt:** Write an interpretive essay about a story you have recently read. As George Eliot suggests, the meaning of a story depends on the key of interpretation. Examine several literary elements in the story, such as plot, characters, setting, mood, dialogue, or point of view. Use details from the story to support your interpretation.

Now write your interpretive essay. The following reminders will help you.

**Reminders**

- Be sure your writing does what the prompt asks.
- Include a thesis statement that identifies the key points of the essay.
- Summarize the interpretation in a conclusion and tell why the story is interesting and important.
- Use precise language to examine and explain the work.
- Check for correct grammar, spelling, and punctuation.

# Unit 5



## Reading Comprehension

**Directions** Wordsworth wrote two poems titled "To a Butterfly," both of which describe the close relationship he shared with his sister when they were children. Read the first and second poems titled "To a Butterfly." Then read "Starlings in Winter" and answer the questions that follow.

**First Poem**
**To a Butterfly**
**William Wordsworth**

I've watched you now a full half hour,
Self-poised upon that yellow flower;
And, little Butterfly! indeed
I know not if you sleep, or feed.
5 How motionless! not frozen seas
More motionless! and then
What joy awaits you, when the breeze
Hath found you out among the trees,
And calls you forth again!

10 This plot of Orchard-ground is ours;
My trees they are, my Sister's flowers;
Stop here whenever you are weary,
And rest as in a sanctuary!
Come often to us, fear no wrong;
15 Sit near us on the bough!
We'll talk of sunshine and of song;
And summer days, when we were young,
Sweet childish days, that were as long
As twenty days are now!

**Second Poem**
**To a Butterfly**
**William Wordsworth**

Stay near me—do not take thy flight!
A little longer stay in sight!
Much converse do I find in Thee,
Historian of my Infancy!
5 Float near me; do not yet depart!
Dead times revive in thee:
Thou bring'st, gay Creature as thou art!
A solemn image to my heart,
My Father's Family!

10 Oh! pleasant, pleasant were the days,
The time, when in our childish plays
My sister Emmeline and I
Together chaced the Butterfly!
A very hunter did I rush
15 Upon the prey:—with leaps and springs
I followed on from brake to bush;
But she, God love her! feared to brush
The dust from off its wings.

**Starlings in Winter**

**Mary Oliver**

Chunky and noisy,
but with stars in their black feathers,
they spring from the telephone wire
and instantly

5 they are acrobats
in the freezing wind.
And now, in the theater of air,
they swing over buildings,

dipping and rising;
10 they float like one stippled star
that opens,
becomes for a moment fragmented,

then closes again;
and you watch
15 and you try
but you simply can't imagine

how they do it
with no articulated instruction, no pause,
only the silent confirmation
20 that they are this notable thing,

this wheel of many parts, that can rise and spin
over and over again,
full of gorgeous life.
Ah, world, what lessons you prepare for us,

25 even in the leafless winter,
even in the ashy city.
I am thinking now
of grief, and of getting past it;

I feel my boots
30 trying to leave the ground,
I feel my heart
pumping hard. I want

to think again of dangerous and noble things.
I want to be light and frolicsome.
35 I want to be improbable beautiful and afraid of nothing,
as though I had wings.



## COMPREHENSION

**Directions** Answer the following questions about the first poem and the second poem titled "To a Butterfly."

**1.** Which of the following words is repeated in lines 5–9 of the first poem titled "To a Butterfly"?

**A.** motionless **C.** joy
**B.** frozen **D.** breeze

**2.** In lines 7–9 of the first poem, the poet personifies the

**A.** butterfly **C.** sea
**B.** breeze **D.** flower

**3.** Which literary element does the poet use in line 2 of the second poem titled "To a Butterfly"?

**A.** simile **C.** alliteration
**B.** repetition **D.** personification

**4.** Based on both poems, you can make the inference that the butterfly reminds the speaker of

**A.** gardening **C.** flying
**B.** childhood **D.** trees

**5.** In both poems, which lines of each stanza rhyme?

**A.** lines 1 and 2 **C.** lines 1 and 5
**B.** lines 2 and 4 **D.** lines 5 and 6

**6.** Which type of poem is "To a Butterfly"?

**A.** lyric poem **C.** limerick
**B.** haiku **D.** humorous poem

## COMPREHENSION

**Directions** Answer the following questions about "Starlings in Winter."

**7.** The imagery in line 1 appeals to the senses of sight and

**A.** taste
**B.** hearing
**C.** touch
**D.** smell

**8.** The metaphor in lines 1–6 compares starlings to

**A.** stars
**B.** feathers
**C.** acrobats
**D.** wires

**9.** The imagery in lines 9–12 appeals to the sense of

**A.** taste
**B.** hearing
**C.** touch
**D.** sight

**10.** The sound device used in lines 14–16 is

**A.** repetition
**B.** onomatopoeia
**C.** rhythm
**D.** rhyme

**11.** The metaphor in line 21 compares a flock of starlings to a

**A.** star
**B.** building
**C.** wheel
**D.** theater

**12.** You can tell that this poem is written in free verse because the lines

**A.** vary in length
**B.** use a pattern of rhyme
**C.** follow a set rhythm
**D.** contain metaphors

**13.** Which type of poem is "Starlings in Winter"?

**A.** narrative poem
**B.** haiku
**C.** lyric poem
**D.** memorial

## COMPREHENSION

**Directions** Answer these questions about all three poems.

**14.** Based on the imagery in all the poems, you can make the inference that the speakers

**A.** admire family members
**B.** respect creatures
**C.** love the winter
**D.** enjoy remembering the past

**15.** You can make an inference that the speakers of all three poems are

**A.** interested in butterflies
**B.** fond of birds
**C.** inspired by nature
**D.** amazed by acrobats

**16.** In all three poems, the speakers express their feelings and thoughts about

**A.** nature
**B.** people
**C.** seasons
**D.** towns

## Written Response

### SHORT RESPONSE

**Directions** Write two or three sentences to answer each question on a separate sheet of paper.

**17.** Identify an example of imagery in lines 1–9 of the first poem titled "To a Butterfly." To which sense does this example appeal?

**18.** In the first "To a Butterfly," the rhyme scheme of stanza 1 is aabbcdccd. Find two pairs of rhyming words that show this rhyme scheme.

### EXTENDED RESPONSE

**Directions** Answer the following question. Write two or more paragraphs on a separate sheet of paper.

**19.** Identify the mood of both poems titled "To a Butterfly." How does the figurative language in each poem create the mood? Give three examples from the poems to support your answer.

## Reading Comprehension

**Directions** Read the following selection. Then answer the questions that follow.

*In the 1930s, author Stanley Kunitz moved from New York City to a farm called Wormwood Hill in the Connecticut countryside.*

**Owls in the Attic**
***from* The Wild Braid**
**Stanley Kunitz**

One day, as I stood under a great chestnut tree deep in the center of the woods, I heard some rustling in the branches. I looked up and saw a family of owls, a mother and four fledglings, all on one branch. The moment I moved, they frantically whisked off.

I vowed I would become a friend of theirs, and realized I must not disturb them in any way. I learned if I approached very quietly, advancing just a few steps, then standing still, then advancing a little more, the owls were not intimidated. And then I would reach the chestnut tree and stand under it absolutely motionless for as long as I could, fifteen minutes, half an hour or so.

10 After doing this day after day for several weeks, I could tell the owls had gained confidence in my presence. Gradually, I dared to raise my arm and lift one of the four babies off its perch and place it on my shoulder for a few minutes and then return it safely. I did that with all of them over a period of weeks and finally made the great maneuver—I extended my arm and lifted them one by one, all five of them, on to my arm. I started with the most familiar one, the mother owl. And then once she was perched there, the others were happy to join. By then they were familiar with my touch. There was no sense of separation; I was part of their life process.

So, with the mother owl and the four little ones perched on my arm I walked
20 gingerly out of the woods and took them home and installed them in the attic where I'd prepared the equivalent of a branch and set out some food to welcome them. They lived there very happily coming and going through the open window, for the remainder of my stay on Wormwood Hill, until eventually I moved on to another small farm in the town of New Hope in Bucks County, Pennsylvania.

My encounter with this family of owls was one of the most intimate of all my experiences with the animal world, a world I consider to be part of our own world, too.

## COMPREHENSION

**Directions** Answer the following questions about "Owls in the Attic."

**20.** The imagery "rustling in the branches" in line 2 appeals to the sense of

**A.** taste **C.** hearing
**B.** touch **D.** smell

**21.** Based on line 4–8, you can make the inference that the author is

**A.** shy **C.** nervous
**B.** patient **D.** scared

**22.** The imagery in lines 9–16 appeals primarily to the sense of

**A.** touch **C.** taste
**B.** hearing **D.** smell

**23.** The imagery in lines 17–19 appeals to the senses of

**A.** hearing and sight **C.** taste and hearing
**B.** smell and taste **D.** sight and touch

# Written Response

## SHORT RESPONSE

**Directions** Write two or three sentences to answer each question on a separate sheet of paper.

**24.** Based on the selection, you can make the inference that the author respects the owls. Give two examples from the selection to support the inference.

**25.** Identify an example of imagery in lines 17–22. To what sense does the example appeal?

## EXTENDED RESPONSE

**Directions** Answer the following question. Write two or more paragraphs on a separate sheet of paper.

**26.** What inference can you make about how the owls feel around the author? Give three examples from the selection to support your inference.

## Vocabulary

**Directions** Use context clues and your knowledge of connotation to answer the following questions.

**1.** The word *sanctuary* in line 13 of the first poem titled "To a Butterfly" suggests a place that is

**A.** lively **C.** safe
**B.** new **D.** popular

**2.** The word *float* in line 24 of the second poem titled "To a Butterfly" suggests a movement that is

**A.** awkward **C.** backward
**B.** invisible **D.** light

**3.** The word *ashy* in line 26 of "Starlings in Winter" suggests that the city is

**A.** crowded **C.** dirty
**B.** noisy **D.** large

**4.** The word *dared* in line 11 of "Owls in the Attic" suggests a decision that is

**A.** irresponsible **C.** risky
**B.** unsuccessful **D.** sudden

## Writing and Grammar

**Directions** Read the personal response and answer the questions that follow.

(1) Do you enjoy being outside in the freezing cold? (2) Most people would answer "no" to this question. (3) However, I love nothing more than being outdoors on a cold, snowy day. (4) Maybe this is why I can relate to Gwendolyn Brooks's poem "Cynthia in the Snow." (5) On snowy days, I have had the same experiences and emotions as the speaker in the poem.

(6) "Cynthia in the Snow" begins with a description of the setting: "It SUSHES. / It hushes / The loudness in the road." (7) For the speaker, the snow has a calming effect and the ability to transform the landscape. (8) It gently falls on the ground and silences the noises of the world. (9) Like the speaker, I also feel calmed by the snow. (10) When I am outside on a snowy day, I often feel like I am the only person awake in the world. (11) I can almost feel the quiet peacefulness when I read the words "SUSHES" and "hushes."

(12) Then the snow is personified by Brooks. (13) She writes, "It flitter-twitters, / And laughs away from me. / It laughs a lovely whiteness." (14) This shows the speaker's playful relationship with the surroundings. (15) As much as the snow can calm me, it can also give me the energy to go sledding and make snow angels and throw snowballs. (16) Brooks conveys the joy and excitement that snow can bring. (17) I never get tired of trying to catch snowflakes on my tongue before they "whitely whir" away.

(18) Finally, the simile "Still white as milk or shirts" is used to describe the silent, pure quality of the snow. (19) In the end, Brooks shows the speaker's emotional response to the snow, writing that the snow is "So beautiful it hurts."

(20) Like the speaker of the poem, I appreciate how a familiar world can be transformed into an "otherwhere" by snow's beauty. (21) Snow makes everything look pure and new again. (22) When I look outside at a world covered by freshly fallen snow, I can understand how something can, indeed, be so beautiful that it hurts.

**1.** How might you revise sentence 2 to make it exclamatory?

**A.** Would you answer "no" to this question?
**B.** Answer "no" to this question.
**C.** I would answer "no" to this question.
**D.** Most would answer "no" to this question!

**2.** Identify the transitional words or phrases used in paragraph 1.

**A.** However, on snowy days
**B.** being outside, I
**C.** Most people, Maybe
**D.** Do you, I can relate

**3.** Which sentence in the essay identifies the title and author of the poem?

**A.** sentence 1 **C.** sentence 4
**B.** sentence 2 **D.** sentence 7

**4.** Which sentence best states the writer's overall response to the poem?

**A.** sentence 1 **C.** sentence 11
**B.** sentence 5 **D.** sentence 12

**5.** What is the literary term used in sentence 6?

**A.** Cynthia **C.** with
**B.** begins **D.** setting

**6.** What is the literary term used in sentence 7?

**A.** speaker **C.** transform
**B.** snow **D.** landscape

**7.** How might you revise sentence 9 to make it interrogative?

**A.** Sometimes, like the speaker, I feel calmed by the snow.
**B.** Like the speaker, why do I feel calmed by the snow?
**C.** Find out why, like the speaker, I also feel calmed by the snow.
**D.** Like the speaker, I also feel calmed by the snow!

**8.** Choose the best way to rewrite sentence 12 by using the active voice.

**A.** The snow is personified by Brooks.
**B.** Personification of the snow is done next.
**C.** The snow is then personified.
**D.** Then Brooks personifies the snow.

**9.** Which of the following sentences uses a quotation to support the idea that snow can be playful?

**A.** sentence 2 **C.** sentence 13
**B.** sentence 8 **D.** sentence 16

**10.** What is the transitional word used in sentence 18?

**A.** Finally **C.** shirts
**B.** milk **D.** snow

**11.** The quotation in sentence 19 supports the key point that

**A.** the speaker relates to the narrator
**B.** Brooks describes snow in her poem
**C.** the speaker appreciates the snow
**D.** snow is calming yet energizing

**12.** Choose the correct way to rewrite the following part of sentence 20 by using the active voice.

**A.** Transforming a familiar world into an "otherwhere" is done by snow's beauty and, like the speaker, I appreciate it.
**B.** Like the speaker, I appreciate how a transformation of a familiar world into an "otherwhere" is done by snow's beauty.
**C.** I appreciate, like the speaker, how a familiar world is being transformed into an "otherwhere" by snow's beauty.
**D.** Like the speaker, I appreciate how snow's beauty can transform a familiar world into an "otherwhere."

## Writing

**Directions** Read the following quotation. Then read the prompt that follows and complete the writing activity.

> "Poetry is, above all, an approach to the truth of feeling . . . . A fine poem will seize your imagination . . ."
>
> Muriel Rukeyser, poet

**Prompt:** Write a personal response to the poem titled "To a Butterfly" or "Starlings in Winter." Does the poem help you understand "the truth of feeling"? Use details and quotations from the poem to support your overall response. Remember to briefly describe the poem so that readers unfamiliar with it can understand your response.

Now write your personal response. Use the reminders that follow to help you write.

**Reminders**

- Be sure your writing does what the prompt asks.
- Identify your overall response to the poem.
- Support your response with specific details and quotes.
- Use a clear organization and include transitions.
- Check for correct grammar, spelling, and punctuation.

## Reading Comprehension

**Directions** Wordsworth wrote two poems titled "To a Butterfly," both of which describe the close relationship he shared with his sister when they were children. Read the first and second poems titled "To a Butterfly." Then read "Starlings in Winter" and answer the questions that follow.

### First Poem
### To a Butterfly
#### William Wordsworth

I've watched you now a full half hour,
Self-poised upon that yellow flower;
And, little Butterfly! indeed
I know not if you sleep, or feed.
5 How motionless! not frozen seas
More motionless! and then
What joy awaits you, when the breeze
Hath found you out among the trees,
And calls you forth again!

10 This plot of Orchard-ground is ours;
My trees they are, my Sister's flowers;
Stop here whenever you are weary,
And rest as in a sanctuary!
Come often to us, fear no wrong;
15 Sit near us on the bough!
We'll talk of sunshine and of song;
And summer days, when we were young,
Sweet childish days, that were as long
As twenty days are now!

**Second Poem**
**To a Butterfly**
**William Wordsworth**

Stay near me—do not take thy flight!
A little longer stay in sight!
Much converse do I find in Thee,
Historian of my Infancy!
5 Float near me; do not yet depart!
Dead times revive in thee:
Thou bring'st, gay Creature as thou art!
A solemn image to my heart,
My Father's Family!

10 Oh! pleasant, pleasant were the days,
The time, when in our childish plays
My sister Emmeline and I
Together chaced the Butterfly!
A very hunter did I rush
15 Upon the prey:—with leaps and springs
I followed on from brake to bush;
But she, God love her! feared to brush
The dust from off its wings.

**Starlings in Winter**

**Mary Oliver**

Chunky and noisy,
but with stars in their black feathers,
they spring from the telephone wire
and instantly

5 they are acrobats
in the freezing wind.
And now, in the theater of air,
they swing over buildings,

dipping and rising;
10 they float like one stippled star
that opens,
becomes for a moment fragmented,

then closes again;
and you watch
15 and you try
but you simply can't imagine

how they do it
with no articulated instruction, no pause,
only the silent confirmation
20 that they are this notable thing,

this wheel of many parts, that can rise and spin
over and over again,
full of gorgeous life.
Ah, world, what lessons you prepare for us,

25 even in the leafless winter,
even in the ashy city.
I am thinking now
of grief, and of getting past it;

I feel my boots
30 trying to leave the ground,
I feel my heart
pumping hard. I want

to think again of dangerous and noble things.
I want to be light and frolicsome.
35 I want to be improbable beautiful and afraid of nothing,
as though I had wings.



## COMPREHENSION

**Directions** Answer the following questions about the first poem and the second poem titled "To a Butterfly."

**1.** Which type of mood does the figurative language in lines 7–9 create in the first poem?

**A.** humorous
**B.** mysterious
**C.** shocking
**D.** cheerful

**2.** Which of the following lines contains alliteration?

**A.** "More motionless!"
**B.** "my Sister's flowers"
**C.** "Stay near me"
**D.** "dust from off its wings"

**3.** In lines 5–9 of the second poem, the speaker conveys the thought that the butterfly

**A.** takes its life too seriously
**B.** once resided around his family
**C.** refuses to rest on one flower
**D.** reminds him of forgotten days

**4.** Which lines should be read together to learn a complete thought of the speaker?

**A.** lines 13–15 in the first poem
**B.** lines 1–2 in the second poem
**C.** lines 10–13 in the second poem
**D.** lines 13–15 in the second poem

**5.** The repetition of "pleasant" in line 10 of the second poem emphasizes the speaker's

**A.** memories of his father
**B.** fear that the butterfly will leave
**C.** happiness as a child
**D.** wish to catch the butterfly

**6.** Based on both poems, you can best make the inference that the speaker

**A.** lives close to his family
**B.** thinks well of his sister
**C.** plans to catch the butterfly
**D.** owns a large amount of land

## COMPREHENSION

**Directions** Answer the following questions about "Starlings in Winter."

**7.** Which line of imagery appeals to the sense of hearing?

**A.** "Chunky and noisy,"
**B.** "they spring from the telephone wire"
**C.** "dipping and rising;"
**D.** "they float like one stippled star"

**8.** The figurative language in line 5 suggests that the starlings

**A.** take to the air in pairs
**B.** fly in a straight line
**C.** move gracefully through the air
**D.** show off their colored feathers

**9.** The varying lengths of lines 8–13 emphasize the starlings'

**A.** talent
**B.** hunger
**C.** sadness
**D.** movement

**10.** In lines 10–13, the speaker expresses the thought that

**A.** birds perform in the air
**B.** starlings form the shape of a star
**C.** acrobats have uneven movements
**D.** nature often confuses people

**11.** The repetition in lines 14–16

**A.** shows the speaker's belief that it is hard to figure out the starlings' movements
**B.** emphasizes how people are connected to the starlings
**C.** illustrates the appearance of the starlings' flight formations
**D.** explains the speaker's opinion that nature is always changing

**12.** Which line contains an example of imagery that appeals to the sense of sight?

**A.** "only the silent confirmation"
**B.** "full of gorgeous life"
**C.** "even in the ashy city"
**D.** "I want to be light and frolicsome"

**13.** In stanza 6, the speaker conveys the thought that

**A.** we can learn a lot from the world
**B.** grief is hard for people to get past
**C.** starlings move with no instruction
**D.** the city is dirty and leafless

## COMPREHENSION

**Directions** Answer these questions about all three poems.

**14.** Based on all three poems, you can best make the inference that the speakers

**A.** prefer the country to the city
**B.** appreciate creatures that fly
**C.** hope to change the natural world
**D.** find the creatures' movements confusing

**15.** Which of the following is found in all the poems?

**A.** rhyme scheme
**B.** onomatopoeia
**C.** metaphor
**D.** free verse

**16.** "Brake to bush" in the second "To a Butterfly" and "stippled star" in "Starlings in Winter" are examples of

**A.** alliteration
**B.** repetition
**C.** similes
**D.** onomatopoeia

# Written Response

## SHORT RESPONSE

**Directions** Write two or three sentences to answer each question on a separate sheet of paper.

**17.** Give one example of figurative language from either "To a Butterfly" poem and one example from "Starlings in Winter." Identify the types of figurative language that you select.

**18.** Is "Starlings in Winter" written in free verse? Give two examples from the poem to support your response.

## EXTENDED RESPONSE

**Directions** Answer one of the following questions. Write two or more paragraphs on a separate sheet of paper.

**19.** What do both poems titled "To a Butterfly" suggest about the speaker and his childhood? How do you think he feels about this time of his life? Support your answer with examples from the poem.

**20.** What feelings or ideas does the imagery in either poem titled "To a Butterfly" suggest? Give examples from the poem to support your response.

## Reading Comprehension

**Directions** Read the following selection. Then answer the questions that follow.

*In the 1930s, author Stanley Kunitz moved from New York City to a farm called Wormwood Hill in the Connecticut countryside.*

### Owls in the Attic
***from* The Wild Braid**

**Stanley Kunitz**

One day, as I stood under a great chestnut tree deep in the center of the woods, I heard some rustling in the branches. I looked up and saw a family of owls, a mother and four fledglings, all on one branch. The moment I moved, they frantically whisked off.

I vowed I would become a friend of theirs, and realized I must not disturb them in any way. I learned if I approached very quietly, advancing just a few steps, then standing still, then advancing a little more, the owls were not intimidated. And then I would reach the chestnut tree and stand under it absolutely motionless for as long as I could, fifteen minutes, half an hour or so.

10 After doing this day after day for several weeks, I could tell the owls had gained confidence in my presence. Gradually, I dared to raise my arm and lift one of the four babies off its perch and place it on my shoulder for a few minutes and then return it safely. I did that with all of them over a period of weeks and finally made the great maneuver—I extended my arm and lifted them one by one, all five of them, on to my arm. I started with the most familiar one, the mother owl. And then once she was perched there, the others were happy to join. By then they were familiar with my touch. There was no sense of separation; I was part of their life process.

So, with the mother owl and the four little ones perched on my arm I walked 20 gingerly out of the woods and took them home and installed them in the attic where I'd prepared the equivalent of a branch and set out some food to welcome them. They lived there very happily coming and going through the open window, for the remainder of my stay on Wormwood Hill, until eventually I moved on to another small farm in the town of New Hope in Bucks County, Pennsylvania.

My encounter with this family of owls was one of the most intimate of all my experiences with the animal world, a world I consider to be part of our own world, too.

## COMPREHENSION

**Directions** Answer the following questions about "Owls in the Attic."

**21.** Which of the following phrases contains an example of imagery?

**A.** "the owls had gained confidence"
**B.** "become a friend of theirs"
**C.** "frantically whisked off"
**D.** "was no sense of separation"

**22.** Which of the following examples of imagery appeals primarily to the sense of hearing?

**A.** "stood under a great chestnut tree"
**B.** "rustling in the branches"
**C.** "I extended my arm and lifted them"
**D.** "set out some food"

**23.** The imagery in lines 9–16 best suggests that the author is responding to the owls with

**A.** respect
**B.** formality
**C.** disinterest
**D.** surprise

**24.** Based on the last paragraph of the selection, you can make the inference that the author

**A.** feels a connection to nature
**B.** loves all kinds of birds
**C.** thinks owls make good pets
**D.** prefers living on farms

# Written Response

## SHORT RESPONSE

**Directions** Write two or three sentences to answer each question on a separate sheet of paper.

**25.** What inference could you make about the author's personality? Give one example from the selection to support your inference.

**26.** What inference can you make about how the author feels about the owls? Provide two details from selection to support your inference.

## EXTENDED RESPONSE

**Directions** Answer one of the following questions. Write two or more paragraphs on a separate sheet of paper.

**27.** What overall picture of nature does the imagery in the selection present? Provide examples from the selection to support your answer.

**28. Challenge** What inferences can you make about the author based on his desire to interact with the owls and include them in his "own world"? Provide examples from the selection to support your answer.

## Vocabulary

**Directions** Use context clues and your knowledge of connotation to answer the following questions.

1. The word *self-poised* in line 2 of the first poem titled "To a Butterfly" suggests that the butterfly is
   - **A.** lost
   - **B.** distracted
   - **C.** young
   - **D.** elegant

2. The word *acrobats* in line 5 of "Starlings in Winter" suggests a being full of
   - **A.** silliness
   - **B.** gracefulness
   - **C.** casualness
   - **D.** mysteriousness

3. The word *whisked* in line 3 of "Owls in the Attic" suggests a movement that is
   - **A.** loud
   - **B.** jumpy
   - **C.** quick
   - **D.** small

4. The word *gingerly* in line 18 of "Owls in the Attic" suggests a movement that is
   - **A.** simple
   - **B.** uncomfortable
   - **C.** graceless
   - **D.** cautious

## Writing and Grammar

**Directions** Read the personal response and answer the questions that follow.

(1) Do you enjoy being outside in the freezing cold? (2) Most people would answer "no" to this question. (3) However, I love nothing more than being outdoors on a cold, snowy day. (4) Maybe this is why I can relate to Gwendolyn Brooks's poem "Cynthia in the Snow." (5) On snowy days, I have had the same experiences and emotions as the speaker in the poem.

(6) "Cynthia in the Snow" begins with a description of the setting: "It SUSHES. / It hushes / The loudness in the road." (7) For the speaker, the snow has a calming effect and the ability to transform the landscape. (8) It gently falls on the ground and silences the noises of the world. (9) Like the speaker, I also feel calmed by the snow. (10) When I am outside on a snowy day, I often feel like I am the only person awake in the world. (11) I can almost feel the quiet peacefulness when I read the words "SUSHES" and "hushes."

(12) Then the snow is personified by Brooks. (13) She writes, "It flitter-twitters, / And laughs away from me. / It laughs a lovely whiteness." (14) This shows the speaker's playful relationship with the surroundings. (15) As much as the snow can calm me, it can also give me the energy to go sledding and make snow angels and throw snowballs. (16) Brooks conveys the joy and excitement that snow can bring. (17) I never get tired of trying to catch snowflakes on my tongue before they "whitely whir" away.

(18) Finally, the simile "Still white as milk or shirts" is used to describe the silent, pure quality of the snow. (19) In the end, Brooks shows the speaker's emotional response to the snow, writing that the snow is "So beautiful it hurts."

(20) Like the speaker of the poem, I appreciate how a familiar world can be transformed into an "otherwhere" by snow's beauty. (21) Snow makes everything look pure and new again. (22) When I look outside at a world covered by freshly fallen snow, I can understand how something can, indeed, be so beautiful that it hurts.

**1.** How might you revise sentence 1 to make it declarative?

**A.** You enjoy being outside in the cold.
**B.** Find out why you enjoy being in the cold.
**C.** You enjoy being outside in the cold!
**D.** Why do you enjoy being in the cold?

**2.** Identify the transition in sentence 3.

**A.** However
**B.** nothing
**C.** being
**D.** snow

**3.** Which sentence identifies the title and author of the poem?

**A.** sentence 1
**B.** sentence 2
**C.** sentence 3
**D.** sentence 4

**4.** Based on the first paragraph, you can tell that the writer

**A.** misunderstood the poem's key ideas
**B.** experienced a strong response to the poem
**C.** questioned the poet's background
**D.** struggled to relate to the poem's narrator

**5.** The word "setting" in sentence 6 strengthens the essay because it is

**A.** intriguing
**B.** simple
**C.** precise
**D.** controversial

**6.** Which sentence contains a quotation that supports the writer's idea that the snow is peaceful?

**A.** sentence 3
**B.** sentence 4
**C.** sentence 5
**D.** sentence 6

**7.** How might you revise sentence 9 to make it interrogative?

**A.** Sometimes, like the speaker, I feel calmed by the snow.
**B.** Like the speaker, why do I feel calmed by the snow?
**C.** Find out why, like the speaker, I also feel calmed by the snow.
**D.** Like the speaker, I also feel calmed by the snow!

**8.** Which literary term should the writer add to strengthen the description in sentence 11?

**A.** speaker
**B.** repetition
**C.** onomatopoeia
**D.** free verse

**9.** Choose the best way to rewrite sentence 12 by using the active voice.

**A.** The snow is personified by Brooks.
**B.** Personification of the snow is done next.
**C.** The snow is then personified.
**D.** Then Brooks personifies the snow.

**10.** Which element does the writer use in sentence 18 to support the key idea of the silencing effects of snow?

**A.** thesis
**B.** conclusion
**C.** quotation
**D.** metaphor

**11.** Identify the transitional word used in sentence 18.

**A.** Finally
**B.** simile
**C.** describe
**D.** quality

**12.** Choose the correct way to rewrite sentence 20 by using the active voice.

**A.** Transforming a familiar world into an "otherwhere" is done by snow's beauty and I appreciate it.

**B.** A transformation of a familiar world into an "otherwhere" is done by snow's beauty.

**C.** The speaker of the poem and I appreciate how a familiar world can be transformed by snow's beauty.

**D.** Like the speaker of the poem, I appreciate how snow's beauty can transform a familiar world into an "otherwhere."

## Writing

**Directions** Read the following quotation. Then read the prompts that follow and complete one of the writing activities.

> "Poetry is, above all, an approach to the truth of feeling . . . . A fine poem will seize your imagination . . ."
>
> Muriel Rukeyser, poet

**Prompt:** Write a personal response to the poems titled "To a Butterfly" or "Starlings in Winter." Begin by describing the feelings the poem causes in you. Considering Rukeyser's quote, how does this poem "seize" or capture your imagination? Use details and quotations to support your overall response.

Now write your personal response. Use the reminders that follow to help you write.

**Challenge Prompt:** Write a personal response to a poem from your textbook. Describe your overall impression of the poem and the feelings it brings to mind. How does the poem's sound devices, figurative language, imagery, or mood influence your response? Then, consider whether—according to Rukeyser's quote—the poem can be considered "fine." Does it present a "truth"? Use details and quotations to support your overall response.

Now write your personal response. Use the reminders that follow to help you write.

**Reminders**

- Be sure your writing does what the prompt asks.
- Identify your overall response to the poem.
- Support your response with specific details and quotes.
- Use a clear organization and include transitions.
- Check for correct grammar, spelling, and punctuation.

## Reading Comprehension

**Directions** Read the following selections. Then answer the questions that follow.

### Athene's City

**Olivia Coolidge**

In the days when Greece was first being settled, Cecrops was king in Attica, a rugged, triangular little country, good mainly for goat farming and the culture of honey bees, and surrounded on two sides by the sea. Here Cecrops planned a city around a steep rock that jutted from the plain a few miles inland. Down on the shore were two fine harbors, while around spread fertile country watered by two streams. The gods, who were always interested in the affairs of men, approved the idea of Cecrops and gave the new city their blessing, foreseeing that it would become in time one of the famous cities of the world. For this reason there was great dispute among the gods as to which of them should be its special patron. 10 Many claims were put forward by this god or by that, but at last, after much arguing, it became clear that the award should lie between Athene, goddess of wisdom, and the sea god, Poseidon. Between these two the gods decided to have a contest. Each should produce some marvel in the Attic land, and each should promise some gift to the city that was to come. The greater gift should win the city.

When the appointed day came, the judges ranged themselves on the rock, and the two gods came before them. Some say that the twelve judges chosen were the spirits of the Attic hills and rivers, and some maintain that they were twelve Olympian gods. Be that as it may, on one side stood Poseidon with 20 flowing dark-blue beard and majestic stature, carrying in his hand the three-pronged trident with which he rules the waves. On the other side stood Athene, grey-eyed and serene, helmet on her golden head and spear in hand. At the word Poseidon raised his trident and struck the ground. Beneath the feet of the judges the whole earth was terribly shaken, and with a mighty rumbling sound it split apart before them. Then appeared the marvel, a salt spring four miles inland where no water had appeared before. To this Poseidon added his gift of sea power, promising the city a great empire, a mighty navy, famed shipwrights, and trading vessels which should make her name known in every corner of the sea.

The judges looked at one another as Poseidon spoke and nodded their heads 30 in approval, thinking the gift indeed a great one and the salt spring and the earthquake fine symbols of Poseidon's power. Grey-eyed Athene said nothing, but smiled gently to herself as she laid aside her spear and quietly kneeling down appeared to plant something in the earth. Between her hands as she worked, there gradually unfolded a little tree, a bush rather, small and unimpressive, with grey-green leaves and grey-green berries about an inch in length. When it had grown to full size, Athene stood up and looked at the judges. That was all.

Poseidon glanced at the dusty looking bush that had grown so quietly. He looked at the hole that had gaped in the earth with the thunder of earthquake, and he threw back his head and laughed. Round the bay rumbled and re-echoed the
40 laughter of the god like distant waves thundering on the rocks, while far out to sea in their deep, green caverns, the old sea gods, his subjects, sent a muffled answering roar. Presently as silence fell, the quiet voice of Athene spoke to the assembled gods.

"This little shrub is the olive, at the same time my marvel and my gift to the city," she said. "With these berries the poor man will flavor his coarse bread and goat's-milk cheese. With scented oil the rich man will deck himself for the feast. Oil poured to the gods shall be among their favorite offerings. With it the housewife will light her lamp and do her cooking, and the athlete will cleanse himself from dust and sweat. This is the ware merchants will carry in the ships
50 Poseidon speaks of, to gain riches and renown for the city which sells what all men use. Moreover, I will make its people skilled in pottery, so that the jars in which the oil is carried shall themselves be a marvel, and the city shall flourish and be famous, not only in trade but in the arts."

She finished, and the judges cried out in surprise at the richness of her dull-looking gift. They awarded the prize to Athene, who called the city Athens. Long afterwards when Athens became famous, celebrated for its beauty and wisdom, the Athenians built a great temple in honor of their patron goddess. This temple was called the Parthenon, or temple of the maiden goddess. Though in ruins, it is still standing and is one of the most famous buildings of the world.

## Uitziton and the First Quarrel *from* The Stolen Fire

**translated by Stella Humphries**

The original home of the Aztecs was a place called Aztlan. When their numbers had increased greatly, Aztlan became too cramped for them. But they did not dare to move elsewhere, because there had been no sign from heaven.

One of their chiefs was named Uitziton. He was a brave man and a clever one. As he sat one day lost in thought, he heard a bird that kept calling,"Tiui-tiui! Tiui-tiui!" In the language of the Aztecs, that meant, "Go forth, go forth!"

Uitziton discussed this with Tecpatzin, who was equally respected by the people. Uitziton thought, "It is easier for two of us to convince the people than one."

10 And that was how it happened. When the bird call was heard again, Uitziton said to the people, "Listen everybody! Listen to what the bird is saying!"

"Go forth, go forth! That is what it is calling," said Tecpatzin.

"Yes," said many of them. "It is calling 'tiui-tiui!'"

"It is a sign from heaven," declared Uitziton. "We have heard it."

"Heaven has sent us a sign," nodded Tecpatzin.

Then many men and women, together with their children, agreed to leave Aztlan, and the future of the Aztec people was assured.

Long before this, Uitziton had sent out scouts, so he knew where there was a land in which they could settle and thrive.

20 But not far from Aztlan, there was a sinister spot which was known as the Snake's Jaws. It was the home of an evil spirit, who tried to harm the Aztecs at every opportunity.

When this spirit observed that the Aztecs were about to part in peace and harmony, he decided to inveigle them into a dispute. He crept into the camp in the dead of night, and left two bundles on the ground. At daybreak, these bundles were discovered. Everyone pushed and jostled to see them. Eagerly, someone opened the first bundle. There came to light an incredibly large emerald, a jewel of incalculable value.

"It belongs to us who are leaving," said some.

30 "No, it belongs to us who are staying," insisted others.

"To us, who are going to found a new home!" cried some.

"To us, who keep faith with the old country!" shouted others.

The quarrel grew more and more violent. Then Uitziton stepped forward and held up the other bundle, which everyone had forgotten in the uproar. "You hotheads!" he cried. "Why are you quarreling over a stone? First let us see what is in the other bundle."

That calmed the shouting throng and they craned their necks as Uitziton unwrapped the other bundle. Two sticks came into sight, a round one and a flat one. A murmur of disappointment ran through the crowd.

40 Uitziton, however, realized that what he held in his hands was worth more than any jewel. To those who were leaving with him, he said, "Leave the emerald here. These two pieces of wood will be much more useful to us on our long march!"

On the trek into the new land, it was shown what a good exchange Uitziton had made when he chose the two sticks instead of the emerald. At the first halt, everyone felt frozen with the cold. So Uitziton brought out the two sticks, placed the round one in the hole in the flat one, and twirled the stick between his palms until the lower end of the round stick began to burn. Now the people had fire and everyone could warm themselves beside it.



## COMPREHENSION

**Directions** Answer the following questions about "Athene's City."

**1.** The presence of gods in this story tells you that the story is a

**A.** legend
**B.** tall legend
**C.** fable
**D.** myth

**2.** What causes the gods to fight after they approve Cecrops' idea for a city?

**A.** Many gods want to be the patron of the new city.
**B.** Certain gods refuse to give the city their blessing.
**C.** The gods disagree about the type of contest they should have.
**D.** Some of the gods do not think Cecrops should be king.

**3.** Which word in lines 10–11 is a clue to the order of events in this story?

**A.** after
**B.** much
**C.** arguing
**D.** clear

**4.** Monitor your understanding of lines 10–15. The patron of the new city will be the god who

**A.** shows the most power
**B.** presents the best gift
**C.** blesses the city first
**D.** impresses Cecrops the most

**5.** Which word in line 16 is a clue to the order of events in this story?

**A.** when
**B.** judges
**C.** on
**D.** and

**6.** Based on the description in lines 22–26, which cultural value does Poseidon represent?

**A.** peace
**B.** obedience
**C.** honesty
**D.** strength

**7.** What does Poseidon do after he speaks to the gods?

**A.** causes an earthquake
**B.** looks at Athene's gift
**C.** strikes the ground
**D.** creates a salt spring

**8.** What question could you ask to best monitor your understanding of lines 31–37?

**A.** Who are the judges?
**B.** Why does Athene carry a spear?
**C.** What does Athene plant?
**D.** How does the tree grow?

**9.** Based on the description in lines 31–37, which cultural value does Athene stand for?

**A.** strength
**B.** love
**C.** kindness
**D.** humbleness

**10.** Athene's gift causes Poseidon to laugh because her gift seems

**A.** alive
**B.** ugly
**C.** loud
**D.** small

**11.** In the end, which character trait helps Athene win the contest?

**A.** wisdom
**B.** humor
**C.** beauty
**D.** strength

## COMPREHENSION

**Directions** Answer the following questions about "Uitziton and the First Quarrel."

**12.** Based on the description in line 4, Uitziton is this legend's

**A.** god
**B.** evil spirit
**C.** hero
**D.** author

**13.** What finally causes Uitziton to leave Aztlan?

**A.** his discussion with Tecpatzin
**B.** a sign from heaven
**C.** the demands of his people
**D.** his fear of evil spirits

**14.** Which word in line 18 is a clue to the order of events in this story?

**A.** before
**B.** this
**C.** Uitziton
**D.** had

**15.** Monitor your understanding of lines 23–24. The evil spirit wants the Aztecs to

**A.** hurt Uitziton
**B.** leave Aztlan
**C.** fight one another
**D.** ignore the bundles

**16.** Lines 20–26 of this legend

**A.** introduce the hero's enemy
**B.** describe an animal character
**C.** emphasize the hero's abilities
**D.** show how spirits came to be

**17.** Immediately after someone opens the first bundle, the Aztecs

**A.** reveal their disappointment
**B.** begin to quarrel
**C.** leave for the new land
**D.** open the other bundle

**18.** Monitor your understanding of lines 43–48. Uitziton uses the sticks in the second bundle to

**A.** dig a hole
**B.** draw a map
**C.** fight the evil spirit
**D.** start a fire

**COMPREHENSION**

**Directions** Answer the following questions about both selections.

**19.** "Athene's City" and "Uitziton and the First Quarrel" are both

**A.** traditional
**B.** Greek
**C.** humorous
**D.** true

**20.** Which cultural value do both stories reflect?

**A.** Love conquers all.
**B.** Wisdom is powerful.
**C.** Respect your elders.
**D.** Treat others with respect.

## Written Response

**SHORT RESPONSE**

**Directions** Write two or three sentences to answer each question on a separate sheet of paper.

**21.** Summarize what happens after Uitziton and some of his people leave for the new land in "Uitziton and the First Quarrel."

**22.** Describe one characteristic from "Athene's City" that the ancient Greeks valued. Use one detail from the story to support your response.

**EXTENDED RESPONSE**

**Directions** Answer the following question. Write two or more paragraphs on a separate sheet of paper.

**23.** How does "Athene's City" show both bad and good behavior? Include two examples of each type of behavior from the story.

## Vocabulary

**Directions** Use context clues and your knowledge of compound words to answer the following questions.

**1.** *Wright* is another word for a worker or builder. In line 27 of "Athene's City," the compound word *shipwrights* refers to people who

**A.** design and build houses
**B.** design and build houses
**C.** construct and repair ships
**D.** make good decisions

**2.** In line 48 of "Athene's City," the compound word *housewife* refers to women who

**A.** maintain a home
**B.** sell goods at markets
**C.** make pottery
**D.** grow olive trees

**3.** Which is the likely definition of the compound word *daybreak* in line 25 of "Uitziton and the First Quarrel"?

**A.** evening
**B.** dawn
**C.** afternoon
**D.** midnight

**4.** In line 36 of "Uitziton and the First Quarrel," the compound word *hotheads* refers to people who are

**A.** hot
**B.** tired
**C.** bored
**D.** angry

**Directions** Use context clues and your knowledge of homographs to answer the following questions.

**5.** Which sentence uses *last* as it is used in line 10 of "Athene's City"?

**A.** We were the last people out of the theater.
**B.** How long will the movie last?
**C.** That is the last thing I want to do.
**D.** At long last, they have arrived!

**6.** Which sentence uses *rock* as it is used in line 16 of "Athene's City"?

**A.** The rumor would rock the town.
**B.** She found a rock in her shoe.
**C.** The rock concert was fun.
**D.** He likes to rock the baby to sleep.

**7.** Which sentence uses *deck* as it is used in line 46 of "Athene's City"?

**A.** She swept the deck of the ship.
**B.** Deck yourself for the party.
**C.** The chairs are on the deck
**D.** He shuffled the deck of cards.

**8.** Which sentence uses *still* as it is used in line 59 of "Athene's City"?

**A.** The show is still on.
**B.** You have to sit still.
**C.** She painted a still life.
**D.** The water was still.

## Writing and Grammar

**Directions** Read the cause-and-effect essay and answer the questions that follow.

(1) The Greek myth "Echo," retold by Alice Low, has a tragic end. (2) In the story, Echo is a mountain nymph who loves to talk. (3) Echo uses talk to distract the goddess Hera. (4) Who wants to punish one of Echo's friends. (5) However, Echo's behavior and actions end up causing her own punishment instead.

(6) When Hera comes looking for her husband's favorite nymph. (7) Echo begins a conversation with the goddess. (8) She hopes to keep Hera from finding and harming one of her friends. (9) Hera tries to get away, but Echo will not stop talking. (10) She continues to ask the goddess question after question. (11) This stalling gives the nymphs time to escape. (12) As a result, Hera reaches the nymphs' pool too late. (13) This, in turn, makes the goddess very angry. (14) She decides to punish Echo for deceiving her. (15) Hera says that because Echo foiled her plans, the nymph can never speak first and can only repeat what others say.

(16) Echo feels the effect of this punishment when she falls in love with Narcissus, a handsome young man. (17) She follows him through the woods in the hope of getting his attention. (18) The nymph cannot call out to Narcissus. (19) She must instead wait for him to speak. (20) When Narcissus does speak, Echo can only repeat his words. (21) The young hunter ignores the nymph's pleading, however. (22) He rejects her and flees into the forest. (23) Clearly, Echo suffers the consequences for her constant talking; she is left in the dark, alone and miserable. (24) Embarrassed, Echo retreats into a cave. (25) The only thing that remains of the nymph is her voice, which echoes the voices of those calling out in the mountains.

**1.** You know that fragment 4 is a dependent clause because it

**A.** does not have a comma
**B.** cannot stand alone
**C.** contains a subject and a verb
**D.** shows a cause of something

**2.** Which of the following best describes sentence 5?

**A.** supportive evidence
**B.** suitable quotation
**C.** thesis statement
**D.** powerful conclusion

**3.** Combining fragment 6 and sentence 7 would create which type of sentence?

**A.** transition
**B.** compound
**C.** simple
**D.** complex

**4.** Sentence 8 describes one of the causes of

**A.** Echo's punishment
**B.** Hera's search
**C.** Narcissus's punishment
**D.** Echo's love

**5.** Which sentence is a compound sentence?

**A.** sentence 8
**B.** sentence 9
**C.** sentence 10
**D.** sentence 11

**6.** Which words in sentence 12 serve as a transition?

**A.** as a result
**B.** Hera reaches
**C.** nymphs' pool
**D.** too late

**7.** Which word shows that sentence 15 contains a cause-and-effect relationship?

**A.** says
**B.** because
**C.** Echo
**D.** first

**8.** Combining sentences 18 and 19 would create which type of sentence?

**A.** thesis
**B.** complex
**C.** simple
**D.** compound

**9.** To present causes and effects in a sensible order, which of the following sentences would need to be switched?

**A.** sentences 1 and 24
**B.** sentences 1 and 25
**C.** sentences 21 and 25
**D.** sentences 23 and 24

**10.** Sentence 23 summarizes the

**A.** organizational pattern
**B.** tone of the essay
**C.** cause-and-effect relationship
**D.** types of evidence

**11.** The tone of this essay is best described as

**A.** angry
**B.** serious
**C.** mysterious
**D.** questioning

**12.** Based on its tone, the essay's purpose is to

**A.** entertain
**B.** reflect
**C.** persuade
**D.** analyze

## Writing

**Directions** Read the following quotation. Then read the prompt that follows and complete the writing activity.

> "Cause and effect are two sides of one fact."
>
> Ralph Waldo Emerson

**Prompt:** Write an essay that describes the cause-and-effect relationships in "Uitziton and the First Quarrel." For example, you might describe the bird call that Uitziton hears. What two sides would Ralph Waldo Emerson see in this event? The cause side is the bird call, and the effect side is what happens as a result of the call. Explain each cause-and-effect relationship that you find by giving facts from the story.

Now write your essay. The following reminders will help you.

**Reminders**

- Be sure your writing does what the prompt asks.
- Introduce and discuss true cause-and-effect relationships.
- Include examples and other details to support your description of each cause-and-effect relationship.
- Use transitions to link causes and effects.
- Check for correct grammar, spelling, and punctuation.

## Reading Comprehension

**Directions** Read the following selections. Then answer the questions that follow.

### Athene's City

**Olivia Coolidge**

In the days when Greece was first being settled, Cecrops was king in Attica, a rugged, triangular little country, good mainly for goat farming and the culture of honey bees, and surrounded on two sides by the sea. Here Cecrops planned a city around a steep rock that jutted from the plain a few miles inland. Down on the shore were two fine harbors, while around spread fertile country watered by two streams. The gods, who were always interested in the affairs of men, approved the idea of Cecrops and gave the new city their blessing, foreseeing that it would become in time one of the famous cities of the world. For this reason there was great dispute among the gods as to which of them should be its special patron.
10 Many claims were put forward by this god or by that, but at last, after much arguing, it became clear that the award should lie between Athene, goddess of wisdom, and the sea god, Poseidon. Between these two the gods decided to have a contest. Each should produce some marvel in the Attic land, and each should promise some gift to the city that was to come. The greater gift should win the city.

When the appointed day came, the judges ranged themselves on the rock, and the two gods came before them. Some say that the twelve judges chosen were the spirits of the Attic hills and rivers, and some maintain that they were twelve Olympian gods. Be that as it may, on one side stood Poseidon with
20 flowing dark-blue beard and majestic stature, carrying in his hand the three-pronged trident with which he rules the waves. On the other side stood Athene, grey-eyed and serene, helmet on her golden head and spear in hand. At the word Poseidon raised his trident and struck the ground. Beneath the feet of the judges the whole earth was terribly shaken, and with a mighty rumbling sound it split apart before them. Then appeared the marvel, a salt spring four miles inland where no water had appeared before. To this Poseidon added his gift of sea power, promising the city a great empire, a mighty navy, famed shipwrights, and trading vessels which should make her name known in every corner of the sea.

The judges looked at one another as Poseidon spoke and nodded their heads
30 in approval, thinking the gift indeed a great one and the salt spring and the earthquake fine symbols of Poseidon's power. Grey-eyed Athene said nothing, but smiled gently to herself as she laid aside her spear and quietly kneeling down appeared to plant something in the earth. Between her hands as she worked, there gradually unfolded a little tree, a bush rather, small and unimpressive, with grey-green leaves and grey-green berries about an inch in length. When it had grown

to full size, Athene stood up and looked at the judges. That was all.

Poseidon glanced at the dusty looking bush that had grown so quietly. He looked at the hole that had gaped in the earth with the thunder of earthquake, and he threw back his head and laughed. Round the bay rumbled and re-echoed the 40 laughter of the god like distant waves thundering on the rocks, while far out to sea in their deep, green caverns, the old sea gods, his subjects, sent a muffled answering roar. Presently as silence fell, the quiet voice of Athene spoke to the assembled gods.

"This little shrub is the olive, at the same time my marvel and my gift to the city," she said. "With these berries the poor man will flavor his coarse bread and goat's-milk cheese. With scented oil the rich man will deck himself for the feast. Oil poured to the gods shall be among their favorite offerings. With it the housewife will light her lamp and do her cooking, and the athlete will cleanse himself from dust and sweat. This is the ware merchants will carry in the ships 50 Poseidon speaks of, to gain riches and renown for the city which sells what all men use. Moreover, I will make its people skilled in pottery, so that the jars in which the oil is carried shall themselves be a marvel, and the city shall flourish and be famous, not only in trade but in the arts."

She finished, and the judges cried out in surprise at the richness of her dull-looking gift. They awarded the prize to Athene, who called the city Athens. Long afterwards when Athens became famous, celebrated for its beauty and wisdom, the Athenians built a great temple in honor of their patron goddess. This temple was called the Parthenon, or temple of the maiden goddess. Though in ruins, it is still standing and is one of the most famous buildings of the world.



**Uitziton and the First Quarrel *from* The Stolen Fire**

**translated by Stella Humphries**

The original home of the Aztecs was a place called Aztlan. When their numbers had increased greatly, Aztlan became too cramped for them. But they did not dare to move elsewhere, because there had been no sign from heaven.

One of their chiefs was named Uitziton. He was a brave man and a clever one. As he sat one day lost in thought, he heard a bird that kept calling, "Tiui-tiui! Tiui-tiui!" In the language of the Aztecs, that meant, "Go forth, go forth!"

Uitziton discussed this with Tecpatzin, who was equally respected by the people. Uitziton thought, "It is easier for two of us to convince the people than one."

10 And that was how it happened. When the bird call was heard again, Uitziton said to the people, "Listen everybody! Listen to what the bird is saying!"

"Go forth, go forth! That is what it is calling," said Tecpatzin.

"Yes," said many of them. "It is calling 'tiui-tiui!'"

"It is a sign from heaven," declared Uitziton. "We have heard it."

"Heaven has sent us a sign," nodded Tecpatzin.

Then many men and women, together with their children, agreed to leave Aztlan, and the future of the Aztec people was assured.

Long before this, Uitziton had sent out scouts, so he knew where there was a land in which they could settle and thrive.

20 But not far from Aztlan, there was a sinister spot which was known as the Snake's Jaws. It was the home of an evil spirit, who tried to harm the Aztecs at every opportunity.

When this spirit observed that the Aztecs were about to part in peace and harmony, he decided to inveigle them into a dispute. He crept into the camp in the dead of night, and left two bundles on the ground. At daybreak, these bundles were discovered. Everyone pushed and jostled to see them. Eagerly, someone opened the first bundle. There came to light an incredibly large emerald, a jewel of incalculable value.

"It belongs to us who are leaving," said some.

30 "No, it belongs to us who are staying," insisted others.

"To us, who are going to found a new home!" cried some.

"To us, who keep faith with the old country!" shouted others.

The quarrel grew more and more violent. Then Uitziton stepped forward and held up the other bundle, which everyone had forgotten in the uproar. "You hotheads!" he cried. "Why are you quarreling over a stone? First let us see what is in the other bundle."

That calmed the shouting throng and they craned their necks as Uitziton unwrapped the other bundle. Two sticks came into sight, a round one and a flat one. A murmur of disappointment ran through the crowd.

40 Uitziton, however, realized that what he held in his hands was worth more than any jewel. To those who were leaving with him, he said, "Leave the emerald here. These two pieces of wood will be much more useful to us on our long march!"

On the trek into the new land, it was shown what a good exchange Uitziton had made when he chose the two sticks instead of the emerald. At the first halt, everyone felt frozen with the cold. So Uitziton brought out the two sticks, placed the round one in the hole in the flat one, and twirled the stick between his palms until the lower end of the round stick began to burn. Now the people had fire and everyone could warm themselves beside it.



## COMPREHENSION

**Directions** Answer the following questions about "Athene's City."

**1.** What causes the gods to decide to hold a contest?

**A.** They need a way to decide which god will be the city's patron.
**B.** Cecrops insists that they hold a contest to entertain the people of the city.
**C.** They want to see Poseidon and Athene compete.
**D.** Poseidon has threatened to harm them unless they hold a contest.

**2.** How can you tell that this story is a myth?

**A.** Judges decide the outcome of the contest.
**B.** Cecrops has a detailed plan for the city.
**C.** The Athenians build a temple for Athene.
**D.** Poseidon displays supernatural powers.

**3.** Reread the sentence contained in lines 25–26. Which words are clues to the order of events in this story?

**A.** appeared, four
**B.** then, before
**C.** marvel, where
**D.** inland, had

**4.** Based on the description in lines 22–28, Poseidon represents

**A.** a positive way of behaving
**B.** the power of men over women
**C.** an explanation of how gods came to be
**D.** the cultural value of strength

**5.** Monitor your understanding of lines 22–28. Poseidon shows the judges how powerful he is by

**A.** creating a large fleet of navy and trading ships
**B.** causing an earthquake and creating an inland salt spring
**C.** using his trident to produce huge ocean waves
**D.** summoning his subjects, the old sea gods, to the contest

**6.** What happens immediately after Poseidon presents his marvel and gift?

**A.** The judges agree on the merit of Poseidon's offering.
**B.** The Athenians build an impressive temple in honor of Athene.
**C.** Poseidon glances down at the olive shrub and laughs.
**D.** Athene explains how her seemingly small gift will benefit the city.

**7.** Monitor your understanding of lines 31–35. When Athene sees Poseidon's marvel she

**A.** becomes frightened
**B.** says nothing
**C.** refuses to compete
**D.** laughs loudly

**8.** After Athene plants the small bush, she

**A.** lays down her spear
**B.** looks at the judges
**C.** smiles to herself
**D.** kneels on the ground

**9.** Based on the description in lines 31–36, Athene represents the cultural value that

**A.** vanity signals wisdom
**B.** power builds societies
**C.** strength brings respect
**D.** simplicity is worthwhile

**10.** Athene's explanation of her gift causes the judges to cry out because they are

**A.** outraged by Athene's arrogance in presenting such a small gift
**B.** startled by Poseidon's earth-shaking laughter
**C.** shocked at the impressive size of the salt spring
**D.** surprised by the significance of Athene's small gift

**11.** In the end, why do the gods choose Athene as the city's patron?

**A.** Athene's gift of the olive tree will benefit the city the most.
**B.** The city does not need Poseidon's sea power.
**C.** Athene modestly hides the full extent of her power.
**D.** Poseidon has been disrespectful of the contest judges.

## COMPREHENSION

**Directions** Answer the following questions about "Uitziton and the First Quarrel."

**12.** Which positive behavior does this legend encourage?

**A.** leaving a crowded place when necessary
**B.** staying loyal to your country
**C.** using wisdom to analyze situations
**D.** following the advice of an outsider

**13.** What is the effect of Uitziton hearing the bird call in lines 5–6?

**A.** The Aztecs decide to get a new leader.
**B.** Uitziton gets the Aztecs to leave Aztlan
**C.** The Aztecs move to Snake's Jaws.
**D.** Uitziton teams up with the evil spirit.

**14.** When does Uitziton hear the bird call?

**A.** before talking to Tecpatzin
**B.** after talking to the people
**C.** before Aztlan becomes too cramped
**D.** after the people agree to move

**15.** Monitor your understanding of lines 20–22. Snake's Jaws is the

**A.** name of the evil spirit
**B.** place where the Aztecs plan to move
**C.** place where the evil spirit lives
**D.** name of the new land

**16.** Lines 20–26 are characteristic of a legend because they

**A.** introduce the hero's enemy
**B.** feature a god with supernatural powers
**C.** include a humorous exaggeration
**D.** tell about a hero with unusual powers

**17.** When do the Aztecs discover the bundles?

**A.** after they reach the new land
**B.** before they begin fighting
**C.** after Uitziton stops the fight
**D.** before the evil spirit enters the camp

**18.** Monitor your understanding of lines 40–48. Uitziton chooses to bring the second bundle because he knows that

**A.** round sticks are hard to find
**B.** valuable jewels are common
**C.** the emerald is a fake
**D.** he can use the sticks to start a fire

## COMPREHENSION

**Directions** Answer these questions about both selections.

**19.** Which statement about cultural values applies to both stories?

**A.** Wisdom and foresight are valuable character traits

**B.** One's true character is revealed in times of crisis.

**C.** People who obey their leaders will be rewarded.

**D.** Do not overlook the value of nature's gifts.

**20.** Athene in "Athene's City" and Uitziton in "Uitziton and the First Quarrel" show that they are alike by

**A.** using supernatural powers

**B.** confronting evil spirits

**C.** portraying positive characteristics

**D.** explaining the origin of something

# Written Response

## SHORT RESPONSE

**Directions** Write two or three sentences to answer each question on a separate sheet of paper.

**21.** Summarize what happens when the Aztecs find the two bundles in "Uitziton and the First Quarrel."

**22.** Based on details in "Athene's City," you can draw the conclusion that the ancient Greeks valued practicality. How does the story support this conclusion?

## EXTENDED RESPONSE

**Directions** Answer one of the following questions. Write two or more paragraphs on a separate sheet of paper.

**23.** How does "Athene's City" show the characteristics of a myth? Support your answer with examples from the story.

**24. Challenge** Choose an Aztec cultural value revealed in "Uitziton and the First Quarrel." Compare and contrast the importance of the value in Aztec society to the importance of the value today in the United States. Include details from the legend and examples from real life in your answer.

## Vocabulary

**Directions** Use context clues and your knowledge of compound words to answer the following questions.

**1.** *Wright* is another word for a worker or builder. In line 27 of "Athene's City," the compound word *shipwrights* refers to people who

**A.** serve in the navy
**B.** fear sea creatures
**C.** construct and repair ships
**D.** prefer the ocean over lakes

**2.** Which of the following words from "Athene's City" is a compound word?

**A.** housewife
**B.** cooking
**C.** athlete
**D.** cleanse

**3.** Which is the likely definition of the compound word *bedrock* in the following sentence? A successful school system is the bedrock of a strong community.

**A.** evidence
**B.** result
**C.** foundation
**D.** downfall

**4.** Which is the likely definition of the compound word *headstrong* in the following sentence? The headstrong child demanded to play with his brother's birthday present.

**A.** possessing an unusually high IQ
**B.** determined to have one's own way
**C.** having difficulty making friends
**D.** being unable to control anger

**Directions** Use context clues and your knowledge of homographs to answer the following questions.

**5.** Which sentence uses *steep* as it is used in line 4 of "Athene's City"?

**A.** Steep the shirt in dye for five minutes.
**B.** Let the tea bag steep.
**C.** We will steep them in our traditions.
**D.** Their driveway is very steep.

**6.** Which sentence uses *plain* as it is used in line 4 of "Athene's City"?

**A.** The child was just plain stubborn.
**B.** They walked for miles on the plain.
**C.** The plain room was nearly empty.
**D.** Her anger was plain to see.

**7.** Which sentence uses *spring* as it is used in line 25 of "Athene's City"?

**A.** She could tell by the flowers that it was finally spring.
**B.** The mineral spring was rumored to cure illnesses.
**C.** The students could not wait for spring break.
**D.** Do not spring such surprising news on your mother.

**8.** Which sentence uses *sign* as it is used in line 3 of "Uitziton and the First Quarrel"?

**A.** He looked to the sky for a sign of what to do next.
**B.** They used sign language to communicate with the students.
**C.** Sign me up to be a volunteer for the walk-a-thon.
**D.** The sign said that the hotel still had rooms available.

## Writing and Grammar

**Directions** Read the cause-and-effect essay and answer the questions that follow.

(1) The Greek myth "Echo," retold by Alice Low, has a tragic end. (2) In the story, Echo is a mountain nymph who loves to talk. (3) Echo uses talk to distract the goddess Hera. (4) Who wants to punish one of Echo's friends. (5) However, Echo's behavior and actions end up causing her own punishment instead.

(6) When Hera comes looking for her husband's favorite nymph. (7) Echo begins a conversation with the goddess. (8) She hopes to keep Hera from finding and harming one of her friends. (9) Hera tries to get away, but Echo will not stop talking. (10) She continues to ask the goddess question after question. (11) This stalling gives the nymphs time to escape. (12) As a result, Hera reaches the nymphs' pool too late. (13) This, in turn, makes the goddess very angry. (14) She decides to punish Echo for deceiving her. (15) Hera says that because Echo foiled her plans, the nymph can never speak first and can only repeat what others say.

(16) Echo feels the effect of this punishment when she falls in love with Narcissus, a handsome young man. (17) She follows him through the woods in the hope of getting his attention. (18) The nymph cannot call out to Narcissus. (19) She must instead wait for him to speak. (20) When Narcissus does speak, Echo can only repeat his words. (21) The young hunter ignores the nymph's pleading, however. (22) He rejects her and flees into the forest. (23) Clearly, Echo suffers the consequences for her constant talking; she is left in the dark, alone and miserable. (24) Embarrassed, Echo retreats into a cave. (25) The only thing that remains of the nymph is her voice, which echoes the voices of those calling out in the mountains.

**1.** Fragment 4 is a

**A.** compound clause
**B.** dependent clause
**C.** simple clause
**D.** independent clause

**2.** What effect does the thesis statement in sentence 5 identify?

**A.** behavior
**B.** actions
**C.** punishment
**D.** instead

**3.** How might you combine fragment 6 and sentence 7 to form a complex sentence?

**A.** When Hera comes looking for her husband's favorite nymph; Echo begins a conversation with the goddess.
**B.** Hera comes looking for her husband's favorite nymph, and Echo begins a conversation with the goddess.
**C.** Echo begins a conversation with Hera; Hera is looking for her husband's favorite nymph.
**D.** When Hera comes looking for her husband's favorite nymph, Echo begins a conversation with the goddess.

**4.** Sentence 8 describes one of the

**A.** causes of Echo's punishment
**B.** effects of Hera's anger
**C.** causes of Hera's search
**D.** effects of Narcissus's actions

**5.** Which kind of sentence is sentence 9?

**A.** simple
**B.** compound
**C.** complex
**D.** dependent

**6.** Which pair of phrases in sentences 12 and 13 serve as transitions?

**A.** as a result; this, in turn
**B.** as a result; very angry
**C.** too late; very angry
**D.** too late; this, in turn

**7.** The word "because" shows that sentence 15 includes a

**A.** thesis statement
**B.** cause-and-effect relationship
**C.** conclusion
**D.** quotation

**8.** How might you combine sentences 18 and 19 to form a compound sentence?

**A.** The nymph cannot call out to Narcissus, she must instead wait for him to speak.
**B.** The nymph, who cannot call out to Narcissus, must wait for him to speak.
**C.** Because the nymph cannot call out to Narcissus, she must wait for him to speak.
**D.** The nymph cannot call out to Narcissus; she must instead wait for him to speak.

**9.** To present causes and effects in a sensible order, you would need to switch which of the following sentences?

**A.** sentences 21 and 25
**B.** sentences 22 and 24
**C.** sentences 22 and 25
**D.** sentences 23 and 24

**10.** Which sentence summarizes the cause-and-effect relationship discussed in this essay?

**A.** sentence 22
**B.** sentence 23
**C.** sentence 24
**D.** sentence 25

**11.** Which of the following words best describes the tone of this essay?

**A.** humorous
**B.** friendly
**C.** formal
**D.** conversational

**12.** Based on its tone, the essay's purpose is to

**A.** persuade
**B.** describe
**C.** express
**D.** analyze

## Writing

**Directions** Read the following quotation. Then read the prompts that follow and complete one of the writing activities.

> "Cause and effect are two sides of one fact."
>
> Ralph Waldo Emerson

**Prompt:** Write an essay that examines the cause-and-effect relationships in either "Athene's City" or "Uitziton and the First Quarrel." Start by discussing the two sides of the bird call: the cause and its effect. Discuss how the characters' interpretations of the facts affect the other cause-and-effect relationships in the story.

Now write your essay. The following reminders will help you.

**Challenge Prompt:** Write an essay that examines the cause-and-effect relationships in a selection from the test or unit. Suggest how the effect "side" of each relationship could turn out differently in the story. Discuss how these changes could affect the final outcome of the story.

Now write your essay. The following reminders will help you.

**Reminders**

- Be sure your writing does what the prompt asks.
- Introduce and discuss true cause-and-effect relationships.
- Include examples and other details to support your description of each cause-and-effect relationship.
- Use transitions to link causes and effects.
- Check for correct grammar, spelling, and punctuation.

## Reading Comprehension

**Directions** Read the following selections. Then answer the questions that follow.

### *from* Jane Goodall: Pioneer Researcher

**Jayne Pettit**

Born in London, England, on April 3, 1934, Jane Goodall fondly remembers being taken on carriage rides through the city's beautiful parks. There, she could watch small groups of ducks swimming on the lakes and ponds. Insects, especially dragonflies, amazed her and she clearly recalls the tears she shed the day a man swatted and killed one that had been lingering overhead. Jane and her mother Vanne often visited the London Zoo, a special place for the blond-haired youngster who at an early age was fascinated with the creatures of the animal world.

When Jane was a little more than a year old, her mother gave her a stuffed chimpanzee toy which had been made in the exact likeness of Jubilee, the first chimp ever to be born in the London Zoo. Despite a number of predictions that the hairy toy would cause the child to have nightmares, "Jubilee" became Jane's constant companion. "I still have the worn old toy," Jane wrote many years later.

Jane's love of animals gave her mother more than an occasional worry. Jane was missing for five hours one day while she hid in a henhouse to find out how eggs were laid. The little "naturalist" lost track of time and arrived home to find that her mother and several others had been looking everywhere for her and had finally called the police.

In 1938, Jane's younger sister Judy was born and the following year, the Goodall family moved to the coastal town of Bournemouth in southern England. With its rocky cliffs nearby to climb and wonderful beaches to explore, Bournemouth was the perfect setting for a curious little girl to spend her childhood. On days when school was not in session, Jane spent hours combing the grounds surrounding The Birches, the big Victorian house where she lived.

By the time Jane was eight years old, she promised herself that when she grew up she would travel to Africa and live among the wild animals. Years later, after she had completed her schooling, she was working in London when she received an invitation to visit an old school friend in Kenya, East Africa. With her dream very much alive, Jane left her job and moved back to Bournemouth to earn enough money to pay for her journey. Living at home to cut expenses and working as a waitress during the busy summer season, she soon had her round-trip ticket in hand.

When Jane Goodall's ship pulled into the harbor at Mombasa, Kenya, in

1957, she was twenty-three years old and eager to explore the land of her dreams. She found it hard to believe that she had finally arrived in Africa after so many years of anticipation.

Second only to Asia in size, the vast continent of Africa is one of great 40 contrasts and climates. From mountains and deserts (the Sahara is the largest) to tropical rain forests and savannahs (broad grasslands such as the Serengeti where antelope, elephants, and giraffes roam), Africa is made up of fifty-three countries. More than 700 million people speaking a thousand different languages inhabit this huge land. Great deposits of diamonds, copper, iron, and other minerals once drew settlers from Europe to make their fortunes. Big-game hunters from around the world wrecklessly exploited the grasslands in search of prized animal trophies such as lion and zebra skins, elephant tusks, and antelope horns. In the process, many species were driven to near extinction. Today, poachers (people who hunt illegally for profit) 50 continue to rob the continent of its wildlife.

Unlike those people however, Jane Goodall had come to Africa to learn of its magnificent wildlife rather than to abuse it. As the visit with her friend drew to a close, she knew that she had to find a way to remain in Kenya.

Within a short time, Jane found work to support herself. One day someone who had learned of her interest in wildlife suggested that she go to see Dr. Louis Leakey. At the time, Leakey was the curator of the National Museum of Natural History in Nairobi, Kenya's capital. Dr. Leakey and his wife Mary were famous paleontologists who studied the fossil remains of creatures that had lived in Africa millions of years ago. The Leakeys were 60 also anthropologists who worked to uncover the bones and artifacts of early humans.

In her interview with Dr. Leakey, Jane described her lifelong dream of studying animals in the wild. As she spoke, the scientist listened quietly and, to Jane's surprise, offered her a job as his secretary.

In *In the Shadow of Man*, researcher Jane Goodall describes her experiences observing chimpanzees in Gombe, Tanzania.

***from* In the Shadow of Man**

**Jane Goodall**

Sometimes at the beginning of a storm a chimpanzee would shelter under an overhanging trunk or tangle of vegetation, but then, when the rain began to drip through, he usually emerged and just sat in the open, hunched and looking miserable. Small infants appeared to fare the best in a heavy storm. Quite often I saw old Flo, who of all the females was least afraid of me at that time, sitting hunched over two-year-old Fifi. At the end of a deluge Fifi would crawl from her mother's embrace looking completely dry. Flo's son Figan, about four years older than Fifi, often swung wildly through the tree on such occasions, dangling from one hand and kicking his legs, leaping from branch to branch, jumping up and down above Flo, until she was showered with debris and she hunched even lower to avoid the twigs that lashed her face. It was a good way of keeping his blood warm-rather like the wild rain display with which older males frequently greeted the start of heavy rain.

As the weeks went by I found that I could usually get closer to a group of chimpanzees when it was cold and wet than when the weather was dry. It was as though they were too fed up with the conditions to bother about me. One day I was moving silently through the dripping forest. Overhead the rain pattered onto the leaves and all around it dripped from leaf to leaf to the ground. The smell of rotten wood and wet vegetation was pungent; under my hands the tree trunks were cold and slippery and alive. I could feel the water trickling through my hair and running warmly into my neck. I was looking for a group of chimps I had heard before the rain began.

Unexpectedly, only a few yards ahead of me, I saw a black shape hunched up on the ground with its back to me. I hunched down onto the ground myself: the chimp hadn't seen me. For a few minutes there was silence save for the pattering of the rain, and then I heard a slight rustle and a soft *hoo* to my right. Slowly I turned my head, but saw nothing in the thick undergrowth. When I looked back, the black shape that had been in front of me had vanished. Then came a sound from above. I looked up and there saw a large male directly overhead: it was Goliath. He stared down at me with his lips tensed and very slightly shook a branch. I looked away, for a prolonged stare can be interpreted as a threat. I heard another rustle to my left, and when I looked I could just make out the black shape of a chimp behind a tangle of vines. Ahead I saw two eyes staring toward me and a large black hand gripping a hanging liana. Another soft *hoo*, this time from behind. I was surrounded.

All at once Goliath uttered a long drawn-out *wraaaa*, and I was showered with rain and twigs as he threatened me, shaking the branches. The call was taken up by the other dimly seen chimps. It is one of the most savage sounds of the African forests, second only to the trumpeting scream of an enraged elephant. All
40 my instincts bade me flee, but I forced myself to stay, trying to appear uninterested and busy eating some roots from the ground. The end of the branch above hit my head. With a stamping and slapping of the ground a black shape charged through the undergrowth ahead, veering away from me at the last minute and running at a tangent into the forest. I think I expected to be torn to pieces. I do not know how long I crouched there before I realized that everything was still and silent again, save for the *drip-drip* of the raindrops. Cautiously I looked around. The black hand and the glaring eyes were no longer there; the branch where Goliath had been was deserted; all the chimpanzees had gone. Admittedly, my knees shook when I got up, but there was the sense of exhilaration
50 that comes when danger has threatened and left one unharmed-and the chimpanzees were surely less afraid of me.



## COMPREHENSION

**Directions** Answer the following questions about the excerpt from *Jane Goodall: Pioneer Researcher.*

**1.** How would you best describe the author's view of Goodall?

**A.** unsure **C.** formal
**B.** admiring **D.** loving

**2.** Based on Goodall's behavior in lines 3–5, you can make the inference that she

**A.** was afraid of insects
**B.** cared for animals
**C.** was mad at her mother
**D.** surprised the man

**3.** When did Goodall travel to Kenya?

**A.** after meeting Dr. Louis Leakey
**B.** before moving to Bournemouth
**C.** after finishing her schooling
**D.** before getting a toy chimpanzee

**4.** Based on the description in lines 30–32, you can make the inference that Goodall was

**A.** sleepy **C.** uninterested
**B.** embarrassed **D.** excited

**COMPREHENSION**

**Directions** Answer the following questions about the excerpt from *In the Shadow of Man.*

**5.** You can tell that this is an autobiography because you learn

**A.** Goliath's view of Goodall
**B.** information from Goodall's friends
**C.** facts about the environment
**D.** Goodall's thoughts and feelings

**6.** Which words or phrases in lines 4–10 help you understand the order of events?

**A.** Flo, Fifi, Figan
**B.** sitting, swung wildly
**C.** At the end, until
**D.** dangling, leaping

**7.** Which words or phrases in lines 21–26 help you understand the order of events?

**A.** When I looked back
**B.** a few yards ahead, I turned
**C.** a black shape, undergrowth
**D.** saw nothing, looked back

**8.** You can make the inference that Goodall continued crouching because she was

**A.** scared
**B.** timid
**C.** lazy
**D.** jealous

**COMPREHENSION**

**Directions** Answer these questions about both selections.

**9.** Both excerpts clearly show

**A.** Goliath's dangerous behavior
**B.** Goodall's interest in animals
**C.** the childhood interests of Goodall
**D.** the way chimpanzees act in the rain

**10.** Based on Goodall's behavior in both excerpts, you can make the inference that she was

**A.** immature
**B.** sloppy
**C.** traditional
**D.** brave

## Written Response

**SHORT RESPONSE**

**Directions** Write two or three sentences to answer each question.

**11.** Summarize the main idea of lines 40–46 in the excerpt from *In the Shadow of Man.*

**12.** Give an example from each excerpt to support the conclusion that Goodall was observant.

**EXTENDED RESPONSE**

**Directions** Answer the following question. Write two or more paragraphs.

**13.** Use the excerpts to synthesize what you learned about the relationship between Goodall and the chimpanzees. Summarize three details from the excerpts to support your conclusion.

## Reading Comprehension

**Directions** Read the following selection. Then answer the questions that follow.

### *from* Crusading for Chimps and Humans

**Peter Miller**

Grabbing roots and vines to keep from sliding, Jane Goodall eases down the steep slope on all fours. It is just before dawn in Tanzania's Gombe National Park, and the 61-year-old primatologist is in a hurry. She wants to find the wild chimpanzees before they waken and climb down from their nests. Stopping beside a sprawling fig tree, whose branches are black fingers against the plum-colored sky, she points to a nest where dark shapes are stirring.

A small face pops up-two bright eyes surrounded by oversize milk-chocolate ears. It's Ferdinand, the three-year-old son of Fifi, the last survivor of the chimpanzees Jane first studied at Gombe 35 years ago. The daughter of
10 ragged-eared, bulbous-nosed Flo, who died in 1972, Fifi has six offspring of her own, including 24-year-old Freud, the dominant, or alpha, male, and Frodo, a 19-year-old bully.

Fifi sits up and stares at Jane, who is wearing her graying hair in her familiar, youthful ponytail. It has been more than six months since Jane's last visit to Gombe. Her days as a field researcher ended a decade ago. She still longs for time with the chimps, but her globe-spanning crusade to promote conservation, create sanctuaries for chimp orphans, and improve conditions for captive chimps keeps her away.

Above us on the ridge, Freud climbs down from his nest. He had decided
20 to wake everybody up. Hooting and screaming at the top of his lungs, he charges down the hillside, tossing up leaves and pounding on the ground in a display of authority. Startled chimps peer down from every tree. Most leave their nests and wander off into the forest.

Most, but not all. Frodo steps out of the shadows. A hundred twenty pounds of bulging shoulders and arms, Frodo stares at Jane belligerently. Chewing on his upper lip as he does before misbehaving, he advances ominously toward us.

"Here he comes," Jane warns, as Frodo rushes ahead. *Slap!* He hits Michael Neugebauer, an Austrian publisher, on the head. *Bang!* He pushes
30 Michio Hoshino, a Japanese photographer, over onto Jane. Leaping over Bill Wallauer, the Gombe videographer, Frodo grabs a small tree with both hands, plants his feet on my back, and kicks me down the hill. Then he circles around for Jane. Seizing her ankle in a viselike grip, he pulls her down the slope for ten feet, then releases her to grab Katrina Fox, another researcher, to drag her against a tree.

And then he is gone.

We are shaken but uninjured. Frodo didn't mean to hurt us. He was only showing off.

"He makes me so angry," Jane says. "I almost wish I knew a lot of swear
40 words."

A spoiled brat at heart, the muscular teenager has jumped Jane before, stamping on her head so hard he nearly broke her neck. Unlike most Gombe chimps, who accept her presence peacefully, he seems to want to dominate Jane, showing that chimps, like people, may be kind or cruel, caring or cold, thoughtful or stupid.

"When I first started at Gombe, I thought the chimps were nicer than we are," Jane recalls wistfully. "But time has revealed that they are not. They can be just as awful."

"Crusading for Chimps and Humans" by Peter Miller. National Geographic, © December 1995, Vol. 188 Issue 6.

## COMPREHENSION

**Directions** Answer the following questions about the excerpt from the article "Crusading for Chimps and Humans."

**14.** The purpose of this article is to

**A.** motivate
**B.** persuade
**C.** inform
**D.** entertain

**15.** This article would be most useful for someone writing a report about Goodall's

**A.** childhood
**B.** education
**C.** research
**D.** publications

**16.** The tone of lines 7–11 is

**A.** direct
**B.** respectful
**C.** lighthearted
**D.** formal

**17.** Which of the following lines would be most useful to someone writing about Goodall's appearance?

**A.** lines 12–13
**B.** lines 14–16
**C.** lines 18–19
**D.** lines 21–22

**18.** Which words or phrases in lines 00–00 help you understand the order of events?

**A.** Here, hits
**B.** as, then
**C.** over, down
**D.** grabs, releases

**19.** The information in lines 21–30 would be most useful when writing a report about

**A.** male chimpanzee behavior
**B.** chimpanzees in Congolese zoos
**C.** videotaping wildlife
**D.** Goodall's followers

## Written Response

### SHORT RESPONSE

**Directions** Write two or three sentences to answer each question on a separate sheet of paper.

**20.** Name two topics in this excerpt from the article.

**21.** Summarize the main idea of the excerpt.

### EXTENDED RESPONSE

**Directions** Answer the following question. Write two or more paragraphs on a separate sheet of paper.

**22.** Why do you think Goodall is considered an important person in our society? Use details from all three excerpts to support your answer.

## /ocabulary

**)irections** Use context clues and the definitions of the Latin words and roots to ınswer the following questions. The line numbers will help you find the words in he excerpts.

**1.** he Latin word *creare* means "to grow." What is the most likely meaning of *creatures* as it is used in line 8 of *Jane Goodall: Pioneer Researcher*?

**A.** human beings **C.** living things
**B.** flying bugs **D.** tall people

**2.** The Latin word *curiosus* means "interested." What is the most likely meaning of *curious* as it is used in line 23 of *Jane Goodall: Pioneer Researcher*?

**A.** questioning **C.** thoughtful
**B.** creative **D.** silly

**3.** The Latin word *fossilis* means "obtained by digging." What is the most likely meaning of *fossil* as it is used in line 58 of *Jane Goodall: Pioneer Researcher*?

**A.** dirty rock **C.** preserved object
**B.** shiny gold **D.** buried plant

**4.** The Latin word *evanescere* means "to go away." What is the most likely meaning of *vanished* as it is used in line 28 of *In the Shadow of Man*?

**A.** disappeared **C.** sickened
**B.** frightened **D.** jumped

**)irections** Use context clues and your knowledge of base words to answer the 'ollowing questions.

**5.** The word *beautiful* is used in line 2 of *Jane Goodall: Pioneer Researcher*. What is the base word of *beautiful*?

**A.** beauty **C.** before
**B.** full **D.** fulfill

**6.** The word *predictions* is used in line 12 of *Jane Goodall: Pioneer Researcher*. What is the base word of *predictions*?

**A.** predict **C.** prepare
**B.** dictate **D.** shuns

**7.** The word *invitation* is used in line 30 of *Jane Goodall: Pioneer Researcher*. What is the base word of *invitation*?

**A.** visit **C.** vivid
**B.** involve **D.** invite

**8.** The word *miserable* is used in line 14 of *In the Shadow of Man*. What is the base word of *miserable*?

**A.** serve **C.** miss
**B.** misery **D.** several

## Writing and Grammar

**Directions** Read the personal narrative and answer the questions that follow.

(1) People waited outside Gordon's Books. (2) Many—appearing just as heaps of winter clothing—clutched foam cups of steaming coffee or hot chocolate to keep their hands warm. (3) I was bundled against the cold, too, but I clutched something much more important: a hardback copy of the novel The Salamander House. (4) I had read the book at least a hundred times, and now I stood only a few feet away from its author and my hero, hans Devon. (5) Mr. Devon had come to my neighborhood bookstore for a signing of his most recent book.

(6) I shivered with excitement while others in line shivered with the cold. (7) I wondered how I could tell Mr. Devon what his writing meant to me. (8) In the distance, I could see the store's large display windows already fogged with the breath of the crowd inside. (9) I stood far back in a line that snaked out the store's door and down the sidewalk. (10) Hugging the book closer, I silently hoped for the line to move faster. (11) Then, the line began to advance, slowly but surely. (12) I stepped up past the sickeningly sweet smell of Donut Explosion! and fielders' flowers—its storefront an explosion of color. (13) Soon, only five people stood between me and the door of the bookstore!

(14) Again, I began to think about what I would say to Mr. Devon. (15) I loved not only his novels but also his short stories, especially Greener Grass. (16) Before I knew it, I was inside, and Mr. Devon sat in front of me. (17) When it was my turn, I inched forward and held out my book.

(18) "A fan of my first novel. (19) What is your name?" Mr. Devon asked, gently taking the book from my hands.

(20) "Muriel," I answered. (21) "Actually, I'm a fan of all your work. (22) Your novels and stories mean a lot to me."

(23) "That is so nice to hear." (24) He smiled and signed, "To Muriel: Thanks for being a loyal reader."

(25) I took the book from his hands and held it again to my chest. (26) I had finally met my hero. (27) Looking back, I realize that this meeting with Mr. Devon, though short, was one of the most exciting moments of my life.

**1.** Choose the best way to rewrite sentence 1 so that it gets the reader's attention.

**A.** People waited outside this great bookstore called Gordon's Books.
**B.** A wet wind whipped the people anxious to get into Gordon's Books.
**C.** I really like buying new books from Gordon's Books.
**D.** Many people waited on the sidewalk outside Gordon's Books.

**2.** The descriptive word *warm* in sentence 2 appeals to the sense of

**A.** sight **C.** touch
**B.** hearing **D.** smell

**3.** Choose the correct way to punctuate the title in sentence 3.

**A.** *The Salamander House*
**B.** The "Salamander" House
**C.** *"The Salamander House"*
**D.** "The Salamander House"

**4.** Which noun should be capitalized in sentence 4?

**A.** read **C.** feet
**B.** times **D.** hans

**5.** Which word in sentence 11 acts as a transition?

**A.** then **C.** began
**B.** line **D.** advance

**6.** Which words should be capitalized in sentence 12?

**A.** stepped, past **C.** fielders', flowers
**B.** up, sickeningly **D.** explosion, color

**7.** Which word is a transition in sentence 14?

**A.** again **C.** would
**B.** what **D.** say

**8.** Choose the correct way to punctuate the title in sentence 15.

**A.** "Greener Grass" **C.** *Greener Grass*
**B.** *"Greener Grass"* **D.** "Greener" Grass

**9.** Which technique does the writer use in sentences 18 through 22 to re-create the event?

**A.** commands **C.** summary
**B.** dialogue **D.** introduction

**10.** Choose the best way to change sentence 22 to a question.

**A.** Do you know how much your novels and stories mean to me?
**B.** Listen to how much your novels and stories mean to me.
**C.** Your novels and stories mean so much to me!
**D.** I want to tell you that your novels and stories mean so much to me.

**11.** Choose the best way to change sentence 26 to an exclamation.

**A.** Did I finally meet my hero?
**B.** I had finally met my hero!
**C.** Watch me meet my hero.
**D.** Finally, I had met my hero.

**12.** Which experience is the writer describing?

**A.** waiting in line for donuts
**B.** applying for an after-school job
**C.** going outside on the first day of winter
**D.** meeting her favorite author

## Writing

**Directions** Read the following quotation. Then read the prompt that follows and complete the writing activity.

> "If you want to understand today, you have to search yesterday."
>
> Pearl S. Buck, author

**Prompt:** Write a personal narrative that describes an incident that happened with your pet or the pet of a neighbor or friend. Tell about something the pet did that amused you or made you happy. Search the past to think of an event.

Now write your personal narrative. The following reminders will help you.

**Reminders**

- Be sure your writing does what the prompt asks.
- Be sure your writing does what the prompt asks.
- Re-create the experience with dialogue, sensory language, and descriptive details.
- Conclude by reflecting on the significance of the experience.
- Check for correct grammar, spelling, and punctuation.

# Unit 7

TEST B/C

## Reading Comprehension

**Directions** Read the following selections. Then answer the questions that follow.

### *from* Jane Goodall: Pioneer Researcher

**Jayne Pettit**

Born in London, England, on April 3, 1934, Jane Goodall fondly remembers being taken on carriage rides through the city's beautiful parks. There, she could watch small groups of ducks swimming on the lakes and ponds. Insects, especially dragonflies, amazed her and she clearly recalls the tears she shed the day a man swatted and killed one that had been lingering overhead. Jane and her mother Vanne often visited the London Zoo, a special place for the blond-haired youngster who at an early age was fascinated with the creatures of the animal world.

When Jane was a little more than a year old, her mother gave her a
10 stuffed chimpanzee toy which had been made in the exact likeness of Jubilee, the first chimp ever to be born in the London Zoo. Despite a number of predictions that the hairy toy would cause the child to have nightmares, "Jubilee" became Jane's constant companion. "I still have the worn old toy," Jane wrote many years later.

Jane's love of animals gave her mother more than an occasional worry. Jane was missing for five hours one day while she hid in a henhouse to find out how eggs were laid. The little "naturalist" lost track of time and arrived home to find that her mother and several others had been looking everywhere for her and had finally called the police.

20 In 1938, Jane's younger sister Judy was born and the following year, the Goodall family moved to the coastal town of Bournemouth in southern England. With its rocky cliffs nearby to climb and wonderful beaches to explore, Bournemouth was the perfect setting for a curious little girl to spend her childhood. On days when school was not in session, Jane spent hours combing the grounds surrounding The Birches, the big Victorian house where she lived.

By the time Jane was eight years old, she promised herself that when she grew up she would travel to Africa and live among the wild animals. Years later, after she had completed her schooling, she was working in
30 London when she received an invitation to visit an old school friend in Kenya, East Africa. With her dream very much alive, Jane left her job and moved back to Bournemouth to earn enough money to pay for her journey. Living at home to cut expenses and working as a waitress during the busy summer season, she soon had her round-trip ticket in hand.

When Jane Goodall's ship pulled into the harbor at Mombasa, Kenya, in

1957, she was twenty-three years old and eager to explore the land of her dreams. She found it hard to believe that she had finally arrived in Africa after so many years of anticipation.

Second only to Asia in size, the vast continent of Africa is one of great
40 contrasts and climates. From mountains and deserts (the Sahara is the largest) to tropical rain forests and savannahs (broad grasslands such as the Serengeti where antelope, elephants, and giraffes roam), Africa is made up of fifty-three countries. More than 700 million people speaking a thousand different languages inhabit this huge land. Great deposits of diamonds, copper, iron, and other minerals once drew settlers from Europe to make their fortunes. Big-game hunters from around the world wrecklessly exploited the grasslands in search of prized animal trophies such as lion and zebra skins, elephant tusks, and antelope horns. In the process, many species were driven to near extinction. Today, poachers (people who hunt illegally for profit)
50 continue to rob the continent of its wildlife.

Unlike those people however, Jane Goodall had come to Africa to learn of its magnificent wildlife rather than to abuse it. As the visit with her friend drew to a close, she knew that she had to find a way to remain in Kenya.

Within a short time, Jane found work to support herself. One day someone who had learned of her interest in wildlife suggested that she go to see Dr. Louis Leakey. At the time, Leakey was the curator of the National Museum of Natural History in Nairobi, Kenya's capital. Dr. Leakey and his wife Mary were famous paleontologists who studied the fossil remains of creatures that had lived in Africa millions of years ago. The Leakeys were
60 also anthropologists who worked to uncover the bones and artifacts of early humans.

In her interview with Dr. Leakey, Jane described her lifelong dream of studying animals in the wild. As she spoke, the scientist listened quietly and, to Jane's surprise, offered her a job as his secretary.

*n* In the Shadow of Man, *researcher Jane Goodalldescribes her experiences observing chimpanzees in Gombe, Tanzania.*

**from In the Shadow of Man**

**Jane Goodall**

Sometimes at the beginning of a storm a chimpanzee would shelter under an overhanging trunk or tangle of vegetation, but then, when the rain began to drip through, he usually emerged and just sat in the open, hunched and looking miserable. Small infants appeared to fare the best in a heavy storm. Quite often I saw old Flo, who of all the females was least afraid of me at that time, sitting hunched over two-year-old Fifi. At the end of a deluge Fifi would crawl from her mother's embrace looking completely dry. Flo's son Figan, about four years older than Fifi, often swung wildly through the tree on such occasions, dangling from one hand and kicking his legs, leaping from branch to branch, jumping up
10 and down above Flo, until she was showered with debris and she hunched even lower to avoid the twigs that lashed her face. It was a good way of keeping his blood warm-rather like the wild rain display with which older males frequently greeted the start of heavy rain.

As the weeks went by I found that I could usually get closer to a group of chimpanzees when it was cold and wet than when the weather was dry. It was as though they were too fed up with the conditions to bother about me. One day I was moving silently through the dripping forest. Overhead the rain pattered onto the leaves and all around it dripped from leaf to leaf to the ground. The smell of rotten wood and wet vegetation was pungent; under my hands the tree trunks
20 were cold and slippery and alive. I could feel the water trickling through my hair and running warmly into my neck. I was looking for a group of chimps I had heard before the rain began.

Unexpectedly, only a few yards ahead of me, I saw a black shape hunched up on the ground with its back to me. I hunched down onto the ground myself: the chimp hadn't seen me. For a few minutes there was silence save for the pattering of the rain, and then I heard a slight rustle and a soft *hoo* to my right. Slowly I turned my head, but saw nothing in the thick undergrowth. When I looked back, the black shape that had been in front of me had vanished. Then came a sound from above. I looked up and there saw a large male directly
30 overhead: it was Goliath. He stared down at me with his lips tensed and very slightly shook a branch. I looked away, for a prolonged stare can be interpreted as a threat. I heard another rustle to my left, and when I looked I could just make out the black shape of a chimp behind a tangle of vines. Ahead I saw two eyes staring toward me and a large black hand gripping a hanging liana. Another soft *hoo*, this time from behind. I was surrounded.

All at once Goliath uttered a long drawn-out *wraaa*, and I was showered with rain and twigs as he threatened me, shaking the branches. The call was taken up by the other dimly seen chimps. It is one of the most savage sounds of the African forests, second only to the trumpeting scream of an enraged elephant. All
40 my instincts bade me flee, but I forced myself to stay, trying to appear uninterested and busy eating some roots from the ground. The end of the branch above hit my head. With a stamping and slapping of the ground a black shape charged through the undergrowth ahead, veering away from me at the last minute and running at a tangent into the forest. I think I expected to be torn to pieces. I do not know how long I crouched there before I realized that everything was still and silent again, save for the *drip-drip* of the raindrops. Cautiously I looked around. The black hand and the glaring eyes were no longer there; the branch where Goliath had been was deserted; all the chimpanzees had gone. Admittedly, my knees shook when I got up, but there was the sense of exhilaration
50 that comes when danger has threatened and left one unharmed-and the chimpanzees were surely less afraid of me.



## COMPREHENSION

**Directions** Answer the following questions about the excerpt from *Jane Goodall: Pioneer Researcher.*

**1.** What does this biography do that an autobiography would not do?

**A.** reveals Goodall's personal thoughts
**B.** uses the word *she* to refer to Goodall
**C.** describes Goodall's life
**D.** includes dialogue throughout the text

**2.** Which inference can you make from Goodall's behavior in lines 2–7?

**A.** London was a difficult city for Goodall to live in.
**B.** Goodall cared for all types of living creatures.
**C.** The animals at the London Zoo intimidated Goodall.
**D.** Goodall liked the park more than she liked the zoo.

**3.** Based on lines 13–16, you can make the inference that Goodall was

**A.** eager to get back to her house
**B.** disrespectful of the police
**C.** anxious when away from her mother
**D.** curious about the natural world

**4.** When did Goodall move home to save money for her trip?

**A.** before finishing school
**B.** after meeting Dr. Louis Leakey
**C.** before visiting the London Zoo
**D.** after living in London

## COMPREHENSION

**Directions** Answer the following questions about the excerpt from *In the Shadow of Man.*

**5.** Which statement best summarizes the main idea of lines 4–12?

**A.** Figan liked to swing from branch to branch, raining debris onto Flo.
**B.** The female chimp Flo had a two-year-old daughter and a four-year-old son.
**C.** Flo protected Fifi from the heavy rain, while Figan swung from branches overhead.
**D.** Fifi crawled out from her mother's protection after the heavy rain had stopped.

**6.** Which words or phrases in lines 13–20 help you understand the order of events?

**A.** As the weeks went by, One day
**B.** get closer, as though, looking for
**C.** silently, pattered, warmly
**D.** Overhead, to the ground

**7.** According to lines 21–32, when did Goodall see Goliath?

**A.** after the black shape charged through the thick undergrowth
**B.** after Goodall got up and found that her knees were shaking
**C.** before Goodall started walking through the dripping forest
**D.** before Goodall heard another rustle to her left

**8.** Which of the following details best helps you understand how Goodall felt in lines 33–46?

**A.** "All at once Goliath uttered a long drawn-out *wraaaa* . . . ."
**B.** "The end of the branch above hit my head."
**C.** "The black hand and the glaring eyes were no longer there . . . ."
**D.** "Admittedly, my knees shook when I got up . . . ."

## COMPREHENSION

**Directions** Answer these questions about both selections.

**9.** Based on the information in both excerpts, you can make the inference that Goodall was

**A.** proud of growing up in London
**B.** determined to observe chimpanzees
**C.** relaxed about her career choices
**D.** used to a life of luxury

**10.** Unlike the excerpt from *Jane Goodall: Pioneer Researcher*, the excerpt from *In the Shadow of Man* gives you

**A.** Goodall's interpretation of events
**B.** an objective picture of Goodall's life
**C.** friends' observations of Goodall
**D.** information from a variety of sources

## Written Response

### SHORT RESPONSE

**Directions** Write two or three sentences to answer each question on a separate sheet of paper.

**11.** Use one example from each excerpt to synthesize the idea that Goodall was courageous.

**12.** How would *In the Shadow of Man* be different if it were a biography?

### EXTENDED RESPONSE

**Directions** Answer one of the following questions. Write two or more paragraphs on a separate sheet of paper.

**13.** Use your own words to summarize the main points of the excerpt from *Jane Goodall: Pioneer Researcher*.

**14.** Analyze Goodall's attitude toward animals and nature, and evaluate her ability to carry out her goals. How did Goodall carry these qualities through from childhood into adulthood? Support your answer with examples from the excerpts.

## Reading Comprehension

**Directions** Read the following selection. Then answer the questions that follow.

***from* Crusading for Chimps and Humans**

**Peter Miller**

Grabbing roots and vines to keep from sliding, Jane Goodall eases down the steep slope on all fours. It is just before dawn in Tanzania's Gombe National Park, and the 61-year-old primatologist is in a hurry. She wants to find the wild chimpanzees before they waken and climb down from their nests. Stopping beside a sprawling fig tree, whose branches are black fingers against the plum-colored sky, she points to a nest where dark shapes are stirring.

A small face pops up-two bright eyes surrounded by oversize milk-chocolate ears. It's Ferdinand, the three-year-old son of Fifi, the last survivor of the chimpanzees Jane first studied at Gombe 35 years ago. The daughter of 10 ragged-eared, bulbous-nosed Flo, who died in 1972, Fifi has six offspring of her own, including 24-year-old Freud, the dominant, or alpha, male, and Frodo, a 19-year-old bully.

Fifi sits up and stares at Jane, who is wearing her graying hair in her familiar, youthful ponytail. It has been more than six months since Jane's last visit to Gombe. Her days as a field researcher ended a decade ago. She still longs for time with the chimps, but her globe-spanning crusade to promote conservation, create sanctuaries for chimp orphans, and improve conditions for captive chimps keeps her away.

Above us on the ridge, Freud climbs down from his nest. He had decided
20 to wake everybody up. Hooting and screaming at the top of his lungs, he charges down the hillside, tossing up leaves and pounding on the ground in a display of authority. Startled chimps peer down from every tree. Most leave their nests and wander off into the forest.

Most, but not all. Frodo steps out of the shadows. A hundred twenty pounds of bulging shoulders and arms, Frodo stares at Jane belligerently. Chewing on his upper lip as he does before misbehaving, he advances ominously toward us.

"Here he comes," Jane warns, as Frodo rushes ahead. *Slap!* He hits Michael Neugebauer, an Austrian publisher, on the head. *Bang!* He pushes
30 Michio Hoshino, a Japanese photographer, over onto Jane. Leaping over Bill Wallauer, the Gombe videographer, Frodo grabs a small tree with both hands, plants his feet on my back, and kicks me down the hill. Then he circles around for Jane. Seizing her ankle in a viselike grip, he pulls her down the slope for ten feet, then releases her to grab Katrina Fox, another researcher, to drag her against a tree.

And then he is gone.

We are shaken but uninjured. Frodo didn't mean to hurt us. He was only showing off.

"He makes me so angry," Jane says. "I almost wish I knew a lot of swear
40 words."

A spoiled brat at heart, the muscular teenager has jumped Jane before, stamping on her head so hard he nearly broke her neck. Unlike most Gombe chimps, who accept her presence peacefully, he seems to want to dominate Jane, showing that chimps, like people, may be kind or cruel, caring or cold, thoughtful or stupid.

"When I first started at Gombe, I thought the chimps were nicer than we are," Jane recalls wistfully. "But time has revealed that they are not. They can be just as awful."

"Crusading for Chimps and Humans" by Peter Miller. National Geographic, © December 1995, Vol. 188 Issue 6.

**COMPREHENSION**

**Directions** Answer the following questions about the excerpt from the article "Crusading for Chimps and Humans."

**15.** The article could be used to write a report on

**A.** chimpanzees **C.** Africa
**B.** photography **D.** Tanzania

**16.** The tone of lines 1–6 is

**A.** angry **C.** mournful
**B.** anxious **D.** frustrated

**17.** Lines 13–16 would be most useful to someone writing a report about

**A.** Goodall's most recent work
**B.** chimpanzee orphans
**C.** Goodall's time at the park
**D.** conserving natural resources

**18.** The scope of this article includes

**A.** Goodall's childhood in London
**B.** Goodall's relationship with Frodo
**C.** the death of Fifi's mother
**D.** the current staff at the park

**19.** In a report on the dangers of working with animals, you could mention

**A.** the plants in Gombe National Park
**B.** Fifi's having six offspring
**C.** the chimpanzees' morning routine
**D.** Frodo's actions toward the group

**20.** When did Frodo attack the group?

**A.** after Freud ran down the hill
**B.** before Freud woke up.
**C.** before Goodall found the nests.
**D.** after he scared Goodall's colleagues

## Written Response

**SHORT RESPONSE**

**Directions** Write two or three sentences to answer each question on a separate sheet of paper.

**21.** You can infer that Goodall cares deeply about chimpanzees, even after she has left the field. Give two details to support this inference.

**22.** Write two or three sentences to summarize the main points of lines 1–16.

**EXTENDED RESPONSE**

**Directions** Answer one of the following questions. Write two or more paragraphs on a separate sheet of paper.

**23.** Describe the treatment and scope of this excerpt. Include its topic, focus, purpose, and overall tone in your answer.

**24. Challenge** Analyze the treatment and scope of the excerpt. What changes might make it more effective? Consider the article's purpose and tone in your response.

## Vocabulary

**Directions** Use context clues and the definitions of the Latin words and roots to answer the following questions. The line numbers will help you find the words in the selections.

**1.** The prefix *pre-* means "before," and the Latin word *dictio* means "speaking." What is the most likely meaning of *predictions* as it is used in line 12 of *Jane Goodall: Pioneer Researcher*?

**A.** forecasts
**B.** arguments
**C.** thoughts
**D.** conclusions

**2.** The Latin word *invitare* means "invite." What is the most likely meaning of *invitation* as it is used in line 30 of *Jane Goodall: Pioneer Researcher*?

**A.** question
**B.** threat
**C.** offer
**D.** present

**3.** The Latin word *familiaris* means "domestic" or "belonging to a family." What is the most likely meaning of *familiar* as it is used in line 14 of "Crusading for Chimps and Humans"?

**A.** oddly made
**B.** quick decision
**C.** often seen
**D.** close relationship

**4.** The Latin word *dominus* means "master." What is the most likely meaning of *dominate* as it is used in line 43 of "Crusading for Chimps and Humans"?

**A.** ignore
**B.** live with
**C.** injure
**D.** rule over

**Directions** Use context clues and your knowledge of base words to answer the following questions.

**5.** The word *extinction* is used in line 49 of *Jane Goodall: Pioneer Researcher*. What is the base word of *extinction*?

**A.** extinct
**B.** exact
**C.** extract
**D.** exit

**6.** The word *miserable* is used in line 4 of *In the Shadow of Man*. What is the base word of *miserable*?

**A.** mystery
**B.** mission
**C.** mixer
**D.** misery

**7.** The word *exhilaration* is used in line 49 of *In the Shadow of Man*. What is the base word of *exhilaration*?

**A.** hilarious
**B.** exhilarate
**C.** ration
**D.** exhale

**8.** The word *primatologist* is used in line 3 of "Crusading for Chimps and Humans." What is the base word of *primatologist*?

**A.** primate
**B.** biologist
**C.** material
**D.** imitate

## Writing and Grammar

**Directions** Read the personal narrative and answer the questions that follow.

(1) People waited outside Gordon's Books. (2) Many—appearing just as heaps of winter clothing—clutched foam cups of steaming coffee or hot chocolate to keep their hands warm. (3) I was bundled against the cold, too, but I clutched something much more important: a hardback copy of the novel The Salamander House. (4) I had read the book at least a hundred times, and now I stood only a few feet away from its author and my hero, hans Devon. (5) Mr. Devon had come to my neighborhood bookstore for a signing of his most recent book.

(6) I shivered with excitement while others in line shivered with the cold. (7) I wondered how I could tell Mr. Devon what his writing meant to me. (8) In the distance, I could see the store's large display windows already fogged with the breath of the crowd inside. (9) I stood far back in a line that snaked out the store's door and down the sidewalk. (10) Hugging the book closer, I silently hoped for the line to move faster. (11) Then, the line began to advance, slowly but surely. (12) I stepped up past the sickeningly sweet smell of Donut Explosion! and fielders' flowers—its storefront an explosion of color. (13) Soon, only five people stood between me and the door of the bookstore!

(14) Again, I began to think about what I would say to Mr. Devon. (15) I loved not only his novels but also his short stories, especially Greener Grass. (16) Before I knew it, I was inside, and Mr. Devon sat in front of me. (17) When it was my turn, I inched forward and held out my book.

(18) "A fan of my first novel. (19) What is your name?" Mr. Devon asked, gently taking the book from my hands.

(20) "Muriel," I answered. (21) "Actually, I'm a fan of all your work. (22) Your novels and stories mean a lot to me."

(23) "That is so nice to hear." (24) He smiled and signed, "To Muriel: Thanks for being a loyal reader."

(25) I took the book from his hands and held it again to my chest. (26) I had finally met my hero. (27) Looking back, I realize that this meeting with Mr. Devon, though short, was one of the most exciting moments of my life.

**1.** Choose the best way to rewrite sentence 1 so that it gets the reader's attention.

**A.** Can you believe all of the people who were waiting outside Gordon's Books?
**B.** A wet wind whipped the people anxious to get into Gordon's Books.
**C.** Tons and tons of people waited outside Gordon's Books.
**D.** One day I joined other people outside this bookstore called Gordon's Books.

**2.** Choose the correct way to punctuate the title in sentence 3.

**A.** *"The Salamander House"*
**B.** The "Salamander House"
**C.** *The Salamander House*
**D.** "The Salamander House"

**3.** Which word should be capitalized in sentence 4?

**A.** book
**B.** author
**C.** hero
**D.** hans

**4.** Choose the best way to change sentence 7 to a question.

**A.** Does Mr. Devon's writing mean anything to me?
**B.** Mr. Devon, what does your writing mean to me?
**C.** How could I tell Mr. Devon what his writing meant to me?
**D.** Should I tell Mr. Devon what I think his writing means?

**5.** The descriptive language in sentence 8 appeals to the sense of

**A.** sight
**B.** hearing
**C.** taste
**D.** smell

**6.** Which of the following words functions as a transition in sentence 11?

**A.** then
**B.** line
**C.** began
**D.** advance

**7.** Which words should be capitalized in sentence 12?

**A.** sweet, fielders
**B.** sweet, smell
**C.** smell, flowers
**D.** fielders', flowers

**8.** Which key writing trait do sentences 13, 19, and 25 illustrate?

**A.** an interesting introduction
**B.** a variety of sentence types
**C.** a relevant flashback
**D.** a reflective conclusion

**9.** Which of the following words functions as a transition in sentence 13?

**A.** soon
**B.** only
**C.** five
**D.** of

**10.** Choose the correct way to punctuate the title in sentence 15.

**A.** *Greener Grass*
**B.** *"Greener Grass"*
**C.** "Greener Grass"
**D.** "Greener" Grass

**11.** Which of the following details most effectively re-creates the event?

**A.** "clutched foam cups of steaming coffee"
**B.** "a hardback copy of the novel"
**C.** "began to think about what I would say"
**D.** "one of the most exciting moments"

**12.** Which experience is the writer describing?

**A.** buying a book by an unfamiliar author
**B.** applying for a job at the bookstore
**C.** waiting to buy a new book
**D.** meeting her favorite author

## Writing

**Directions** Read the following quotation. Then read the prompts that follow and complete one of the writing activities.

> "If you want to understand today, you have to search yesterday."
>
> Pearl S. Buck, author

**Prompt:** Write a personal narrative about an event that you would like to experience again. As the quote suggests, try to understand the event. Perhaps you would like the chance to do something differently this time.

Now write your personal narrative. The following reminders will help you.

**Challenge Prompt:** Write a personal narrative about an event that was different from what you expected it to be. As the quote suggests, try to understand the event. Explain why you expected the event to be a certain way.

Now write your personal narrative. The following reminders will help you.

**Reminders**

- Be sure your writing does what the prompt asks.
- Focus on a single experience.
- Re-create the event with dialogue, sensory language, and descriptive details.
- Conclude by reflecting on the significance of the event.
- Check for correct grammar, spelling, and punctuation.

# Unit 8

TEST A

## Reading Comprehension

**Directions** Read the following selections. Then answer the questions that follow

**Barbara Jordan: Congresswoman *from* Toucan Valley Publications**

**Barbara Jordan**

Born: February 21, 1936 Houston, Texas
Died: January 17, 1996 Austin, Texas

Barbara Jordan was the first black woman to serve in the Texas State Senate, and the first black to be elected from any southern state to the U.S. House of Representatives. She worked to improve the lives of the poor and the working class, and encouraged both blacks and whites to work together in unity. One of her favorite mottoes, often included in her speeches, was "e pluribus unum" (in unity we are one).

**Childhood**

Barbara Charline Jordan was born on February 21, 1936, in Houston, Texas. Her parents, Benjamin and Arlyne (Patten) Jordan were poor people. Her father 10 worked as a warehouse clerk, and later became a Baptist preacher. The family lived in the Fifth Ward, one of Houston's long-standing communities of African-Americans.

Barbara's grandfather, John Ed Patten, often encouraged Barbara. They spent many weekend afternoons together, working at his junkyard business. John told Barbara that she could be different, and that she did not need to settle for an ordinary life. As a result, she refused to allow poverty, or other people's prejudices about race, or the fact that she was a woman keep her from succeeding in what she chose to do.

At an early age, Barbara was often asked to recite poems and stories at her 20 church. She had a strong voice, and a lively manner of speaking. She used this talent throughout her work.

**Education**

Barbara's parents believed education would help their children to rise above their circumstances. Often when Barbara came home from school with all A's and one B, her father would ask, "Why did you get a B?" Barbara saw this as a challenge, and did her best.

At Phillis Wheatley High School in Houston, Barbara participated in the school's debate team and easily became a winner in various contests. In 1953 she won first place in the Texas State Ushers Oratorical Contest. As a result, she 30 attended a national oration contest in Chicago, which she won. Barbara graduated in the top 5% of her high school class.

After high school she attended Texas Southern University, an all-black university in Houston. Barbara majored in government and history, determined to become a lawyer. Tom Freeman, the school's speech coach, recognized her abilities, and coached her in public speaking skills. Barbara learned to defend her ideas by speaking more clearly and sharpening her thinking. She graduated from Texas Southern in 1956 *magna cum laude* (with great honor).

From 1956 until 1959, Barbara studied to be a lawyer at Boston University. In 1959, she passed the bar exams in both Texas and Massachusetts.

40 **Career**

For a time, Jordan taught at the Tuskegee Institute in Alabama. She returned to Houston in 1960 and started a law practice, working out of her parents' home. For three years she saved money, preparing to open her own office.

At the same time, Jordan became active in politics. She worked towards the nomination of John F. Kennedy as the Democratic Party candidate for president, and urged blacks to register to vote.

***In the Texas Senate***

Wanting to make a difference in the lives of people, Jordan ran for the Texas Legislature. Although she lost her first elections in 1962 and 1964, she was

50 determined. She won a seat in the Texas Senate in 1966. She was the first black woman to be voted into the Senate, and the first black to be elected to the Texas Legislature since 1883. Reporters asked Jordan if she was afraid to work in the Senate as the only black woman. Jordan replied, "I know how to read and write and think, so I have no fear."

During her tenure in the Texas Senate, Jordan conducted herself with dignity, which earned the respect of her colleagues and the voters. In 1972 she was voted *president pro tempore* (temporary president) of the Senate. As chair of the Labor and Management Relations Committee, she authored the state's first successful minimum wage bill. She also worked on legislation supporting and

60 encouraging voter rights. President Lyndon B. Johnson consulted her in matters of national civil rights.

***In the U.S. House of Representatives***

In 1973 Jordan began her career in the U.S. House of Representatives. Again, her election was a "first," the first black elected to the U.S. House of Representatives from any of the southern states. She served on the House Ways and Means Committee and the House Judiciary Committee.

Jordan was a member of the House Judiciary Committee during the investigation of President Richard Nixon and the Watergate scandal in 1974. She

became nationally known for her persuasive speaking skills, particularly after
70 giving a compelling speech in favor of the impeachment of President Nixon. She spoke about the duty of elected officials to the public they serve and to the Constitution. In 1976 Jordan became the first female keynote speaker at the Democratic National Convention, as well as the first black keynote speaker.

By 1978, Jordan had decided that she had little desire to be a long-term politician. She chose not to run for reelection. After leaving Washington, D.C. she taught at the University of Texas in Austin, in the L.B.J. School of Public Affairs. In 1982 she was awarded the University's LBJ National Chair of Policy. She taught courses on government, political values, and ethics.

In 1979, she published her autobiography: *Barbara Jordan: A Self-Portrait.*
80 During the early 1990s she served as an ethics advisor to Governor Ann Richards of Texas. Jordan delivered the keynote address at the 1992 Democratic convention. Her speech was praised for its views against racial prejudice among both blacks and whites.

Jordan suffered from multiple sclerosis during her later years and was confined to a wheelchair. In 1988, she came close to drowning at her home in Austin, but survived. On January 17, 1996, Barbara Jordan died from pneumonia and leukemia. She was buried at the state cemetery in Austin, Texas.

**Remembering Barbara Jordan**

Jordan received many honors for her work, including an Honorary Doctorate
90 from Harvard University. She was named to the Texas Women's Hall of Fame in 1990, and is also honored in the National Women's Hall of Fame in Seneca, New York. In 1992 Jordan received the Eleanor Roosevelt Val-Kill Medal for humanitarianism and the Springarn Medal from the National Association for the Advancement of Colored People (NAACP). In 1994 she was awarded the Presidential Medal of Freedom, the nation's highest civilian award.



*Barbara Jordan gave this speech at the 1992 Democratic National Convention.*

## All Together Now

**Barbara Jordan**

When I look at race relations today I can see that some positive changes have come about. But much remains to be done, and the answer does not lie in more legislation. We have the legislation we need: we have the laws. Frankly, I don't believe that the task of bringing us all together can be accomplished by government. What we need now is soul force—the efforts of people working on a small scale to build a truly tolerant, harmonious society. And parents can do a great deal to createthat tolerant society.

We all know that race relations in America have had a very rocky history. Think about the 1960s when Dr. Martin Luther King Jr., was in his heyday and
10 there were marches and protests against segregation and discrimination. The movement culminated in 1963 with the March on Washington.

Following that event, race relations reached an all-time peak. President Lyndon B. Johnson pushed through the Civil Rights Act of 1964, which remains the fundamental piece of civil rights legislation in this century. The Voting Rights Act of 1965 ensured that everyone in our country could vote. At last, black people and white people seemed ready to live together in peace.

But that is not what happened. By the 1990's the good feelings had diminished. Today the nation seems to be suffering from compassion fatigue, and issues such as race relations and civil rights have never regained momentum.

20 Those issues, however, remain crucial. As our society becomes more diverse, people of all races and backgrounds will have to learn to live together. If we don't think this is important, all we have to do is look at the situation in Bosnia today.

How do we create a harmonious society out of so many kinds of people? The key is tolerance—the one value that is indispensable in creating community.

If we are concerned about community, if it is important to us that people not feel excluded, then we have to do something. Each of us can decide to have one friend of a different race or background in our mix of friends. If we do this, we'll be working together to push things forward.

30 One thing is clear to me: We, as human beings, must be willing to accept people who are different from ourselves. I must be willing to accept people who don't look as I do and don't talk as I do. It is crucial that I am open to their feelings, their inner reality.

What can parents do? We can put our faith in young people as a positive force. I have yet to find a racist baby. Babies come into the world as blank as slates and, with their beautiful innocence, see others not as difficult but as enjoyable companions. Children learn ideas and attitudes from the adults who nurture them. I absolutely believe that children do not adopt prejudices unless they absorb them from their parents or teachers.

40 The best way to get this country faithful to the American dream of tolerance and equality is to start small. Parents can actively encourage their children to be in the company of people who are of other racial and ethnic backgrounds. If a child thinks, "Well, that person's color is not the same as mine, but she must be okay because she likes to play with the same things I like to play with," that child willgrow up with a broader view of humanity.

I'm an incurable optimist. For the rest of the time that I have left on this

planet I want to bring people together. You might think of this as a labor of love. Now, I know that love means different things to different people. But what I mean is this: I care about you because you are a fellow human being and I find it
50 okay in my mind, in my heart, to simply say to you, I love you. And maybe that would encourage you to love me in return.

It is possible for all of us to work on this-at home, in our schools, at our jobs. It is possible to work on human relationships in every area of our lives.

Courtesy-Congresswoman Barbara Jordan Archives-Robert J. Terry Library-
Texas Southern University-Special Collections

## COMPREHENSION

**Directions** Answer the following questions about "Barbara Jordan: Congresswoman."

**1.** The subheadings show that the main pattern of organization in the article is

**A.** compare and contrast
**B.** cause-and-effect organization
**C.** classification
**D.** chronological order

**2.** The boxed text feature at the beginning of the article introduces the dates of Barbara Jordan's

**A.** book publications
**B.** election victories
**C.** birth and death
**D.** keynote speeches

**3.** Which source could you best use to verify the facts in lines 1–2?

**A.** reliable print or online source
**B.** personal observation
**C.** discussion with an adult
**D.** scientific experiment

**4.** Which signal words in lines 12–15 show cause-and-effect organization?

**A.** "she did not"
**B.** "As a result"
**C.** "the fact that"
**D.** "chose to do"

**5.** Which statement from lines 11–26 best shows the author's bias?

**A.** "Barbara's grandfather, John Ed Patten, often encouraged Barbara."
**B.** "At an early age, Barbara was often asked to recite poems and stories at her church."
**C.** "She had a strong voice, and a lively manner of speaking."
**D.** "In 1953 she won first place in the Texas State Ushers Oratorical Contest."

6. Under the subheading "Education," you learn that Barbara Jordan attended
   - A. University of Texas
   - B. Texas Southern University
   - C. Tuskegee Institute
   - D. Texas State

7. Which pattern of organization do lines 77–80 use?
   - A. chronological order
   - B. classification
   - C. compare and contrast
   - D. cause-and-effect organization

8. Under the subheading "Remembering Barbara Jordan," you learn that Barbara Jordan received the Eleanor Roosevelt Val-Kill Medal for
   - A. patriotism
   - B. ethics
   - C. humanitarianism
   - D. citizenship

## COMPREHENSION

**Directions** Answer the following questions about "All Together Now."

9. The main idea of lines 1–7 is that people must
   - A. create more laws and legislation
   - B. work together to make a better society
   - C. find new forms of government
   - D. acknowledge positive changes

10. In lines 3–7, the author supports her claim with
    - A. statistics
    - B. questions
    - C. opinions
    - D. research

11. Which of the following statements is a fact?
    - A. "But much remains to be done, and the answer does not lie in more legislation."
    - B. "Following that event, race relations reached an all-time peak."
    - C. "The Voting Rights Act of 1965 ensured that everyone in our country could vote."
    - D. "By the 1990's the good feelings had diminished."

12. Which persuasive technique does the author use in lines 17–19?
    - A. emotional appeal
    - B. appeal by association
    - C. logical appeal
    - D. appeal to authority

**13.** In lines 20–21, the author most appeals to your

**A.** personal experiences
**B.** sense of pride
**C.** family values
**D.** common sense

**14.** The author most likely included lines 21–22 to

**A.** support her claim
**B.** create a sense of anger
**C.** show her view on war
**D.** offer a history lesson

**15.** Which phrase contains an example of loaded language?

**A.** "race relations and civil rights"
**B.** "different race or background"
**C.** "a baby's beautiful innocence"
**D.** "people and human relationships"

**16.** Which phrase from lines 29–30 gives the best clue that those lines contain an opinion?

**A.** One thing is clear to me
**B.** "We, as human beings
**C.** must be willing to accept people
**D.** who are different from ourselves

**17.** Which words best indicate that lines 35–37 contain an opinion?

**A.** I, believe
**B.** children, adopt
**C.** prejudices, absorb
**D.** they, from

**18.** Which pattern of organization does the author use in lines 38–43?

**A.** compare and contrast
**B.** chronological
**C.** classification
**D.** cause and effect

**19.** Lines 38–43 show the author's bias that parents affect

**A.** children's games
**B.** small communities
**C.** racial tolerance
**D.** historical events

**20.** The author's claim in the selection is that people must

**A.** work toward a tolerant society
**B.** find diverse playmates for children
**C.** remember the situation in Bosnia
**D.** create more civil rights laws

**COMPREHENSION**

**Directions** Answer these questions about both selections.

**21.** What similar main idea is reflected in the first paragraph of each selection?

**A.** The lives of the poor and working class need to be improved.

**B.** Jordan thinks people need to work together to create a better society.

**C.** The answer to fixing race relations lies with parents.

**D.** Jordan's favorite motto is *"e pluribus unum."*

**22.** What pattern of organization is used in each selection?

**A.** chronological order

**B.** counterarguments

**C.** complex sentences

**D.** critical analysis

## Written Response

**SHORT RESPONSE**

**Directions** Write two or three sentences to answer each question on a separate sheet of paper.

**23.** Identify one opinion in lines 44–56 of "All Together Now."

**24.** Identify one piece of information discussed under the subheading "Childhood" in "Barbara Jordan: Congresswoman."

**EXTENDED RESPONSE**

**Directions** Answer the following question. Write two or more paragraphs on a separate sheet of paper.

**25.** Identify the main idea of "All Together Now." How does the author use persuasive techniques to support the main idea? Provide two details from the selection to support your response.

## Vocabulary

**Directions** Use context clues and your knowledge of idioms to choose the best definition of the underlined idiom in each sentence.

**1.** Barbara Jordan hoped that listeners would go along with her plan for a better society.

**A.** visit with
**B.** dance with
**C.** sing with
**D.** agree with

**2.** Jordan wanted tolerance in the worst way.

**A.** very much
**B.** extremely slowly
**C.** mainly used
**D.** especially now

**3.** When Jordan's speech is over with, we can discuss her main points.

**A.** covered
**B.** printed
**C.** reviewed
**D.** finished

**Directions** Use your knowledge of prefixes and Latin roots and words to answer the following questions.

**4.** The Latin prefix *re-* means "again," and the Latin word *citare* means "to summon." What is the most likely meaning of the word *recite* as it is used in line 16 of "Barbara Jordan: Congresswoman"?

**A.** call from a phone
**B.** speak from memory
**C.** learn from a teacher
**D.** sing in a choir

**5.** The Latin prefix *re-* means "again," and the Latin root *lect* means "choose." What is the most likely meaning of the word *reelection* as it is used in line 68–69 of "Barbara Jordan: Congresswoman"?

**A.** selection one more time
**B.** management for awhile
**C.** assortment daily
**D.** schedule for two weeks

**6.** The Latin prefix *re-* means "again," and the Latin root *cre* means "grow." What is the most likely meaning of the word *recreate* as it is used in the following sentence? Jenna will recreate the broken diorama of the March on Washington.

**A.** provide water
**B.** show two times
**C.** plant a tree
**D.** make once more

## Writing and Grammar

**Directions** Read the persuasive essay and answer the questions that follow.

(1) Poplar Park the oldest park in Grantville is no longer a pleasant place to picnic or play. (2) Its large grassy areas towering trees and winding paths once attracted visitors from far and wide. (3) Lately the park has experienced an increase in litter, vandalism, and crime. (4) Because of the vandalism and crime, the city changed the park's closing time to 700 p.m. (5) This is why the city needs to spend more money to clean up Poplar Park, to repair its features, and to make it a safe place to visit. (6) Improving the condition of the park will bring more people to the area and provide visitors—as well as residents of Grantville—with a great place to enjoy.

(7) The first way the city could improve the condition of Poplar Park is by repairing the tennis courts. (8) Damage such as large cracks on the courts' surface, torn nets, and missing wind screens have discouraged people from coming to the park to play. (9) If the city spent the money to fix the courts, more people would be drawn to the park. (10) Also, tournament directors would be more likely to hold their tennis events at well-maintained courts.

(11) Another way the city could improve Poplar Park's condition is by painting over the graffiti that covers the back wall of the concessions stand and the side of the soccer bleachers. (12) By giving these structures a coat of fresh paint, the park would look more appealing and would consequently attract more visitors. (13) The Grantville Gophers the community group that runs the stand would undoubtedly benefit from an increase in concessions customers.

(14) The last way that the city could improve the condition of Poplar Park is by adding the following floodlights security cameras and park police. (15) Flood lights would help light areas that are dark and unsafe. (16) Security cameras would help catch people throwing garbage on the ground instead of in trash cans. (17) Park police would help create a safer environment for people who want to relax in the park during the evening. (18) Park police would also help catch people who vandalize buildings and equipment in the park.

(19) Many Grantville residents say that the city's money is better spent on planting flowers and trees along Main Street. (20) Although these new plantings would be attractive, they would not benefit the public. (21) They would not help make the park safer. (22) In fact, people who vandalize the buildings and equipment might also destroy the flowers. (23) This is why money should go to improving Poplar Park. (24) If given the care and attention it needs and deserves, this beautiful Grantville landmark will give people a safe place to enjoy for years to come.

1. To punctuate the appositive phrase in sentence 1, place commas after
   - A. "Poplar" and "Park"
   - B. "Park" and "Grantville"
   - C. "Grantville" and "pleasant"
   - D. "is" and "picnic"

2. To punctuate the items in a series in sentence 2, place commas after
   - A. "large" and "far"
   - B. "grassy" and "winding"
   - C. "areas" and "trees"
   - D. "once" and "visitors"

3. Choose the correct way to punctuate the beginning of sentence 3 with a comma.
   - A. Lately the park has,
   - B. Lately the, park has
   - C. Lately, the park has
   - D. Lately the park, has

4. Choose the correct place to insert a colon in sentence 4.
   - A. time:
   - B. 7:00 P.M.
   - C. closes:
   - D. 700 P.M.:

5. Sentences 5 and 6 present this persuasive essay's
   - A. counterclaim
   - B. thesis statement
   - C. sentence pattern
   - D. conclusion

6. Sentence 8 supports the writer's position by
   - A. presenting opposing arguments
   - B. explaining children's concerns
   - C. providing convincing details
   - D. issuing a call to action

7. Identify the transition in sentence 11.
   - A. Another way
   - B. painting over
   - C. back wall
   - D. soccer bleachers

8. Which words from sentence 12 are examples of persuasive language?
   - A. giving, structures
   - B. look, would
   - C. appealing, attract
   - D. these, coat

9. To punctuate the appositive phrase in sentence 13, place commas after
   - A. "stand" and "increase"
   - B. "Gophers" and "stand"
   - C. "Grantville" and "Gophers"
   - D. "group" and "benefit"

**10.** Choose the correct way to punctuate sentence 14 with a colon and commas.

**A.** The last way the city could improve the condition of Poplar Park: is by adding the following floodlights security cameras, and park police.

**B.** The last way: the city could improve the condition of Poplar Park, is by adding the following floodlights, security cameras, and park police.

**C.** The last way the city could improve the condition of Poplar Park is by adding the following: floodlights, security cameras, and park police.

**D.** The last way the city could improve the condition of Poplar Park is: by adding the following, floodlights, security cameras and park police.

**11.** Which sentences include the summary of the writer's position and a call to action?

**A.** 15 and 16

**B.** 18 and 19

**C.** 20 and 21

**D.** 23 and 24

**12.** Which words from sentence 24 are examples of persuasive language?

**A.** Grantville, people

**B.** care, deserves

**C.** for, come

**D.** it, this

## Writing

**Directions** Read the following quotation. Then read the prompt that follows and complete the writing activity.

> "He who wants to persuade should put his trust not in the right argument, but in the right word.".
>
> Joseph Conrad

**Prompt:** Write a persuasive essay in which you try to persuade a family member or friend to agree with your point of view on an issue. As the quote suggests, use precise words and convincing details to support your ideas.

Now write your persuasive essay. Use the reminders that follow to help you write.

**Reminders**

- Be sure your writing does what the prompt asks.
- Present a thesis statement that takes a clear stand on an issue.
- Use convincing details to support the thesis.
- Use persuasive language effectively.
- Check for correct grammar, spelling, and punctuation.

## Reading Comprehension

**Directions** Read the following selections. Then answer the questions that follow.

**Barbara Jordan: Congresswoman *from* Toucan Valley Publications**

**Barbara Jordan**

Born: February 21, 1936 Houston, Texas
Died: January 17, 1996 Austin, Texas

Barbara Jordan was the first black woman to serve in the Texas State Senate, and the first black to be elected from any southern state to the U.S. House of Representatives. She worked to improve the lives of the poor and the working class, and encouraged both blacks and whites to work together in unity. One of her favorite mottoes, often included in her speeches, was "e pluribus unum" (in unity we are one).

**Childhood**

Barbara Charline Jordan was born on February 21, 1936, in Houston, Texas. Her parents, Benjamin and Arlyne (Patten) Jordan were poor people. Her father
10 worked as a warehouse clerk, and later became a Baptist preacher. The family lived in the Fifth Ward, one of Houston's long-standing communities of African-Americans.

Barbara's grandfather, John Ed Patten, often encouraged Barbara. They spent many weekend afternoons together, working at his junkyard business. John told Barbara that she could be different, and that she did not need to settle for an ordinary life. As a result, she refused to allow poverty, or other people's prejudices about race, or the fact that she was a woman keep her from succeeding in what she chose to do.

At an early age, Barbara was often asked to recite poems and stories at her
20 church. She had a strong voice, and a lively manner of speaking. She used this talent throughout her work.

**Education**

Barbara's parents believed education would help their children to rise above their circumstances. Often when Barbara came home from school with all A's and one B, her father would ask, "Why did you get a B?" Barbara saw this as a challenge, and did her best.

At Phillis Wheatley High School in Houston, Barbara participated in the school's debate team and easily became a winner in various contests. In 1953 she won first place in the Texas State Ushers Oratorical Contest. As a result, she
30 attended a national oration contest in Chicago, which she won. Barbara graduated

in the top 5% of her high school class.

After high school she attended Texas Southern University, an all-black university in Houston. Barbara majored in government and history, determined to become a lawyer. Tom Freeman, the school's speech coach, recognized her abilities, and coached her in public speaking skills. Barbara learned to defend her ideas by speaking more clearly and sharpening her thinking. She graduated from Texas Southern in 1956 *magna cum laude* (with great honor).

From 1956 until 1959, Barbara studied to be a lawyer at Boston University. In 1959, she passed the bar exams in both Texas and Massachusetts.

40 **Career**

For a time, Jordan taught at the Tuskegee Institute in Alabama. She returned to Houston in 1960 and started a law practice, working out of her parents' home. For three years she saved money, preparing to open her own office.

At the same time, Jordan became active in politics. She worked towards the nomination of John F. Kennedy as the Democratic Party candidate for president, and urged blacks to register to vote.

***In the Texas Senate***

Wanting to make a difference in the lives of people, Jordan ran for the Texas Legislature. Although she lost her first elections in 1962 and 1964, she was
50 determined. She won a seat in the Texas Senate in 1966. She was the first black woman to be voted into the Senate, and the first black to be elected to the Texas Legislature since 1883. Reporters asked Jordan if she was afraid to work in the Senate as the only black woman. Jordan replied, "I know how to read and write and think, so I have no fear."

During her tenure in the Texas Senate, Jordan conducted herself with dignity, which earned the respect of her colleagues and the voters. In 1972 she was voted *president pro tempore* (temporary president) of the Senate. As chair of the Labor and Management Relations Committee, she authored the state's first successful minimum wage bill. She also worked on legislation supporting and
60 encouraging voter rights. President Lyndon B. Johnson consulted her in matters of national civil rights.

***In the U.S. House of Representatives***

In 1973 Jordan began her career in the U.S. House of Representatives. Again, her election was a "first," the first black elected to the U.S. House of Representatives from any of the southern states. She served on the House Ways and Means Committee and the House Judiciary Committee.

Jordan was a member of the House Judiciary Committee during the investigation of President Richard Nixon and the Watergate scandal in 1974. She

became nationally known for her persuasive speaking skills, particularly after
70 giving a compelling speech in favor of the impeachment of President Nixon. She spoke about the duty of elected officials to the public they serve and to the Constitution. In 1976 Jordan became the first female keynote speaker at the Democratic National Convention, as well as the first black keynote speaker.

By 1978, Jordan had decided that she had little desire to be a long-term politician. She chose not to run for reelection. After leaving Washington, D.C. she taught at the University of Texas in Austin, in the L.B.J. School of Public Affairs. In 1982 she was awarded the University's LBJ National Chair of Policy. She taught courses on government, political values, and ethics.

In 1979, she published her autobiography: *Barbara Jordan: A Self-Portrait.*
80 During the early 1990s she served as an ethics advisor to Governor Ann Richards of Texas. Jordan delivered the keynote address at the 1992 Democratic convention. Her speech was praised for its views against racial prejudice among both blacks and whites.

Jordan suffered from multiple sclerosis during her later years and was confined to a wheelchair. In 1988, she came close to drowning at her home in Austin, but survived. On January 17, 1996, Barbara Jordan died from pneumonia and leukemia. She was buried at the state cemetery in Austin, Texas.

**Remembering Barbara Jordan**

Jordan received many honors for her work, including an Honorary Doctorate
90 from Harvard University. She was named to the Texas Women's Hall of Fame in 1990, and is also honored in the National Women's Hall of Fame in Seneca, New York. In 1992 Jordan received the Eleanor Roosevelt Val-Kill Medal for humanitarianism and the Springarn Medal from the National Association for the Advancement of Colored People (NAACP). In 1994 she was awarded the Presidential Medal of Freedom, the nation's highest civilian award.



*Barbara Jordan gave this speech at the 1992 Democratic National Convention.*

**All Together Now**

**Barbara Jordan**

When I look at race relations today I can see that some positive changes have come about. But much remains to be done, and the answer does not lie in more legislation. We have the legislation we need: we have the laws. Frankly, I don't believe that the task of bringing us all together can be accomplished by government. What we need now is soul force—the efforts of people working on a small scale to build a truly tolerant, harmonious society. And parents can do a great deal to createthat tolerant society.

We all know that race relations in America have had a very rocky history. Think about the 1960s when Dr. Martin Luther King Jr., was in his heyday and
10 there were marches and protests against segregation and discrimination. The movement culminated in 1963 with the March on Washington.

Following that event, race relations reached an all-time peak. President Lyndon B. Johnson pushed through the Civil Rights Act of 1964, which remains the fundamental piece of civil rights legislation in this century. The Voting Rights Act of 1965 ensured that everyone in our country could vote. At last, black people and white people seemed ready to live together in peace.

But that is not what happened. By the 1990's the good feelings had diminished. Today the nation seems to be suffering from compassion fatigue, and issues such as race relations and civil rights have never regained momentum.

20 Those issues, however, remain crucial. As our society becomes more diverse, people of all races and backgrounds will have to learn to live together. If we don't think this is important, all we have to do is look at the situation in Bosnia today.

How do we create a harmonious society out of so many kinds of people? The key is tolerance—the one value that is indispensable in creating community.

If we are concerned about community, if it is important to us that people not feel excluded, then we have to do something. Each of us can decide to have one friend of a different race or background in our mix of friends. If we do this, we'll be working together to push things forward.

30 One thing is clear to me: We, as human beings, must be willing to accept people who are different from ourselves. I must be willing to accept people who don't look as I do and don't talk as I do. It is crucial that I am open to their feelings, their inner reality.

What can parents do? We can put our faith in young people as a positive force. I have yet to find a racist baby. Babies come into the world as blank as slates and, with their beautiful innocence, see others not as difficult but as enjoyable companions. Children learn ideas and attitudes from the adults who nurture them. I absolutely believe that children do not adopt prejudices unless they absorb them from their parents or teachers.

40 The best way to get this country faithful to the American dream of tolerance and equality is to start small. Parents can actively encourage their children to be in the company of people who are of other racial and ethnic backgrounds. If a child thinks, "Well, that person's color is not the same as mine, but she must be okay because she likes to play with the same things I like to play with," that child willgrow up with a broader view of humanity.

I'm an incurable optimist. For the rest of the time that I have left on this

planet I want to bring people together. You might think of this as a labor of love. Now, I know that love means different things to different people. But what I mean is this: I care about you because you are a fellow human being and I find it
50 okay in my mind, in my heart, to simply say to you, I love you. And maybe that would encourage you to love me in return.

It is possible for all of us to work on this-at home, in our schools, at our jobs. It is possible to work on human relationships in every area of our lives.

Courtesy-Congresswoman Barbara Jordan Archives-Robert J. Terry Library-
Texas Southern University-Special Collections

## COMPREHENSION

**Directions** Answer the following questions about "Barbara Jordan: Congresswoman."

**1.** The title "Barbara Jordan: Congresswoman" tells you that this article will most likely

**A.** list the educational accomplishments of Barbara Jordan
**B.** analyze a speech given by Barbara Jordan in Congress
**C.** discuss Barbara Jordan's childhood and family life
**D.** explore Barbara Jordan's career as a politician

**2.** The subheadings in the article best reveal that

**A.** events will be told in chronological order
**B.** causes and effects will be stated
**C.** events will be classified by importance
**D.** people will be compared and contrasted

**3.** In lines 11–15, the author uses cause-and-effect organization to

**A.** illustrate the meaning of love
**B.** compare Jordan and her grandfather
**C.** explain a bias about education
**D.** show the relationship of events

**4.** Which piece of information would you find under the subheading "Education"?

**A.** John Ed Patten encouraged Jordan.
**B.** Jordan won an oratorical contest.
**C.** She won a seat in the Texas Senate.
**D.** Jordan taught at the Tuskegee Institute.

**5.** Which piece of information from lines 24–27 contains an opinion?

**A.** Jordan was part of the debate team at Phillis Wheatley High School.
**B.** During high school, Jordan easily won various debate contests
**C.** In Chicago, Jordan won a national oration contest.
**D.** When she graduated, Jordan was in the top 5% of her high school class.

**6.** Under the subheading "Career," you learn that Jordan taught

**A.** at Phillis Wheatley High School
**B.** in a small school in Boston
**C.** at Tuskegee Institute in Alabama
**D.** from her parents' home

**7.** Which piece of information would you find under the subheading "Career"?

**A.** Jordan used to recite poems at her church.
**B.** Tom Freeman coached Jordan.
**C.** Jordan started a law practice in Houston.
**D.** The NAACP gave Jordan a medal.

**8.** The word *compelling* in lines 62–64 best reveals the author's bias that

**A.** Jordan was an effective public speaker
**B.** effective speaking skills take practice
**C.** President Nixon deserved to be impeached
**D.** elected officials must respect their duties

**9.** Under the subheading "Remembering Barbara Jordan," you learn that Jordan received

**A.** a recognition of excellence
**B.** an Honorary Doctorate from Harvard
**C.** a medal for citizenship
**D.** an award from the University of Texas

## COMPREHENSION

**Directions** Answer the following questions about "All Together Now."

**10.** Which statement from the selection is a fact?

**A.** "But much remains to be done, and the answer does not lie in more legislation."
**B.** "And parents can do a great deal to create that tolerant society."
**C.** "The Voting Rights Act of 1965 ensured that everyone in our country could vote."
**D.** "It is possible for all of us to work on this—at home, in our schools, at our jobs."

**11.** In lines 3–6, Barbara Jordan addresses the counterargument that

**A.** government must fix race relations
**B.** parents are too lazy to take action
**C.** leaders must make new rules
**D.** people lack the time to better society

**12.** Jordan most likely included lines 3–7 to

**A.** explain her opinion of segregation
**B.** appeal to common sense
**C.** reveal the effects of discrimination
**D.** suggest feelings of fear

**13.** Lines 8–16 support the author's claim by

**A.** revealing the achievements of Dr. Martin Luther King Jr.
**B.** showing that people need to work together to achieve tolerance
**C.** showing that people need to work together to achieve tolerance
**D.** pointing out that the fight against segregation has been a long battle

14. Which phrase from the selection contains an example of loaded language?

A. "When I look at race relations"
B. "Think about the 1960s"
C. "indispensable in creating community"
D. "work on this—at home"

15. Jordan most likely uses chronological order in lines 8–16 to

A. list the people involved in the 1963 March
B. restate the dates of the protests
C. state the steps taken by Dr. King
D. show the order of events in race relations

16. The word *crucial* in line 20 reveals the author's bias about the

A. effects of the Voting Rights Act
B. importance of fixing race relations
C. loss of good feelings in the 1990's
D. impact of parents on children

17. Jordan's mention of making a friend of a different race or background supports the main idea that

A. people can take small steps
B. people often feel excluded
C. babies are born without prejudices
D. children should be influenced

18. Which statement best expresses the main idea of lines 32–37?

A. Children adopt their attitudes from adults.
B. People need to take steps to end racism.
C. Babies are blank as slates when born.
D. Most children enjoy companions.

19. Jordan most likely uses a logical appeal in lines 32–37 to

A. explain her views on raising children
B. support her claim about taking small steps
C. encourage teachers to teach more history
D. show parents the effect of racism

20. In lines 44–48, Jordan most likely uses an emotional appeal to

A. explain discrimination to her audience
B. create a community of friends
C. persuade her audience to act as she does
D. illustrate that she is an optimist

## COMPREHENSION

**Directions** Answer these questions about both selections.

**21.** What similar main idea is reflected in the first paragraph of each selection?

**A.** The lives of the poor and working class need to be improved.
**B.** Jordan thinks people need to work together to create a better society.
**C.** The remedy for fixing race relations lies with parents.
**D.** Jordan was the first black woman to fight for equal rights.

**22.** What pattern of organization is used in each selection?

**A.** chronological order
**B.** counterarguments
**C.** complex sentences
**D.** critical analysis

# Written Response

## SHORT RESPONSE

**Directions** Write two or three sentences to answer each question.

**23.** Explain how lines 20–21 of "All Together Now" appeal to common sense on a separate sheet of paper.

**24.** Identify two facts included under the subheading "Remembering Barbara Jordan" in "Barbara Jordan: Congresswoman."

## EXTENDED RESPONSE

**Directions** Answer one of the following questions. Write two or more paragraphs on a separate sheet of paper.

**25.** What does the loaded language in "Barbara Jordan: Congresswoman" reveal about the author's biases? Provide examples from the selection to support your answer.

**26. Challenge** Based on the information in "Barbara Jordan: Congresswoman," why do you think Jordan thinks as she does in "All Together Now"? Give examples from both selections to support your response.

## Vocabulary

**Directions** Use context clues and your knowledge of idioms to choose the best definition of the underlined idiom in each sentence.

**1.** People would not face up to the fact that race relations still needed to be improved.

**A.** review
**B.** confront
**C.** defend
**D.** analyze

**2.** At long last, people recognized that they must work together to build a tolerant society.

**A.** prior to a meeting
**B.** around a similar instance
**C.** after much time
**D.** before morning

**3.** How come it took so long to improve race relations?

**A.** when will that
**B.** how is it that
**C.** where does
**D.** what is the purpose

**Directions** Use context clues and your knowledge of prefixes and Latin roots and words to answer the following questions.

**4.** The Latin prefix *re-* means "again," and the Latin word *citare* means "to summon." What is the most likely meaning of the word *recite* as it is used in line 16 of "Barbara Jordan: Congresswoman"?

**A.** describe from knowledge
**B.** speak from memory
**C.** explain from experience
**D.** create from imagination

**5.** The Latin prefix *re-* means "again," and the Latin root *lect* means "choose." What is the most likely meaning of the word *reelection* as it is used in line 68–69 of "Barbara Jordan: Congresswoman"?

**A.** selection once more
**B.** repeated gathering
**C.** meeting another time
**D.** several collections

**6.** The Latin prefix *re-* means "again," and the Latin root *uni* means "one." What is the most likely meaning of the word *reunite* as it is used in the following sentence? We will reunite the group for a discussion of Jordan's accomplishments.

**A.** show many people around
**B.** combine one rule with another
**C.** explain one idea twice
**D.** bring together once more

## Writing and Grammar

**Directions** Read the persuasive essay and answer the questions that follow.

(1) Poplar Park the oldest park in Grantville is no longer a pleasant place to picnic or play. (2) Its large grassy areas towering trees and winding paths once attracted visitors from far and wide. (3) Lately the park has experienced an increase in litter, vandalism, and crime. (4) Because of the vandalism and crime, the city changed the park's closing time to 700 p.m. (5) This is why the city needs to spend more money to clean up Poplar Park, to repair its features, and to make it a safe place to visit. (6) Improving the condition of the park will bring more people to the area and provide visitors—as well as residents of Grantville—with a great place to enjoy.

(7) The first way the city could improve the condition of Poplar Park is by repairing the tennis courts. (8) Damage such as large cracks on the courts' surface, torn nets, and missing wind screens have discouraged people from coming to the park to play. (9) If the city spent the money to fix the courts, more people would be drawn to the park. (10) Also, tournament directors would be more likely to hold their tennis events at well-maintained courts.

(11) Another way the city could improve Poplar Park's condition is by painting over the graffiti that covers the back wall of the concessions stand and the side of the soccer bleachers. (12) By giving these structures a coat of fresh paint, the park would look more appealing and would consequently attract more visitors. (13) The Grantville Gophers the community group that runs the stand would undoubtedly benefit from an increase in concessions customers.

(14) The last way that the city could improve the condition of Poplar Park is by adding the following floodlights security cameras and park police. (15) Flood lights would help light areas that are dark and unsafe. (16) Security cameras would help catch people throwing garbage on the ground instead of in trash cans. (17) Park police would help create a safer environment for people who want to relax in the park during the evening. (18) Park police would also help catch people who vandalize buildings and equipment in the park.

(19) Many Grantville residents say that the city's money is better spent on planting flowers and trees along Main Street. (20) Although these new plantings would be attractive, they would not benefit the public. (21) They would not help make the park safer. (22) In fact, people who vandalize the buildings and equipment might also destroy the flowers. (23) This is why money should go to improving Poplar Park. (24) If given the care and attention it needs and deserves, this beautiful Grantville landmark will give people a safe place to enjoy for years to come.

**1.** To correctly punctuate the appositive phrase in sentence 1, place commas after

**A.** "Park" and "park"
**B.** "Park" and "Grantville"
**C.** "Grantville" and "place"
**D.** "longer" and "picnic"

**2.** To punctuate the items in a series in sentence 2 place commas after

**A.** "towering" and "winding"
**B.** "large" and "paths"
**C.** "areas" and "trees"
**D.** "areas" and "trees"

**3.** Choose the correct way to punctuate the beginning of sentence 3 with a comma.

**A.** Lately the park has,
**B.** Lately the, park has
**C.** Lately, the park has
**D.** Lately the park, has

**4.** Choose the correct place to insert a colon in sentence 4.

**A.** 70:0 P.M.
**B.** 700: P.M.
**C.** 7:00 P.M.
**D.** 700 P.M.:

**5.** The purpose of sentences 5 and 6 is to

**A.** explain a counterclaim
**B.** state the thesis statement
**C.** show a sentence pattern
**D.** describe the conclusion

**6.** The purpose of sentence 8 is to

**A.** support the author's opinion
**B.** transition between improvements
**C.** summarize the author's position
**D.** answer an opposing argument

**7.** Identify the transition in sentence 11.

**A.** Another way
**B.** could improve
**C.** over the
**D.** side of

**8.** In sentence 12, the writer includes language such as "more appealing" and "attract more visitors" to

**A.** set an honest tone
**B.** give you a summary
**C.** persuade you
**D.** show the organization

**9.** To punctuate the appositive phrase in sentence 13, place commas after

**A.** "Gophers" and "stand"
**B.** "stand" and "benefit"
**C.** "Grantville" and "Gophers"
**D.** "group" and "increase"

**10.** Choose the correct place to insert a colon in sentence 14.

**A.** Park:
**B.** following:
**C.** way:
**D.** is:

**11.** The writer's call to action states that

**A.** residents want to plant flowers and trees
**B.** new trees would not benefit the public
**C.** money should be used for improvements
**D.** people need a place to enjoy

**12.** The writer includes language such as "car and attention" and "beautiful Grantville landmark" to

**A.** persuade you
**B.** summarize the essay
**C.** entertain you
**D.** transition ideas

## Writing

**Directions** Read the following quotation. Then read the prompts that follow and complete one of the writing activities.

> "He who wants to persuade should put his trust not in the right argument, but in the right word."
>
> Joseph Conrad

**Prompt:** Write a persuasive essay based on an issue addressed in a movie you have seen. Clearly identify the issue and your position. As the quote suggests, use precise words and support your ideas.

Now write your persuasive essay. Use the reminders that follow to help you write.

**Challenge Prompt:** Write a persuasive essay in which you take a position regarding Conrad's quote. Does an effective argument rely on the substance of its argument or the power of its word? Support your position.

Now write your persuasive essay. Use the reminders that follow to help you write.

**Reminders**

- Be sure your writing does what the prompt asks.
- Present a thesis statement that takes a clear stand on an issue.
- Use convincing details to support the thesis.
- Use persuasive language effectively.
- Check for correct grammar, spelling, and punctuation

## Using the Internet

**Directions** Use the Web site to answer the questions that follow.

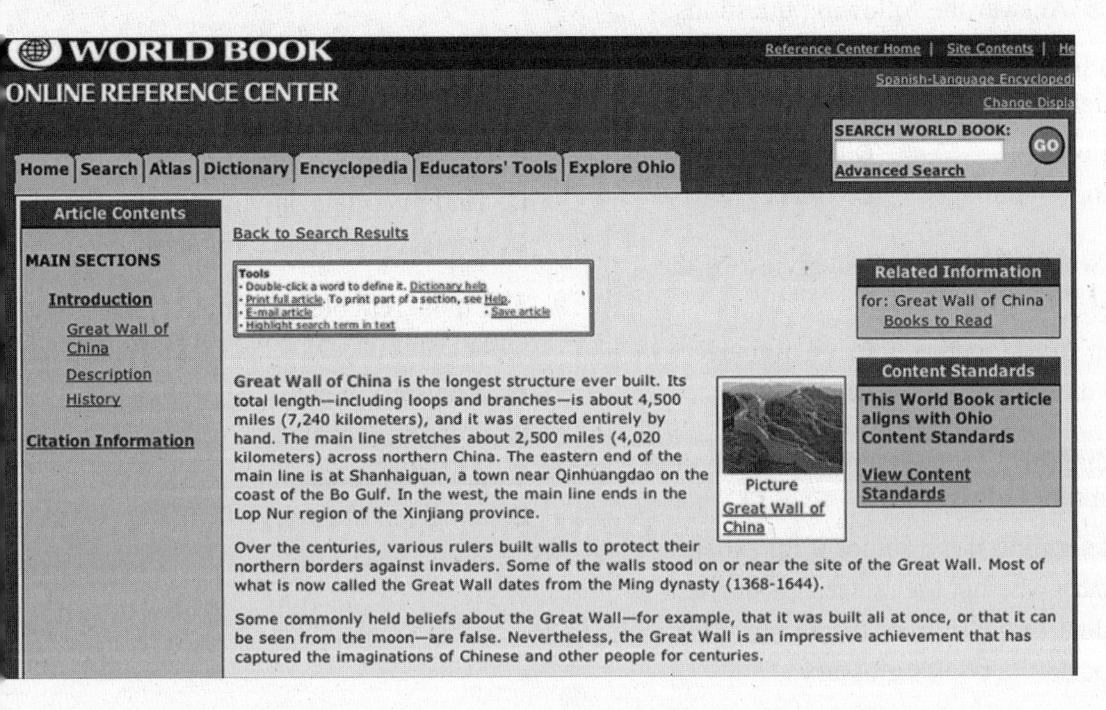
WORLD BOOK
ONLINE REFERENCE CENTER
Reference Center Home | Site Contents | He
Spanish-Language Encycloped
Change Displa
SEARCH WORLD BOOK: GO
Advanced Search
Home | Search | Atlas | Dictionary | Encyclopedia | Educators' Tools | Explore Ohio

Article Contents
MAIN SECTIONS
Introduction
Great Wall of China
Description
History
Citation Information

Back to Search Results

Tools
- Double-click a word to define it. Dictionary help
- Print full article. To print part of a section, see Help.
- E-mail article
- Save article
- Highlight search term in text

Related Information
for: Great Wall of China
Books to Read

Content Standards
This World Book article aligns with Ohio Content Standards
View Content Standards

Picture
Great Wall of China

**Great Wall of China** is the longest structure ever built. Its total length—including loops and branches—is about 4,500 miles (7,240 kilometers), and it was erected entirely by hand. The main line stretches about 2,500 miles (4,020 kilometers) across northern China. The eastern end of the main line is at Shanhaiguan, a town near Qinhuangdao on the coast of the Bo Gulf. In the west, the main line ends in the Lop Nur region of the Xinjiang province.

Over the centuries, various rulers built walls to protect their northern borders against invaders. Some of the walls stood on or near the site of the Great Wall. Most of what is now called the Great Wall dates from the Ming dynasty (1368-1644).

Some commonly held beliefs about the Great Wall—for example, that it was built all at once, or that it can be seen from the moon—are false. Nevertheless, the Great Wall is an impressive achievement that has captured the imaginations of Chinese and other people for centuries.

**Directions** Answer the following questions about the Web site.

**1.** From which keyword search would you most likely find this Web site?

**A.** Chinese rulers
**B.** walls AND forts
**C.** border protection
**D.** China AND wall

**2.** Which link would you click to learn when the Great Wall of China was completed?

**A.** Home
**B.** Dictionary
**C.** History
**D.** Citation Information

**3.** Which link would you click to find an article about another topic?

**A.** Home
**B.** Atlas
**C.** Description
**D.** History

## USING THE LIBRARY AND REFERENCE SOURCES; EVALUATING SOURCES AND SITES

**Directions** Answer the following questions.

**4.** Which part of a book tells you the publication date?

**A.** glossary **C.** table of contents
**B.** copyright page **D.** index

**5.** You would find the best overview of the Great Wall of China in

**A.** an encyclopedia **C.** an almanac
**B.** a dictionary **D.** an atlas

**6.** Reading background information about the author helps you

**A.** determine if the author is an expert
**B.** learn whether the material is current
**C.** identify the sources the author uses
**D.** locate the book's glossary

**7.** A library catalog allows you to

**A.** read online magazines
**B.** ask research questions
**C.** find materials on your topic
**D.** contact a reference librarian

**8.** The most reliable information about the Great Wall of China would be found in

**A.** a mystery novel
**B.** a personal Web site
**C.** a history magazine
**D.** an adventure story

# Written Response

## SHORT RESPONSE

**Directions** Write two or three sentences to answer the following question.

**9.** Describe two details to check when evaluating a source.

# Primary and Secondary Sources

**Directions** Read the following selections. Then answer the questions that follow.

### Secondary Source

*The following excerpt describes how rulers during the Ming dynasty accomplished the enormous task of building the Great Wall.*

***from* The Great Wall of China**

**Louise Chipley Slavicek**

### The High Costs of Ming Wall Building

Constructing the strongest and most elaborate border fortifications in the history of Chinese defensive wall building required massive investments of money and manpower. Utilizing bricks and stone blocks to construct the wall and its thousands of forts, beacon towers, watchtowers, and other structures substantially increased the cost of the Middle Kingdom's border defenses since the employment of brickmakers, stone masons, and other specialized craftsmen was now required. Adding to the government's expenses, a "considerable network of brick-kilns, quarries, and transportation routes" also would have had to be developed.

10 In addition to the teams of skilled craftsmen who worked on the Ming Great Wall, millions of soldiers and convicted criminals also toiled on the sprawling defense line. "Worker numbers mushroomed during the Ming dynasty, in order to cope with the vastly increased scale and extent of construction," writes a modern expert on the Great Wall:

> Armies were enlarged and a new penal code established to ensure a constant supply of manpower for the work. Scores of offenses were met with sentences of labor on the Great Wall. Even petty criminals were given life terms of work on the structure. More serious offenders received "perpetual" sentences. This meant that after the convict died 20 working on the Great Wall, a member of his family-a son, brother, cousin, or nephew-was sought as a replacement, inheriting the sentence. During the Ming dynasty, censuses gave officials accurate information on the populace and family relationships, thus providing the administrative basis for operating such a draconian penal system.



**Primary Source**

*For more than twenty years, Mendes Pinto traveled extensively. His autobiography, originally published in 1614 tells his observations and adventures. In this excerpt, he describes the use of forced labor in the construction of the Great Wall.*

### *from* The Travels of Mendes Pinto

**Fernão Mendes Pinto; edited and translated by Rebbeca D. Catz**

By order of the king the prison population is maintained at a constant level of 300,000 men ranging in age from seventeen to fifty-a startling piece of information which naturally came as a great surprise to us. When we asked the Chinese why they had built such a huge prison and why so many men were kept there, they told us that not long after the Chinese king called Crisnagol Dacotay had finished sealing off the frontier between China and Tartary with a wall that extended for three hundred leagues, as mentioned above, he gave orders, with the approval of the peoples who were summoned to a national assembly of the estates convoked for that purpose, that all those who had been condemned to the penalty 10 of exile by the courts of justice should be sent to serve a sentence of forced labor

on the wall, in exchange for which they would only receive their food and keep, without any obligation on the part of the king to compensate them for their labor, since they were serving that sentence as a penalty for their crimes, and that after they had served for six consecutive years, they would be free to go on their way, without being forced by law to serve the rest of their original sentence, because the king chose to pardon them as compensation for what in all good conscience he would have had to pay them for their labor; but if before the end of the six years they should in any way distinguish themselves by some outstanding deed or show themselves superior to others, or be wounded three times in their border
20 forays, or succeed in killing one of the enemy, then they will receive an immediate pardon for the rest of the time they would have served, with the chaem issuing them a certificate to that effect, describing the circumstances that had won them their freedom, wherein all could see that he had satisfied the law, in conformity with the statutes of war.



## IDENTIFYING PRIMARY AND SECONDARY SOURCES; COLLECTING DATA

**Directions** Answer the following questions.

**10.** You can tell that the first selection is a secondary source because it

**A.** includes ideas from a modern expert
**B.** describes events seen by the author
**C.** contains detailed information
**D.** resides in a library database

**11.** The primary source gives you firsthand information about the

**A.** lifestyles of ancient Chinese kings
**B.** Great Wall's building materials
**C.** use of prisoners to build the Great Wall
**D.** traveling conditions in ancient China

**12.** The secondary source would be most helpful to a person writing about the

**A.** location of the Great Wall of China
**B.** enemies who tried to overcome the wall
**C.** Chinese army's uniforms and weapons
**D.** resources used to build the wall

**13.** Who is the best person to interview for information about the Great Wall of China?

**A.** a Chinese history expert
**B.** a tour leader in China
**C.** a professional bricklayer
**D.** a museum employee

4. An example of field research is
   A. reading and summarizing encyclopedia articles
   B. visiting a museum and recording observations
   C. using an Internet search engine and library catalog
   D. comparing information from several published sources

15. To conduct an interview, you should first
   A. prepare specific questions in advance
   B. write notes to your interview subjects
   C. make a chart or table of your findings
   D. use note cards to record answers

## 'araphrasing, Summarizing, and Plagiarizing

**irections** Read the following selection. Then answer the questions that follow.

*The following excerpt describes how ordinary citizens as well as lawbreakers ere forced to labor on the Great Wall.*

***rom* The Great Wall of China**

**ousie Chipley Slavicek**

**'he Human Costs of Building the First Great Wall**

Historians can only speculate regarding the First Emperor's true motives and frame of mind when he ordered the creation of his "10,000-li" northern defense line. They have a much clearer conception of the horrific toll that the first Great Wall's construction took on Qin Shi Huang Di's downtrodden subjects.

According to Sima Qian in his Records of the Grand Historian, some 300,000 soldiers and 500,000 civilians toiled on the artificial boundary that Qin Shi Huang Di was determined to create between the Chinese people and their nomadic neighbors. Peasants, who composed the vast majority of China's population during Qin Shi Huang Di's reign (and throughout most of Chinese 10 history), made up the bulk of the Wall's half million-strong civilian work force. By order of the emperor, soldiers rounded up males from farming communities all over China and marched them off to the northern frontiers for months or even years at a stretch. As Qin Shi Huang Di had decreed that any male over the height of four feet could be drafted to build his border wall, even boys were compelled to leave their homes and families for long periods to help with the emperor's monstrous construction project. Women may also have been part of the wall's civilian work force. One ancient chronicler reported that Qin Shi Huang Di required the widows of men who had died while toiling on the northern rampart to labor in their late husbands' places.

20 Although most of the first Great Wall's civilian labor force consisted of law-abiding peasants, many convicted lawbreakers also toiled on the fortifications.

Indeed, lawbreakers were plentiful in China during the Qin dynasty, and condemned criminals provided a vital source of labor not only for Qin Shi Huang Di's 10,000-li wall but also for the emperor's other ambitious building projects from his vast highway system to his magnificent mausoleum.



**Directions** Answer the following questions about paraphrasing, summarizing, and plagiarizing.

**16.** Which is the correct way to use the author's idea in the sentence in lines 1–2 without plagiarizing?

**A.** Slavicek writes that the First Emperor's frame of mind is unclear (Slavicek).
**B.** No one really knows the Emperor's "true motives" for creating the wall.
**C.** We "can only speculate" about why the Emperor built the wall (Slavicek 33).
**D.** A great deal of speculation exists about the Emperor's motives (page 33).

**17.** Which is the best way to paraphrase the sentence contained in lines 3–4?

**A.** Historians know that people suffered during the building of the first Great Wall.
**B.** Qin Shi Huang Di's subjects helped construct the first Great Wall.
**C.** Experts clearly understand how the first Great Wall was constructed.
**D.** Qin Shi Huang Di mistreated many of the people in his kingdom.

**18.** Which is the correct way to use the author' idea in the sentence contained in lines 16–17 without plagiarizing?

**A.** The "civilian work force" probably included women (page 34).
**B.** Slavicek notes that women probably worked on the wall, too (34).
**C.** Women may have been part of the work force (Slavicek).
**D.** Women were part of the "wall's civilian work force."

**19.** Which is the best way to summarize the sentence contained in lines 17–19?

**A.** Ancient historians often had varying accounts about the Great Wall.
**B.** Some men died while working on the northern part of wall.
**C.** An ancient historian said that widows worked on the northern part of the wall.
**D.** Widows may have had to take their husbands' places and work on the wall.

20. Which is the best way to paraphrase the sentence contained in lines 20–21?
   A. Criminals as well as honest people worked on the wall.
   B. Many convicted criminals contributed to the construction of the wall.
   C. Different kinds of people helped construct the Great Wall of China.
   D. Many peasants worked on the wall,, but lawbreakers joined first.

## Written Response

### SHORT RESPONSE

**Directions** Write the answer to the following question on a separate sheet of paper.

21. Summarize the last sentence of the excerpt.

**Research Data:** **Directions** Read the information shown for each topic. Then answer the questions.

**Topic: Ellis Island**

**Facts, Figures, and Details**

- Ellis Island is located in New York Harbor, near the Statue of Liberty.
- From 1892 to 1954, over 12 million immigrants came through it.
- Before it was an immigration center, Ellis Island was home to Fort Gibson, part of the defense system for New York Harbor.
- The first major groups to come through Ellis Island were from England, Ireland, Germany, and Scandinavia. From 1880 to 1930, Italian, Russian, and Austro-Hungarian immigrants also arrived in large numbers.
- Ellis Island's immigration building burned to the ground in 1897.
- Other immigration ports at the time included Boston, Philadelphia, Baltimore, San Francisco, Miami, and New Orleans.
- During World War I, the number of immigrants decreased.
- Ellis Island closed in 1954 but later reopened as a historical site.

**Sources**

**World Wide Web**

"Ellis Island History—A Brief Look" by the National Park Service.
http://www.nps.gov/stli/serv02.htm#Ellis

"Ellis Island Immigrant Records Search Engine" by Ancestor Hunt.
http://www.ancestorhunt.com/ellis_island_records_search.html

**Library**

Ellis Island: An Illustrated History of the Immigrant Experience by Ivan Chermayeff, Fred Wasserman, and Mary J. Shapiro, copyright 1991 (call number: 325.1 CHE)

Gateway to Liberty: The Story of the Statue of Liberty & Ellis Island by Mary J. Shapiro, copyright 1986 (call number: 974.71 SHA)

Strangers at the Door: Ellis Island, Castle Garden, & The Great Migration to America by Ann Novotny, copyright 1971 (call number: 325.73 NOV)

**Original Source**

The federal immigration depot could inspect thousands of people a day. On April 17, 1907, the island's busiest day, 11,747 immigrants were processed; 1907 was also the island's busiest year, with over one million arrivals.

*Ellis Island: An Illustrated History of the Immigrant Experience* (page 109)

**Topic: Pyramids of Ancient Egypt**

**Facts, Figures, and Details**

- Pyramids exist in Ethiopia, Greece, India, and Mexico, as well as in Egypt.
- Egyptian pyramids contain burial chambers for members of royal families.
- Thieves have stolen stones and artifacts from the Egyptian pyramids.
- Pyramids were part of complexes that had temples and other buildings.
- The most prominent Egyptian pyramids are those at Giza.
- The three Pyramids of Giz—built about 2575–2465 b.c.—were built and named for kings: Khufu, Khafre, and Menkaure.
- Khufu, the Great Pyramid, is the largest pyramid. It contains approximately 2.3 million stone blocks weighing over five million tons.
- One ancient historian believed that over 100,000 people worked on the Great Pyramid. Modern experts think that perhaps 20,000 people built it.

**Sources**

**World Wide Web**

"The Great Pyramid of Giza" by Alaa K. Ashmawy, http://ce.eng.usf.edu/pharos/wonders/pyramid.html

"Cairo, Egypt" (no author) http://www.cairotourist.com

**Library**

The Mystery of the Pyramids by Humphrey Evans, copyright 1979 (call number 932.01 EVA)

The Pyramids of Egypt by I.E.S. Edwards; copyright 1947 (call number 932 EDW)

Voyages of the Pyramid Builders: The True Origins of the Pyramids, from Lost Egypt to Ancient America by Robert M. Schoch, copyright 2003 (call number 970.011 SCH)

**Original Source**

When it was first complete, Khufu's Pyramid was a sight we can now only imagine. It was finished with a layer of fitted, polished white limestone that gleamed like a thousand full moons. Long after the Old Kingdom had passed, people who knew nothing of that lost glory pulled the limestone off and carried it away to build Cairo.

*Voyages of the Pyramid Builders: The True Origins of the Pyramids, from Lost Egypt to Ancient America* (page 30)

## PREWRITING AND RESEARCHING

**Directions** Use the Research Data to answer these questions.

**22.** Which topic could you best cover in a research paper?

**A.** immigrants in history
**B.** importance of Ellis Island
**C.** historical sites of America
**D.** various languages of Europe

**23.** Which topic could you best cover in a research paper?

**A.** Pyramids of Giza
**B.** styles of buildings
**C.** ancient artifacts
**D.** Greek architecture

**24.** Which is the best research question for a report on Ellis Island?

**A.** How many people immigrated in 1880?
**B.** Was another port close to Ellis Island?
**C.** How were people treated at Ellis Island?
**D.** What is another historical site?

**25.** Which is the best research question for a report on the Pyramids at Giza?

**A.** What is the closest major city?
**B.** How can I build a model pyramid?
**C.** Where else do pyramids exist?
**D.** Why did the Egyptians build pyramids?

**26.** The most likely reason to reject the source "Cairo, Egypt" is that it is

**A.** an outdated book
**B.** a student's school report
**C.** an unreliable Web site
**D.** a book with an unreliable author

**27.** A source that most likely has little detailed information on Ellis Island's history is

**A.** "Ellis Island History—A Brief Look"
**B.** "Ellis Island Immigrant Records Search Engine"
**C.** *Ellis Island: An Illustrated History of the Immigrant Experience*
**D.** *Gateway to Liberty*

**28.** Which information would you include on a source card for *Strangers at the Door*?

**A.** description of book cover
**B.** library call number
**C.** Web site address
**D.** number of pages

**29.** The following source card is missing one part. Choose the missing part. Novotny, Ann. *Strangers at the Door*. Riverside, Connecticut: Chatham Press, 1971.

**A.** call number
**B.** publisher
**C.** year of publication
**D.** author's name

**30.** Which detail would be best to include on a note card for *Ellis Island: An Illustrated History of the Immigrant Experience*?

**A.** Millions of people immigrated.
**B.** The center opened in January.
**C.** Ellis Island often saw thousands each day.
**D.** The island was a very busy place.

**31.** Which detail would be best to include on a note card for *Voyages of the Pyramid Builders*?

**A.** It is hard to imagine seeing Khufu's pyramid.
**B.** The builders carefully polished the white limestone.
**C.** After the Old Kingdom ended, people climbed the Pyramids.
**D.** People took the Pyramid's limestone to build Cairo.

**32.** Which subheading would you use in an outline for a report on Ellis Island?

**A.** Islands
**B.** Defending New York Harbor
**C.** Where Immigrants Came From
**D.** World War I

**33.** Which subheading would you use in an outline for a report on the Pyramids of Giza?

**A.** 2575–2465 b.c.
**B.** Greece
**C.** Construction
**D.** Egypt

## Written Response

### SHORT RESPONSE

**Directions** Write the answer to the following question on a separate sheet of paper.

**34.** Which source of information about Ellis Island is from a reliable government source?

### DRAFTING, REVISING, AND EDITING

**Directions** Use the Research Data to answer these questions.

**35.** In a report on Ellis Island, which sentence would work best in the introduction?

**A.** Defending the harbor was important.
**B.** Millions started new lives at Ellis Island.
**C.** The main building burned down.
**D.** Boston was home to an immigration port.

**36.** In a report on the Pyramids of Giza, which sentence would work best in the introduction?

**A.** Mexico, India, and Greece also have pyramids.
**B.** Thieves stole many things from the pyramids.
**C.** No one really knows how many Egyptians built the pyramids.
**D.** The Pyramids of Giza are the most well-known of the Egyptian pyramids.

**37.** Which sentence would work best in the conclusion of a report on Ellis Island?

**A.** At the time of World War I, immigration decreased.
**B.** People from all over Europe came to Ellis Island.
**C.** Ellis Island remains an important part of U.S. history.
**D.** The Statue of Liberty is another historical site.

**38.** Which sentence would work best in the conclusion of a report on the Pyramids of Giza?

**A.** Pyramids exist in India, as well.
**B.** The Pyramids are still an amazing sight.
**C.** There are other pyramids to see, too.
**D.** The Great Pyramid is the largest.

**39.** Which Works Cited entry shows the correct way to cite the source?

**A.** Gateway to Liberty by Mary J. Shapiro. New York: Random House, 1986.
**B.** Shapiro, Mary J. Gateway to Liberty. New York: Random House, 1986.
**C.** Shapiro, Mary J. Gateway to Liberty. Random House, 1986.
**D.** Gateway to Liberty by Mary J. Shapiro. New York: Random House.

**40.** A Works Cited list is arranged by

**A.** author's first name
**B.** title of the source
**C.** author's last name
**D.** publication date

**41.** A Works Cited list includes

**A.** all of the sources
**B.** library call numbers
**C.** key words from the outline
**D.** charts and diagrams

**42.** Which introduction to a report on Ellis Island best grabs the reader's attention?

**A.** They must have felt fear right away.
**B.** The trip was long and tiring.
**C.** New York Harbor was full of ships.
**D.** Later Ellis Island closed its doors.

**43.** Which introduction to a report on pyramids best grabs the reader's attention?

**A.** Tourists enjoy visiting pyramids.
**B.** The Pyramids are interesting structures.
**C.** Some might like to live in a pyramid.
**D.** Desert surrounds the Pyramids.

**44.** Which sentence is the best thesis statement for a report on the Pyramids of Giza?

**A.** The Pyramids are monuments that reveal an ancient culture.
**B.** The Egyptian pyramids have survived for a long time.
**C.** Many people built the Pyramids.
**D.** Pyramids contain burial chambers.

**45.** Which of the following best shows a logical connection between ideas?

**A.** The immigration center was open from 1892 to 1954. It burned down.
**B.** Many got a new start at Ellis Island, so it symbolizes hope and opportunity.
**C.** Thousands visit each year, even though the main building was rebuilt.
**D.** Traveling to America was hard, but 1907 was the busiest year.

**46.** What is wrong with this sentence? San Francisco was a major port, although Fort Gibson was located on Ellis Island.

**A.** unrelated to the topic of the paper
**B.** short, choppy sentence
**C.** missing transitional word
**D.** unclear connection between ideas

**47.** Which of the following best shows a logical connection between ideas?

**A.** Historians say that thousands built the Pyramids, and thieves stole artifacts.
**B.** The Pyramids are southwest of Cairo, and pyramids exist in India.
**C.** Khufu's white limestone shone brightly, so it was surely a magnificent sight.
**D.** The Pyramids at Giza are famous. Limestone was taken to build Cairo.

**48.** Which detail best supports the idea that the Pyramids contained valuable materials?

**A.** Thieves took stones and artifacts.
**B.** Temples were also nearby.
**C.** Pyramids were part of complexes.
**D.** Ancient Egyptians built the Pyramids.

**49.** Which detail supports the idea that Ellis Island is an important American symbol?

**A.** Workers rebuilt the main building.
**B.** Ships arrived in New York Harbor.
**C.** Ellis Island is now a historical site.
**D.** The center closed in 1954.

**50.** Which detail supports the idea that Ellis Island was often crowded and noisy?

**A.** The journey from Europe was long.
**B.** Other immigration ports existed.
**C.** People came from many countries.
**D.** Thousands of people arrived each day.

## Using the Internet

**Directions** Use the Web site to answer the questions that follow.

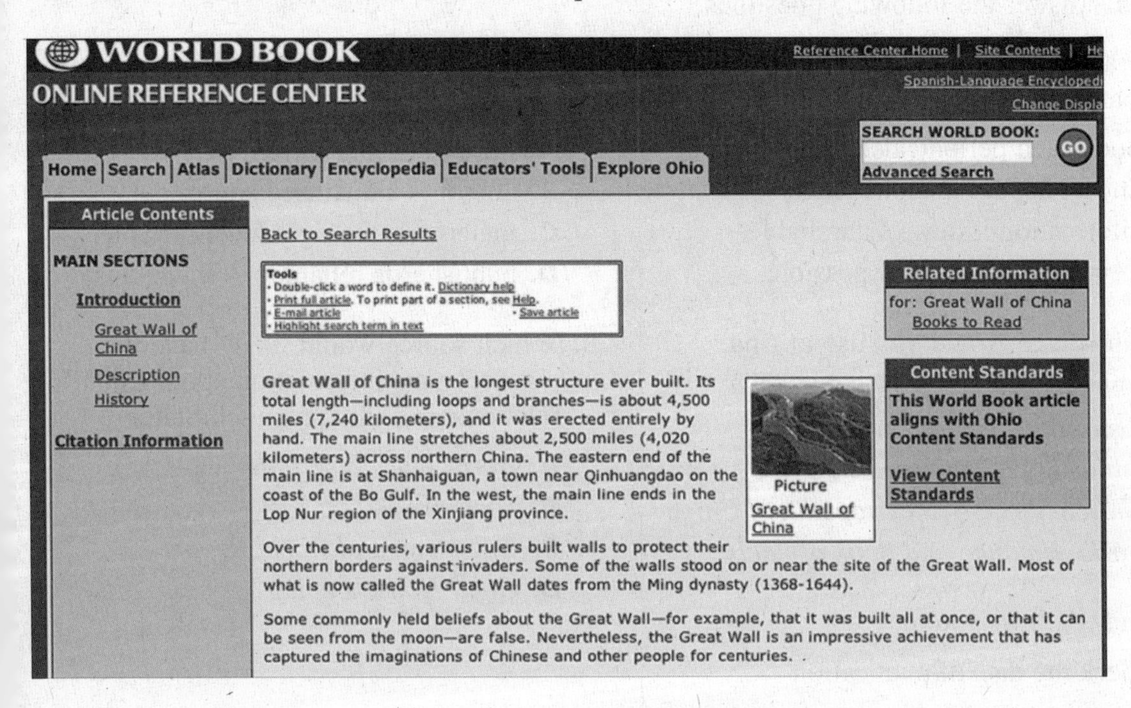
WORLD BOOK
ONLINE REFERENCE CENTER

Reference Center Home | Site Contents |
Spanish-Language Encyclopedi
Change Displa

SEARCH WORLD BOOK:
GO
Advanced Search

Home | Search | Atlas | Dictionary | Encyclopedia | Educators' Tools | Explore Ohio

Article Contents

MAIN SECTIONS
Introduction
Great Wall of China
Description
History
Citation Information

Back to Search Results

Tools
- Double-click a word to define it. Dictionary help
- Print full article. To print part of a section, see Help.
- E-mail article
- Save article
- Highlight search term in text

Related Information
for: Great Wall of China
Books to Read

Content Standards
This World Book article aligns with Ohio Content Standards
View Content Standards

Picture
Great Wall of China

**Great Wall of China** is the longest structure ever built. Its total length—including loops and branches—is about 4,500 miles (7,240 kilometers), and it was erected entirely by hand. The main line stretches about 2,500 miles (4,020 kilometers) across northern China. The eastern end of the main line is at Shanhaiguan, a town near Qinhuangdao on the coast of the Bo Gulf. In the west, the main line ends in the Lop Nur region of the Xinjiang province.

Over the centuries, various rulers built walls to protect their northern borders against invaders. Some of the walls stood on or near the site of the Great Wall. Most of what is now called the Great Wall dates from the Ming dynasty (1368-1644).

Some commonly held beliefs about the Great Wall—for example, that it was built all at once, or that it can be seen from the moon—are false. Nevertheless, the Great Wall is an impressive achievement that has captured the imaginations of Chinese and other people for centuries.

**Directions** Answer the following questions about the Web site.

**1.** From which keyword search would you most likely find this Web site?

**A.** China AND history
**B.** rulers AND protection
**C.** China AND wall
**D.** Ming AND dynasty

**2.** Which link would you click to find a map of China?

**A.** Home
**B.** Dictionary
**C.** Encyclopedia
**D.** Atlas

**3.** This site would be most useful to someone looking for

**A.** an overview of the Great Wall of China
**B.** information about modern Chinese culture
**C.** biographies of Chinese rulers
**D.** descriptions of major cities in China

**USING THE LIBRARY AND REFERENCE SOURCES; EVALUATING SOURCES AND SITES**

**Directions** Answer the following questions.

**4.** How are searching the Internet and searching a library catalog similar?

**A.** Books and periodicals appear first.
**B.** Entries appear in alphabetical order.
**C.** Information is always unreliable.
**D.** Keyword searches are possible.

**5.** Which source would you use to find additional information on the Great Wall?

**A.** *Exploring Ancient Civilizations*
**B.** *Anthology of Chinese Literature*
**C.** *The Cambridge Encyclopedia of China*
**D.** *World Almanac and Book of Facts*

**6.** An index allows you to

**A.** check the date of publication
**B.** skim for terms and topics of interest
**C.** find meanings of technical terms
**D.** review the author's sources

**7.** Checking the copyright date helps you evaluate whether the

**A.** information is current
**B.** author is a qualified source
**C.** material is the right level for you
**D.** publisher is reliable

**8.** Which source would likely have the most relevant information about China's relationship with the United States?

**A.** *World Literature Today*
**B.** *Southern Living*
**C.** *U.S. News and World Report*
**D.** *Good Housekeeping*

## Written Response

### SHORT RESPONSE

**Directions** Write two or three sentences to answer the following question on a separate sheet of paper.

**9.** Tell two items to check when evaluating a source. Give a brief explanation of why you should check each item.

## Primary and Secondary Sources

**Directions** Read the following selections. Then answer the questions that follow.

**Secondary Source**

*The following excerpt describes how rulers during the Ming dynasty accomplished the enormous task of building the Great Wall.*

***from* The Great Wall of China**

**Louise Chipley Slavicek**

**The High Costs of Ming Wall Building**

Constructing the strongest and most elaborate border fortifications in the history of Chinese defensive wall building required massive investments of money and manpower. Utilizing bricks and stone blocks to construct the wall and its thousands of forts, beacon towers, watchtowers, and other structures substantially increased the cost of the Middle Kingdom's border defenses since the employment of brickmakers, stone masons, and other specialized craftsmen was now required. Adding to the government's expenses, a "considerable network of brick-kilns, quarries, and transportation routes" also would have had to be developed.

10 In addition to the teams of skilled craftsmen who worked on the Ming Great Wall, millions of soldiers and convicted criminals also toiled on the sprawling defense line. "Worker numbers mushroomed during the Ming dynasty, in order to cope with the vastly increased scale and extent of construction," writes a modern expert on the Great Wall:

> Armies were enlarged and a new penal code established to ensure a constant supply of manpower for the work. Scores of offenses were met with sentences of labor on the Great Wall. Even petty criminals were given life terms of work on the structure. More serious offenders received "perpetual" sentences. This meant that after the convict died
> 20 working on the Great Wall, a member of his family-a son, brother, cousin, or nephew-was sought as a replacement, inheriting the sentence. During the Ming dynasty, censuses gave officials accurate information on the populace and family relationships, thus providing the administrative basis for operating such a draconian penal system.

**Primary Source**

*For more than twenty years, Mendes Pinto traveled extensively. His autobiography, originally published in 1614 tells his observations and adventures. In this excerpt, he describes the use of forced labor in the construction of the Great Wall.*

***from* The Travels of Mendes Pinto**

**Fernão Mendes Pinto; edited and translated by Rebbeca D. Catz**

By order of the king the prison population is maintained at a constant level of 300,000 men ranging in age from seventeen to fifty-a startling piece of information which naturally came as a great surprise to us. When we asked the Chinese why they had built such a huge prison and why so many men were kept there, they told us that not long after the Chinese king called Crisnagol Dacotay had finished sealing off the frontier between China and Tartary with a wall that extended for three hundred leagues, as mentioned above, he gave orders, with the approval of the peoples who were summoned to a national assembly of the estates convoked for that purpose, that all those who had been condemned to the penalty
10 of exile by the courts of justice should be sent to serve a sentence of forced labor on the wall, in exchange for which they would only receive their food and keep, without any obligation on the part of the king to compensate them for their labor, since they were serving that sentence as a penalty for their crimes, and that after they had served for six consecutive years, they would be free to go on their way, without being forced by law to serve the rest of their original sentence, because the king chose to pardon them as compensation for what in all good conscience he would have had to pay them for their labor; but if before the end of the six years they should in any way distinguish themselves by some outstanding deed or show themselves superior to others, or be wounded three times in their border
20 forays, or succeed in killing one of the enemy, then they will receive an immediate pardon for the rest of the time they would have served, with the chaem issuing them a certificate to that effect, describing the circumstances that had won them their freedom, wherein all could see that he had satisfied the law, in conformity with the statutes of war.

## IDENTIFYING PRIMARY AND SECONDARY SOURCES; COLLECTING DATA

**Directions** Answer the following questions.

**10.** You can tell that the second selection is a primary source because

**A.** Mendes Pinto describes what he saw
**B.** it discusses how the king chose laborers.
**C.** Mendes Pinto knows much about China
**D.** it describes Mendes Pinto's return.

**11.** Which of the following statements is supported by both sources?

**A.** The Great Wall was constructed mainly by skilled craftsmen.
**B.** Prisoners could earn pardons while working on the Great Wall.
**C.** Building the Great Wall required the effort of many people.
**D.** The Great Wall includes forts, prisons, and watchtowers.

**12.** The secondary source clarifies information from the primary source by

**A.** describing the materials the workers used to build the Great Wall
**B.** providing information about Mendes Pinto's travels through Asia
**C.** telling how many people actually worked on the Great Wall
**D.** explaining why Chinese rulers imprisoned so many people

**13.** Which is the best way to collect data about the building of the Great Wall?

**A.** Interview an expert in Chinese history.
**B.** Visit a Chinese restaurant.
**C.** Survey people who have visited China.
**D.** Conduct a museum field study.

**14.** One advantage of interviewing an expert is that

**A.** your research is complete after the interview.
**B.** it can help you think about a topic in a new way
**C.** you do not have to prepare for the interview
**D.** you can do field research during the interview

**15.** For which research topic would your observations be the best source of information?

**A.** differences in modern governments
**B.** types of people who go to a local park
**C.** youth activities in several states
**D.** popularity of country music

## Paraphrasing, Summarizing, and Plagiarizing

**Directions** Read the following selection. Then answer the questions that follow.

*The following excerpt describes how ordinary citizens as well as lawbreakers were forced to labor on the Great Wall.*

***from* The Great Wall of China**

**Lousie Chipley Slavicek**

### The Human Costs of Building the First Great Wall

Historians can only speculate regarding the First Emperor's true motives and frame of mind when he ordered the creation of his "10,000-li" northern defense line. They have a much clearer conception of the horrific toll that the first Great Wall's construction took on Qin Shi Huang Di's downtrodden subjects.

According to Sima Qian in his Records of the Grand Historian, some 300,000 soldiers and 500,000 civilians toiled on the artificial boundary that Qin Shi Huang Di was determined to create between the Chinese people and their nomadic neighbors. Peasants, who composed the vast majority of China's population during Qin Shi Huang Di's reign (and throughout most of Chinese 10 history), made up the bulk of the Wall's half million-strong civilian work force. By order of the emperor, soldiers rounded up males from farming communities all over China and marched them off to the northern frontiers for months or even years at a stretch. As Qin Shi Huang Di had decreed that any male over the height of four feet could be drafted to build his border wall, even boys were compelled to leave their homes and families for long periods to help with the emperor's monstrous construction project. Women may also have been part of the wall's civilian work force. One ancient chronicler reported that Qin Shi Huang Di required the widows of men who had died while toiling on the northern rampart to labor in their late husbands' places.

20 Although most of the first Great Wall's civilian labor force consisted of law-abiding peasants, many convicted lawbreakers also toiled on the fortifications. Indeed, lawbreakers were plentiful in China during the Qin dynasty, and condemned criminals provided a vital source of labor not only for Qin Shi Huang Di's 10,000-li wall but also for the emperor's other ambitious building projects from his vast highway system to his magnificent mausoleum.

**Directions** Answer the following questions.

**16.** Which is the best way to summarize the sentence contained in lines 5–8?

**A.** Many soldiers labored to build the wall between China and its neighbors.
**B.** Qin Shi Huang Di wanted to create a wall surrounding China.
**C.** Hundreds of thousands of soldiers and civilians worked on the border wall.
**D.** In Records of the Grand Historian, Sima Qian lists who built the wall.

**17.** Which is the correct way to use the author's idea in lines 11–16 without plagiarizing?

**A.** The emperor forced males from "farming communities" to work on the wall (page 34).
**B.** Males were forced to work for "months or even years at a stretch" (Slavicek 34).
**C.** Slavicek writes that soldiers took males from farms to work on the wall.
**D.** Soldiers "rounded up males" because the emperor needed more workers.

**18.** Which is the best way to paraphrase the sentence contained in lines 16–17?

**A.** Women might have worked on the wall.
**B.** Civilians were part of the wall's work force.
**C.** Women were ready to work on the wall.
**D.** Many people were laborers.

**19.** Which is the best paraphrase of the sentence in lines 17–19?

**A.** The emperor said that if a man died while working, someone had to take his place.
**B.** Ancient sources have given historians much information about the Great Wall.
**C.** Qin Shi Huang Di had unfair policies toward women.
**D.** According to one report, wives had to replace husbands who died while working.

**20.** Which is the correct way to use the author's idea in lines 22–25 without plagiarizing?

**A.** Slavicek notes that criminals worked on many of the emperor's ventures (34).
**B.** Criminals were a "vital source" of labor, according to Louise Slavicek.
**C.** The emperor used lawbreakers to build his highways (Slavicek).
**D.** The emperor's projects required labor from convicted criminals.

## WRITTEN RESPONSE

### Short Response

**Directions** Write the answer to the following question on a separate sheet of paper.

**21.** Summarize the sentence that starts in line 13 and ends in line 16.

**Research Data:** **Directions** Read the information shown for each topic. Then answer the questions.

**Topic: Ellis Island**

**Facts, Figures, and Details**

- Ellis Island is located in New York Harbor, near the Statue of Liberty.
- From 1892 to 1954, over 12 million immigrants came through it.
- Before it was an immigration center, Ellis Island was home to Fort Gibson, part of the defense system for New York Harbor.
- The first major groups to come through Ellis Island were from England, Ireland, Germany, and Scandinavia. From 1880 to 1930, Italian, Russian, and Austro-Hungarian immigrants also arrived in large numbers.
- Ellis Island's immigration building burned to the ground in 1897.
- Other immigration ports at the time included Boston, Philadelphia, Baltimore, San Francisco, Miami, and New Orleans.
- During World War I, the number of immigrants decreased.
- Ellis Island closed in 1954 but later reopened as a historical site.

**Sources**

**World Wide Web**

"Ellis Island History—A Brief Look" by the National Park Service. http://www.nps.gov/stli/serv02.htm#Ellis

"Ellis Island Immigrant Records Search Engine" by Ancestor Hunt. http://www.ancestorhunt.com/ellis_island_records_search.html

**Library**

Ellis Island: An Illustrated History of the Immigrant Experience by Ivan Chermayeff, Fred Wasserman, and Mary J. Shapiro, copyright 1991 (call number: 325.1 CHE)

Gateway to Liberty: The Story of the Statue of Liberty & Ellis Island by Mary J. Shapiro, copyright 1986 (call number: 974.71 SHA)

Strangers at the Door: Ellis Island, Castle Garden, & The Great Migration to America by Ann Novotny, copyright 1971 (call number: 325.73 NOV)

**Original Source**

The federal immigration depot could inspect thousands of people a day. On April 17, 1907, the island's busiest day, 11,747 immigrants were processed; 1907 was also the island's busiest year, with over one million arrivals.

*Ellis Island: An Illustrated History of the Immigrant Experience* (page 109)

**Topic: Pyramids of Ancient Egypt**

**Facts, Figures, and Details**

- Pyramids exist in Ethiopia, Greece, India, and Mexico as well as in Egypt.
- Egyptian pyramids contain burial chambers for members of royal families.
- Thieves have stolen stones and artifacts from the Egyptian pyramids.
- Pyramids were part of complexes that had temples and other buildings.
- The most prominent Egyptian pyramids are those at Giza.

- The three Pyramids of Giza—built about 2575–2465 b.c.—were built and named for kings: Khufu, Khafre, and Menkaure.
- Khufu, the Great Pyramid, is the largest pyramid. It contains approximately 2.3 million stone blocks weighing over five million tons.
- One ancient historian believed that over 100,000 people worked on the Great Pyramid. Modern experts think that perhaps 20,000 people built it.

**Sources**

**World Wide Web**

"The Great Pyramid of Giza" by Alaa K. Ashmawy, http://ce.eng.usf.edu/pharos/wonders/pyramid.html"Cairo, Egypt" (no author) http://www.cairotourist.com

**Library**

The Mystery of the Pyramids by Humphrey Evans, copyright 1979 (call number 932.01 EVA)

The Pyramids of Egypt by I.E.S. Edwards; copyright 1947 (call number 932 EDW)

Voyages of the Pyramid Builders: The True Origins of the Pyramids, from Lost Egypt to Ancient America by Robert M. Schoch, copyright 2003 (call number 970.011 SCH)

**Original Source**

When it was first complete, Khufu's Pyramid was a sight we can now only imagine. It was finished with a layer of fitted, polished white limestone that gleamed like a thousand full moons. Long after the Old Kingdom had passed, people who knew nothing of that lost glory pulled the limestone off and carried it away to build Cairo.

*Voyages of the Pyramid Builders: The True Origins of the Pyramids, from Lost Egypt to Ancient America* (page 30)

## PREWRITING AND RESEARCHING

**Directions** Use the Research Data to answer these questions.

**22.** Which topic related to Ellis Island could you best cover in a research paper?

**A.** immigration patterns in other countries
**B.** immigrants' experiences upon arrival
**C.** New York Harbor's defense systems
**D.** various immigrant languages

**23.** Which topic related to pyramids could you best cover in a research paper?

**A.** the building of the Pyramids of Giza
**B.** South American pyramids
**C.** finding the Pyramids' lost artifacts
**D.** Khufu's geographic location

**24.** A source that is most likely not related to the history of Egyptian pyramids is

**A.** "The Great Pyramid of Giza"
**B.** "Cairo, Egypt"
**C.** *The Mystery of the Pyramids*
**D.** *The Pyramids of Egypt*

**25.** Which detail would you include under the heading "Pyramid Cities" in an outline?

**A.** built from 2575–2465 b.c.
**B.** burial chambers for royal families
**C.** temples, tombs, and workers' buildings
**D.** removal of stones and artifacts

**26.** Which is the best research question for a report on Ellis Island?

**A.** How many people passed through Ellis Island?
**B.** When did the main immigration building burn to the ground?
**C.** What did immigrants experience when they arrived at Ellis Island?
**D.** How many people visit the historical site at Ellis Island each year?

**27.** Which is the best research question for a report on the Pyramids at Giza?

**A.** Are Mexican pyramids well built?
**B.** Why did people take artifacts and materials from the Pyramids?
**C.** Where are the pyramids in India?
**D.** How did the ancient Egyptians build the giant pyramids?

**28.** One reason to use the source "Ellis Island History—A Brief Look" is that it is

**A.** the only source you can trust
**B.** the home page of a historian
**C.** a reliable government Web site
**D.** a book with a credible author

**29.** The most likely reason to reject *The Pyramids of Egypt* is that the source

**A.** may contain outdated information
**B.** comes from an unreliable publisher
**C.** may be trying to sell something
**D.** does not state the author

**30.** What information would you include on a source card for "Ellis Island History—A Brief Look"?

**A.** library call number
**B.** name of the organization responsible
**C.** page numbers of article
**D.** name and year of encyclopedia

**31.** Which source card entry is correct?

**A.** Novotny, Ann. *Strangers at the Door*. Riverside, Connecticut: Chatham Press, 1971. 325.73 NOV
**B.** *Strangers at the Door*. Riverside, Connecticut: Chatham Press. NOV
**C.** Novotny, *Strangers at the Door*. Riverside, Connecticut: Chatham Press, pages 72-–76, 1971.
**D.** Novotny, Ann. *Strangers at the Door*. Connecticut: Chatham, 325.73 NOV

**32.** Which detail would be best to include on a note card for *Ellis Island: An Illustrated History of the Immigrant Experience*?

**A.** The immigration stations were busy.
**B.** One April 17 was a very busy day.
**C.** On Ellis Island's busiest day, over 11,000 immigrants came through.
**D.** It was not unusual to see many immigrants in one day at Ellis Island.

**33.** Which is the best paraphrase of information for the note card*Voyages of the Pyramid Builders?*

**A.** Now we can only imagine how Khufu's Pyramid looked.
**B.** Polished limestone covered Khufu's Pyramid, so it must have been a spectacular sight.
**C.** Khufu's Pyramid was finished with a layer of polished white limestone.
**D.** Years later, people took the shiny limestone from the Great Pyramid and used it for buildings in Cairo.

**34.** Which detail belongs under "Immigrants' Backgrounds" in an outline?

**A.** New York Harbor's defense system
**B.** Statue of Liberty
**C.** English, Irish, German
**D.** Boston, Philadelphia, New Orleans

## RAFTING, REVISING, AND EDITING

**irections** Use the Research Data to answer these questions.

5. Which sentence should be included in the introduction of a report on Ellis Island?
   - **A.** Fort Gibson played an important part in the defense of New York Harbor.
   - **B.** Over 12 million people began their new lives in America at Ellis Island.
   - **C.** In 1897, the main immigration building burned, but it was quickly rebuilt.
   - **D.** Other immigration ports existed in Philadelphia and Boston.

6. Which statement should be included in the introduction of a report on Egyptian pyramids?
   - **A.** Other countries, including Mexico, India, and Greece, also have pyramids.
   - **B.** The Great Pyramid has approximately 2.3 million stone blocks.
   - **C.** Experts still debate how many people were needed to build the pyramids.
   - **D.** The three Pyramids of Giza are the most famous Egyptian pyramids.

7. Which conclusion would be the best ending for a report on Ellis Island?
   - **A.** By the time World War I was raging, immigration had slowed.
   - **B.** Many Europeans came to America.
   - **C.** Immigrants no longer arrive at Ellis Island, yet it is key to our history.
   - **D.** The Statue of Liberty, near Ellis Island, is an important American landmark.

8. Which introduction best grabs the reader's attention?
   - **A.** People visit these structures.
   - **B.** The Pyramids tower over the desert.
   - **C.** Pyramids are ancient buildings.
   - **D.** People still wonder about the Pyramids.

39. Which sentence would best conclude a report on the history of Egyptian pyramids?
   - **A.** The ancient Egyptians named the Pyramids of Giza after kings.
   - **B.** These amazing structures bridge the ancient and modern worlds.
   - **C.** The royal families used the pyramids to bury their loved ones.
   - **D.** The oldest and largest of the Pyramids of Giza is known as the Great Pyramid.

40. Which Works Cited entry shows the correct way to cite the source?
   - **A.** National Park Service. 20 Mar. 2008 http://www.nps.gov/stli/serv02.htm#Ellis "Ellis Island History—A Brief Look"
   - **B.** "Ellis Island History—A Brief Look." National Park Service. 20 Mar. 2008 http://www.nps.gov/stli/serv02.htm#Ellis
   - **C.** National Park Service. "Ellis Island History—A Brief Look." 20 Mar. 2008 http://www.nps.gov/stli/serv02.htm#Ellis
   - **D.** "Ellis Island History—A Brief Look." http://www.nps.gov/stli/serv02.htm#Ellis National Park Service.

41. Which sentence is the best thesis statement for a report on Ellis Island?
   - **A.** Ellis Island is vital to American history.
   - **B.** Millions have come to America.
   - **C.** Ellis Island stories are interesting.
   - **D.** The process of immigrating was scary.

**42.** Which introduction best grabs the reader's attention?

**A.** Imagine how exhausted immigrants felt when they reached Ellis Island.
**B.** Ellis Island is a great place that is located in New York Harbor.
**C.** Ellis Island was many immigrants' first experience with the United States.
**D.** Plenty of people arrived in the United States by coming through Ellis Island.

**43.** Which of the following best shows a logical connection between ideas?

**A.** Ellis Island is in New York Harbor. Boston had an immigration port, too.
**B.** Immigration declined during World War I. Many tourists visit Ellis Island.
**C.** Many immigrants came from England, and 1907 was a very busy year.
**D.** The trip to America was long and difficult, so immigrants were tired.

**44.** What is wrong with this sentence? Pyramids were built for kings, although they are massive structures.

**A.** unrelated to the topic of the paper
**B.** short, choppy sentence
**C.** unclear connection between ideas
**D.** missing transitional word

**45.** Which of the following best shows a logical connection between ideas?

**A.** The Great Pyramid weighs almost six million tons. It has chambers.
**B.** Khufu is one of the Pyramids at Giza Pyramids exist in India.
**C.** Khufu is the largest pyramid, so it is known as the Great Pyramid.
**D.** Workers in Cairo used limestone fron Khufu. Tourists visit Cairo, too.

## WRITTEN RESPONSE

### Short Response

**Directions** Write the answers to the following questions on a separate sheet of paper.

**46.** Write a Works Cited entry for *Gateway to Liberty*. Random House published this book in New York.

**47.** Write a Works Cited entry for *The Mystery of the Pyramids*, which was published in New York by Thomas Y. Crowell, Publishers.

**48.** Which detail supports the idea that pyramids were more than tombs?

**49.** Which detail shows that our nation recognizes Ellis Island's historical importance?

**50.** Which detail supports the idea that Ellis Island was often crowded and noisy?

# Contents

## Benchmark Tests

Benchmark Test 1 221
Benchmark Test 2 246
Benchmark Test 3 271
Benchmark Test 4 296

# Benchmark Test 1

UNITS 1–2

## Reading Comprehension

**Directions** Read the following selection. Then answer the questions that follow.

***from* Fast Sam, Cool Clyde, and Stuff**

**Walter Dean Myers**

It was a dark day when we got our report cards. The sky was full of gray clouds and it was sprinkling rain. I was over to Clyde's house and Gloria and Kitty were there. Sam probably would have been there too, only he had got a two-week job in the afternoons helping out at Freddie's. Actually he only did it so that his mother would let him be on the track team again. Sam and his mother had this little system going. He would do something good-doing and she'd let him do something that he wanted to.

Clyde's report card was on the kitchen table and we all sat around it like it was some kind of a big important document. I had got a pretty good report card 10 and had wanted to show it off but I knew it wasn't the time. Clyde pushed the card toward me and I read it. He had all satisfactory remarks on the side labeled Personal Traits and Behavior. He had also received B's in music and art appreciation. But everything else was either a C or a D except mathematics. His mathematics mark was a big red F that had been circled. I don't know why they had to circle the F when it was the only red mark on the card. In the Teacher's Comments section someone had written that Clyde had "little ability to handle an academic program."

"A little ability is better than none," I said. No one said anything so I figured it probably wasn't the right time to cheer Clyde up.

20 I knew all about his switching from a commercial program to an academic program, but I really hadn't thought he'd have any trouble.

"I saw the grade adviser today. He said I should switch back to the commercial program." Clyde looked like he'd start crying any minute. His eyes were red and his voice was shaky. "He said that I had to take mathematics over and if I failed again or failed another required subject I couldn't graduate. The way it is now I'm going to have to finish up in the summer because I switched over."

"I think you can pass it if you really want to," Kitty said. Clyde's sister was so pretty I couldn't even look at her. If I did I started feeling funny and couldn't 30 talk right. Sometimes I daydreamed about marrying her.

Just then Clyde's mother came in and Clyde gave a quick look at Kitty. Sam breezed in right behind her, happy that his job was over for the day.

"Hi, young ladies and young gentlemen." Mrs. Jones was a kind of heavy woman but she was pretty too. You could tell she was Kitty's mother if you looked close. She put her package down and started taking things out. "I heard you people talking when I first came in. By the way you hushed up I guess you don't want me to hear what you were talking about. I'll be out of your way in a minute, soon as I put the frozen foods in the refrigerator."

"I got my report card today," Clyde said. His mother stopped taking the
40 food out and turned toward us. Clyde pushed the report card about two inches toward her. She really didn't even have to look at the card to know that it was bad. She could have told that just by looking at Clyde. But she picked it up and looked at it a long time. First she looked at one side and then the other and then back at the first side again.

"What they say around the school?" she asked, still looking at the card.

"They say I should drop the academic course and go back to the other one." I could hardly hear Clyde he spoke so low.

"Well, what you going to do, young man?" She looked up at Clyde and Clyde looked up at her and there were tears in his eyes and I almost started
50 crying. I can't stand to see my friends cry. "What are you going to do, Mr. Jones?"

"I'm—I'm going to keep the academic course," Clyde said.

"You think it's going to be any easier this time?" Mrs. Jones asked.

"No."

"Things ain't always easy. Lord knows that things ain't always easy." For a minute there was a faraway look in her eyes, but then her face turned into a big smile. "You're just like your father, boy. That man never would give up on anything he really wanted. Did I ever tell you the time he was trying to learn to play the trombone?"

60 "No." Clyde still had tears in his eyes, but he was smiling, too. Suddenly everyone was happy. It was like seeing a rainbow when it was still raining.

"Well, we were living over across from St. Nicholas Park in this little rooming house. Your father was working on a job down on Varick Street that made transformers or some such nonsense—anyway, he comes home one day with this long package all wrapped up in brown paper. He walks in and sits it in the corner and doesn't say boo about what's in the bag. So at first I don't say anything either, and then I finally asks him what he's got in the bag, and he says, "What bag?" Now this thing is about four feet long if it's an inch and he's asking *what* bag." Mrs. Jones wiped the crumbs from Gloria's end of the table
70 with a quick swipe of the dish cloth, leaving a swirling pattern of tiny bubbles. Gloria tore off a paper towel and wiped the area dry.

"Now I look over at him and he's trying to be nonchalant. Sitting there, a grown man, and big as he wants to be and looking for all the world like somebody's misplaced son. So I says, 'The bag in the corner.' And he says, 'Oh, that's a trombone I'm taking back to the pawn shop tomorrow.' Well, I

naturally ask him what he's doing with it in the first place, and he says he got carried away and bought it but he realized that we really didn't have the thirty-five dollars to spend on foolishness and so he'd take it back the next day. And all the time he's sitting there scratching his chin and rubbing his nose and trying
80 to peek over at me to see how I felt about it. I just told him that I guess he knew what was best. Only the next day he forgot to take it back, and the next day he forgot to take it back, and finally I broke down and told him why didn't he keep it. He said he would if I thought he should.

"So he unwraps this thing and he was just as happy with it as he could be until he tried to get a tune out of it. He couldn't get a sound out of it at first, but then he started oomping and woomping with the thing as best he could. He worked at it and worked at it and you could see he was getting disgusted. I think he was just about to give it up when the lady who lived under us came upstairs and started complaining about the noise. It kept her Napoleon awake,
90 she said. Napoleon was a dog. Little ugly thing, too. She said your father couldn't play, anyway.

"Well, what did she say that for? That man played that thing day and night. He worked so hard at that thing that his lips were too sore for him to talk right sometime. But he got the hang of it."

"I never remember Pop playing a trombone," said Clyde.

"Well, your father had a streak in him that made him stick to a thing," she said, pouring some rice into a colander to wash it off, "but every year his goals got bigger and bigger and he had to put some things down so that he could get to others. That old trombone is still around here some place. Probably in one of
100 them boxes under Kitty's bed. Now, you children, excuse me, young ladies and gentlemen, get on out of here and let me finish supper."

We all went to Clyde's living room.

"That was my mom's good-doing speech," Clyde said. "She gets into talking about what a great guy my father was and how I was like him and whatnot."

"You supposed to be like your father," Sam said. "He was the one that raised you, right?"

"She wants me to be like him, and I want to be like him, too, I guess. She wants me to keep on trying with the academic thing."

110 "What do you want to do," Sam asked, "give it up?"

"No. Not really. I guess I want people like my mother to keep on telling me that I ought to do it, really. Especially when somebody tells me I can't do it."

"Boy," Sam said, sticking his thumbs in his belt and leaning back in the big stuffed chair, "you are just like your father."

Then we all went into Clyde's room and just sat around and talked for a while. Mostly about school and stuff like that, and I wanted to tell Clyde that I thought I could help him if he wanted me to. I was really getting good grades in school, but I thought that Clyde might get annoyed if I mentioned it. But then Gloria said that we could study together sometime and that was cool too.



## COMPREHENSION

**Directions** Answer the following questions about the excerpt from *Fast Sam, Cool Clyde, and Stuff.*

**51.** In the first paragraph, the narrator uses foreshadowing to suggest that Clyde will

**A.** graduate soon
**B.** have a bad report card
**C.** be late for school
**D.** play with his friends

**52.** Lines 8–17 are part of the story's

**A.** exposition
**B.** rising action
**C.** climax
**D.** falling action

**53.** The setting at the beginning of the story is

**A.** a math classroom
**B.** the guidance counselor's office
**C.** a local pawn shop
**D.** the kitchen in Clyde's house

**54.** Which of the following characters is a minor character?

**A.** Kitty
**B.** Mrs. Jones
**C.** Clyde
**D.** Sam

**55.** Which of these lines helps you visualize the opening scene?

**A.** "Sam probably would have been there too, only he had got a two-week job"
**B.** "he only did it so that his mother would let him be on the track team"
**C.** "we all sat around it like it was some kind of a big important document"
**D.** "He said I should switch back to the commercial program"

**56.** Based on lines 9–10, you can infer that the narrator is

**A.** eager to brag about his own success
**B.** concerned about hurting Clyde's feelings
**C.** shy about making conversation with Kitty
**D.** anxious to get away from Clyde's house

57. Which sentence shows that the story is told from a first-person point of view?

**A.** "The sky was full of gray clouds and it was sprinkling rain."
**B.** "I was over to Clyde's house and Gloria and Kitty were there."
**C.** "Sam and his mother had this little system going."
**D.** "His mathematics mark was a big red F that had been circled."

58. Lines 13–17 show a conflict between Clyde and his

**A.** friends **C.** math class
**B.** mother **D.** conscience

59. According to the sequence of events, Mrs. Jones enters the room before

**A.** Clyde talks to his grade adviser
**B.** she shops for groceries
**C.** the narrator gets his report card
**D.** Clyde starts crying

60. Based on lines 41–42, you can infer that Clyde looks

**A.** disappointed **C.** confused
**B.** irritated **D.** sick

61. The falling action of the story occurs when the children

**A.** receive their report cards
**B.** go into Clyde's living room
**C.** listen to Mrs. Jones's story
**D.** visit their grade advisers

62. Mrs. Jones's story about Clyde's father is an example of

**A.** flashback **C.** resolution
**B.** falling action **D.** climax

63. You can predict that Clyde will work hard in math because

**A.** Mrs. Jones contacts his teacher
**B.** he is afraid of changing programs
**C.** the narrator offers to help him study
**D.** he wants to be like his father

## Written Response

### SHORT RESPONSE

**Directions** Write two or three sentences to answer each question on a separate sheet of paper.

**64.** Describe an internal conflict that the narrator faces in the excerpt from *Fast Sam, Cool Clyde, and Stuff.*

**65.** Identify the resolution of the story and explain how the conflict is resolved.

### EXTENDED RESPONSE

**Directions** Write a short paragraph to answer this question on a separate sheet of paper.

**66.** How is Clyde's experience in school similar to his father's experience playing the trombone? Explain how their experiences reveal a common character trait, and support your answer with examples from the story.

## Reading Comprehension

**Directions** Read the following selection. Then answer the questions that follow.

### from *Sons from Afar*

**Cynthia Voigt**

He lay back and looked at the sky. The stars were coming out, little pale pinpricks of light. He knew they weren't really coming out, that they'd been burning away out in the darkness of space all day long; but it looked like they were coming out, like flowers coming into bloom. Sammy had his head against the stiff splintery boards of the dock, and he was looking out into space so deep it might as well be endless. He thought it would be great to explore space: sailing out among the stars, discovering . . . you couldn't even begin to imagine what you might discover. If there were huge winds that blew across the vast empty reaches, and your ship had a big metal sail . . . but he didn't think there were space winds. He could ask James, but he didn't want to. "I'm good at math and science. I could be an astronaut," he said to the stars.

"I thought you were going to play tennis," James answered.

"I'll do both," Sammy said. The sky turned darker, and darker still. The stars burned white, making the sky look crowded. You could put a tennis court in a spaceship; the ship would have to be large, anyway, and people would have to have something to do, to fill in the vast stretches of time, and to keep in shape. "Why shouldn't I do both?"

"Because they're both careers for young men—too short-lived," James's voice informed him. "Be practical."

That was pretty funny, coming from James. Sammy thought. Now James was getting going on being a lawyer, and Sammy was letting his brother's words blow away on the wind. He'd heard it all before, about a 4.0 average so you could get a scholarship to a good college; about the right major, something to do with history or political science, to prepare you for the three-year course in law school; about the best schools and the scholarships they offered to the best students. After that, the voice went on—Sammy had heard it all before—you just chose how you wanted to make your money.
Government work was secure but paid the least. If you did corporate law, working for a big corporation, you earned big bucks but the job wasn't that secure. Or you could work for a law firm, criminal law or property law, or handling wills and estates. You could do whatever you wanted, whatever you were good at, in a law firm, as you worked your way up to being a partner and taking a percentage of the firm's earnings. With a law degree you could even go

into politics—although Sammy couldn't see anybody voting for James. He didn't think *he* would.

"International law, international banking law," James's voice said. "I think I'd be good at that."

"I wouldn't," Sammy said. "I wouldn't like something where you didn't do anything."

40 James sputtered and Sammy was afraid he'd start explaining how important banking was, but he didn't.

James had heard the boredom in Sammy's voice and reminded himself that Sammy was still young, still just a kid, only twelve. "What about your homework?" he asked.

"What I don't get done tonight I can finish on the bus."

James shrugged: Sammy just didn't care about grades. He just didn't know how important they were; he didn't care about knowing things either.

"You know," Sammy's voice said, "it always looks like the stars are coming out, even if they aren't."

50 "They're really suns," James told him. He looked up at the sky then. It was black, silky black, with no moon yet so the suns burned clear out there. James picked out the constellations he knew: Orion, by his belt, he could always, always find Orion; the big dipper, like a geometric figure, like a rhomboid; the little dipper, a smaller rhomboid, his eyes searched it out. Then the North Star, Polaris. The Pleiades, the sisters, crowded together, the seventh sister burning faintly. "Every one of them is a sun, a mass of burning gases. Do you know how hot the sun burns?"

"So what," Sammy's uninterested voice said.

"Neither do I," James admitted. He used to know, but he'd forgotten.

60 Sammy's laugh sounded friendly. "Tell you a story," James offered. "You want to hear a story?" Sammy always liked being told stories.

"Good-o."

James identified the story's source, first. "This is from Greek mythology. There was an inventor, named Daedalus, a famous inventor. Everybody knew about him. So when King Minos of Crete wanted a labyrinth built—a maze—where he'd keep his son, the Minotaur, in the middle—"

"I remember the Minotaur," Sammy interrupted. "It was in my book of monsters. It was half man, half bull."

"Yeah. So Minos hired Daedalus to design and build this labyrinth.

70 Daedalus took his son Icarus with him to Crete. But when the job was finished, Minos kept them prisoners in a high tower."

"Why?"

"Because they knew how to get out of the maze and Minos wanted that to be a secret. In the tower, they had to haul their food up in baskets, and they had candles for light. The only things that could get into the tower were birds. They were prisoners there for a long time. There was no way to escape, but Daedalus figured out a way. See, when the birds flew in they'd shed their feathers. So he and Icarus collected the feathers. They stuck them together with wax, to make huge wings. When they had enough - it must have taken years—they were
80 ready to fly out, away, to fly free. Before they left, Daedalus warned Icarus that he shouldn't fly too close to the sun, because the heat of it would melt the wax that was holding the wings together. But Icarus didn't pay attention. Or he forgot, maybe. Because when they were out and flying, he went up, and up, until the heat was too great. His wings fell apart and he fell—he fell out of the sky into the ocean. He drowned." James never could tell a story the way it should be told; when he told it, he could hear it sound like a series of facts, like a history book, not like a story.

"I can see why he did that," Sammy said. "If you could really fly, you'd always want to go higher, once you started flying. Wouldn't you?"

## COMPREHENSION

**Directions** Answer the following questions about the excerpt from *Sons from Afar*.

**67.** Lines 1–6 are part of the excerpt's

**A.** exposition
**B.** rising action
**C.** climax
**D.** falling action

**68.** The main setting of the excerpt is a

**A.** lawyer's office
**B.** field behind a house
**C.** guarded tower
**D.** dock near the water

**69.** At what time of day does the excerpt begin?

**A.** sunrise
**B.** midday
**C.** twilight
**D.** midnight

**70.** The first paragraph is written from which point of view?

**A.** first person
**B.** second person
**C.** third person limited
**D.** third person omniscient

**71.** Which method of characterization does Cynthia Voigt use in lines 6–10?

**A.** Sammy's thoughts
**B.** the narrator's comments
**C.** James's thoughts
**D.** Sammy's actions

**72.** Based on lines 6–10, you can infer that Sammy

**A.** has a powerful imagination
**B.** is good at making friends
**C.** does well in school
**D.** follows directions well

**73.** In lines 42–43, the point of view shifts from

**A.** James's thoughts to the narrator's voice
**B.** James's thoughts to Sammy's thoughts
**C.** the narrator's voice to Sammy's thoughts
**D.** Sammy's thoughts to James's thoughts

**74.** Lines 50–56 help you visualize

**A.** the night sky
**B.** Minos's labyrinth
**C.** the setting sun
**D.** James's expression

**75.** In line 61, Voigt characterizes Sammy through

**A.** the narrator's actions
**B.** Sammy's speech
**C.** the narrator's comments
**D.** James's thoughts

**76.** According to the sequence of events, James offers to tell a story

**A.** before he tells Sammy about the stars
**B.** after he talks to Sammy about law
**C.** before he asks about Sammy's homework
**D.** after he tells Sammy about Icarus

**77.** According to the sequence of events in James's story, Icarus' wings fall apart

**A.** after he flies too close to the sun
**B.** before Daedalus designs the maze
**C.** after he falls into the ocean
**D.** before Daedalus escapes from the tower

## Written Response

### SHORT RESPONSE

**Directions** Write two or three sentences to answer each question on a separate sheet of paper.

**78.** Explain one of the conflicts in the story that James tells. Then identify it as an internal or an external conflict.

**79.** Predict how James would respond to Sammy's question at the end of the excerpt. Explain your response.

### EXTENDED RESPONSE

**Directions** Write a short paragraph to answer this question on a separate sheet of paper.

**80.** Discuss how Voigt uses characterization to develop James's character in the excerpt from *Sons from Afar*. Support your response with two examples from the excerpt.

## Reading Comprehension

**Directions** Read the following selections. Then answer the questions that follow.

### Lifesaver

**John DiConsiglio**

Having grown up in San Diego, California, Mack Lothian knows a lot about the beach—in particular, Newport Beach. He is aware that the best place to avoid crowds is three miles north of the jetty. The area is so deserted that lifeguards are stationed there only during the peak summer months. "It's so peaceful out there," Mack, 15, tells Choices. "You look around and all you see are miles of sand and water."

But on an April afternoon in 2004, Mack saw more than waves. He saw a little boy being swept out to sea, and Mack sprang into action to save him. Mack never expected to be a lifesaver. He had gone to the beach that day with 10 other family members to relax. While his relatives were lying on the sand, Mack waded out into the water to bodysurf.

He noticed two boys playing just a few yards from the shore. They seemed to be about 8 or 9 years old. As Mack floated nearby, he noticed a troubling sign in the water. On either side of the boys, steady waves lapped the shore. But the boys were standing in oddly calm water. Mack knew what that meant: rip current.

**Deadly Waters**

A rip current is a powerful flow of water away from the shore. It is caused by waves traveling from deep to shallow water. Sometimes those waves break 20 in different ways. Some break strongly, others weakly. That makes the water move in narrow, fast-moving belts. The ground under the current can drop from 3 feet to more than 20 in one step. And the current can sweep you out to sea in as fast as 8 feet per second.

Rip currents are deadly. More people die every year from rip currents than from shark attacks, tornadoes, lightning, or hurricanes. According to the United States Lifesaving Association, 80 percent of beach rescues are due to rip currents—and more than 100 people drown each year when they can't escape the current.

As Mack watched, the head of one of the boys bobbed under the water. 30 Within seconds, the current started dragging him out to sea. Mack yelled out to the boy. When he didn't answer, Mack swam toward him—right into the current.

Mack grabbed the panicky boy's arm and tried to calm him. They were about 15 yards from the beach, but Mack knew that the current could sweep them out 100 yards - the length of a football field—in minutes. Mack also knew the beach led to the mouth of the Santa Ana River. If the current pulled them into the powerful river, they might never make it back. He began to tread water and told the boy to grab his legs. They were going to swim to shore.

**Treading Water**

40 Mack, who learned how to swim at age 4, knows how to swim in a rip current. "It's useless to fight it and swim headlong to shore," he says. "You won't make any progress. The current will push you backward." The boy kicked and flailed. Mack told him to hold on.

But the current was too strong. Mack was getting tired and a little worried. They were moving out to sea fast. The boy jumped on Mack's shoulders, pushing him into the water. Mack knew that swimming wasn't the answer. The best thing to do, he realized, was to wait.

Mack held the boy and assured him that everything would be OK. He kept treading forward in the current, allowing the water to slowly move him 50 backward. "We were out there for maybe 10 minutes, but it seemed like 10 days," Mack says. In the spring, few lifeguards patrol the beach. The current had already pulled them far away from Mack's family. He began to wonder if anyone would ever find them.

Finally, Mack saw a lifeguard Jeep along the shore. He called out and waved his right arm. "We're going to be all right," he told the boy. Within moments, a team of lifeguards with buoys made their way to Mack and the boy. The lifeguards took the boy to shore as Mack swam beside them. When the boy was safe, a lifeguard turned to Mack, but he was already gone.

**Worn Out**

60 Mack slowly walked along the beach toward his family's camp. He dropped down on a towel, exhausted. "My arms and legs felt like lead," he says. "I felt like I'd just run a mile" None of his family knew what had happened and Mack didn't tell them.

"That's just Mack," says his father, who's also named Mack. "He never wants to take credit." Soon, the lifeguard Jeep came by. The lifeguard told Mack that he had probably saved the boy's life. "If you hadn't gone out to get him, no one would have reached him in time," the lifeguard said.

Mack still doesn't think of himself as a hero even after he won the U.S Lifeguard Association's Heroic Acts Award. And he never saw the boy's 70 family again. "Lifeguards are the real heroes," he says. "They do this stuff every day. I was just in the right place at the right time."

## Rip Current Safety

**National Weather Service**

### Why Rip Currents Form

As waves travel from deep to shallow water, they will break near the shoreline. When waves break strongly in some locations and weakly in others, this can cause circulation cells which are seen as rip currents: narrow, fast-moving belts of water traveling offshore.

### Why Rip Currents Are Dangerous

Rip currents are the leading surf hazard for all beachgoers. They are particularly dangerous for weak or non-swimmers. Rip current speeds are typically 1-2 feet per second. However, speeds as high as 8 feet per second have been
10 measured—this is faster than an Olympic swimmer can sprint! Thus, rip currents can sweep even the strongest swimmer out to sea.

Over 100 drownings due to rip currents occur every year in the United States. More than 80% of water rescues on surf beaches are due to rip currents.

Rip currents can occur at any surf beach with breaking waves, including the Great Lakes.

### When Rip Currents Form

Rip currents can be found on many surf beaches every day. Under most tide and sea conditions the speeds are relatively slow. However, under certain wave, tide, and beach profile conditions the speeds can quickly increase to become
20 dangerous to anyone entering the surf. The strength and speed of a rip current will likely increase as wave height and wave period increase. **They are most likely to be dangerous during high surf conditions as the wave height and wave period increase.**

### Where Rip Currents Form

Rip currents most typically form at low spots or breaks in sandbars, and also near structures such as jetties and piers. Rip currents can be very narrow or extend in widths to hundreds of yards. The seaward pull of rip currents varies: sometimes the rip current ends just beyond the line of breaking waves, but sometimes rip currents continue to push hundreds of yards offshore.

30 **How to Identify Rip Currents**

Look for any of these clues:

• a channel of churning, choppy water
• an area having a notable difference in water color
• a line of foam, seaweed, or debris moving steadily seaward
• a break in the incoming wave pattern

None, one, or more of the above clues may indicate the presence of rip currents. Rip currents are often not readily or easily identifiable to the average beachgoer. For your safety, be aware of this major surf zone hazard. Polarized sunglasses make it easier to see the rip current clues provided above.

40 **How to Avoid and Survive Rip Currents**

**Learn how to swim!**

• Never swim alone.
• Be cautious at all times, especially when swimming at unguarded beaches. If in doubt, don't go out!
• Whenever possible, swim at a lifeguard protected beach.
• Obey all instructions and orders from lifeguards.
• If caught in a rip current, remain calm to conserve energy and think clearly.
• Don't fight the current. Swim out of the current in a direction following the shoreline. When out of the current, swim towards shore.
50 • If you are unable to swim out of the rip current, float or calmly tread water. When out of the current, swim towards shore.
• If you are still unable to reach shore, draw attention to yourself: face the shore, wave your arms, and yell for help.

If you see someone in trouble, get help from a lifeguard. If a lifeguard is not available, have someone call 9-1-1. Throw the rip current victim something that floats and yell instructions on how to escape. **Remember, many people drown while trying to save someone else from a rip current.**

## COMPREHENSION

**Directions** Answer the following questions about "Lifesaver."

**1.** The details in lines 13–15 help you visualize the

**A.** nearby lifeguard station
**B.** offshore rip current
**C.** coastline near San Diego
**D.** families on the beach

**2.** According to the article, what causes water to move in narrow, fast-moving belts?

**A.** changes in water temperature
**B.** differences in the way waves break
**C.** patches of oddly calm water
**D.** waves traveling along the coastline

**3.** According to lines 48–53, the effect of the current was to

**A.** sweep Mack and the boy farther away from shore
**B.** attract the attention of several lifeguards with buoys
**C.** encourage Mack to start swimming against it
**D.** make the waves become choppy and white

**4.** Which words in lines 48–58 show that the two paragraphs are written in chronological order?

**A.** 10 minutes, 10 days
**B.** In the spring, slowly
**C.** kept treading, already gone
**D.** Finally, within moments

**5.** From lines 62–65, you can draw the conclusion that Mack is

**A.** respectful
**B.** honest
**C.** creative
**D.** modest

**6.** According to the chronological order of events, the lifeguards talked to Mack

**A.** minutes before he swam back to shore
**B.** soon after he found his family's camp
**C.** months after he received the award
**D.** seconds before he met the boy's family

**7.** Which line from the excerpt shows the writer's position?

**A.** "Mack Lothian knows a lot about the beach"
**B.** "the best place to avoid crowds is three miles north of the jetty"
**C.** "He began to wonder if anyone would ever find them"
**D.** "I was just in the right place at the right time"

**8.** You can predict that the next time Mack sees someone caught in a rip current he will

**A.** tell the person to swim toward shore
**B.** look to see whether the water is calm
**C.** swim with the current to save the person
**D.** find the nearest lifeguard on duty

## COMPREHENSION

**Directions** Answer the following questions about "Rip Current Safety."

**9.** Rip currents are likely to be most dangerous as a result of increased

**A.** wave height and period
**B.** water temperature
**C.** sandbar and beach depth
**D.** tides and surf

**10.** Based on lines 31–39, you can draw the conclusion that rip currents are

**A.** rare in warm climates
**B.** difficult to identify
**C.** harmless in most cases
**D.** always a different color

**11.** Which sentence best describes the writer's position?

**A.** Rip currents are safe only if you know how to handle them
**B.** Surfing in rip currents is allowable if a lifeguard is nearby.
**C.** Rip currents are dangerous and should be avoided by everyone.
**D.** Slow or weak swimmers should use caution near rip currents.

**12.** After failing to swim out of a rip current, what should a swimmer do next?

**A.** call 911
**B.** tread water
**C.** fight the current
**D.** call a lifeguard

## COMPREHENSION

**Directions** Answer these questions about both selections.

**13.** Synthesize the two selections. Both authors stress the idea that rip currents

**A.** can be deadly for swimmers
**B.** are often found on surf beaches
**C.** form in deep, uneven water
**D.** are dangerous in bad weather

**14.** Synthesize both selections. The most important thing Mack did to survive was

**A.** pull the boy in
**B.** remain calm
**C.** fight the current
**D.** float on his back

**15.** From reading both selections, you can conclude that the most dangerous part of rip currents is their

**A.** frequency
**B.** speed
**C.** appearance
**D.** depth

## Written Response

### SHORT RESPONSE

**Directions** Write two or three sentences to answer each question on a separate sheet of paper.

**16.** Synthesize both selections. What typical signs of a rip current did Mack Lothian see? Use one detail from each selection to support your answer.

**17.** Analyze the writer's position about rip currents in "Lifesaver." Support your analysis with one detail from the text.

### EXTENDED RESPONSE

**Directions** Write a short paragraph to answer this question on a separate sheet of paper.

**18.** According to "Rip Current Safety," did Mack Lothian follow the rules for surviving rip currents? Synthesize details from both selections to support your answer.

## Vocabulary

**Directions** Use your knowledge of prefixes and suffixes to answer the following questions. The line numbers will help you find the words in the excerpt from *Fast Sam, Cool Clyde, and Stuff.*

**1.** Which prefix can be added to the adjective *satisfactory* in line 11 to form an adjective meaning "not suitable"?

**A.** *un-*
**B.** *dis-*
**C.** *in-*
**D.** *re-*

**2.** Which suffix can be added to the adjective *academic* in line 17 to form an adverb that means "in a scholarly way"?

**A.** *-eous*
**B.** *-ally*
**C.** *-ness*
**D.** *-ial*

**3.** Adding the suffix *-er* to the word *advise* produces a word that means

**A.** quality of needing advice
**B.** action or process of giving advice
**C.** relating to advice
**D.** one who gives or offers advice

**4.** Adding the prefix *un-* to the word *wrap* produces a word that means to

**A.** wrap again
**B.** do the opposite of wrap
**C.** wrap before
**D.** almost wrap something

**Directions** Use context clues to answer the following questions. The line numbers will help you find the words in the excerpt from *Sons from Afar.*

**5.** Which is the most likely meaning of *corporation* in line 29?

**A.** government
**B.** criminal
**C.** company
**D.** factory

**6.** Which is the most likely meaning of *percentage* in line 33?

**A.** small fraction
**B.** free education
**C.** varying degree
**D.** honest attempt

**7.** Which is the most likely meaning of *constellations* in line 52?

**A.** geometric figures
**B.** groups of stars
**C.** visible planets
**D.** clusters of moons

**8.** Which is the most likely meaning of *labyrinth* in line 65?

**A.** wing
**B.** monster
**C.** tower
**D.** maze

**Directions** Use your knowledge of multiple-meaning words to answer the following questions. The line numbers will help you find the words in "Rip Current Safety."

**9.** Which meaning of *break* is used in line 2?

**A.** exceed a record
**B.** interrupt an activity
**C.** emerge above a surface
**D.** shatter into small pieces

**10.** Which meaning of *sweep* is used in line 11?

**A.** carry away forcibly
**B.** destroy completely
**C.** brush lightly
**D.** pass over quickly

**11.** Which meaning of *wave* is used in line 18?

**A.** surge or rush
**B.** curved pattern
**C.** rising trend
**D.** ridge of water

**12.** Which meaning of *period* is used in line 23?

**A.** division of time in a sport or game
**B.** point at which something is ended
**C.** time between repeating events
**D.** punctuation mark indicating a full stop

**Directions** Use your knowledge of synonyms and antonyms to answer the following questions.

**13.** Choose the word that is an antonym for *deserted* in line 3 of "Lifesaver."

**A.** protected
**B.** busy
**C.** convenient
**D.** humid

**14.** Choose the word that is a synonym for *flailed* in line 43 of "Lifesaver."

**A.** breathed
**B.** swam
**C.** thrashed
**D.** cried

**15.** Choose the word that is an antonym for *required* in line 25 of the excerpt from *Fast Sam, Cool Clyde, and Stuff.*

**A.** difficult
**B.** commercial
**C.** creative
**D.** optional

**16.** Choose the word that is a synonym for *nonchalant* in line 72 of the excerpt from *Fast Sam, Cool Clyde, and Stuff*

**A.** casual
**B.** sneaky
**C.** bold
**D.** suspicious

## Writing and Grammar

**Directions** Read the descriptive essay and answer the questions that follow.

(1) Nature has always played an important role in my life. (2) Some of my fondest memories are of my parents' farm, where I grew up. (3) I loved exploring the quiet ponds and peaceful woods, and I learn much about the natural world. (4) That farm will always have a special place in my heart.

(5) Most days after school I would walk down a long dirt road that snaked through the grounds. (6) I would enter the big gate, I would cross a bridge to the far side of the pond. (7) On some days a blue heron would greet me. (8) Flapping noisily as she circled above.

(9) The pond was always a calming place. (10) Closing my eyes, I would concentrate on the frogs's croaking. (11) When I opened my eyes, I would take in the scenery. (12) There were bright yellow flowers perched atop clusters of large green lily pads. (13) Dragonflies flew through the air while moths flew around my head. (14) On the surface of the water, tiny flying bugs scooted in all directions. (15) Dropping from a nearby tree, ripples spread through the still water.

(16) The dirt path continued beyond the bridge. (17) Usually, I would stay on it until I reached a large oak tree. (18) The old trees trunk formed a perfect seat where they split into three branches. (19) Of all the nearby trees, it was the better for climbing. (20) Frequently I would hoist myself into the sturdy branches to observe my surroundings. (21) Bushy-tailed squirrels darted from tree to tree as fuzzy-capped acorns fall from the trees. (22) I would often take a pen and notebook from my schoolbag and bring it into the tree to write or sketch. (23) Around me I'd hear an owl clicking. (24) Below me I'd smell fresh sap wafting. (25) I still have all of the stories and drawings I made while sitting in that tree.

(26) I don't live on that farm anymore. (27) My parents sold them and we moved to a big city. (28) Now I have a whole new set of sights and sounds to explore. (29) I'll always remember the farm and what it taught me. (30) Those walks down the dirt road taught me to appreciate nature and brought out my creative side.

**1.** The introduction is effective because it

**A.** describes an important event
**B.** explains things that will be compared
**C.** identifies the place being described
**D.** establishes a serious tone

**2.** To correct the verb tense in sentence 3, change "learn" to

**A.** learned
**B.** will learn
**C.** learning
**D.** had learned

**3.** The words "long dirt road" in sentence 5 appeal to which of the following senses?

**A.** smell
**B.** sight
**C.** sound
**D.** taste

**4.** Choose the best way to rewrite sentence 6 so that it is no longer a run-on sentence

**A.** I would enter the big gate I would cross a bridge to the far side of the pond.
**B.** I would enter the big gate; so I would cross a bridge to the far side of the pond.
**C.** I would enter the big gate, I would, cross a bridge to the far side of the pond.
**D.** I would enter the big gate, and I would cross a bridge to the far side of the pond.

**5.** What is the best way to revise sentences 7 and 8 to avoid having a sentence fragment?

**A.** On some days a blue heron would greet me flapping noisily as she circled above.
**B.** On some days a blue heron would greet me; flapping noisily as she circled above.
**C.** On some days a blue heron would greet me, flapping noisily as she circled above.
**D.** On some days a blue heron would greet me flapping, noisily as she circled above.

**6.** To punctuate the plural possessive in sentence 10 correctly, change *frogs's* to

**A.** frogs'
**B.** frogs
**C.** frogses
**D.** frog's

**7.** Choose the best transition to add to the beginning of sentence 11.

**A.** However
**B.** Then
**C.** Therefore
**D.** Although

**8.** Which words in sentences 11–12 demonstrate sensory details?

**A.** "opened my eyes"
**B.** "take in the scenery"
**C.** "atop clusters of"
**D.** "bright yellow flowers"

**9.** Choose the best way to rewrite sentence 13 using precise words.

**A.** Big dragonflies whizzed through the air while little tiny moths flew all around my head.
**B.** Shiny blue dragonflies chased one another through the air while white and yellow moths danced patterns around my head.
**C.** Large dragonflies flew all through the air while little tiny moths buzzed around my head.
**D.** Shiny blue dragonflies flew through the air while white and yellow moths flew around my head.

**10.** Choose the best way to revise the misplaced modifier in sentence 15.

**A.** Ripples, dropping from a nearby tree, spread through the still water.
**B.** Dropping from a nearby tree, ripples spread from a leaf through the still water.
**C.** Ripples spread through the still water, dropping from a nearby tree.
**D.** Dropping from a nearby tree, a leaf spread ripples through the still water.

**11.** In the fourth paragraph, the writer uses a

**A.** variety of sentence lengths
**B.** forceful and persuasive tone
**C.** quotation to support the thesis
**D.** series of declarative statements

**12.** To punctuate the plural possessive in sentence 18 correctly, change *trees* to

**A.** tree's  **C.** trees'
**B.** trees's  **D.** treeses

**13.** To maintain pronoun-antecedent agreement in sentence 18, change "they" to

**A.** he  **C.** its
**B.** it  **D.** you

**14.** Choose the correct way to use the superlative form in sentence 19.

**A.** Of all the nearby trees, it was more good for climbing.
**B.** Of all the nearby trees, it was the most good for climbing.
**C.** Of all the nearby trees, it was the best for climbing.
**D.** Of all the nearby trees, it was more better for climbing.

**15.** To correct the verb tense in sentence 21, change "fall" to

**A.** fell  **C.** had fallen
**B.** will fall  **D.** falls

**16.** To maintain pronoun-antecedent agreement in sentence 22, change "it" to

**A.** its  **C.** them
**B.** him  **D.** you

**17.** Choose the best way to vary the structure of sentences 23 and 24.

**A.** I'd hear an owl clicking around me. I'd smell fresh sap wafting from below.
**B.** Around me an owl would be clicking. Below me fresh sap would be wafting.
**C.** I'd hear an owl clicking around me. I'd smell the waft of fresh sap below me.
**D.** Around me I'd hear an owl clicking. The smell of fresh sap would waft from below.

**8.** To maintain pronoun-antecedent agreement in sentence 27, change "them" to

**A.** her
**B.** you
**C.** it
**D.** me

**9.** Choose the best transition to add to the beginning of sentence 29.

**A.** Therefore
**B.** However
**C.** Instead
**D.** Furthermore

**20.** The conclusion is effective because it

**A.** explains why the farm is important to the writer
**B.** provides additional details about how the farm looked
**C.** introduces a new idea about the writer's argument
**D.** describes what the farm is like many years later

## Vriting

**irections** Read the following quotation. Then read the prompt that follows and omplete the writing activity.

> "The two most engaging powers of an author are to make new things familiar, familiar things new."
>
> William Makepeace Thackeray

**rompt:** Write an essay that compares and contrasts two familiar people or things. .s Thackeray suggests, you have the power to consider your subjects in a new or ifferent way. Explore alternative ways of viewing your subjects as you compare nd contrast them.

Now write your essay. Use the reminders that follow to help you write.

**eminders**

- Be sure your writing does what the prompt asks.
- Clearly state the activities being compared and contrasted.
- Include a focused thesis statement.
- Support your points with explanations and details.
- Use transitions to connect ideas.
- Check for correct grammar, spelling, and punctuation.

# Benchmark Test 2

## Reading Comprehension

**Directions** Read the following selection. Then answer the questions that follow.

**If I Forget Thee, On Earth . . .**
**Arthur C. Clarke**

When Marvin was ten years old, his father took him through the long, echoing corridors that led up through Administration and Power, until at last they came to the uppermost levels of all and were among the swiftly growing vegetation of the Farmlands. Marvin liked it here: it was fun watching the great, slender plants creeping with almost visible eagerness toward sunlight as it filtered down through the plastic domes to meet them. The smell of life was everywhere, awakening inexpressible longings in his heart: no longer was he breathing the dry, cool air of the residential levels, purged of all smells but the faint tang of ozone. He wished he could stay here for a little while, but Father would not let him. They went onward until they had reached the entrance to the Observatory, which he had never visited: but they did not stop, and Marvin knew with a sense of rising excitement that there could be only one goal left. For the first time in his life, he was going Outside.

There were a dozen of the surface vehicles, with their wide balloon tires and pressurized cabins, in the great servicing chamber. His father must have been expected, for they were led at once to the little scout car waiting by the huge circular door of the airlock. Tense with expectancy, Marvin settled himself down in the cramped cabin while his father started the motor and checked the controls. The inner door of the lock slid open and then closed behind them: he heard the roar of the great air pumps fade slowly away as the pressure dropped to zero. Then the "Vacuum" sign flashed on, the outer door parted, and before Marvin lay the land which he had never yet entered.

He had seen it in photographs, of course: he had watched it imaged on television screens a hundred times. But now it was lying all around him, burning beneath the fierce sun that crawled so slowly across the jet-black sky. He stared into the west, away from the blinding splendor of the sun-and there were the stars, as he had been told but never quite believed. He gazed at them for a long time, marveling that anything could be so bright and yet so tiny. They were intense unscintillating points, and suddenly he remembered a rhyme he had once read in one of his father's books:

*Twinkle, twinkle, little star,*
*How I wonder what you are.*

Well, *he* knew what stars were. Whoever asked that question must have been very stupid. And what did they mean by "twinkle"? You could see at a glance that all the stars shone with the same steady, unwavering light. He abandoned the puzzle and turned his attention to the landscape around him.

They were racing across a level plain at almost a hundred miles an hour, the great balloon tires sending up little spurts of dust behind them. There was no sign of the Colony: in the few minutes while he had been gazing at the stars, its 40 domes and radio towers had fallen below the horizon. Yet there were other indications of man's presence, for about a mile ahead Marvin could see the curiously shaped structures clustering round the head of a mine. Now and then a puff of vapor would emerge from a squat smokestack and would instantly disperse.

They were past the mine in a moment: Father was driving with a reckless and exhilarating skill as if—it was a strange thought to come into a child's mind—he were trying to escape from something. In a few minutes they had reached the edge of the plateau on which the Colony had been built. The ground fell sharply away beneath them in a dizzying slope whose lower stretches were 50 lost in shadow. Ahead, as far as the eye could reach, was a jumbled wasteland of craters, mountain ranges, and ravines. The crests of the mountains, catching the low sun, burned like islands of fire in a sea of darkness: and above them the stars still shone as steadfastly as ever.

There could be no way forward—yet there was. Marvin clenched his fists as the car edged over the slope and started the long descent. Then he saw the barely visible track leading down the mountainside, and relaxed a little. Other men, it seemed, had gone this way before.

Night fell with a shocking abruptness as they crossed the shadow line and the sun dropped below the crest of the plateau. The twin searchlights sprang 60 into life, casting blue-white bands on the rocks ahead, so that there was scarcely need to check their speed. For hours they drove through valleys and past the foot of mountains whose peaks seemed to comb the stars, and sometimes they emerged for a moment into the sunlight as they climbed over higher ground.

And now on the right was a wrinkled, dusty plain, and on the left, its ramparts and terraces rising mile after mile into the sky, was a wall of mountains that marched into the distance until its peaks sank from sight below the rim of the world. There was no sign that men had ever explored this land, but once they passed the skeleton of a crashed rocket, and beside it a stone cairn surmounted by a metal cross.

70 It seemed to Marvin that the mountains stretched on forever: but at last, many hours later, the range ended in a towering, precipitous headland that rose steeply from a cluster of little hills. They drove down into a shallow valley that curved in a great arc toward the far side of the mountains: and as they did so, Marvin slowly realized that something very strange was happening in the land ahead.

The sun was now low behind the hills on the right: the valley before them should be in total darkness. Yet it was awash with a cold white radiance that came spilling over the crags beneath which they were driving. Then, suddenly, they were out in the open plain, and the source of the light lay before them in all
80 its glory.

It was very quiet in the little cabin now that the motors had stopped. The only sound was the faint whisper of the oxygen feed and an occasional metallic crepitation as the outer walls of the vehicle radiated away their heat. For no warmth at all came from the great silver crescent that floated low above the far horizon and flooded all this land with pearly light. It was so brilliant that minutes passed before Marvin could accept its challenge and look steadfastly into its glare, but at last he could discern the outlines of continents, the hazy border of the atmosphere, and the white islands of cloud. And even at this distance, he could see the glitter of sunlight on the polar ice.

90 It was beautiful, and it called to his heart across the abyss of space. There in that shining crescent were all the wonders that he had never known—the hues of sunset skies, the moaning of the sea on pebbled shores, the patter of falling rain, the unhurried benison of snow. These and a thousand others should have been his rightful heritage, but he knew them only from the books and ancient records, and the thought filled him with the anguish of exile.

Why could they not return? It seemed so peaceful beneath those lines of marching cloud. Then Marvin, his eyes no longer blinded by the glare, saw that the portion of the disk that should have been in darkness was gleaming faintly with an evil phosphorescence: and he remembered. He was looking upon the
100 funeral pyre of a world-upon the radioactive aftermath of Armageddon. Across a quarter of a million miles of space, the glow of dying atoms was still visible, a perennial reminder of the ruinous past. It would be centuries yet before that deadly glow died from the rocks and life could return again to fill that silent, empty world.

And now Father began to speak, telling Marvin the story which until this moment had meant no more to him than the fairy tales he had once been told. There were many things he could not understand: it was impossible for him to picture the glowing, multicolored pattern of life on the planet he had never seen. Nor could he comprehend the forces that had destroyed it in the end, leaving the
110 Colony, preserved by its isolation, as the sole survivor. Yet he could share the agony of those final days, when the Colony had learned at last that never again would the supply ships come flaming down through the stars with gifts from home. One by one the radio stations had ceased to call: on the shadowed globe the lights of the cities had dimmed and died, and they were alone at last, as no men had ever been alone before, carrying in their hands the future of the race.

Then followed the years of despair, and the long-drawn battle for survival in this fierce and hostile world. That battle had been won, though barely: this little oasis of life was safe against the worst that Nature could do. But unless there was a goal, a future toward which it could work, the Colony would lose
120 the will to live, and neither machines nor skill nor science could save it then.

So, at last, Marvin understood the purpose of this pilgrimage. He would never walk beside the rivers of that lost and legendary world, or listen to the thunder raging above its soft rounded hills. Yet one day—how far ahead?—his children's children would return to claim their heritage. The winds and the rains would scour the poisons from the burning lands and carry them to the sea, and in the depths of the sea they would waste their venom until they could harm no living things. Then the great ships that were still waiting here on the silent, dusty plains could lift once more into space, along the road that led to home.

That was the dream: and one day, Marvin knew with a sudden flash of
130 insight, he would pass it on to his own son, here at this same spot with the mountains behind him and the silver light from the sky streaming into his face.

He did not look back as they began the homeward journey. He could not bear to see the cold glory of the crescent Earth fade from the rocks around him, as he went to rejoin his people in their long exile.

## COMPREHENSION

**Directions** Answer the following questions about "If I Forget Thee, Oh Earth . . ."

**1.** The story's main setting is

**A.** in a space ship
**B.** on the Earth
**C.** in another galaxy
**D.** on the moon

**2.** Which sentence best summarizes Marvin's actions in lines 1–13?

**A.** When Marvin was ten, his father took him to the Farmlands, Marvin's favorite place.
**B.** After asking for years, Marvin finally convinced his father to bring him Outside.
**C.** When Marvin was ten, his father led him through the colony to bring him Outside.
**D.** After searching the Colony, Marvin's father finally found him in the Farmlands.

**3.** Which word best describes the mood of lines 10–13?

**A.** peaceful
**B.** serious
**C.** suspenseful
**D.** terrifying

**4.** Monitor your understanding of lines 26–28. Marvin is fascinated with the stars because he

**A.** does not believe stars exist
**B.** wants to know why they twinkle
**C.** has never seen the sky before
**D.** is afraid of the dark night

**5.** From Marvin's reaction in lines 33–35 to the nursery rhyme, you can infer that

**A.** children in Marvin's world do not learn the same rhymes we learn
**B.** Marvin's world is so different from ours that the stars do not twinkle
**C.** children in Marvin's world learn about science earlier than we do
**D.** Marvin's world has stars that are bigger and brighter stars than ours

**6.** Based on lines 35–44, which phrase best describes Marvin's character?

**A.** curious about his environment
**B.** frightened by the new things he sees
**C.** confused about what is happening
**D.** eager to learn the journey's purpose

**7.** The details of the setting in lines 47–53 show that the world outside the Colony is

**A.** beautiful
**B.** threatening
**C.** exciting
**D.** barren

**8.** Marvin's ride into the Outside is the plot stage known as

**A.** exposition
**B.** rising action
**C.** climax
**D.** resolution

9. The author's word choice in lines 77–80 creates which kind of style?

**A.** informal
**B.** journalistic
**C.** descriptive
**D.** exciting

0. Which sentence best summarizes Marvin and his father's drive outside the Colony?

**A.** Marvin's father drives for many hours and stops in the silver light of Earth.
**B.** They reach the edge of the plateau, and Marvin's father drives over it.
**C.** They drive far from the Colony to a place where a rocket from Earth will land.
**D.** Marvin's father seems to be lost, but then Marvin notices faint tire tracks.

1. Which words in lines 81–85 help create a mood of loneliness?

**A.** little cabin, great silver crescent"
**B.** motors had stopped, pearly light
**C.** faint whisper, no warmth at all
**D.** metallic crepitation, far horizon

2. The details of the setting in lines 85–89 reveal that Marvin is

**A.** seeing the moon from the Earth
**B.** looking up at the Earth
**C.** thinking about Earth for the first time
**D.** longing to escape life on Earth

3. In lines 90–93, the "shining crescent" symbolizes

**A.** the beauty of space
**B.** fear of the unknown
**C.** the memory of Earth
**D.** life in the Colony

**14.** Which word best describes the mood of lines 93–95?

**A.** mysterious
**B.** romantic
**C.** sorrowful
**D.** peaceful

**15.** Which sentence best summarizes the story that Marvin's father tells in lines 105–120?

**A.** After disaster ended life on Earth, the people of the Colony struggled to survive.
**B.** The people of the Colony were in despair, but they found the strength to go on.
**C.** A war on Earth left the people of the Colony stranded, hoping to be rescued.
**D.** When the supply ships stopped coming, the people of the Colony lost hope.

**16.** Which words contribute most to the formal, serious style of lines 110–115?

**A.** those final days, through the stars
**B.** one by one, dimmed and died
**C.** lights of the cities, in their hands
**D.** flaming down, supply ships

**17.** The long sentences and use of the word *would* in lines 121–127 create a style that is

**A.** objective and appropriate for science
**B.** journalistic and reflective of tragic events
**C.** flowery and full of rich and vivid details
**D.** formal and suited to imagining the future

**18.** The climax of the story occurs when

**A.** the light of Earth shines on Marvin
**B.** Marvin's father drives off the plateau
**C.** Marvin realizes the loss of his heritage
**D.** Marvin's father tells the Colony's story

**19.** Marvin's journey with his father is a symbol of

**A.** the desire to explore and learn
**B.** a father's love for his son
**C.** the dream of a better future
**D.** a child's becoming an adult

**20.** Which statement best describes the character of Marvin's father?

**A.** Earth is his greatest goal.
**B.** He wants to recapture his youth.
**C.** Speed is his only pleasure.
**D.** He plans everything carefully.

**21.** Lines 121–128 represent which plot stag

**A.** exposition
**B.** rising action
**C.** climax
**D.** resolution

**22.** Lines 129–131 help express the story's theme by showing that

**A.** Marvin understands his father's drean
**B.** Earth is precious to all human beings
**C.** humans' actions threaten Earth's futu
**D.** the people of the Colony will survive

**23.** What does Earth symbolize for Marvin a the end of the story?

**A.** hope for the future
**B.** pride in his heritage
**C.** regret over the past
**D.** a return to innocence

## Written Response

### SHORT RESPONSE

**Directions** Write two or three sentences to answer each question on a separate sheet of paper.

**24.** Describe the author's style in "If I Forget Thee, Oh Earth . . ." Support your response with two details from the story.

**25.** What does the narrator reveal about Marvin's character in lines 107–113? Include one detail from these lines to support your response.

### EXTENDED RESPONSE

**Directions** Write a short paragraph to answer this question on a separate sheet of paper.

**26.** Explain the theme of the story, and discuss how it is different from the topic of the story. Support your response with details from the story.

## Reading Comprehension

**Directions** Read the following selections. Then answer the questions that follow.

### *from* Cesar's Way

**Cesar Millan**

There's a unique neediness in American dogs—I've seen it in their eyes and felt it in their energies from the first day I crossed over the border into the United States. America's pet dogs long to have what most dogs in the wild have naturally: the ability simply to *be dogs*, to live in a stable, balanced *pack*. American dogs struggle with an issue unknown to most of the world's dogs—the need to "unlearn" their owners' lovingly motivated but ultimately destructive efforts to transform them into four—legged people with fur.

As a kid in Mexico, I watched *Lassie* and *Rin Tin Tin* and dreamed of becoming the world's greatest dog "trainer." I don't call what I do "training"
10 anymore. There are plenty of great trainers out there-people who can teach your dog to respond to such commands as "sit," "stay," "come," and "heel." That's not what I do. I do heavy-duty rehab. I deal with dog psychology: trying to connect with the dog's mind and natural instincts to help correct unwanted behavior. I don't use words or commands. I use energy and touch. When I come to a client's house, the owner usually thinks the problem lies with the dog. I always have in the back of my mind that the issue is most likely with the owner. I often tell my clients, "I rehabilitate dogs, but I train people."

The key to my method is what I call "the power of the pack." Having
20 grown up on a farm, around dogs that were work dogs but not house pets, I had years of experience interacting with and observing dogs in their natural "pack" societies. The concept of a "pack" is ingrained in your dog's DNA. In a pack, there are only two roles: the role of leader and the role of follower. If you don't become your dog's pack leader, he will assume that role and try to dominate you. In America, most pet owners spoil their dogs and give them constant affection, thinking that this is enough for the dog. Simply stated, it's not

enough. In a dog's world, getting only affection upsets his natural balance. By teaching my clients how to "speak" their dog's language—the language of the pack—I open up a whole new world for *them*. My goal in working with clients
30 is to ensure that both the human and the dog end up healthier and happier.

There are more than sixty-five million pet dogs in America. Over the past ten years, the pet industry has doubled in size, with an income of about $34 billion—yes, billion! American dog owners pamper their pets with such things as $5,700 green crocodile leather travel bags for miniature Yorkshire terriers and $30,000 insurance policies. On the average, dog owners can spend as much as $11,000 or more on their pet in that pet's lifetime-and that's one of the more conservative figures! This country definitely has the most spoiled dogs in the world. But are they the happiest?

My answer, sadly, is no.

***from* Dog Training Basics**

**Miriam Field-Babineau**

Dogs go through many physical and social stages. The best training time is from two to four months of age, because their minds are like sponges soaking up all the experiences, making them both impressionable and responsive. Everything they learn at this age will remain with them throughout their lives.

Several things are happening during this formative time. First, they are acclimating to their new family pack. Second, their baby teeth are being replaced by their permanent teeth. This is a very "oral" time, just as it would be for a two-year-old human. Everything goes in the mouth to discover whether it might be edible or fun to play with.

10 The first year of a pup's social development can be likened to that of a human from age one to 21. A young puppy (two to four months) is socially similar to a child aged four to seven years. While the attention span may be short, the amount of information learned is at its highest point. The more fun a youngster has while learning, the less resistant he will be to new input as he gets older. Parents also tend to be more tolerant of mistakes, allowing disruption and incorrect responses to some extent, in order to encourage the correct response.

This is the best time to begin training. Although the pup's attention span and tolerance of work will be short, you will make more progress. Keeping the 20 training session short and fun will yield the best responses.

In dog packs, domestic or wild, older dogs tolerate a variety of indiscretions on the part of the younger pack members. They understand the puppies have no knowledge of the social order. Through socialization with other pack members, puppies learn which dogs are dominant or submissive. A pup will begin as a subordinate but is driven, through instinct, to work his way up the hierarchical ladder, testing other pack members. As he reaches adolescence, the other canines will begin putting him in his place with quick, decisive reprimands. As the dog gets older, the reprimands will become increasingly firmer.

Just as the puppy learns social behaviors from his dog pack, he must also 30 learn the proper behavior in his new family pack. He will look to you for guidance, seeing you as leader. If you are consistent, reinforcing all proper behaviors and correcting the bad ones, your puppy will be happy to comply. He won't know any other way.

A puppy from five to six months of age is similar to a preadolescent child. He begins to experience hormonal changes, as well as having enormous teething pain with his back teeth coming in. This is when the worst chewing begins. There is also a marked increase in activity, although the attention span remains short.

When your puppy reaches six to seven months of age, he has entered his
40 most difficult developmental period. The hormones are in full swing, making the dog do things that he *knows* are incorrect. Most of the dog's dominance testing occurs at this time, occasionally making the animal difficult to live with. His energy level is very high, causing lots of mischievous behavior-much the same as you might expect from a human teenager.

At eight to ten months, your dog will still be testing your authority. However, if you have maintained your dominant position and consistency up to this point, you will see a slow decrease in the difficult behavior. Remain watchful, however, for devious behavior that occurs behind your back.

By the time your pet reaches ten months the teething is over, he understands
50 his environment, and will behave properly most of the time. You can expect to experience a few bad days now and then.

Throughout this developmental period there are several ages in particular that you should be aware of. The ages four months and nine months present certain behaviors that can ultimately lead to difficulties later on. These are fear imprint periods. During this time, any bad experiences are imprinted on the canine's brain, causing a phobic reaction throughout its life. It is, therefore, particularly important to make sure all experiences are positive and enjoyable, especially the training.

## COMPREHENSION

**Directions** Answer the following questions about the excerpt from *Cesar's Way.*

**27.** From what the author says about American dogs in lines 1–3, you can infer that he

**A.** dislikes American dogs
**B.** helps uniquely needy dogs
**C.** misses dogs he knew in Mexico
**D.** understands how dogs feel

**28.** Monitor your understanding of lines 5–7. According to the author, American dogs struggle with

**A.** owners who treat them like people
**B.** the same issues all other dogs face
**C.** owners who refuse to train them
**D.** the destructiveness of dog packs

**29.** The author's method for training dogs is different from that of other trainers because the author

**A.** gives dogs whatever they want
**B.** corrects a dog's bad behavior
**C.** makes dogs want to obey him
**D.** uses touch instead of commands

**30.** Which quotation from the excerpt expresses the author's opinion?

**A.** "As a kid in Mexico, I watched *Lassie* and *Rin Tin Tin* and dreamed of becoming the world's greatest dog 'trainer.'" (lines 8–9)
**B.** "I deal with dog psychology: trying to connect with the dog's mind and natural instincts" (lines 12–13)
**C.** "In America, most pet owners spoil their dogs and give them constant affection, thinking that this is enough" (lines 25–26)
**D.** "American dog owners pamper their pets with such things as $5,700 green crocodile leather travel bags" (lines 33–34)

**31.** Monitor your understanding of lines 15–18. According to the author, problems with dog behavior stem from

**A.** poor training
**B.** the pack's power
**C.** difficult dogs
**D.** the dog's owner

**32.** Which statement best describes the author's position in lines 22–27?

**A.** American dogs want to be leaders.
**B.** Dogs need more than just affection.
**C.** People want to dominate their dogs.
**D.** People should give dogs more affection.

**33.** According to the author, what effect does constant affection have on a dog?

**A.** It makes a dog mean and aggressive.
**B.** Dogs become confused and anxious.
**C.** It upsets a dog's natural balance.
**D.** Dogs no longer obey commands.

**34.** Which quotation from the excerpt expresses one of the author's opinions?

**A.** "The concept of a 'pack' is ingrained in your dog's DNA." (line 22)
**B.** "In a pack, there are only two roles" (lines 22–23)
**C.** "Over the past ten years, the pet industry has doubled in size" (lines 31–32)
**D.** "This country definitely has the most spoiled dogs in the world." (lines 37–38)

**35.** Which statement is a fact based on the information in the excerpt?

**A.** In America, there are more than 65 million pet dogs.
**B.** American dog-owners are harming their pets.
**C.** Usually the owner, not the dog, is the problem.
**D.** Americans do not know how to speak to their dogs.

**36.** Which sentence best describes the writer's position on American dogs?

**A.** Dogs in America need more time with their packs.
**B.** American owners should take better care of their dogs.
**C.** Dogs in America are more aggressive than dogs in Mexico.
**D.** American dogs have lost the ability simply to be dogs.

## COMPREHENSION

**Directions** Answer the following questions about the excerpt from *Dog Training Basics.*

**37.** What causes puppies to be easily trained when they are from two to four months old?

**A.** They are too young to have long attention spans.
**B.** Puppies at this age are very responsive and impressionable.
**C.** They are too young to know their place in a pack.
**D.** Puppies at this age are more interested in having fun.

**38.** How does the author compare and contrast two- to four-month-old puppies and two-year-old humans in lines 5–9?

**A.** It is a formative time for puppies, but not for humans.
**B.** Both puppies and humans are acclimating to their packs.
**C.** It is a very "oral" time for puppies, but not for humans.
**D.** Both puppies and humans want to put things in their mouths.

**39.** From the description of young children and their parents in lines 13–17, you can infer that

**A.** puppies always have fun learning
**B.** children are capable of behaving perfectly
**C.** children must be trained like puppies
**D.** puppies' mistakes should be tolerated

**40.** Monitor your understanding of lines 20–28. According to the author, older dogs in a pack socialize puppies by

**A.** reprimanding them more as they get older
**B.** allowing them to make many mistakes
**C.** biting them more and more firmly
**D.** rewarding their aggressive behavior

**41.** What causes a puppy to chew between the ages of six and seven months?

**A.** the puppy's rebelliousness
**B.** great pain from teething
**C.** an increase in activity level
**D.** the puppy's hormonal changes

**42.** Which word in lines 39–42 shows that the author uses chronological order?

**A.** when
**B.** period
**C.** Most
**D.** occasionally

**43.** According to the chronological order in the article, a dog should be fully trained by the age of

**A.** two months
**B.** five months
**C.** ten months
**D.** one year

**44.** Which inference can you make from the author's advice in lines 52–58?

**A.** Four- to nine-month-old puppies are very difficult.
**B.** It is helpful to be very strict when training puppies.
**C.** Four- to nine-month-old puppies are highly phobic.
**D.** It is important to keep puppies from being frightened.

**45.** Which statement best describes the writer's position on dog training?

**A.** Dogs can be trained only by using the language of the pack.
**B.** Training should start early and stay consistent and positive.
**C.** Dogs will misbehave no matter how well they are trained.
**D.** Training is most effective when it uses affection and rewards.

## COMPREHENSION

**Directions** Answer these questions about both selections.

**46.** Which statement best describes the difference between the two authors' methods of training dogs?

**A.** Cesar Millan uses the power of the pack, but Miriam Fields-Babineau does not.

**B.** Miriam Fields-Babineau focuses on dogs, and Cesar Millan focuses on owners.

**C.** Cesar Millan rehabilitates dogs, and Miriam Fields-Babineau trains puppies.

**D.** Miriam Fields-Babineau accepts bad behavior, but Cesar Millan does not.

**47.** Which sentence best synthesizes ideas from both selections about the proper relationship between dogs and owners?

**A.** Owners should maintain a dominant position with their dogs.

**B.** Dogs will misbehave no matter how their owners treat them.

**C.** Owners should always give their dogs unlimited affection.

**D.** Dogs should never be pampered with expensive things.

## Written Response

### SHORT RESPONSE

**Directions** Write two or three sentences to answer each question on a separate sheet of paper.

**48.** Describe two chronological stages of puppy development from the excerpt from *Dog Training Basics.*

**49.** According to the two excerpts, what causes dogs to misbehave? Support your response with one detail from each selection.

### EXTENDED RESPONSE

**Directions** Write a short paragraph to answer this question on a separate sheet of paper.

**50.** Synthesize information from the two excerpts to explain the role of the pack in dog behavior. Support your response with details from both selections.

## Vocabulary

**Directions** Read the dictionary entry and answer the questions that follow. The line numbers will help you find the words in "If I Forget Thee, Oh Earth . . ."

> abandon (ə-băn′dən) *v.* 1. To withdraw one's support or help from; desert. 2. To give up by leaving or ceasing to operate or inhabit. 3. To surrender one's claim to or right to; give up entirely. 4. To cease trying to continue. 5. To yield completely, as to an emotion. *n.*1.Unbounded enthusiasm. 2. A complete surrender of inhibitions. **Synonyms:** relinquish, resign, give up, forgo, surrender, leave, quit, evacuate, desert, maroon, discard

**1.** Which definition best matches the meaning of the word *abandoned* as it is used in lines 35–36?

**A.** verb definition 1
**B.** verb definition 2
**C.** verb definition 3
**D.** verb definition 4

**2.** In which sentence is *abandon* used as a noun?

**A.** He danced with abandon when he heard his favorite song.
**B.** He could not abandon the dance floor until it was over.
**C.** They wanted to abandon him before the song ended.
**D.** When it finished, he was ready to abandon the dance.

**3.** Which synonym best matches the meaning of the word *abandoned* as it is used in lines 35–36?

**A.** resign
**B.** surrender
**C.** quit
**D.** maroon

**4.** Which synonym best matches the meaning of the word *abandon* as it is used in the following sentence?
We should abandon this sinking ship right away.

**A.** give up
**B.** evacuate
**C.** surrender
**D.** discard

**Directions** Use context clues and your knowledge of literal and figurative meanings to answer the following questions about words from "If I Forget Thee, Oh Earth . . ."

**5.** Which is the most likely meaning of *burning* in lines 25?

**A.** on fire
**B.** very hot
**C.** melting
**D.** darkened

**6.** Which is the most likely meaning of the phrase *comb the stars* in lines 62?

**A.** blend into the sky
**B.** hide stars from view
**C.** glow with starlight
**D.** be as high as the stars

**7.** Which is the most likely meaning of the phrase *called to his heart* in line 90?

**A.** communicated to him in words
**B.** made his heart beat faster
**C.** caused an emotional reaction
**D.** made him feel a great sorrow

**8.** Which is the most likely meaning of the phrase *oasis of life* in lines 117–118?

**A.** only place anything survives
**B.** body of water in a desert
**C.** warm and comfortable home
**D.** place to escape one's cares

**Directions** Use context clues and your knowledge of connotation and denotation to answer the following questions.

**9.** The denotation of *blinding* in line 26 of "If I Forget Thee, Oh Earth . . ." is "depriving of sight." Which phrase best describes its connotation?

**A.** dangerous
**B.** destructive
**C.** awesome
**D.** beautiful

**10.** The denotation of *steady* in line 35 of "If I Forget Thee, Oh Earth . . ." is "fixed." Which word best describes its connotation?

**A.** eternal
**B.** weak
**C.** flickering
**D.** bright

**11.** The denotation of *issue* in line 16 of the excerpt from *Cesar's Way* is "essential point." Which word best describes its connotation?

**A.** debate
**B.** problem
**C.** question
**D.** confusion

**12.** The denotation of *pamper* in line 33 of the excerpt from *Cesar's Way* is "give excessive care and attention." Which word best describes its connotation?

**A.** fatten
**B.** discipline
**C.** encourage
**D.** spoil

**Directions** Use context clues and your knowledge of Latin roots to answer the following questions about words in the excerpt from *Dog Training Basics.*

**13.** The Latin word *similis* means "like." What is the most likely meaning of *similar* in line 12?

**A.** identical to
**B.** fond of
**C.** growing faster than
**D.** related in nature

**14.** The Latin word *rumpere* means "to break," and the prefix *dis-* means "apart." The word *disruption* in line 15 most likely means

**A.** interruption or confusion
**B.** separation or division
**C.** anger or fighting
**D.** mistakes or errors

**15.** The Latin word *ordinare* means "to set in order," and the prefix *sub-* means "under." The word *subordinate* in line 23 most likely means

**A.** someone who moves up
**B.** a very orderly person
**C.** someone of lower rank
**D.** a disorganized person

**16.** The Latin word *dominari* means "to rule over." What is the most likely meaning of *dominance* in line 39?

**A.** aggression
**B.** authority
**C.** weakness
**D.** measurement

## Writing and Grammar

**Directions** Read this short story and answer the questions that follow.

(1) It all started when his owner, Lee, started her new job. (2) Life had been good before that. (3) Lee took him for walks. (4) She played with him. (5) She gave him attention. (6) Now, every morning, she tied him to a run in the backyard and left him there all day. (7) Sometimes she didn't get home until night.

(8) Cody was a beautiful reddish color and had deep brown eyes. (9) Even though he was small—only 18 pounds—he knew he was handsome and loved to flaunt his long fur and gorgeous tail. (10) He liked other dogs and loved being around people, but running and playing ball was his favorite things in the world. (11) No matter where Lee threw that ball. (12) Cody would catch it and bring it back.

(13) Now, everything was different, and Cody didn't like it. (14) Being in the yard all day by himself were just plain boring. (15) There was nothing to do but dig holes. (16) That only made Lee angry. (17) He tried to play, but it was hard to play all by himself. (18) He had to do something. (19) He had to try barking.

(20) No one paid attention when he started barking. (21) He barked some more. (22) Soon, he was barking all day long. (23) People in the area were not happy with all the noise. (24) Cody thought, "I'm just going to keep on barking, no matter how hoarse and sore my throat gets. (25) "If I keep on barking, someone is bound to notice and come play with me."

(26) One day an irritated neighbor, Thelma, called the police. (27) "You've got to stop this dog from barking!" she told them. (28) The police contacted the owner. (29) They told her she must control her dog. (30) Nothing happened. (31) Thelma decided to see Cody's owner. (32) Because Thelma was upset when she arrived. (33) Lee took her outside to meet Cody. (34) Cody ran right up to Thelma with the ball in his mouth, asking her to throw it for him. (35) It was almost love at first sight. (36) "What a beautiful dog!" Thelma thought. (37) "If someone could get him to stop barking, he would probably make a wonderful pet. (38) I wonder if I could help."

(39) Thelma telephoned Lee. (40) "I'd like to adopt Cody on a trial basis" Thelma said with some hesitation. (41) "I think maybe he misses being around people during the day, and I work at home. (42) Would you let me try?"

(43) Lee breathed a sigh of relief. (44) "Oh, I know he's been unhappy since I started this job. (45) Cody and I would both be grateful."

(46) So Cody got what he needed. (47) With Thelma, he can walk and play every day. (48) He's a very good dog again.

**1.** Choose the best sentence to add to the beginning of paragraph 1 to introduce the character of Cody.

**A.** Once there was a dog whose name was Cody.

**B.** Cody was a good dog, but then things changed.

**C.** Cody was happiest when Lee stayed at home.

**D.** When Lee wanted to get a dog, she found Cody.

**2.** Choose the best way to combine sentences 3, 4, and 5.

**A.** Lee took him for walks, she played with him, and she gave him attention.

**B.** Lee took him for walks and played with him. She gave him attention.

**C.** Lee took him for walks, played with him, and gave him attention.

**D.** Lee took him for walks, played with him, or gave him attention.

**3.** Which words in the second paragraph provide descriptive detail?

**A.** "beautiful reddish color"

**B.** "he was handsome"

**C.** "He liked other dogs"

**D.** "his favorite things"

**4.** To maintain subject verb-agreement in sentence 10, you should change "was" to

**A.** am

**B.** were

**C.** is

**D.** have

**5.** Choose the best way to combine the clauses in fragment 11 and sentence 12.

**A.** No matter where Lee threw that ball; but Cody would catch it and bring it back.

**B.** No matter where Lee threw that ball, and Cody would catch it and bring it back.

**C.** No matter where Lee threw that ball; Cody would catch it and bring it back.

**D.** No matter where Lee threw that ball, Cody would catch it and bring it back.

**6.** To maintain subject verb-agreement in sentence 14, you should change "were" to

**A.** are

**B.** is

**C.** was

**D.** would

**7.** Which sentence best helps introduce the story's plot?

**A.** sentence 8

**B.** sentence 10

**C.** sentence 13

**D.** sentence 15

**8.** Choose the best way to vary the structures of sentences 18 and 19.

**A.** He had to do something. Finally, he decided to try barking.

**B.** Something had to be done. That something was barking.

**C.** He had to do something. He had to try something like barking.

**D.** There was something to be done. There was barking to be done.

**9.** Choose the best way to combine sentences 20 and 21.

**A.** No one paid attention when he started barking, and he barked some more.
**B.** No one paid attention when he started barking, so he barked some more.
**C.** No one paid attention when he started barking, but he barked some more.
**D.** No one paid attention when he started barking, when he barked some more.

**10.** The words "hoarse and sore" in sentence 24 appeal to your sense of

**A.** sight
**B.** sound
**C.** taste
**D.** touch

**11.** Choose the correct way to punctuate the dialogue in sentence 25.

**A.** If I keep on barking, someone is bound to notice and come play with me.
**B.** If I keep on barking, someone is bound to notice and come play with me."
**C.** "If I keep on barking, someone is bound to notice and come play with me".
**D.** "If I keep on barking, someone is bound to notice and come play with me.

**12.** In sentences 24 and 25, the writer reveals that the character Cody is

**A.** determined to get attention
**B.** independent and stubborn
**C.** obnoxious and irritating
**D.** extremely well-behaved

**13.** Choose the best way to vary the lengths of sentences 28, 29, and 30.

**A.** The police contacted Lee. They told her that she must control her dog, but nothing happened.
**B.** The police contacted the owner. They told her to control her dog. Nothing happened after that.
**C.** Nothing happened when they contacted the owner. The police told her she must control her dog.
**D.** Then the police contacted Lee. They told her to control her dog. However, nothing happened.

**14.** Choose the best word or phrase to add to the beginning of sentence 31 to make the sequence of events clearer.

**A.** Someday
**B.** Finally
**C.** However
**D.** Before that

**15.** Choose the best way to combine the clauses in fragment 32 and sentence 33.

**A.** Thelma was upset when she arrived, and Lee took her outside to meet Cody.
**B.** Although Thelma was upset when she arrived, Lee took her outside to meet Cody.
**C.** Thelma was upset when she arrived, because Lee took her outside to meet Cody.
**D.** Because Thelma was upset when she arrived, Lee took her outside to meet Cody.

**16.** What do Thelma's thoughts and dialogue in the fifth paragraph reveal about her character?

**A.** Because she works at home, she is often lonely.

**B.** Although she does not like dogs, she puts up with Cody.

**C.** She does not have a dog, but she wants one.

**D.** Although she gets irritated, she is kindhearted.

**17.** Choose the best word or phrase to add to the beginning of sentence 39 to make the sequence of events clearer.

**A.** The next day

**B.** Nevertheless

**C.** One day

**D.** Whenever

**18.** Choose the correct way to punctuate the dialogue in sentence 40.

**A.** I'd like to adopt Cody on a trial basis, Thelma said with some hesitation.

**B.** "I'd like to adopt Cody on a trial basis," Thelma said with some hesitation.

**C.** "I'd like to adopt Cody on a trial basis, Thelma said with some hesitation."

**D.** "I'd like to adopt Cody on a trial basis." Thelma said with some hesitation.

**19.** In which sentence does the story reach its resolution?

**A.** sentence 38

**B.** sentence 41

**C.** sentence 42

**D.** sentence 45

**20.** The writer concludes the story by

**A.** Telling why Cody finally stopped barking

**B.** showing that Thelma was a good owner

**C.** telling how Cody's problems were solved

**D.** explaining that Lee was happy for Cody

## Writing

**Directions** Read the following quotation. Then read the prompt that follows and complete the writing activity.

> "For those who have seen the Earth from space, and for the hundreds and perhaps thousands more who will, the experience most certainly changes your perspective."
>
> Donald Williams

**Prompt:** Write an interpretive essay about "If I Forget Thee, Oh Earth . . ." Explain how Marvin changes his perspective after he sees Earth. How does viewing Earth affect the way Marvin sees life in the Colony? Use details from the story to support your ideas.

**Reminders**

- Be sure your writing does what the prompt asks.
- Include a thesis statement that identifies the key points of the essay.
- Summarize the interpretation in a conclusion and tell why the story is interesting or important.
- Use precise language to examine and explain the work.
- Check for correct grammar, spelling, and punctuation.

# Benchmark Test 3

## Reading Comprehension

**Directions** Read the following selections. Then answer the questions that follow.

### Baucis and Philemon

**A Retelling**

Long ago in a land called Phrygia, an old couple lived in a tiny cottage among gently rolling hills. Baucis and Philemon lived modestly and without complaint. Their marriage was sound, and their love for each other remained as strong as it had been on their wedding day.

One day Jupiter, king of the gods, traveled to Earth to test the Phrygians. Disguised as mortals, he and Mercury, the messenger god, walked from one home to the next asking for shelter. At each home, the Phrygians heartlessly turned the gods away. Finally, the gods came to the cottage of Baucis and Philemon, where the couple welcomed the strangers warmly. After arranging a
10 place for their guests to rest, the couple prepared a meal. Baucis and Philemon brought out their finest dishes and carefully set the table, paying attention to even the most minute details. As the meal began, Philemon poured the wine. To his surprise, he saw that the bottle refilled itself. Frightened, he and Baucis apologized for being poor hosts, but Jupiter stopped them. "We caused the wine to be replenished," he said, "for we are gods. We came to Phrygia to test the kindness of its citizens. You and Baucis alone have passed. The rest will be punished as they deserve."

Baucis and Philemon followed the gods up a nearby hill. Upon reaching the top, they were shocked to see that a lake stood where their neighbors' houses
20 had been. The couple wept, but when they looked closer, they saw that their own cottage had been transformed into a temple with a roof of glimmering gold. "Worthy couple," said Jupiter, "we thank you for your generosity. Name what it is you desire and it shall be yours."

The couple spoke privately for a moment. Then Philemon said, "We wish to be guardians of this temple and to serve you for the rest of our days. Also, we wish never to be separated, even in death."

In the years that followed, Baucis and Philemon cared for the temple and served the gods faithfully. One day, Baucis noticed leaves sprouting from Philemon's hair. Philemon turned to Baucis and saw her wrinkled skin turning
30 to bark. Realizing that their end was drawing near, they bid each other farewell. At that moment, Philemon was transformed into a sturdy oak and Baucis turned into a graceful linden. The couple's wish was fulfilled, for the two trees grew from a single trunk. For centuries, people have marveled at the intertwined trees, a symbol of the devoted couple that passed the test of the gods.

**Pirate Grace**

**Retold by Richard Walker**

Grace O'Malley was no ordinary pirate; she was a member of the O'Malley family, a powerful Irish clan who owned several castles and a mighty fleet of merchant ships. Grace liked nothing better than to be out on the high seas, and when she set sail, everyone on the west coast of Ireland recognized her, for she was famous across land and sea.

One spring evening, Grace was a long way from home when she began to feel particularly tired and hungry. She and her men were on their way back from a long trading expedition; the ship's supply of food had run low and the crew were soaked to the skin by heavy rain. Grace needed a break and a meal. 10 So when she saw the lights of Howth glittering in the distance, she ordered her helmsman to sail into the harbor; the castle there would be as good a place as any for her and her men to stop awhile.

Now in those days, it was the custom for all Gaelic chieftains to offer hospitality to any member of another friendly clan who was passing through their territory. But when Grace and her men approached the castle gates, they were surprised to find them locked and barred.

"Is anyone home?" Grace bellowed, and she rattled on the gates until a servant came running up.

"Who is it?" called a timid voice from the other side of the gate.

20 "It's Grace O'Malley come to visit His Lordship. Go and tell your master he has some visitors. We're wet and hungry and we need a decent meal. Be quick about it, now!"

The servant did not need to be asked twice. He had never met Grace, but he knew it would not be wise to fall out with her. So he hurried away through the corridors of the castle to announce her arrival.

In the dining room, the Lord of Howth was about to start his evening meal. The table was groaning with succulent meats.

"Excuse me, my lord. Grace O'Malley is at the door. She wants to come in and dine with you. Shall I bring her to you?"

30 But his master's face darkened. "Certainly not!" he roared. "Can't you see I'm eating? Tell her I'm too busy to be disturbed. Besides, it's almost nighttime. She'll have to go away."

"But . . ."

"But what?"

"But surely we should do something for her. After all, isn't she the most famous pirate in the land? It wouldn't do to fall out with her; it wouldn't do at all."

"Do you think I'm frightened of Grace O'Malley? Humph! Tell her to clear off and stop standing there shaking in your socks! Now, let me enjoy my 40 meal in peace."

With that, the lord picked up his knife and started to carve a juicy side of beef for himself.

The poor servant scuttled nervously back to the front door. He knew how dangerous Grace could be. He had even heard a rumor that she slept with a rope that led from her favorite ship to her big toe. In the event of any trouble, a pull on the rope would bring her running. So he stood well back from the gates and called out:

"I'm sorry, Mistress Grace. My master says that he is too busy to see you. Can you come another time perhaps?"

50 "Another time? Doesn't he know that it's pouring rain? What's he doing that's so important? Has he forgotten the rule of hospitality?"

Even with the gate between them, the servant was so scared that he blurted out the truth:

"He's in the middle of his dinner, Miss. He says he wants to enjoy it in peace and quiet."

"He's having a meal!" Grace roared back. "And he won't share it! Well, he may live to regret it!"

Then she spun around on her heels and led her crew back down to the harbor. Through the half-light, she could see a young boy dragging his boat 60 onto the beach, alongside her own. Grace stopped in her tracks.

"Who are you?" she demanded.

"I live here," the boy answered simply. "This is my father's castle. Who are you?"

Without stopping to explain, Grace seized the lad and dragged him onto her boat. The boy kicked and screamed and tried to bite, but she was more than a match for him. She used an old rope to bind his arms and legs, and a kerchief to gag him. Now she had a hostage that would bring the Lord of Howth to his senses! Swiftly and silently, Grace and her men sailed out of the harbor. They kept sailing right through the night until they came to Clare Island Castle, the 70 O'Malleys' stronghold.

Back at Howth, no one could understand what had happened to the lord's heir; but the servant who had answered the gate to Grace had his suspicions. Search parties were sent up and down the coast, but although the boy's rowing boat was found safely moored, there was no sign of the child. The Lord of Howth was beside himself with fear. What had happened to his beloved son? Had he been drowned, kidnapped or murdered?

He did not have to wait long to find out. After a few days, a message was delivered to the castle. "If you wish to see your son alive," it read, "Grace O'Malley invites you to visit him at her home on Clare Island."

80 Now the Lord of Howth regretted his folly, for the waters around Clare Island were known to be treacherous and many sailors had lost their lives on the rocks there. Before he embarked, he found a local fisherman to act as his guide. The fisherman's boat bobbed like a cork on the waves: the Lord of Howth turned green and then he turned grey. At last, the fisherman steered the boat safely into the bay. A servant greeted them and led them in solemn silence to meet Grace.

The Lord of Howth entered with as much dignity as he could muster. He was sick as a dog and his legs were nearly collapsing beneath him, but he looked Grace O'Malley straight in the eye:

90 "Forgive me for sending you away," he said. "Name your price and whatever it is, I shall pay it. Only let me take my dear son home with me!"

Grace looked back at him. She was still smarting with fury, but she felt sorry for the man, and for his child. She smiled quietly, holding his gaze.

"I don't want your money, or your son," she replied slowly. "Instead, I demand an apology . . ."

"You have it, you have it!"

". . . and not just an apology, but a vow."

"Yes?"

"From this day on, the doors of your castle must never be barred to anyone

100 looking for shelter. Not only that . . . in future, you must always lay a spare place at your dining table in case anyone should need it."

Then the Lord of Howth bowed his head and made the vow. His son was returned to him, safe and well, and Grace even offered him a meal before they left.

Maybe the Lord of Howth had got away with his foolishness lightly, but he honored his promise and so, in his turn, did his son. In fact, I am told that even to this day, there is always a spare place at the dinner table of his castle.

## COMPREHENSION

**Directions** Answer the following questions about "Baucis and Philemon."

**1.** The setting at the beginning of the myth is a

**A.** hilltop **C.** temple
**B.** cottage **D.** lake

**2.** Lines 1–4 create a mood that is

**A.** hopeful **C.** peaceful
**B.** silly **D.** mysterious

**3.** Which cultural value do Baucis and Philemon represent in lines 3–4?

**A.** devotion **C.** bravery
**B.** hard work **D.** generosity

**4.** Which plot stage do lines 5–8 contain?

**A.** exposition **C.** climax
**B.** rising action **D.** falling action

**5.** Which lines from the myth help you visualize the scene in which Baucis and Philemon prepare a meal for the gods?

**A.** "where the couple welcomed the strangers warmly" (line 9)
**B.** "brought out their finest dishes and carefully set the table" (line 11)
**C.** "paying attention to even the most minute details" (lines 11–12)
**D.** "apologized for being poor hosts, but Jupiter stopped them" (line 14)

**6.** The gods turn the neighborhood houses into a lake because they want to

**A.** provide water for the temple
**B.** beautify the Phrygian landscape
**C.** impress Baucis and Philemon
**D.** punish the citizens of Phrygia

## COMPREHENSION

**Directions** Answer the following questions about "Pirate Grace."

**7.** Which part of the plot do lines 1–5 contain?

**A.** exposition **C.** climax
**B.** rising action **D.** falling action

**8.** Which character trait best describes Grace in lines 50–70?

**A.** calm **C.** threatening
**B.** forgiving **D.** intelligent

**9.** Which character trait best describes the Lord of Howth's servant?

**A.** crafty
**B.** industrious
**C.** loyal
**D.** fearful

**10.** Which words in lines 58–79 show that the paragraphs are written in chronological order?

**A.** down to the harbor, alongside her own
**B.** onto her boat, Back at Howth
**C.** through the night, After a few days
**D.** onto the beach, up and down the coast

**11.** Reread lines 64–72 and monitor your understanding. The Lord of Howth's servant suspects that

**A.** the Lord of Howth's son has run away from home
**B.** Pirate Grace has kidnapped the Lord of Howth's son
**C.** the Lord of Howth's son is alive but lost at sea
**D.** Pirate Grace wants to take over the Lord of Howth's throne

**12.** Which statement is one possible theme of "Pirate Grace"?

**A.** It takes courage to apologize.
**B.** Kindness is its own reward.
**C.** Trust is a dangerous thing.
**D.** Friendship is better than riches.

### COMPREHENSION

**Directions** Answer these questions about both selections.

**13.** Which cultural value do both the myth and the legend uphold?

**A.** Be courageous in the face of danger.
**B.** Love your partner always and forever.
**C.** Treat guests with warmth and kindness.
**D.** Never resolve disputes with violence.

**14.** Jupiter, Mercury, and Pirate Grace inflict punishment on others because they are

**A.** kidnapped by mortals
**B.** spoken to rudely
**C.** disobeyed by others
**D.** refused shelter

## Written Response

### SHORT RESPONSE

**Directions** Write two or three sentences to answer each question on a separate sheet of paper.

**15.** Explain two cultural values that "Baucis and Philemon" and "Pirate Grace" share. Support your response with details from both selections.

**16.** Describe one of the conflicts in "Pirate Grace." Identify it as an internal or an external conflict, and explain your reasoning.

### EXTENDED RESPONSE

**Directions** Write a short paragraph to answer this question on a separate sheet of paper.

**17.** Identify a universal theme that "Baucis and Philemon" and "Pirate Grace" share. Support your response with details from both stories.

## Reading Comprehension

**Directions** Read the following selections. Then answer the questions that follow.

### Hound on the Church Porch

**Robert P. Tristram Coffin**

The farmer knew each time a friend went past
Though he was deep in Sunday and his eyes
Were on the preacher or the azure squares
The high church sashes cut out of the skies
5 And on the dark blue serge upon his thighs.

Every time a man the farmer knew
Went by upon the road, the farmer's hound
On the church's wooden porch outside
Would thump his tail and make a pleasant sound,
10 His tail struck every time that it went round.

The farmer knew how well he knew each friend
Going by, he counted up the score;
If the passer-by were a plain friend,
There would be three thumps, or maybe four,
15 But if it was a good friend, it was more.

That would be Sam Rogers passing now,
And that would be Dave Merryman, all right,
For the hound-dog's joy flowed down his tail
And made it pound the planks with all its might,
20 He could not stop it going for delight.

The man in church sat back and glowed all through,
He heard the sermon, but it did not hide
The rhythm of the comforting old hymn
Of friendship that was going on outside,
25 And every inch of him filled out with pride.

**A Man in Our Village**

**Leslie Norris**

A man in our village,
a village high in the hills,
often among clouds,
a poor village with little money,
5 this man had a dog.

She was not a pretty dog.
Her coat was unkempt black and tan
and she was small and thin.
You wouldn't have looked twice at her—
10 unless you had noticed how closely
she stayed behind the man,
watching his every step, staying
close to his heels, watching him.
It was clear she loved the man.

15 The dog's eyes were brown
and very, very bright. Her name
was Betsy. Someone told me that.
I never heard anyone call her by name,
nobody patted her or fondled her ears.
20 Once a child bent down to speak to her
where she sat near the man
as he spoke to a friend in the street.
But she growled quietly, not in anger,
just to say she didn't want to be spoken to.
25 The man was just a man.

There was a high path over the hills,
a short cut to the next valley.
One day people saw the man and his dog
walk out along the path. It was winter,
30 the hill pools had been solid ice for a month,
the ground was hard as a bone.
The man vanished around a bend
and his dog was as frail behind him
as his winter shadow. And soon it grew dark.

Not only evening dark, not only the natural dusk.
Clouds heavy with snow grew bleakly under the moon
and in an hour the hills, the village,
the white countryside, all lay under the muffling
snow. All night it fell. Everything
40 was altered. All paths were hidden under
that fallen sky. We began to worry
about the man and his little dog.

In the morning we set out over the changed hills,
in a long line, calling one to the other,
to keep in touch. Blue shadows filled
the hollows, and we swung our arms in the cold
and we shouted. All morning we searched
but we did not find them, nor any sign of them.

A bitter wind filled our eyes with tears
50 and we moved slowly, with great weariness,
through the deep snow. We gave up hope,
We stumbled back along the tracks we had made.

But a great shout stopped us. They were found!
We knew they were found by the joy
of the loud call, by the waving of arms
near a crop of rocks. They lay under
what shelter the rocks could have given them
and they were alive. The man could not hear us,
he was insensible with cold. But his little dog
60 had crept and curled herself over his heart
and kept him warm. She had saved his life.
We brought them down, step by step, through snow,
and into a house blazing with comfort.
We praised the little dog, made much of her,
gave her warm milk to drink, for the first time
spoke her name.

When summer came again and the hills
turned kind and pink with heather,
the man sold his dog to a passing visitor.
70 He sold her, although she had saved his life.
Would you have done that, would you?
I didn't think anyone could have done that.



## COMPREHENSION

**Directions** Answer the following questions about "Hound on the Church Porch."

**1.** Which lines in each stanza rhyme?

**A.** first, third, and fifth
**B.** second and fifth only
**C.** second, fourth, and fifth
**D.** fourth and fifth only

**2.** How many stressed syllables are in each line of the poem?

**A.** five
**B.** six
**C.** eight
**D.** ten

**3.** Which word from the poem is an example of onomatopoeia?

**A.** "azure" (line 3)
**B.** "sashes" (line 4)
**C.** "pleasant" (line 9)
**D.** "thumps" (line 14)

**4.** Which type of figurative language does the poet use in lines 23–24?

**A.** personification
**B.** metaphor
**C.** imagery
**D.** simile

## COMPREHENSION

**Directions** Answer the following questions about "A Man in Our Village."

**5.** The rhythm of the words "and she was small and thin" in line 8 is

**A.** alternating unstressed and stressed syllables
**B.** random patterns of stressed and unstressed syllables
**C.** alternating stressed and unstressed syllables
**D.** all stressed syllables and no unstressed syllables

**6.** The repetition of "watching" in lines 12 and 13 emphasizes the dog's

**A.** intelligence
**B.** devotion
**C.** shyness
**D.** courage

**7.** Which line from the poem contains a simile?

**A.** "patted her or fondled her ears" (line 19)
**B.** "she didn't want to be spoken to" (line 24)
**C.** "hill pools had been solid ice" (line 30)
**D.** "the ground was hard as a bone" (line 31)

**8.** Lines 33–34 help you visualize the dog as

**A.** threatening
**B.** fragile
**C.** annoyed
**D.** sluggish

**9.** The imagery in lines 35–42 creates what kind of mood?

**A.** dreadful
**B.** confusing
**C.** worrying
**D.** mysterious

**10.** Which phrase from the poem contains alliteration?

**A.** "a crop of rocks" (line 56)
**B.** "crept and curled" (line 60)
**C.** "blazing with comfort" (line 63)
**D.** "milk to drink" (line 65)

**11.** In lines 67–68, the poet personifies

**A.** pink
**B.** heather
**C.** summer
**D.** hills

**12.** Which sentence best describes the speaker's point of view?

**A.** "Her coat was unkempt black and tan and she was small and thin." (lines 8–9)
**B.** "Not only evening dark, not only the natural dusk." (line 35)
**C.** "All paths were hidden under that fallen sky." (lines 40–41)
**D.** "I didn't think anyone could've done that." (line 72)

## COMPREHENSION

**Directions** Answer these questions about both poems.

**13.** Which sentence tells how the two poems are alike in structure?

**A.** The lines are all of equal length.
**B.** Rhymes are arranged in couplets.
**C.** Lines are arranged in stanzas.
**D.** The rhythm follows a regular pattern.

**14.** Which character trait do the two dogs have in common?

**A.** friendliness
**B.** devotion
**C.** youthfulness
**D.** confidence

# Written Response

## SHORT RESPONSE

**Directions** Write two or three sentences to answer each question.

**15.** Reread lines 11–20 of "Hound on the Church Porch" and monitor your understanding. How does the farmer know that Sam Rogers and Dave Merryman are passing by outside? Use details from the poem to support your answer.

**16.** How does the speaker in "A Man in Our Village" feel about the dog throughout the poem? Use details from the poem to support your answer.

## EXTENDED RESPONSE

**Directions** Write a short paragraph to answer this question on a separate sheet of paper.

**17.** Explain how the imagery in both poems reveals the relationships between the dogs and their owners. Use details from both poems to support your response.

## Reading Comprehension

**Directions** Read the following selections. Then answer the questions that follow.

### Book Review of *The Prairie Builders: Reconstructing America's Lost Grasslands*

*The Prairie Builders* is an exciting and informative book. It begins with a suspenseful scene: a group of people is deliberately starting a large grass fire. A few miles east of Des Moines, Iowa, these workers and volunteers are taking land that has been plowed for cornfields and returning it to its natural condition. They are patiently building a tallgrass prairie full of wildflowers, butterflies, and buffalo, trying to recreate the prairie that existed 150 years ago—before the land was farmed. Author Sneed B. Collard III weaves colorful narrative and vivid description with gorgeous photographs, helpful maps, and informative sidebars. He helps readers visualize the prairies of the mid-1800s, and he
10 illustrates the idea that nature can indeed be restored.

Collard's writing is wonderful. He condenses years of complicated history and conveys scientific information in clear and simple terms. He mentions briefly how the prairie was lost, placing his main emphasis on the narrative of restoration. He makes the narrative personal, using relevant dialogue and letting the participants speak for themselves. He quotes Neal Smith, an Iowa Congressman who helped turn the farmland into a National Wildlife Refuge, and he profiles biologists Pauline Drobney and Diane Debinski. Collard also depicts children working as volunteers, scattering seeds and "dancing" them into the ground.

20 *The Prairie Builders* is useful, beautiful, and inspiring. In addition to the color photographs and maps, Collard includes a number of noteworthy resources, including an index, a glossary of terms, and a list for further reading. Although it was written for children, *The Prairie Builders* will appeal to adults, as well. Collard's work is a smart investment for anyone interested in nature and the environment.

## *from* The Prairie Builders: Reconstructing America's Lost Grassland

**Sneed B. Collard III**

It is a fall day on the Neal Smith National Wildlife Refuge in central Iowa. The weather is cool and the humidity is high. The wind blows gently, creating ideal conditions for what biologist Pauline Drobney and her crew want to do. Still, Pauline wants to double-check that everything and everyone is in place. On her two-way radio, she calls the rest of her team. "How's it look?" she asks. "Everyone ready? The wind staying in check?"

After a pause, a male voice responds. "We're all set."

Pauline takes a deep breath. Then she picks up a smoking can of fuel called a drip torch and shouts to several other people gathered along a meadow's edge.

10 "Let's go!"

Pauline and another crew member begin moving in opposite directions, dripping dabs of burning fuel onto the ground. The dry prairie grasses quickly pick up the flames. Fanned by the day's gentle breezes, a crackling orange wall five, ten, fifteen feet high quickly climbs toward the sky. Men and women carrying tools called "flappers" rush along the line, smothering stray embers that threaten to burn in the wrong direction. Two fire engines and their crews also stand ready, waiting to leap into action if the blaze gets out of control.

But today, the burn goes well. The fire stretches a quarter-, then a half-mile long, consuming any dry plant material in front of it. It churns the raw fuel into

20 a dancing mixture of smoke, flame, and heat as it marches across the meadow.

The fire crew pauses and stares, mesmerized by the flames. But for Pauline and her team, the fire is much more than entertainment. It is a vital step in an experiment that has never been attempted before—the creation from scratch of a large, functioning tallgrass prairie.

### The Vanished Grasslands

The tallgrass prairie that Pauline and her colleagues are trying to create is an ecosystem that has almost completely vanished from the North American continent. Tallgrass prairie once dominated the central part of our nation. According to the National Park Service, it covered 400,000 square miles from

30 Ohio to North Dakota and Minnesota to Texas. An explosion of plant and animal species thrived on this expanse. Grasses up to twelve feet tall fed elk, deer, pronghorn, and between 30 and 75 *million* bison, or buffalo. Native Americans, wolves, grizzly bears, and coyotes hunted this bounty. Thousands of bird and insect species also made their homes here, including hundreds of kinds of butterflies.

Amazingly, when Europeans first saw the prairie, they thought it was a wasteland and called it "The Great American Desert." By the mid–1800s, though, white Americans smartened up. They realized that the deep prairie soils would make world-class farmland. The U.S. government signed a series of 40 treaties with Native American tribes to remove them from prairie lands and resettle them onto small reservations. Later, the government broke many of its promises to the tribes. It wasn't fair, but the treaties opened the way for white settlers and the destruction of the prairie.

By the early 1900s more than 96 percent of America's tallgrass prairie had been turned into farms and grazing lands. In Iowa, the numbers were even more dramatic. Of the 36 million acres of prairie in Iowa, less than *one tenth of one percent* survived the plow. If you imagine that the original prairie was the size of a football field, all that remained was a little patch eight feet long and seven feet wide.

50 Of course, when the prairie disappeared, most prairie plants and animals disappeared with it. And for almost a century, no one seemed to miss them.

**Reawakening**

Beginning in the 1960s, though, many people gained a new concern for tallgrass prairie. They realized that most of the tallgrass prairie had been destroyed, but they began working to protect the little patches—called *prairie remnants*—that remained.

The problem was that most prairie remnants were simply too small to support all of their original plants and animals. Some remnants were a few hundred acres in size. Most were only a few acres or smaller. What were 60 needed were some large prairies—prairies that covered thousands of acres. Prairies that stretched across the horizon.

In the 1980s, a congressman named Neal Smith spearheaded a drive to create just such a large prairie in his home state of Iowa. Iowa had lost more of its original prairie than any other state, and Congressman Smith felt that the children of Iowa deserved to know what their native land had once looked like.

"We looked for five or six years before we found the land," Neal Smith remembers. "Then one day, I received a call from an engineer at Iowa Light and Power. He told me they had decided they were never going to build the nuclear power plant they had planned out at a place called Walnut Creek. He 70 asked if we were interested in the land and I asked him if he could hold it for a day or two."

Congressman Smith rushed to write a bill to purchase the land along with surrounding farmland for a new National Wildlife Refuge. He got his bill passed by Congress that same year, 1989. At first, many people in the National Wildlife Refuge system opposed the idea. After all, other wildlife refuges *already* had wildlife on them, and this refuge was just cornfields. Was it possible to build a prairie from scratch? they wondered. Was it even a smart thing to do?



## COMPREHENSION

**Directions** Answer the following questions about the book review.

**1.** Which words from the first paragraph express the writer's opinion?

**A.** "exciting and informative" (line 1)
**B.** "deliberately starting" (line 2)
**C.** "its natural condition" (line 4)
**D.** "visualize the prairies" (line 9)

**2.** Reread the first paragraph and monitor your understanding. A crew is starting a fire in order to

**A.** prepare the land for planting corn
**B.** get rid of some prairie wildflowers
**C.** restore the prairies of the mid-1800s
**D.** prevent buffalo from taking over

**3.** Which words from the first paragraph help you visualize the natural prairie?

**A.** "A few miles east of Des Moines, Iowa, these" (lines 2–3)
**B.** "taking land that has been plowed for cornfields" (lines 3–4)
**C.** "full of wildflowers, butterflies, and buffalo" (lines 5–6)
**D.** "vivid description with gorgeous photographs" (lines 7–8)

**4.** From lines 9–10, you can conclude that some people

**A.** think that nature is not worth saving
**B.** believe that the prairie is not in danger
**C.** support the destruction of the prairie
**D.** doubt that the prairie can be restored

**5.** Which words from the third paragraph reveal the writer's opinion?

**A.** useful, beautiful, inspiring
**B.** number, resources, further
**C.** index, glossary, adults
**D.** appeal, investment, nature

## COMPREHENSION

**Directions** Answer the following questions about the excerpt from *The Prairie Builders.*

**6.** Which words from the excerpt help you visualize the movement of the fire?

**A.** "dripping dabs of burning fuel onto the ground" (line 12)
**B.** "embers that threaten to burn in the wrong direction" (lines 15–16)
**C.** "leap into action if the blaze gets out of control" (line 17)
**D.** "dancing mixture of smoke, flame, and heat" (line 20)

**7.** According to the excerpt, what once allowed thousands of animal species to thrive on the prairie?

**A.** plentiful water
**B.** tall grasses
**C.** high humidity
**D.** cool weather

**8.** According to lines 26–57, what happened after the new Americans realized that the prairie would make good farmland?

**A.** Europeans declared the surrounding area a wasteland.
**B.** Native Americans were moved to reservations.
**C.** Plant and animal species experienced a population boom.
**D.** People realized that most of the prairies had been destroyed.

**9.** According to the excerpt, what happened when the prairie was opened to white settlers?

**A.** Some prairie land was converted into reservations.
**B.** Prairie land dominated the central part of the country.
**C.** Many prairie plants and animals vanished from the prairie.
**D.** Settlers decided that the prairie was mostly infertile.

**10.** The section entitled "Reawakening" is mainly organized by

**A.** cause and effect
**B.** chronological order
**C.** opinion and support
**D.** comparison and contrast

**COMPREHENSION**

**Directions** Answer these questions about both selections.

**11.** From reading the two selections, you can conclude that both writers

**A.** think that children should not take part in prairie restoration

**B.** oppose the views of Congressman Neal Smith

**C.** agree that people should not try to change nature

**D.** believe that prairie restoration is a worthwhile topic

**12.** By synthesizing both selections, you can tell that the land at Walnut Creek likely

**A.** lost much of its wildlife in the fire

**B.** became a successful tallgrass prairie

**C.** was denied refuge status by Congress

**D.** housed a large nuclear power plant

## Written Response

**SHORT RESPONSE**

**Directions** Write two or three sentences to answer each question on a separate sheet of paper.

**13.** The author of the book review states that *The Prairie Builders* is written for children. Provide two details from the review that support this position.

**14.** What conclusion can you draw about the fire crew's level of experience and preparation from the information in lines 1–26 of the excerpt from *The Prairie Builders*? Include details from the text to support your response.

**EXTENDED RESPONSE**

**Directions** Write a short paragraph to answer this question on a separate sheet of paper.

**15.** Based on the excerpt from *The Prairie Builders,* explain why you agree or disagree with the reviewer's analysis of the book in the second paragraph of the review. Synthesize details from both selections to support your response.

## Vocabulary

**Directions** Use context clues and your knowledge of homographs to answer the following questions.

**1.** Which sentence uses *sound* as it is used in line 3 of "Baucis and Philemon"?

**A.** The captain prepared to sound his horn when he spotted the fishers.
**B.** Her guidance counselor gave her sound advice about how to handle stress.
**C.** Picking up the tuba, he was barely able to produce a constant sound.
**D.** A narrow sound connects the lake with the open ocean.

**2.** What is the likely meaning of *minute* as it is used in line 12 of "Baucis and Philemon"?

**A.** moment
**B.** sixty seconds
**C.** meeting notes
**D.** insignificant

**3.** Which sentence uses *match* as it is used in line 66 of "Pirate Grace"?

**A.** After years of being undefeated, the boxer finally met his match.
**B.** The tennis player lost his first match but won the second and third.
**C.** She looked all over the house but could not find a match to light the candle.
**D.** With their floppy ears and big brown eyes, the puppies made a perfect match.

**4.** What is the meaning of *bay* as it is used in line 85 of "Pirate Grace"?

**A.** opening in a wall
**B.** type of tree
**C.** body of water
**D.** sound made by dogs

**Directions** Read the dictionary entries and answer the questions that follow. The line references will help you find the words in "Pirate Grace."

| **decent** (dĭ-sĕnt′) *adj.* **1.** upstanding or moral. **2.** meeting accepted standards. **3.** kind or obliging. **4.** properly or suitably dressed |
|---|

**5.** Which definition matches the meaning of the word *decent* as it is used in line 21?

**A.** definition 1 **C.** definition 3
**B.** definition 2 **D.** definition 4

**6.** Which word is a synonym for *decent* in the following sentence? She is a decent neighbor and always lends me what I need.

**A.** considerate **C.** fashionable
**B.** ethical **D.** satisfactory

**parties** (pärt′ez) *n., pl.* **1.** social gatherings for pleasure or amusement. **2.** established political groups. **3.** groups of people who take part in an activity. **4.** people involved in a legal proceeding.

**7.** Which definition matches the meaning of the word *parties* as it is used in line 73?

**A.** definition 1
**B.** definition 2
**C.** definition 3
**D.** definition 4

**8.** Which word is a synonym for *parties* in the following sentence? We have two parties in our homeroom each year: one in December and the other in June.

**A.** organizations
**B.** defendants
**C.** partners
**D.** celebrations

**Directions** Use context clues to answer the following questions.

**9.** Which is the most likely meaning of *unkempt* in line 7 of "A Man in Our Village"?

**A.** short
**B.** messy
**C.** thick
**D.** spotted

**10.** Which is the most likely meaning of *insensible* in line 59 of "A Man in Our Village"?

**A.** angry
**B.** tired
**C.** numb
**D.** quiet

**11.** Which is the most likely meaning of *deliberately* in line 2 of the book review of *The Prairie Builders*?

**A.** intentionally
**B.** mysteriously
**C.** fortunately
**D.** peacefully

**12.** Which is the most likely meaning of *depicts* in line 17 of the book review of *The Prairie Builders*?

**A.** studies a subject
**B.** interviews briefly
**C.** praises eagerly
**D.** gives a picture of

**Directions** Use context clues and your knowledge of compound words to answer the following questions.

**13.** Which is the likely definition of *sidebars* in line 9 of the book review of *The Prairie Builders*?

**A.** maps showing additional views of a specialized location

**B.** groups of photographs that appear within a book

**C.** boxes in the margins of a book containing extra information

**D.** lists of helpful words and phrases and their definitions

**14.** Which is the likely definition of *noteworthy* in line 21 of the book review of *The Prairie Builders*?

**A.** winning awards

**B.** attracting fame

**C.** showing examples

**D.** deserving attention

**15.** Which is the likely definition of *wasteland* in line 38 of the excerpt from *The Prairie Builders*?

**A.** useless soil

**B.** dull scenery

**C.** open space

**D.** unsettled territory

**16.** Which is the likely definition of *spearheaded* in line 62 of the excerpt from *The Prairie Builders*?

**A.** sent a message

**B.** acted as a leader

**C.** delivered a speech

**D.** worked as an advisor

## Writing and Grammar

**Directions** Read the cause-and-effect essay and answer the questions that follow.

(1) Last Sunday night, I was doing homework in my room when I heard the weirdest noise I'd ever heard. (2) At first I thought it was my dog, Cricket. (3) She growls when she plays with her toys. (4) I glanced around and saw her staring at the wall, ears perked and tail quivering. (5) "What is it, girl?" I asked. (6) The eerie sound, something between a growl and a cough, was coming from inside the wall! (7) I let out a yelp, and Cricket started yipping loudly. (8) My dad came running. (9) He realized right away what the noise was. (10) The noise turned out to be my fault. (11) While rushing to finish my chores earlier that day. (12) I had neglected to lock the storage shed, which is attached to our house. (13) Then a pesky possum got in the shed and found a small opening in the wall of our house. (14) Before the night was over, my efforts to hurry had caused the disruption of the entire neighborhood, the loss of a good night's sleep, and my forfeiture of a week's allowance.

(15) Stray cats are adopted by our neighbors, the Mitchells. (16) They have one of those special traps that doesn't harm animals. (17) As soon as Dad figured out that the intruder was a possum, he dashed across the street to the Mitchells' house. (18) Running in his pajamas with his hair all a mess was such a funny sight. (19) My mother suffered a fit of laughter and, for a time, was unable to regain her composure. (20) Meanwhile, the commotion had roused some of our neighbors, who were standing in their front yards, wondering what was going on.

(21) It was late when we went to bed. (22) When he got back, Dad and I set the trap and baited it with some canned tuna. (23) When I stumbled into the kitchen for breakfast, and Dad pointed to the back porch. (24) There in the trap was the possum. (25) When it saw me, the possum made the noise and showed its teeth. (26) Dad left for work. (27) Before he left, he carefully slid a bowl of water into the trap.

(28) "When I get home," he said, "we'll drive to Smithson Valley and let it loose. (29) Then, your allowance will be spent by us on materials to repair that hole."

(30) That old saying "Haste makes waste" sure is true. (31) In my rush to finish my chores, I caused a lot of people to lose sleep and gave up a whole week's allowance. (32) Now I know that a few extra seconds can mean a great deal. (33) I won't forget to lock the shed any time soon!

**1.** The introduction is effective because it

**A.** summarizes key points
**B.** asks the reader a question
**C.** presents a logical argument
**D.** grabs the reader's attention

**2.** How might you combine sentence 2 and sentence 3 to form a complex sentence?

**A.** At first I thought it was Cricket, and my dog growls when she plays with her toys.
**B.** At first I thought it was my dog, Cricket, who growls when she plays with her toys.
**C.** At first I thought it was my dog, Cricket; she growls when she plays with her toys.
**D.** At first I thought it was Cricket; my dog growls when she plays with her toys.

**3.** Sentence 6 is an example of which kind of sentence?

**A.** declarative
**B.** imperative
**C.** exclamatory
**D.** interrogative

**4.** Which words in the first paragraph contribute to the essay's informal tone?

**A.** noise, running, small
**B.** fault, opening, hurried
**C.** yelp, yipping, pesky
**D.** chores, rushing, entire

**5.** Choose the best way to combine sentences 8 and 9 to form a compound sentence.

**A.** My dad came running, and he knew right away what the noise was.
**B.** Running, my dad knew right away what the noise was.
**C.** My dad came running he knew right away what the noise was.
**D.** Right away my dad, who was running, knew what the noise was.

**6.** Which transition word belongs at the beginning of sentence 10?

**A.** Nevertheless
**B.** Therefore
**C.** Although
**D.** Unfortunately

**7.** Which line from the essay is a fragment?

**A.** "I glanced around and saw her staring at the wall, ears perked and tail quivering."
**B.** "I let out a yelp, and Cricket started yipping loudly."
**C.** "While rushing to finish my chores earlier that day."
**D.** "They have one of those special traps that doesn't harm animals."

**8.** Sentence 14 is important to the introduction because it

**A.** offers a possible solution to a problem
**B.** establishes a mood of suspense
**C.** identifies a cause-and-effect relationship
**D.** resolves the writer's internal conflict

**9.** Choose the best way to rewrite sentence 15 in the active voice.

**A.** Adoption of cats is done by our neighbors, the Mitchells.
**B.** Cats, adopted by our neighbors, the Mitchells, are stray.
**C.** Stray cats have adoption by the Mitchells, our neighbors.
**D.** The Mitchells, our neighbors, adopt stray cats.

**10.** For the second paragraph to make sense, sentences 15 and 16 should follow

**A.** sentence 17
**B.** sentence 18
**C.** sentence 19
**D.** sentence 20

**11.** Choose the correct way to rewrite sentence 18 to avoid a dangling modifier

**A.** Dad was running in his pajamas with his hair all a mess was such a funny sight.
**B.** Running in Dad's pajamas with his hair all a mess was such a funny sight.
**C.** In his pajamas and with Dad's hair all a mess, he was such a funny sight.
**D.** Running in his pajamas with his hair all a mess, Dad was such a funny sight.

**12.** Sentence 19 does not fit with the rest of the essay because it

**A.** has an inappropriately formal tone
**B.** disproves the writer's thesis
**C.** contains grammatical mistakes
**D.** weakens the cause-and-effect relationship

**13.** Sentence 20 strengthens the cause-and-effect relationship by

**A.** identifying multiple causes
**B.** addressing counterarguments
**C.** providing supporting details
**D.** resolving the main conflict

**14.** Choose the best way to rewrite sentence 21 using precise language.

**A.** It was extremely late when we finally decided to go to bed.
**B.** It was nearly one o'clock when Dad and I went to bed, exhausted.
**C.** It was very late at night when the two of us went to sleep.
**D.** It was a lot later when Dad and I decided to go to bed.

**15.** For the third paragraph to make sense, sentence 22 should come before

**A.** sentence 21
**B.** sentence 24
**C.** sentence 26
**D.** sentence 28

**16.** Which sentence, if added to the third paragraph, would support the cause-and-effect relationship?

**A.** The back porch was bright red with white tables and chairs.
**B.** I woke up to the smells of pancakes and frying bacon.
**C.** The next morning I was so tired that I could barely get out of bed.
**D.** Staying up that late was a new experience for me.

**17.** Choose the best way to rewrite sentence 25 using precise language

**A.** Seeing me, the possum made the noise I had heard before and showed its teeth.
**B.** When it saw me, the possum growled and bared its pointed, yellow teeth.
**C.** When the possum saw me, it made the awful noise and showed me its teeth.
**D.** The possum, when it saw me, made the noise and showed its large teeth.

**18.** Choose the best way to combine sentences 26 and 27 to form a complex sentence.

**A.** Dad left for work, but before he did he carefully slid a bowl of water into the trap.
**B.** Sliding a bowl of water into the trap, Dad carefully left for work.
**C.** Before he left for work, Dad carefully slid a bowl of water into the trap.
**D.** Dad, having left for work, carefully slid a bowl of water into the trap.

**19.** Choose the best way to rewrite sentence 29 in the active voice.

**A.** Then, your allowance on materials to repair that hole will be spent by us.
**B.** Then, we'll spend your allowance on materials to repair that hole.
**C.** Then, materials will be bought by us with your allowance to repair that hole.
**D.** Then, to repair that hole we'll get materials bought by your allowance.

**20.** Choose the best way to rewrite sentence 33 as an interrogative sentence.

**A.** Do you think I'll ever forget to lock the shed again?
**B.** You can bet I won't forget to lock the shed any time soon!
**C.** I wonder how long it will be before I forget to lock the shed.
**D.** It will be a long time before I forget to lock the shed.

## Writing and Grammar

**Directions** Read the following quotation. Then read the prompt that follows and complete the writing activity.

> "I would hope that people, no matter what age, would find something to identify with in my books, pick one up and experience a personal sense of discovery."
>
> Shel Silverstein

**Prompt:** Write a personal response to "A Man in Our Village." Explain why the poem makes you feel a certain way. Silverstein would call these feelings your "personal sense of discovery."
Now write your response. Use the reminders that follow to help you write.

**Reminders**

- Be sure your writing does what the prompt asks.
- Identify your overall response to the poem.
- Support your response with specific details and quotes.
- Use a clear organization and include transitions.
- Check for correct grammar, spelling, and punctuation.

# Benchmark Test 4



## Reading Comprehension

**Directions** Read the following short story. Then answer the questions that follow.

### A Secret For Two

**Quentin Reynolds**

Montreal is a very large city, but, like all large cities, it has some very small streets. Streets, for instance, like Prince Edward Street, which is only four blocks long, ending in a cul-de-sac. No one knew Prince Edward Street as well as did Pierre Dupin, for Pierre had delivered milk to the families on the street for thirty years now.

During the past fifteen years the horse which drew the milk wagon used by Pierre was a large white horse named Joseph. In Montreal, especially in that part of Montreal which is very French, the animals, like children, are often given the names of saints. When the big white horse first came to the
10 Provincale Milk Company, he didn't have a name. They told Pierre that he could use the white horse henceforth. Pierre stroked the softness of the horse's neck; he stroked the sheen of its splendid belly, and he looked into the eyes of the horse.

"This is a kind horse, a gentle and a faithful horse," Pierre said, "and I can see a beautiful spirit shining out of the eyes of the horse. I will name him after good St. Joseph, who was also kind and gentle and faithful and a beautiful spirit."

Within a year Joseph knew the milk route as well as Pierre. Pierre used to boast that he didn't need reins—he never touched them. Each morning Pierre
20 arrived at the stables of the Provincale Milk Company at five o'clock. The wagon would be loaded and Joseph hitched to it. Pierre would call "*Bon jour, vieille ami,*[1]" as he climbed into his seat and Joseph would turn his head and the other drivers would smile and say that the horse would smile at Pierre. Then Jacques, the foreman, would say, "All right, Pierre, go on," and Pierre would call softly to Joseph, "*Avance, mon ami*[2]," and the splendid combination would stalk proudly down the street.

The wagon, without any direction from Pierre, would roll three blocks down St. Catherine Street, then turn right two blocks along Roslyn Avenue: then left, for that was Prince Edward Street. The horse would stop at the first
30 house, allow Pierre perhaps thirty seconds to get down from his seat and put a bottle of milk at the front door and would then go on, skipping two houses and stopping at the third. So down the length of the street. Then Joseph, still

---

1. **Bon jour, vieille ami** French for "Hello, old friend."
2. **Avance, mon ami** French for "Go forward, my friend."

without any direction from Pierre, would turn around and come back along the other side. Yes, Joseph was a smart horse.

Pierre would boast at the stable of Joseph's skill. "I never touch the reins. He knows just where to stop. Why, a blind man could handle my route with Joseph pulling the wagon."

So it went on for years—always the same. Pierre and Joseph both grew old together, but gradually, not suddenly. Pierre's huge walrus mustache was

40 pure white now and Joseph didn't lift his knees so high or raise his head quite as much. Jacques, the foreman of the stables, never noticed that they were both getting old until Pierre appeared one day carrying a heavy walking stick.

"Hey, Pierre," Jacques laughed. "Maybe you got the gout, hey?"

"*Mais oui,* [3] Jacques," Pierre said uncertainly. "One grows old. One's legs get tired."

"You should teach the horse to carry the milk to the front door for you," Jacques told him. "He does everything else."

He knew every one of the forty families he served on Prince Edward Street. The cooks knew that Pierre could neither read nor write, so instead of

50 following the usual custom of leaving a note in an empty bottle if an additional quart of milk was needed they would sing out when they heard the rumble of his wagon wheels over the cobbled street, "Bring an extra quart this morning, Pierre."

"So you have company for dinner tonight," he would call back gaily.

Pierre had a remarkable memory. When he arrived at the stable he'd always remember to tell Jacques, "The Paquins took an extra quart this morning; the Lemoines bought a pint of cream."

Jacques would note these things in a little book he always carried. Most of the drivers had to make out the weekly bills and collect the money, but Jacques,

60 liking Pierre, had always excused him from this task. All Pierre had to do was to arrive at five in the morning, walk to his wagon, which was always in the same spot at the curb, and deliver his milk. He returned some two hours later, got stiffly from his seat, called a cheery "*Au 'voir*[4]" to Jacques and then limped slowly down the street.

One morning the president of the Provincale Milk Company came to inspect the early morning deliveries. Jacques pointed Pierre out to him and said, "Watch how he talks to that horse. See how the horse listens and how he turns his head toward Pierre? See the look in that horse's eyes? You know, I think those two share a secret. I have often noticed it. It is as though they both

---

3. **Mais oui** French for "but yes."
4. **Au 'voir** French for "until we meet again"; "goodbye."

70 sometimes chuckle at us as they go off on their route. Pierre is a good man, *Monsieur*[5] President, but he gets old. Would it be too bold for me to suggest that he be retired and be given perhaps a small pension?" he added anxiously.

"But of course," the president laughed, "I know his record. He has been on this route now for thirty years and never once has there been a complaint. Tell him it is time he rested. His salary will go on just the same."

But Pierre refused to retire. He was panic-stricken at the thought of not driving Joseph every day. "We are two old men," he said to Jacques. "Let us wear out together. When Joseph is ready to retire—then I, too, will quit."

Jacques, who was a kind man, understood. There was something about

80 Pierre and Joseph which made a man smile tenderly. It was as though each drew some hidden strength from the other. When Pierre was sitting in his seat, and when Joseph was hitched to the wagon, neither seemed old. But when they finished their work, then Pierre would limp down the street slowly, seeming very old indeed, and the horse's head would drop and he would walk very wearily to his stall.

Then one morning Jacques had dreadful news for Pierre when he arrived. It was a cold morning and still pitch-dark. The air was like iced wine that morning and the snow which had fallen during the night glistened like a million diamonds piled together.

90 Jacques said, "Pierre, your horse, Joseph, did not wake this morning. He was very old, Pierre, he was twenty-five, and that is like seventy-five for a man."

"Yes," Pierre said, slowly. "Yes. I am seventy-five. And I cannot see Joseph again."

"Of course you can," Jacques soothed. "He is over in his stall, looking very peaceful. Go over and see him."

Pierre took one step forward then turned. "No . . . no . . . you don't understand, Jacques."

Jacques clapped him on the shoulder. "We'll find another horse just as

100 good as Joseph. Why, in a month you'll teach him to know your route as well as Joseph did. We'll . . ."

The look in Pierre's eyes stopped him. For years Pierre had worn a heavy cap, the peak of which came low over his eyes, keeping the bitter morning wind out of them. Now Jacques looked into Pierre's eyes and he saw something which startled him. He saw a dead, lifeless look in them. The eyes were mirroring the grief that was in Pierre's heart and his soul. It was as though his heart and soul had died.

---

5. **Monsieur** French for "mister" or "sir."

"Take today off, Pierre," Jacques said, but already Pierre was hobbling off down the street, and had one been near one would have seen tears streaming
110 down his cheeks and have heard half-smothered sobs. Pierre walked to the corner and stepped into the street. There was a warning yell from the driver of a huge truck that was coming fast and there was a scream of brakes, but Pierre apparently heard neither.

Five minutes later an ambulance driver said, "He's dead. Was killed instantly."

Jacques and several of the milk-wagon drivers had arrived and they looked down at the still figure.

"I couldn't help it," the driver of the truck protested, "he walked right into my truck. He never saw it, I guess. Why, he walked into it as though he was
120 blind."

The ambulance doctor bent down. "Blind? Of course the man was blind. See those cataracts? This man has been blind for five years." He turned to Jacques. "You say he worked for you? Didn't you know he was blind?"

"No . . . no . . ." Jacques said softly. "None of us knew. Only one knew—a friend of his named Joseph . . . . It was a secret, I think, just between those two."



## COMPREHENSION

**Directions** Answer the following questions about "A Secret for Two."

**1.** The main setting of the story is

**A.** the office of Provincale Milk
**B.** a horse farm in Canada
**C.** the house of Pierre Dupin
**D.** a small street in Montreal

**2.** Lines 1–13 represent the story's

**A.** exposition **C.** falling action
**B.** rising action **D.** resolution

**3.** Which word best describes the mood of lines 21–26?

**A.** tense **C.** pleasant
**B.** humorous **D.** awkward

**4.** The details about the setting in lines 27–34 suggest that Pierre and Joseph

**A.** avoid relationships with the people on their route
**B.** know Prince Edward Street as well as they know each other
**C.** have difficulty trusting one another on the milk route
**D.** are eager to complete their routine on Prince Edward Street

**5.** In lines 39–42, the author shows that the characters are growing old mainly by

**A.** showing how Pierre and Joseph act toward others
**B.** describing Pierre and Joseph's physical appearance
**C.** including what Pierre says to Joseph about himself
**D.** describing others' reactions to Pierre and Joseph

**6.** Lines 48–53 reveal which detail about Pierre

**A.** the degree to which he enjoys his job
**B.** his frustration at being unable to read
**C.** the worry he feels about growing old
**D.** his relationship with the community

**7.** The climax of the story occurs when

**A.** Joseph begins to grow weak with age
**B.** Jacques requests a pension for Pierre
**C.** Pierre is hit by a passing truck
**D.** Jacques learns that Pierre is blind

**8.** In lines 124–126, Jacques's final words help express the story's theme by showing that

**A.** relationships are built on dependency
**B.** trust between friends can be very strong
**C.** animals can feel love just as people can
**D.** secrets between people can be destructive

## Written Response

### SHORT RESPONSE

**Directions** Write two or three sentences to answer each question.

**9.** What does Pierre's first interaction with Joseph reveal about Pierre's character? Support your response with information from the story.

**10.** Identify the main conflict in the story and explain how it is resolved. Support your response with details from the story.

### EXTENDED RESPONSE

**Directions** Write a short paragraph to answer this question.

**11.** What is the theme of the story? How does Pierre's relationship with Joseph reflect this theme? Cite details from the story to support your response.

## Reading Comprehension

**Directions** Read the following selection. Then answer the questions that follow.

### Burning Out at Nine?

**Nadya Labi**

Steven Guzman is only 12, but he's booked solid. He wakes up at 6 every weekday morning, downs a five-minute breakfast, reports to school at 7:50, returns home at 3:15, hits the books from 5 to 9 (with a break for dinner) and goes to sleep at 10:30. Saturdays are little better: from 9 to 5 he attends a prep program in the hope of getting a scholarship to a private school. Then there are piano lessons and a couple of hours of practice a week. If he's lucky, he'll squeeze in his friends on Sunday. "Sometimes I think, like, since I'm a kid, I need to enjoy my life," he says. "But I don't have time for that."

Remember when enjoying life seemed like the point of childhood? Hah! 10 Researchers at the University of Michigan's Institute for Social Research compiled the 1997 time diaries of 3,586 children nationwide, ages 12 and under. The participants came from virtually every ethnic background and all kinds of households—rich, poor, single parent, dual income. But funnily enough, they all sounded a little like Steven.

On average, kids ages 3 to 12 spent 29 hours a week in school, eight hours more than they did in 1981, when a similar study was conducted. They also did more household chores, accompanied their parents on more errands and participated in more of such organized activities as soccer and ballet.

Involvement in sports, in particular, rose almost 50% from 1981 to 1997: 20 boys now spend an average of four hours a week playing sports; girls log half that time. All in all, however, children's leisure time—defined as time left over after sleeping, eating, personal hygiene and attending school or day care—dropped from 40% of the day in 1981 to 25%.

"Children are affected by the same time crunch that affects their parents," says Sandra Hofferth, the sociologist who headed the study. A chief reason, she says, is that more mothers are working outside the home. (Nevertheless, children in both dual-income and "male breadwinner" households spent comparable amounts of time interacting with their parents, 19 hours and 22 hours respectively. In contrast, children spent only 9 hours with their single 30 mothers.)

All work and no play could make for some very messed-up kids. Child experts, usually a divided bunch, agree: fun is good. "Play is the most powerful way a child explores the world and learns about himself," says T. Berry Brazelton, a pediatrician at Harvard Medical School who has written a number of books on parenting. Unstructured play encourages independent thinking and allows the young to negotiate their relationships with their peers, but kids ages 3 to 12 spent only 12 hours a week engaged in it. Brazelton warns, "If we don't pay attention to this, we're going to create obsessive-compulsive people."

The children sampled spent a quarter of their rapidly diminishing "free
40 time" watching television. But that, believe it or not, was one of the findings parents might regard as good news. Kids watched TV for an average of an hour and a half each weekday, the study found, a 25% decline since 1981. The drop parallels the Nielsen ratings, which show that TV viewership by kids ages 2 to 11 has reached its lowest level since the mid-'70s.

But if they're spending less time in front of the TV set, kids aren't replacing it with reading. Despite the campaigning by parents, teachers and Hilary Clinton to get kids more interested in books, the children surveyed spent just over an hour a week reading, little changed from 1981. Let's face it, who's got the time?



## COMPREHENSION

**Directions** Answer the following questions about "Burning Out at Nine?"

**12.** Which persuasive technique does the author use in lines 7–8?

**A.** appeal to fear
**B.** testimonial
**C.** bandwagon appeal
**D.** loaded language

**13.** Based on the word "Hah!" in line 9, which sentence best describes the author's bias?

**A.** Research studies do not reflect children's behavior.
**B.** Private school programs are too demanding.
**C.** Children no longer have time to enjoy themselves.
**D.** Activities are more important than friendships.

**14.** Which sentence best summarizes the findings of the Michigan survey mentioned in line 10?

**A.** Time diaries completed by children in 1997 revealed that type of household affected how much free time children had.
**B.** Ethnic background was a minor factor in determining family income for most children under the age of 12.
**C.** Of the 3,586 children surveyed, most participated in private school programs and took piano lessons as Steven Guzman did.
**D.** Family income level and ethnic background did not strongly influence the amount of free time children had.

**15.** Which statement from the essay expresses the author's opinion?

**A.** "they all sounded a little like Steven" (line 15)

**B.** "kids ages 3 to 12 spend 29 hours a week in school" (line 16)

**C.** "They also did more household chores" (lines 16–17)

**D.** "Involvement in sports, in particular, rose almost 50%" (line 19)

**16.** The information in lines 16–19 supports the author's argument by showing that

**A.** parents require their children to do too many chores

**B.** children have busier schedules today than they did years ago

**C.** children suffer physical side effects when they are too busy

**D.** parents expect more from children than they used to

**17.** Which statement is a fact based on the information in lines 19–23?

**A.** In 1997, children had less than 50% of the free time they had in 1981.

**B.** In 1981, children spent more than half of their free time playing sports.

**C.** In 1997, children had 15% less free time than they did in 1981.

**D.** In 1981, children spent more time playing sports than they did in 1997.

**18.** Which counterargument does the author address in lines 39–44?

**A.** Parents are unhappy with many current television programs.

**B.** Children are watching less television than they used to.

**C.** Parents are glad that their children are watching television.

**D.** Children today have more free time than they did years ago.

**19.** The author avoids plagiarism in lines 24–26 by

**A.** citing sociologist Sandra Hofferth as the source of information

**B.** crediting a book on sociology in parentheses

**C.** using her own words to paraphrase Sandra Hofferth's findings

**D.** using a footnote to indicate the source of the quotation

**20.** The persuasive technique that the author uses in lines 32–35 is an appeal to

**A.** pity

**B.** authority

**C.** vanity

**D.** fear

**21.** The phrase "believe it or not" in line 40 suggests that the author believes

**A.** parents should be happy that children watch so little television

**B.** children are more interested in reading than in watching television

**C.** parents should worry about how much television children watch

**D.** children spend too much of their free time watching television

**22.** Which sentence is an effective paraphrase of the sentence in lines 46–48?

**A.** Parents, teachers, and politicians have all tried to get children to read more books.

**B.** Although adults have tried to get children to read more, their efforts have failed.

**C.** Since 1981, reading habits among young children have improved only slightly.

**D.** Children today are too busy with other activities to spend much time reading.

**23.** Which sentence best describes the author's use of facts and opinions in the essay?

**A.** She supports her opinions with research studies and statements from experts.

**B.** The essay contains many strong opinions but very few supporting details.

**C.** She includes only facts based on research and does not include personal opinions.

**D.** It is difficult to distinguish which statements are facts and which are opinions.

## Written Response

### SHORT RESPONSE

**Directions** Write two or three sentences to answer each question.

**24.** Identify the author's main claim in "Burning Out at Nine?" Support your response with a specific quotation from the essay.

**25.** Cite two examples of loaded language that indicate the author's bias about the demands on children's free time.

### EXTENDED RESPONSE

**Directions** Write a short paragraph to answer this question.

**26.** Explain whether or not the author uses one type of persuasive technique more frequently than others to support her argument. Support your response with specific examples from the essay.

## Reading Comprehension

**Directions** Read the following selections. Then answer the questions that follow.

### Lighting

**Ways of Producing Light Artificially, from Candles to Lightbulbs to Neon Lights**

Before people made artificial light, human activities started at sunrise and stopped at sunset. When cave dwellers built fires for warmth, they also created artificial light. Ancient civilizations burned animal fats and rushes for light. By the 4th century B.C.E., candles were used to light temples and homes. Candle wax was derived from seeds or insects, or skimmed from boiling cinnamon. Medieval candlemakers dipped thick cotton wicks in tallow, made by heating animal fats, or beeswax. Candles were unsuitable for night journeys, so travelers used flaming torches-sticks with a rag soaked in tar or wax at one end. From the 1500s, wealthy people used oil lamps with metal reflectors to
10 direct more light into the room. The vegetable and animal fats used in these lamps produced a lot of smoke. Kerosene, a cheaper fuel that gave better light, began to be used in the mid-19th century.

**Lighting by Gas**

Gas lighting was invented in 1792. The world's first gasworks opened in London, England, in 1805, and by 1823 gas lit 215 miles (346 km) of London's streets. Town dwellers enjoyed the extended hours of light. Gaslit halls made entertainment and evening classes possible. In 1885, the invention of the Welsbach gas mantle brought practical gas lighting into the home. The light from these mantles came not from the flame but from a ceramic surround,
20 which glowed as it grew hot.

*The thin tungsten wire filaments in this argon gas-filled lightbulb glow white-hot when an electric current passes through them.*

**Electricity**

In 1809, English chemist Sir Humphry Davy (1778-1829) produced a brilliant white arc of electricity between two charged blocks of carbon or metal, called electrodes. It took another 40 years to build a practical arc lamp. The first practical electric light was fitted to a lighthouse on the south coast of England in 1858. However, early electric light was not suitable for private houses. Buildings with electric lights required costly electric generators, and the glare of electric light was too harsh for small rooms.

**Bulbs and Filaments**

30 Lightbulbs were invented in 1879 by U.S. inventor Thomas Alva Edison (1847-1931). They contain a thin wire, or filament, that glows when an electric current passes through it. Filaments burn away quickly if exposed to the air, so Edison encased the filament inside a glass bulb with the air pumped out.

Lightbulbs were perfected in 1913 when lengths of the sturdy metal tungsten were coiled into tight filaments. These were placed inside glass bulbs filled with the gas argon, which does not react with the hot tungsten to burn it out.

**PEOPLE**

**Thomas Alva Edison**

U.S inventor Thomas Alva Edison (1847–1931) was a shrewd businessman who patented 1, 093 inventions. Although other inventors were working on lightbulbs, Edison beat the field to deomonstrate the first practical electric light on Decemeber 31, 1879. Edison developed a successful filament, which glowed when electric power passed through it and lasted a long time. He quickly capatalized on his invention, and he devised a system to make electricity and distribute it to many homes. Edison set up the Pearl Street generating station in New York City. He also set up a company to mass-produce his lightbulbs.

Fluorescent lamps do not have filaments, but use electric current to create light. Fluorescent discharge tubes were developed in the 1930s. The tube is 40 coated with materials called phosphors that glow when an electric current passes between electrodes at each end. A popular type of tube contains argon gas and mercury. As electricity flows, a surge of particles called electrons travels between the electrodes. When the electrons collide with mercury atoms, they release invisible ultraviolet light. This light makes the phosphor crystals glow. Different light colors can be made by filling fluorescent tubes with different gasses and phosphors. Tubes that contain neon gas glow red, for example. Street lights are usually lit by tubes containing sodium vapor, which produces bright yellow light.

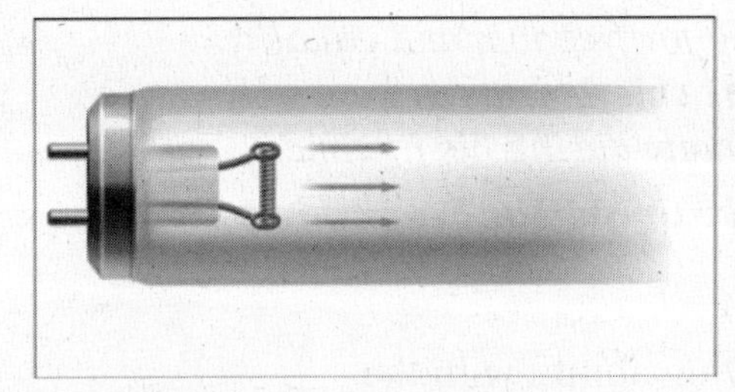

*Electrons moving between the electrodes collide with mercury atoms, causing them to emit invisible ultraviolet (UV) light. This makes the phosphors emit visible light.*

**Special-Purpose Lighting**

50 Lights can illuminate cosmetic counters and refrigerators, spotlight actors on stage, or be used for advertisements. Searchlights have a very long range and illuminate targets at night. Powerful floodlights illuminate sports fields at night. Laser lights, the most intense lights of all, can cut through diamond, the hardest material on Earth. Lasers are used for many purposes, from eye surgery and laser shows to scanning bar codes.

HIGHLIGHTS

- Until the invention of gas lights in the 18th century, people relied on candles for light.
- Modern lighting serves many different purposes, from illuminating the contents of refrigerators to laser shows.
- The basic lightbulb design has changed little since its invention by Thomas Alva Edison in 1879.

*Now Is Your Time!* tells the stories of people striving for freedom and equality. In this excerpt, author Walter Dean Myers describes the achievements of Lewis H. Latimer, an inventor, draftsman, and poet who inspired many during his lifetime.

**from Now Is Your Time! The African-American Struggle for Freedom**

**Walter Dean Myers**

Latimer liked to draw, and he combined his drawing ability with the willingness to apply himself as he established himself as one of the finest draftsmen in the country. He believed in himself and in his own mental capacities. He felt that he could do anything that involved just his mind and the willingness to work. As he saw others applying for patents, he wondered if they were really more inventive than he was. Before his twenty-sixth birthday, Latimer received a patent for one of his own inventions-a device that improved the bathroom facilities on trains. Perhaps his hat had been stolen once, for he also received a patent on a hat rack that could prevent hats from
10 being stolen in restaurants.

In 1879 Thomas Alva Edison invented the incandescent light bulb. The light was a marvelous invention, and it fascinated Latimer. Just as he had studied art in his spare time, and later drafting, now he began to study electricity. He read as much as he could about the uses of electricity and conducted his own experiments.

His reputation as a draftsman was outstanding, and in 1880 he was hired by Hiram Stevens Maxim, the chief engineer of the United States Electric Lighting Company. Latimer worked as a draftsman for Maxim and continued his own studies of electricity. In 1881 Lewis H. Latimer received a patent for
20 inventing, with Joseph V. Nichols, a way of attaching filaments in lamps. In 1882 he received his most important patent, for an improved process of manufacturing filaments.

Before incandescent lighting most large buildings had gaslights. Gas was piped into the building and regulated by a nozzle. A glass bulb was placed over the nozzle and the gas ignited with a match. Incandescent lighting was safer, cleaner, and much more convenient. The few men who understood this lighting were in high demand. Latimer was an African American who had knowledge and talents that people needed.

The work done by people like Edison, Maxim, and to an extent Latimer
30 changed the way we now live in cities. It was Latimer who helped install the lights in some of the first electrically lighted buildings, such as the old Equitable Building in New York. He also supervised the installation of electric lighting in Philadelphia; London, England; and Montreal, Canada. He learned enough French to speak it to Canadians. (He was proud of his ability to speak French but was disappointed in his German.)

Lewis Latimer, son of a man held in bondage, was sent by Maxim to England to set up an incandescent-lamp department in Maxim's factory there. Latimer thought he would have little difficulty in England. He was wrong. His English co-workers were not used to taking orders from Americans, especially 40 not black Americans. Eventually, though, they realized that Latimer knew his business, and the department was established. Latimer's ability outweighed all other factors.

It is not unusual for the top experts in any field to work together at some point in their careers. It is no wonder, then, that Latimer would one day work for Thomas Edison. He worked largely in the legal department, as an expert in electricity, using his knowledge of patent law to defend the rights of the Edison company, which had become the General Electric company. In 1918, to further the advances he had already made in the field, Edison put together a band of experts in electricity and electrical lighting called the Edison Pioneers. One of 50 those Pioneers was Lewis H. Latimer.



## COMPREHENSION

**Directions** Answer the following questions about the excerpt from "Lighting."

**27.** Which statement best expresses the main idea of the first paragraph?

**A.** Early forms of artificial lighting included fire, candles, torches, and kerosene lamps.
**B.** Before artificial lighting most activities stopped when the sun went down.
**C.** Vegetable and animal fats produced a lot of smoke when they were burned.
**D.** Artificial lighting was one of the most important inventions in history.

**28.** The headings "Lighting by Gas," "Electricity," and "Bulbs and Filaments" help to show

**A.** why candles, torches, and oil lamps are no longer used
**B.** how artificial lighting developed from 1792 to 1913
**C.** what special purposes artificial lighting can be used for
**D.** how incandescent and fluorescent lightbulbs work

**29.** Which sentence is an effective paraphrase of the sentence in lines 18–20?

**A.** Gas lights were often placed on the mantle so that they would not start a fire.
**B.** Welsbach mantles burned ceramic pieces, not wood, to produce light.
**C.** A ceramic piece surrounded the flame in order to protect the flame inside.
**D.** The Welsbach gas mantle gave off light from a ceramic part, not a flame.

**30.** Which detail from the third paragraph best supports the idea that "early electric light was not suitable for private houses"?

**A.** Sir Humphry Davis produced an arc of electricity in 1809.
**B.** It took forty years to build a practical arc lamp.
**C.** The glare of early electric light was too harsh for small rooms.
**D.** The first practical arc lamp was used on a lighthouse.

**31.** The graphic aid "An Incandescent Electric Lightbulb" is important to the selection because it

**A.** explains that gas argon is used in lightbulbs
**B.** illustrates how electricity is used to make artificial light
**C.** demonstrates that air is pumped out of a lightbulb
**D.** shows how the parts of a lightbulb work together

**32.** Choose the best way to use information from lines 34–37 without plagiarizing.

**A.** Tungsten and argon are crucial elements of a modern light bulb ("Lighting" 411).
**B.** Lightbulbs were perfected in 1913 by using tungsten "coiled into tight filaments."
**C.** According to "Lighting," argon does not react with hot tungsten to burn it out (411).
**D.** Tungsten is coiled into tight filaments and placed inside a bulb filled with argon.

**33.** Which pattern of organization does the author use in lines 47–57?

**A.** compare and contrast
**B.** cause-and-effect
**C.** chronological order
**D.** classification

**34.** The function of the bulleted list labeled "Highlights" is to

**A.** give facts not covered in the selection
**B.** persuade people to read more on lighting
**C.** sum up the selection's important points
**D.** provide interesting, attention-getting facts

## COMPREHENSION

**Directions** Answer the following questions about the excerpt from *Now Is Your Time!*

**35.** Lines 1–10 express the main idea that Latimer felt

**A.** afraid that others were stealing his ideas
**B.** confident in his abilities and talent
**C.** angry that people would steal hats
**D.** proud to be the country's best draftsman

**36.** You can tell from the first paragraph that this excerpt comes from a biography because the author

**A.** tells what Latimer thought and felt
**B.** guesses about Latimer's motivation
**C.** writes using the first person
**D.** draws from a variety of sources

**37.** In lines 11–15, the author describes the effects of

**A.** Latimer's meeting Thomas Edison
**B.** Edison's deciding to hire Latimer
**C.** Latimer's working in a factory
**D.** Edison's inventing the lightbulb

**38.** Which words in the third paragraph indicate that it is written in chronological order?

**A.** in 1880, In 1881, In 1882
**B.** was hired, Latimer worked, he received
**C.** draftsman, engineer, inventing
**D.** worked, continued, improved process

**39.** Which detail best supports the idea that Latimer and others "changed the way we now live in cities"?

**A.** Joseph V. Nichols helped Latimer receive a patent for filaments.
**B.** Latimer was an African American who had valuable knowledge.
**C.** Latimer helped install some of the first indoor electric lights.
**D.** Hiram Stevens Maxim hired Latimer to work in a factory in England.

**40.** Which statement best paraphrases the words "Lewis Latimer, son of a man held in bondage" in line 36?

**A.** The father of Lewis Latimer was once held for ransom.
**B.** Lewis Latimer was an enslaved person early in life.
**C.** The son of Lewis Latimer worked in the bond industry.
**D.** Lewis Latimer's father was an enslaved person.

**41.** The sentences in lines 36–40 illustrate which characteristic of a biography?

**A.** examples of how others viewed Latimer important
**B.** aspects of Latimer's personality
**C.** facts about where Latimer was born
**D.** opinions from the writer about Latimer

**42.** Choose the best way to use the information in lines 45–48 without plagiarizing.

**A.** According to Myers, Latimer worked largely in the legal department, as an expert in electricity, at General Electric.
**B.** Latimer's experience with electricity and patents helped him succeed in General Electric's legal department (Myers 226).
**C.** According to Myers, Latimer worked as an expert, using his knowledge of patent law to defend the rights of the Edison company.
**D.** Latimer was "an expert in electricity" and used his "knowledge of patent law" as an employee of General Electric (226).

**43.** Which word best describes the author's feelings about Latimer, the subject of this biography?

**A.** admiring
**B.** critical
**C.** envious
**D.** objective

**Directions** Answer the following question about both selections.

**44.** How are the main ideas of "Lighting" and *Now Is Your Time!* similar?

**A.** Both selections are about the importance of incandescent lighting.
**B.** The article and the biography both focus on Lewis H. Latimer's career.
**C.** Both selections explain how people used lighting before the 18th century.
**D.** The article and the biography both tell about the General Electric company.

## Written Response

### SHORT RESPONSE

**Directions** Write two or three sentences to answer each question.

**45.** Identify the main idea of the excerpt from *Now Is Your Time!* Support your response with one detail from the selection.

**46.** Which details from "Lighting" and the excerpt from *Now Is Your Time!* support the idea that electric lighting changed the way people live today? Include one detail from each selection in your response.

## EXTENDED RESPONSE

**Directions** Write a short paragraph to answer this question.

**47.** Synthesize the information from "Lighting" and the excerpt from *Now Is Your Time!* to explain Thomas Edison's role in the development of electric lighting. Support your response with details from both selections.

## Vocabulary

**Directions** Use context clues and your knowledge of connotation and denotation to answer the following questions. The line numbers will help you find the words in "A Secret for Two."

**1.** The denotation of *softly* in line 26 is "in a quiet way." Which word best describes its connotation?

**A.** grandly
**B.** shyly
**C.** gently
**D.** eagerly

**2.** The denotation of *boast* in line 36 is "to glorify oneself in speech." Which word best describes its connotation?

**A.** overconfidence
**B.** cleverness
**C.** impatience
**D.** happiness

**3.** The denotation of *remarkable* in line 55 is "worthy of notice." Which word best describes its connotation?

**A.** boring
**B.** desirable
**C.** amazing
**D.** secretive

**4.** The denotation of *stiffly* in line 63 is "in a rigid manner." Which phrase best describes its connotation?

**A.** weak with age
**B.** slow with patience
**C.** cold with fear
**D.** firm with bitterness

**Directions** Use context clues and your knowledge of idioms to answer the following questions. The line numbers will help you find the words in "Burning Out at Nine?"

**5.** The idiom *hits the books* in line 3 means

**A.** gets frustrated easily
**B.** reads quietly
**C.** strikes forcefully
**D.** studies hard

**6.** In line 21, the idiom *all in all* means

**A.** despite everything else
**B.** more important than that
**C.** taking everything into account
**D.** without counting that detail

**7.** The idiom *messed-up* in line 31 refers to

**A.** being careless
**B.** having problems
**C.** looking sloppy
**D.** acting mature

**8.** In line 48, the idiom *face it* means

**A.** accept the truth
**B.** admit one's mistakes
**C.** examine the argument
**D.** change one's mind

**Directions** Use context clues and your understanding of specialized vocabulary to answer the following questions. The line numbers will help you find the words in "Lighting."

**9.** In line 18, the word *mantle* most likely refers to a

**A.** loose coat worn over other layers
**B.** sheath that gives off light when heated
**C.** shelf for decorations over a fireplace
**D.** zone of hot gases around a flame

**10.** In line 19, the word *surround* most likely refers to a

**A.** device that heats large areas
**B.** flame that is created by electricity
**C.** metal plate that conducts heat
**D.** piece that encloses something

**11.** In line 27, the word *generators* most likely refers to

**A.** anything that releases energy
**B.** cables that carry electricity
**C.** machines that make electricity
**D.** people who invent things

**12.** In line 39, the word *discharge* most likely refers to

**A.** carrying a flow of electricity
**B.** getting rid of something
**C.** creating an electricity source
**D.** altering the form of something

**Directions** Use your knowledge of Latin roots and base words to answer the following questions about the excerpt from *Now Is Your Time!*

**13.** The Latin word *candēscere* means "to glow." What is the most likely meaning of *incandescent* as it is used in line 11?

**A.** capable of producing heat
**B.** made up of rays of light
**C.** giving off light when heated
**D.** unable to light up or glow

**14.** The Latin word *ignis* means "fire." The word *ignited* in line 25 most likely means

**A.** became excited
**B.** made bright
**C.** heated intensely
**D.** lit on fire

**15.** The word *installation* in line 32 comes from which base word?

**A.** still
**B.** install
**C.** station
**D.** tall

**16.** The word *disappointed* in line 35 comes from which base word?

**A.** disease
**B.** appoint
**C.** sapped
**D.** pointed

## Writing and Grammar

**Directions** Read the research report below and answer the questions that follow.

(1) Franklin Delano Roosevelt was the 32nd president of the United States. (2) He was elected in November of 1932. (3) Before that, he was a lawyer (whitehousekids.gov). (4) Roosevelt's folks were really well off. (5) When he became president, though, millions of people were poor and out of work. (6) This was a terrible period in American history known as The Great Depression. (7) During his presidency, Roosevelt helped Americans survive a difficult period.

(8) At the beginning of 1929, the country had seemed very rich. (9) In "The Great Depression: An Eyewitness history," David Burg says that people were making more money and buying more stock than ever. (10) Then suddenly the investors began selling their stock, which created a panic. (11) On October 28, the stock market crashed, and billions of dollars were lost (48). (12) By the time Roosevelt was elected, 12 million people were out of work. (13) To make things worse, there was no unemployment insurance or social security to help people (Freedman 74).

(14) One of Roosevelt's first tasks was to help the people of the United States. (15) Many people were homeless, and factories and banks had closed (Goodwin). (16) Roosevelt needed to do two things; feed and house people, and create new jobs. (17) One program he developed was the Civilian Conservation Corps. (18) It gave jobs in the national forests and parks to young men who were out of work. (19) The men received pay and they were also given food clothing and a place to live. (20) In addition, because many of them had very little education, they were taught to read and write (Freedman 95).

(21) The National Youth Administration was another program that helped young people. (22) It gave people in high school and college part-time jobs in libraries and also jobs as research assistants. (23) This way, they were able to stay in school (Freedman 95). (24) They learned some new skills, too, that could help them get jobs when they finished school.

(25) One of the things president Roosevelt created was Social security, from which we still benefit today. (26) This program protects people when they got old, become disabled, or lose their jobs. (27) Both employers and the people who work for them pay a tax on what they earn. (28) This money goes to the federal government. (29) The government then pays people if they are out of work or can't work because they are disabled. (30) It also pays people a pension when they get old and retire (Encarta 13).

(31) Roosevelt created many other programs that helped the United States recover from the Great Depression. (32) There were, programs that built schools roads and libraries. (33) There were programs that supported artists. (34) There were programs that protected mortgages so people wouldn't become homeless (Goodwin). (35) These programs cost the government a lot of money, which came from higher taxes for big companies and for rich people (Freedman 102).

(36) There were many people who didn't like Roosevelt and what he was doing. (37) However enough people liked his programs to re-elect him in 1936. (38) In fact, he got the most votes ever and won by almost 11 million votes (Freedman 105–06). (39) Franklin Delano Roosevelt got re-elected: two more times in 1940 and in 1944. (40) He was the president of the United States during World War Two, another terrible time in history when the American people trusted Roosevelt to help them survive.

**Works Cited**

Burg, David F. The Great Depression: An Eyewitness History. New York: Facts On File, Inc., 1996.

"Franklin D. Roosevelt." www.whitehousekids.gov. White House. 5 Sep. 2006 {http://www.whitehouse.gov/kids/presidents/franklindroosevelt.html}.

Freedman, Russell. Franklin Delano Roosevelt. New York: Clarion Books, 1990.

Goodwin, Doris Kearns. "Person of the Century Runner-Up: Franklin Delano Roosevelt." Time 100: Person of the Century. Time 3 Jan. 2000. 5 Sep. 2006. {http;//whitehouse.gov/kids/presidents/franklindroosevelt.html}.

"Roosevelt, Franklin Delano." Microsoft Encarta Reference Library 2004. CD-ROM. Redmond, WA: Microsoft Corporation, 2004.

**1.** Choose the most suitable question for further research on Franklin Delano Roosevelt.

**A.** How did Roosevelt boost the United States' economy?

**B.** In what year was Franklin Delano Roosevelt born?

**C.** What was the president's salary when Roosevelt served?

**D.** Was Franklin Delano Roosevelt a good president?

**2.** Which topic would help you narrow research for this report?

**A.** the life of Franklin Delano Roosevelt

**B.** an economic history of the United States

**C.** problems people have finding jobs

**D.** which steps Roosevelt took to create jobs

**3.** Which sentence identifies the writer's thesis statement?

**A.** sentence 1
**B.** sentence 4
**C.** sentence 6
**D.** sentence 7

**4.** Choose the best way to correct the punctuation and capitalization in sentence 9.

**A.** In "The Great Depression; an Eyewitness History," David Burg says that people were making more money and buying more stock than ever.

**B.** In The Great Depression: An Eyewitness History, David Burg says that people were making more money and buying more stock than ever.

**C.** In "The Great Depression: An Eyewitness History," David Burg says that people were making more money and buying more stock than ever.

**D.** In The Great Depression, an eyewitness history, David Burg says that people were making more money and buying more stock than ever.

**5.** Which sentence has a tone that is inappropriate for a research report?

**A.** sentence 4
**B.** sentence 6
**C.** sentence 11
**D.** sentence 12

**6.** The third paragraph helps support the writer's thesis by

**A.** explaining the reasons why banks and factories closed

**B.** describing steps Roosevelt took to help people who lost their jobs

**C.** explaining the challenges Roosevelt faced as president

**D.** describing the significance of national forests and parks

**7.** Choose the best way to punctuate sentence 16 using a colon.

**A.** Roosevelt needed: to do two things; feed and house people, and create new jobs.

**B.** Roosevelt needed to do two things feed and house people: and create new jobs.

**C.** Roosevelt needed to do two things: feed and house people and create new jobs.

**D.** Roosevelt needed to do: two things; feed and house people and create new jobs.

**8.** Choose the best way to rewrite sentence 19 using commas correctly.

**A.** The men received pay, and they were also given food, clothing, and places to live.

**B.** The men received pay, and they were also given food clothing and places to live.

**C.** The men received pay and they were also given food, clothing, and places to live.

**D.** The men received pay, and they were also given food, clothing and places to live.

**9.** Which research question would help you learn more about the National Youth Administration?

**A.** What are some programs that are similar to the National Youth Administration?

**B.** What percentage of the population was under 21 in the 1930s?

**C.** What was it like to be a student in the National Youth Administration?

**D.** What other programs for young people did Roosevelt launch?

**10.** Choose the best way to correct the capitalization in sentence 25.

**A.** One of the things President Roosevelt created was Social Security, from which we still benefit today.
**B.** One of the things president Roosevelt created was Social security, from which we still benefit today.
**C.** One of the things President Roosevelt created was social security, from which we still benefit today.
**D.** One of the things president Roosevelt created was Social Security, from which we still benefit today.

**11.** Choose the best way to correct the comma errors in sentence 32.

**A.** There were programs that built, schools, roads, and libraries.
**B.** There were programs, that built schools roads, and libraries.
**C.** There were programs that built schools, roads and libraries.
**D.** There were programs that built schools, roads, and libraries.

**12.** The best place to find information about the people mentioned in sentence 36 is a

**A.** Web site about presidential programs
**B.** biography about Roosevelt and his family
**C.** journal article about the 1930s
**D.** book about Roosevelt's political career

**13.** To punctuate sentence 37 correctly, a comma should follow

**A.** However
**B.** people
**C.** programs
**D.** him

**14.** How should you revise sentence 39 so that it is punctuated correctly?

**A.** Insert a second colon after the word "times."
**B.** Delete the colon, and insert a comma after the word "times."
**C.** Change the colon after "elected" to a comma.
**D.** Delete the colon, and add a semicolon after "times."

**15.** Which source on the Works Cited list likely describes life during the Great Depression?

**A.** The Great Depression: An Eyewitness History
**B.** "Person of the Century Runner-Up: Franklin Delano Roosevelt"
**C.** Franklin Delano Roosevelt, by Russell Freedman
**D.** "Roosevelt, Franklin Delano" from Microsoft Encarta

**16.** The Web site "Franklin D. Roosevelt" is not an appropriate source for this report because it likely

**A.** contains outdated information
**B.** is intended for young children
**C.** includes inaccurate statements
**D.** reveals the author's bias

**17.** Which of the following sources would be least reliable for a report on Roosevelt's career?

**A.** an article in a magazine about the long-term effects of Roosevelt's programs
**B.** a newspaper article about Roosevelt written during the Great Depression
**C.** an Internet site with an essay that opposes Roosevelt's economic ideas
**D.** a book on Roosevelt's career in political life.

**18.** Which word best describes the tone of this report?

**A.** sarcastic
**B.** lighthearted
**C.** formal
**D.** enthusiastic

**19.** The writer's tone is appropriate because the purpose of the report is to

**A.** inform readers about Roosevelt and the Great Depression
**B.** persuade readers that Roosevelt was a great president
**C.** express feelings about the causes of the Great Depression
**D.** entertain readers with stories about life in the 1930s

**20.** Which topic would most likely be too narrow for a research report?

**A.** policies created during Roosevelt's second term
**B.** the size of the National Youth Administration
**C.** factors that led to the 1929 stock market crash
**D.** the development of unemployment insurance

## Writing

**Directions** Read the following quotation. Then read the prompt that follows and complete the writing activity.

> "And so, my fellow Americans: ask not what your country can do for you—ask what you can do for your country."
>
> John F. Kennedy

**Prompt:** Write a persuasive essay in which you argue that even one person can make a great difference in the United States. As Kennedy suggests, consider how an individual can contribute to his or her country. Use evidence and persuasive appeals to support your argument.

Now write your persuasive essay. Use the reminders that follow to help you write.

**Reminders**

- Be sure your writing does what the prompt asks.
- Present a thesis statement that takes a clear stand on an issue.
- Use convincing details to support the thesis. .
- Use persuasive language effectively.
- Check for correct grammar, spelling, and punctuation

# Answer Key

## Unit 1, Test A

### Comprehension

**1.** D
**2.** B
**3.** A
**4.** B
**5.** D
**6.** A
**7.** B
**8.** D
**9.** D

### Comprehension

**10.** B
**11.** A
**12.** A
**13.** B
**14.** A
**15.** C
**16.** D

### Comprehension

**17.** A
**18.** B
**19.** B

### Written Response

### Short Response

**20.** Responses will vary. Students may identify the following descriptions of the setting: a. In the beginning of the selection, the setting is Base Camp on Mt. Everest (lines 01–10). b. Another part of the setting is a crevasse with a bridge made out of a ladder. Laurie describes the width of the crevasse and the length of the bridge (lines 20–24). c. Laurie mentions the settings of Camp One and a Camp Two (line 46).

**21.** Responses will vary. Students may suggest two of the following details: a. In *Banner in the Sky*, Rudi overcomes an internal conflict about whether he should continue climbing. He is determined to climb to the top of the Citadel despite what others think (lines 16–29). b. In *Banner in the Sky*, Rudi continues climbing even though he knows the danger of being alone without food or a tent (lines 18–20). c. In *Banner in the Sky*, Rudi is so determined to climb the mountain that he remains cautious and moves slowly throughout his climb (lines 38–44). d. In *To the Top of Everest*, Laurie is so determined to climb Everest that he continues despite Bill's warnings (lines 01–10). e. In *To the Top of Everest*, Laurie shows his determination when he spends over an hour looking for a place to cross (lines 25–27). f. In *To the Top of Everest*, Laurie is so determined to climb that he risks his life jumping the crevasse (lines 30–40).

### Extended Response

**22.** Responses will vary. The exposition introduces the setting and characters. It may also include setup for the conflict. The rising action builds suspense and shows how the conflict unfolds. The climax is the turning point of a selection. It is often the most exciting moment. The falling action eases suspense. It also shows how the main character begins to resolve the conflict. The resolution ties up any loose ends in a story. It sometimes offers an unexpected twist in the plot. Students may suggest the following plot stage examples: a. One example of exposition is that the reader learns about two people involved in the selection—Laurie and Bill (lines 01–03). b. In the exposition, the reader learns that the setting is Base Camp on Mt. Everest (lines 01–07). c. The exposition also sets up the conflict by telling the reader that the climb is dangerous (lines 01–10). d. An example of rising action is when the reader learns that the climb becomes more difficult (lines 16–19). e. An example of rising action is when Laurie discovers that he cannot find a new place to cross. This complicates the conflict (lines 25–27). f. The climax of the selection occurs when Laurie jumps from the ladder to the other side of the crevasse (lines 33–40). g. An example of falling action is Laurie's explanation of how he feels after making the jump (lines 41–45). h. An example of falling action is Laurie's climb from Camp One to Camp Two (lines 46–47). g. The resolution of the selection occurs when

Laurie discovers that Bill is happy that Laurie made the climb (lines 51–56).

**Vocabulary**

1. B
2. C
3. A
4. D
5. A
6. C
7. D
8. A
9. D

1. C
2. A
3. A
4. B
5. C
6. C
7. B
8. D
9. B
10. A
11. C
12. C

**Writing**

Rubric: Describing People and Places
Identifies the topic
Explains why the topic is significant
Follows a clear organizational pattern, with an introduction, a body, and a conclusion
Uses transitions to connect ideas
Provides background information for the reader if it is needed
Shows the writer's or the character's personality and style
Uses sensory details to show the reader what the person or place is like
Holds reader interest by using different sentence lengths
Uses correct grammar, spelling, and punctuation

## Unit 1, Test B/C

**Comprehension**

1. D
2. B
3. C
4. A
5. D
6. A
7. B
8. D
9. D

**Comprehension**

10. A
11. A
12. B
13. A
14. D
15. B
16. A

**Comprehension**

17. B
18. C
19. A

**Written Response**

**Short Response**

20. Responses will vary. Students should recognize that each man is struggling to prove something to himself. Students may offer two of the following details to support their answers: a. Rudi pushes himself in order to follow in his father's footsteps and to prove that he is capable of more than washing dishes (Lines 17–25). b. Rudi says that the need to reach the top pushed him to climb on. He needed to prove to himself that he could climb the mountain because it was his dream (Lines 19–22). b. Laurie wants to use his knowledge of climbing to help others on Everest (Lines 4–8). c. Laurie wants to prove that he has given more than his best effort on the mountain (Lines23–27).
21. Responses will vary. Students should recognize that the falling action occurs after Laurie makes the jump across the crevasse. The resolution occurs after Laurie arrives at Camp Two. Students may offer two of the following details to support their answers: a. One example of falling action is when Laurie lays panting on the far side after he jumps the crevasse (Line 35). b. A second example of falling action is when Laurie climbs to Camp One and on toward Camp Two (Line 40.) c. The resolution occurs when Bill and Laurie talk. Bill tells Laurie that he needed him but could not risk Laurie's life by telling him to climb (Lines 44–49).

**Extended Response**

22. Responses will vary. Students should recognize that the setting in both selections contributes to different plot stages.

Students may use any of the following examples in their responses: *Banner in the Sky* a. The setting helps build suspense in the rising action of the plot. Descriptions, such as "the steep maze of the icefall" and "avalanche area," add suspense to Rudi's climb up the mountain (Lines 12–13; 34–36.) b. The setting helps complicate the external conflict of the story. Descriptions, such as "great crevasse," "steep maze," and "deep drifts," show the difficulty of Rudi's climb up the mountain (Lines 11–12; 12–13; 48–49). c. The setting is part of the climax. The climax occurs when Rudi reaches the Citadel (Lines 51–53.) *To the Top of Everest* d. The setting builds suspense in the rising action. Descriptions, such as "the route was in much worse shape" and "the bridge ended 1.5 m (5 ft.) from the far wall," increase the suspense of the selection (Lines 14–15; 17–18). e. The setting complicates the conflict of the selection. The setting of the treacherous mountain landscape and unusable ladder bridges complicate Laurie's external conflict with Everest 14–22. f. The setting is part of the climax. Laurie has to jump across a wide crevasse by jumping from a ladder bridge (Lines 16–34). g. The setting is also part of the falling action. Laurie's climb to Camp One and Camp Two are the main descriptions in the falling action of the selection 40.

**23.** Responses will vary. Students should recognize that the external conflict is Laurie vs. the mountain. The internal conflict is Laurie vs. himself. Students may use the following examples to support the response that the external conflict is more important to the plot: a. The external conflict builds suspense in the rising action of the selection. Descriptions, such as "the route was in much worse shape" and "the bridge ended 1.5 m (5 ft.) from the far wall," increase the suspense of the selection by showing what Laurie is up against (Lines 14–15; 17–18.) b. The external conflict complicates the conflict by showing the increasing difficulty of climbing Everest. The descriptions of a treacherous mountain landscape and unusable ladder bridges show this difficulty (Lines 14–22.) c. The climax is Laurie's triumph over his external conflict with the mountain (Lines 16–34.) Students may use the following examples to support the response that the internal conflict is more important to the plot: d. It is Laurie's internal conflict that pushes him to climb the mountain despite Bill's warning. This internal conflict plays a role in the exposition and the rising action of the selection (Lines 4–8.) e. Laurie's internal conflict builds suspense in the rising action. He is ready to climb back down to Base Camp, but then he asks himself if he had given the crevasse more than his best. He decides he had not, so he chooses to jump from the ladder(Lines 21–27.) f. Laurie's internal conflict about whether to climb the mountain is a main part of the resolution. He learns that Bill needed his help but did not want Laurie's possible death on his conscience (Lines 40–49.)

**Vocabulary**

**1.** D
**2.** A
**3.** C
**4.** B
**5.** C
**6.** A
**7.** B
**8.** A
**9.** D

**Writing and Grammar**

**1.** A
**2.** B
**3.** C
**4.** A
**5.** B

**6.** C
**7.** B
**8.** C
**9.** B
**10.** C
**11.** D
**12.** C

**Writing**

1. Identifies the topic
2. Explains why the topic is significant
3. Follows a clear organizational pattern, with an introduction, a body, and a conclusion
4. Uses transitions to connect ideas
5. Provides background information for the reader if it is needed
6. Shows the writer's or the character's personality and style
7. Uses sensory details to show the reader what the person or place is like
8. Holds reader interest by using different sentence lengths
9. Uses correct grammar, spelling, and punctuation

## Unit 2, Test A

**Comprehension**

**1.** B
**2.** A
**3.** B
**4.** C
**5.** D
**6.** B
**7.** A
**8.** D
**9.** A
**10.** C

**Comprehension**

**11.** C
**12.** A
**13.** C
**14.** D
**15.** A
**16.** B
**17.** B
**18.** D

**Comprehension**

**19.** C
**20.** A

**Written Response**

**Short Response**

**21.** Responses will vary. Students should visualize Mina as barely able to control her excitement. Students may give two of the following details as support: a. During the slow ride to camp, Mina's heart is beating so fast that she imagines it can be seen under her shirt. As they near the camp, Mina has to force herself to be patient (lines 1–4). b. Immediately after arriving at camp, Mina "burst[s] out" of the car and then waits for her father to finish talking to Miss Maddinton (lines 7–9). c. During the adults' conversation, Mina has to restrain herself from running around the camp to touch all the items she remembers so fondly (lines 10–14. d. Mina has to force herself to "stand and wave" as her father drives away (lines 20–21).

**22.** Responses will vary. Students might use one of the following details: a. Instead of accusing the narrator of being afraid of girls, the father uses his own experiences as a seventh-grader and his own fears at that time of his life (lines 51–64). age…having a great time"b. The father lets the narrator make his own decision, instead of telling him what to do (line 64). c. The narrator takes the time to think about what his father says. He makes the decision to go to the dance after listening to his father (lines 65–67).

**Extended Response**

**23.** Responses will vary. Students may say that they learn that the narrator is self-conscious, wants to make a good impression, is thoughtful, and has a good sense of humor. Students might use three of the following details: a. The narrator has a sense of humor about the chain of events leading up to his deciding to go to the dance (lines 1–6). b. The narrator thinks it is embarrassing to be seen dancing with a girl who is taller than he is (lines 7–12). c. The narrator teases Myron about Myron's "mustard sandwich" (lines 31–40). d. The narrator thoughtfully listens to what his father has to say, and he thinks about it afterward. Their talk helps him decide to go to the dance (lines

65–67). e. The narrator has a sense of humor about his nervousness in the hours leading up to the dance (lines 68–72). f. Before the dance, the narrator takes the time to put on after-shave, hairgel, and deodorant. He wants to make a good impression (lines 73–76).

**Vocabulary**

1. D
2. B
3. D
4. C
5. B
6. A
7. D
8. C

**Writing and Grammar**

1. B
2. C
3. A
4. B
5. A
6. D
7. B
8. A
9. C
10. B
11. D
12. C

## Unit 2, Test B/C

**Comprehension**

1. B
2. A
3. C
4. B
5. C
6. A
7. D
8. A
9. D
10. C

**Comprehension**

11. A
12. B
13. C
14. A
15. C
16. A
17. B
18. D

**Comprehension**

19. C
20. A

**Written Response**

**Short Response**

21. Responses will vary. Students may give one of the following characteristics and examples: a. Mina is sensitive to her father's feelings. She forces herself to wave as her father drives away (lines 20–22) b. Mina is friendly. She smiles and laughs around Miss Maddinton, even though the woman is not friendly in return (lines 22–31). c. Mina is oblivious to Miss Maddinton's coldness. She laughs at Miss Maddinton's comment, even though it was not a friendly one (lines 29–31).
22. Responses will vary. Students should conclude that Tansy is not a good friend to Mina. Tansy does not want to be Mina's roommate because Mina is black. Even though the girls were friends last year at camp, Tansy is not even there to say hello to Mina. Students might point out that a good friend would focus on the kind of person Mina is rather than the color of her skin.

**Extended Response**

23. Response will vary. Students should note that Schwartz uses the following methods of characterization: physical appearance; a character's thoughts, speech, and actions; other characters' reactions to a character. Students might use the following examples: a. Character's actions and physical appearance: You learn that the narrator wants to make a good impression at the dance because he takes extra care with his appearance. He wears hair gel, after-shave, and "musky deodorant." He also spends an excessive amount of time in the bathroom (lines 68–75) b. Character's thoughts: You learn that the narrator thinks it is embarrassing to be seen dancing with a girl who is taller than him (lines 7–12). c. Character's speech: You see the narrator's sense of humor in his conversation with Myron (lines 18–40). d. Character's thoughts and actions: You learn that the narrator seriously thinks about what his father says when he stays in the den for a long time after their talk (lines 65–67). e. Other characters' reactions to the

character: From the father's speech, you learn that the narrator is intimidated by girls and afraid to go to the dance (lines 50–64).

**24.** Responses will vary. Students should recognize that the third-person omniscient point of view would reveal all of the characters' thoughts and feelings—not just Mina's. Students might say this would be less effective because it might give away the end of the excerpt sooner. Seeing the story through Mina's eyes alone makes the ending more powerful and shocking. Students might say they can sympathize more with Mina's character by having the focus be on her. Other students might think that the third-person omniscient point of view would make the excerpt more effective because the reader would learn more about the other characters. Perhaps they would gain a better understanding of Tansy's behavior or Mina's father's worries about how Mina will be treated. Readers would also learn more about Miss Maddinton's thoughts and feelings, instead of just interpreting her actions as cold and distant.

**Vocabulary**

**1.** D
**2.** B
**3.** D
**4.** C
**5.** B
**6.** A
**7.** D
**8.** C

**Writing and Grammar**

**1.** D
**2.** C
**3.** A
**4.** B
**5.** C
**6.** B
**7.** C
**8.** B
**9.** C
**10.** D
**11.** A
**12.** C

**Writing**

Rubric: Comparison-Contrast Essay
Identifies the characters or subjects being compared and/or contrasted
Includes a thesis statement that identifies similarities and/or differences
Supports key ideas with examples
Includes a strong introduction and a satisfying conclusion
Follows a clear organizational pattern
Connects ideas with transitions
Uses language that is appropriate for the audience and purpose
Uses precise words to explain similarities and differences
Varies sentence beginnings
Uses correct grammar, spelling, and punctuation

## Unit 3, Test A

**Comprehension**

**1.** C
**2.** B
**3.** B
**4.** A
**5.** C
**6.** D
**7.** A
**8.** B
**9.** D
**10.** C
**11.** D

**Comprehension**

**12.** A
**13.** B
**14.** D
**15.** C
**16.** B
**17.** A
**18.** B

**Comprehension**

**19.** C
**20.** B

**Written Response**

**Short Response**

**21.** Responses will vary. Students may offer the following details: a. They both enjoy exploring the outdoors (line 16). . The blue cat is fearless, and likes to parade around the field. The ruddy is more timid and stays near the edges of the field. (lines 28–33). c. The blue easily climbs trees, but the ruddy cannot climb as easily (lines 38–39). d. The ruddy captures a small bird, but the blue does not. (lines 43–44)

**22.** Students should recognize that the natural elements Jan Skiba lists represent true beauty.

**Extended Response**

**23.** Responses will vary. Students may provide the following examples for support: a. The Skiba women become obsessed with their looks and consequently neglect their familial duties (lines 23–41). b. The Skibas' awareness of their physical faults causes them to worry and to question the family's status in society (lines 49–50). c. The mirror causes the pets to turn against each other (lines 51–65). d. The Skibas forget about the beauty of nature (lines 67–69). e. The Skibas forget the "true" image they should be observing: the image of the soul (lines 74–78).

**Vocabulary**

**1.** D
**2.** B
**3.** A
**4.** C
**5.** B
**6.** A
**7.** B
**8.** D

**Writing and Grammar**

**1.** B
**2.** A
**3.** D
**4.** C
**5.** A
**6.** B
**7.** B
**8.** A
**9.** B
**10.** C
**11.** A
**12.** D

**Writing**

1. Has an interesting plot and one or more characters
2. Develops and resolves a central conflict
3. Includes descriptive details that reveal the setting and characters
4. Uses dialogue to show characters' personalities
5. Introduces the characters, the setting, or the action in a way that gets a reader's attention
6. Follows a clear sequence of events
7. Resolves the conflict with a convincing conclusion
8. Shows the writer's individual style
9. Uses sensory language to show what fictional characters and places are like
10. Varies sentence lengths
11. Uses correct grammar, spelling, and punctuation

## Unit 3, Test B/C

**Comprehension**

**1.** A
**2.** B
**3.** B
**4.** D
**5.** D
**6.** C
**7.** A
**8.** C
**9.** D
**10.** D

**Comprehension**

**11.** C
**12.** A
**13.** B
**14.** A
**15.** C
**16.** B
**17.** A
**18.** C

**Comprehension**

**19.** D
**20.** B

**Written Response**

**Short Response**

**21.** Responses will vary. Students may support the theme with the following examples: a. The addition of the mirror to the household causes the family sadness and anxiety (lines 31–50). b. The mirror causes the women to neglect the housework (lines 39–41). c. The mirror causes the pets to turn against each other (lines 51–65). d. The mirror causes the family to forget the beauty of nature (lines 67–69). e. The mirror causes the family to value exterior images and to ignore their souls (lines 75–78).

**22.** Responses will vary. Students should recognize that the cat and dog represent the family. With the appearance of the mirror, the animals—like the Skiba family—begin to focus on appearance. The animals first react violently to their own reflections and then turn on each other. The animals symbolize the extreme consequences of vanity.

**Extended Response**

**23.** Responses will vary. Students should recognize the following causes and effects: a. A peddler visits the Skibas' hut and shows the women many items, including a mirror (lines 16–23). b. The women become interested in the mirror and make an offer for it (lines 23–25). c. The peddler sells the women the mirror, knowing that they are trustworthy (lines 27–30). d. The Skibas become obsessed with looking in the mirror (line 31). e. The women are so focused on their physical flaws that they begin to neglect their duties (lines 33–41). f. The family members begin to doubt their worth and become jealous of the rich (lines 49–50). g. Another effect of the addition of the mirror is that Burek and Kot react negatively to their own reflections (lines 51–59). h. The animals turn against each other and must be separated (lines 59–65). i. Jan Skiba recognizes the problems caused by the mirror and removes it from the hut (lines 66–70). j. Jan returns the mirror to the peddler and buys gifts for the women (lines 70–71). k. In the absence of the mirror, Burek and Kot become friends again (lines 72–73). l. The daughters forget their flaws and find husbands (lines 73–74). m. The episode with the mirror prompts a visit from the village priest, who reminds the family members of what their concerns should be (lines 74–78).

**24.** Students should recognize that the characters' reactions to the mirror effectively demonstrate the theme "Vanity is destructive." Students may provide the following examples to support their answers. a. The Skiba women become obsessed with their looks and consequently neglect their familial duties (lines 33–41). b. The Skibas' awareness of their physical faults causes them to worry and to question the family's status in society (lines 49–50). c. The dog and cat become aware of their physical differences, turn on each other, and bring chaos to the once peaceful household (lines 59–65). d. The Skibas forget about the beauty of nature (lines 67–69). e. The Skibas forget the "true" image they should be observing: the image of the soul (lines 74–78).

**Vocabulary**

**1.** A
**2.** C
**3.** B
**4.** D
**5.** A
**6.** B
**7.** D
**8.** A

**Writing and Grammar**

**1.** B
**2.** A
**3.** C
**4.** A
**5.** B
**6.** A
**7.** D
**8.** B
**9.** C
**10.** D
**11.** A
**12.** D

**Writing**

1. Has an interesting plot and one or more characters
2. Develops and resolves a central conflict
3. Includes descriptive details that reveal the setting and characters
4. Uses dialogue to show characters' personalities
5. Introduces the characters, the setting, or the action in a way that gets a reader's attention
6. Follows a clear sequence of events
7. Resolves the conflict with a convincing conclusion
8. Shows the writer's individual style
9. Uses sensory language to show what fictional

characters and places are like
10. Varies sentence lengths
11. Uses correct grammar, spelling, and punctuation

## Unit 4, Test A

### Comprehension

1. A
2. A
3. B
4. A
5. D
6. B
7. B
8. D

### Written Response

### Short Response

9. Responses will vary. Students may suggest that the dialogue reveals that Bob is friendly, cheerful, or arrogant. Students may use one of the following examples as support: a. Bob readily offers an explanation for his presence on the street to the police officer (lines 13–17). This readiness shows his friendliness. b. Bob's warm description of his friend shows his cheerful nature (lines 22–24). c. Bob boasts to the police officer about his sharp wit and "razor-edge" (lines 43–46). This boasting reveals Bob's arrogant nature.
10. Responses will vary. Students should include the following information in their responses: a. Jimmy tells Bob that he had kept their appointment (line 92). b. When Bob lit his match, Jimmy recognized him as a wanted criminal from Chicago (lines 92–93). c. Jimmy could not bring himself to arrest his old friend, so he found a plain clothes police officer to arrest Bob (lines 93–94).

### Extended Response

11. Responses will vary. Students may include the following points in their summaries: a. A police officer patrols an empty street at night. The police officer meets a man waiting in a darkened doorway (lines 1–13). b. The man explains that he is waiting for a friend he has not seen for twenty years. As young men, the two friends agreed to meet at the restaurant where they had last seen each other. The waiting man, Bob, had gone West while his friend Jimmy remained in New York (lines 14–46). c. The police officer wishes Bob luck and leaves. A few minutes later a man shows up claiming to be Bob's former friend Jimmy. Bob is excited to see his friend and begins to tell him about his success in the West (lines 47–77). d. The two men begin to walk to a restaurant, but Bob realizes that the man is not his former friend. The man tells Bob that Bob is under arrest. The man hands him a note from Jimmy. The note says that Jimmy was the police officer who had talked to Bob earlier. He had recognized Bob as a wanted criminal. Jimmy found a plain clothes officer to arrest Bob (lines 78–95).

### Comprehension

1. A
2. B
3. B
4. A
5. C
6. D
7. B
8. B

### Written Response

### Short Response

9. Responses will vary. Students may provide two of the following examples that help create an upbeat mood: a. The author uses vivid language to describe the colors she wears, such as "beautiful reds and oranges, and greens and pinks, and teals and turquoise" (lines 4–7). This word choice creates an upbeat mood b. The author uses positive words, such as "loving," "beautiful," "confident," "enhances," and "comfortable" (lines 4,30,38,41). These words help create an upbeat mood. c. The author uses words such as "tickled," "glad," and "delighted" (lines 21–23). These happy words create an upbeat mood.
10. Responses will vary. Students may identify two of the following

opinions: a. ". . . I kept us nicely dressed in discoveries bought at the Salvation Army and other secondhand shops" (lines 3–4). b. "When people are young, they desperately need to conform, and no one can embarrass a young person in public so much as an adult to whom he or she is related" (lines 25–26). c. "I think I know what looks good on me, and I certainly know what feels good in me" (lines 33–34). d. "Then I am so comfortable that whatever I wear looks good on me even to the external fashion arbiters" (lines 43–44). e. "You will always be in fashion if you are true to yourself, and only if you are true to yourself" (lines 56–57).

**Extended Response**

11. Responses will vary. Students may suggest that the author's imagery and word choice reveal a descriptive style. Students may use three of the following examples as support: a. In lines 4–5, the author's style is descriptive because she uses imagery that appeals to the sense of sight. She describes the bright colors of her clothing b. In lines 12–14, the author's style is descriptive because she describes her "colorful regalia" and beads and head wraps. She uses imagery that appeals to the sense of sight. c. In lines 15–16, the author uses imagery that appeals to sight. She describes her son's eyes as "an old man's eyes." This imagery reveals a descriptive style. d. In lines 15–16, the author uses imagery that appeals to sound. She says a "young boy's voice." This imagery shows a descriptive style. e. The author's precise, vivid words reveal a descriptive style. Examples of the author's descriptive word choice include "beautiful," "concocted," "quite solemnly," "puzzled," "huffily," "tickled," and "imprisoned" (lines 4,7,14,16,19,21,45).

**Vocabulary**

1. B
2. A
3. D
4. A
5. D
6. C
7. D
8. B

1. A
2. C
3. B
4. C
5. A
6. D
7. B
8. A
9. B
10. B
11. C
12. B

**Writing**

Rubric: Interpretive Essay

Includes a thesis statement that identifies the key points the writer will discuss
Supports key points with evidence—details, examples, or quotations from the text
Identifies the author and title of the work in an interesting introduction
Provides plot details as needed to help the reader understand the interpretation
Summarizes the interpretation in a conclusion and tells why the story is interesting or important
Has an appropriate tone for the audience and purpose
Uses precise language to examine and explain the work
Varies sentence structures
Uses correct grammar, spelling, and punctuation

## Unit 4, Test B/C

**Comprehension**

1. D
2. A
3. A
4. C
5. D
6. A
7. A
8. B

**Written Response**

**Short Response**

9. Responses will vary. Students may suggest that the dialogue reveals that the plain clothes officer is clever, calm, sarcastic, or authoritative. Students may

use one of the following examples as support: a. The plain clothes officer is clever because he is able to fool Bob into believing that he is Jimmy Wells (lines 71). b. The officer is sarcastic when he calls Bob "Silky Bob" in lines 84–85. c. The officer is calm and authoritative when he arrests Bob and gives Bob the note to read. The officer says, "'Going quietly, are you? That's sensible.'" (lines 86–87) d. The officer is authoritative when he tells Bob what to do and where Bob can read the note (lines 87–88).

**10.** Responses will vary. Students should include the following points in their summaries: a. Jimmy Wells stayed in New York and became a police officer (lines 25–26, 89–96). b. "Silky" B ob went West and became a criminal (lines 34–35 85–94).

**Extended Response**

**11.** Responses will vary. Students may suggest that the overall mood is suspenseful or mysterious. Students may use any of the following examples to support their responses: a. The setting is a dark, empty street on a cold, damp night (lines 1–4). This setting creates a mysterious and suspenseful mood. b. The first character introduced is a policeman, which suggests that there may be something unsafe or criminal about to happen (lines 1–4). This character introduction helps build a suspenseful and mysterious mood. c. The other main character is described as standing in a darkened doorway. This character description creates a suspenseful and mysterious mood (lines 1–13). d. The waiting man explains through dialogue that he is waiting for a friend he has not seen in twenty years. This dialogue creates a suspenseful mood. (lines 14–17). e. O. Henry describes Bob's appearance. Bob has a scar over his eye and "keen" eyes. He also wears a diamond scarfpin and a diamond watch. These descriptions add to the mysterious mood because Bob's appearance is shady or criminal (lines 19–21). f. The third character turns out to be a plain clothes police officer and not Jimmy Wells, Bob's former friend. This character introduction helps create a suspenseful and mysterious mood (lines 80–82).

**12.** Responses will vary. Students may suggest that the word choice, sentence structure, and tone reveal an informal, conversational, or descriptive style. Students may use any of the following examples as support for their responses: a. Throughout the story, O. Henry uses colorful words and phrases to give detailed descriptions of the setting, characters, and characters' actions. Some examples of descriptive words and phrases are "chilly gusts of wind with a taste of rain in them," "intricate and artful movements," "suddenly slowed," and "spoke up quickly" (lines 3,5,11,13). These descriptions show a descriptive style b. O. Henry describes how the policeman walks with a "slight swagger" and how he moves his club. He describes the policeman as "stalwart" with a "watchful eye." He is a "fine picture of the guardian of the peace." These descriptions contribute to O. Henry's descriptive style (lines 5–7). c. In lines 19–21, O. Henry describes Bob's "square-faced jaw," "keen eyes" and "little white scar near his eyebrow." This imagery reveals a descriptive style. d. O. Henry's sentence structure is varied throughout the story. He uses a combination of long and short sentences that results in an informal, conversational style. e. O. Henry's use of colloquial terms and phrases in the dialogue also adds to the conversational, informal style. Examples of slang terms and phrases include "my chum, and the finest chap in the world," "it seems to me," "You bet!" and "Bless my heart!" (lines 22,32,43,64). f. O. Henry's tone toward Bob in lines 22–30 of the story is humorous or amused. This reveals an informal style.

**Comprehension**

**1.** C
**2.** A
**3.** C
**4.** D
**5.** D
**6.** D
**7.** A
**8.** A

**Written Response**

**Short Response**

**9.** Responses will vary. Students may suggest one of the following opinions and explanations: a. "I kept us nicely dressed in discoveries bought at the Salvation Army and other secondhand shops" (lines 3–4). This statement is an opinion because a person could argue that Angelou and her son were not nicely dressed. b. "When people are young, they desperately need to conform, and no one can embarrass a young person in public so much as an adult to whom he or she is related" (lines 25–26). This is an opinion because a person could argue that young people do not want to conform and that relatives do not easily embarrass them. c. "I think I know what looks good on me, and I certainly know what feels good in me" (lines 33–34). This is an opinion because it is what Angelou thinks and cannot be proven. d. "You will always be in fashion if you are true to yourself, and only if you are true to yourself" (lines 56–57). This is an opinion because a person could argue that being true to yourself does not make a person fashionable.

**10.** Responses will vary. Students should suggest that the son wanted Angelou to wear matching sweaters like the other mothers. He wanted her to wear the sweaters when she came to visit him. Angelou's clothing embarrassed him (lines 16–26).

**Extended Response**

**11.** Responses will vary. Students may suggest that Angelou's word choice and sentence structure reveal an informal, conversational, or descriptive style. Students may use any of the following examples to support their responses: a. Throughout the selection, Angelou uses descriptive language. Some examples are "beautiful," "concocted," "quite solemnly," "puzzled," "huffily," "tickled," and "imprisoned" (lines 4,7,14,16,19,21,45). These words reveal a descriptive style b. Angelou also uses vivid language to describe the colors she wears, such as "beautiful reds and oranges, and greens and pinks, and teals and turquoise"(lines 4–7). This language reveals her descriptive style. c. Angelou's word choice reveals an informal or conversational style. Some examples of informal word choice are "'getups,'" "I am happy to say," "maybe a little huffily," and "to be a little more" (lines 8,11,18,19,29). c. Angelou's word choice reveals an informal or conversational style. Some examples of informal word choice are "'getups,'" "I am happy to say," "maybe a little huffily," and "to be a little more" (lines 9, 12, 21, 31) Angelou uses first person pronouns and directly addresses the reader as "you" in the second half of the selection. This use creates a conversational style (lines 60–68). e. Angelou's sentence structure gives the selection an informal, conversational style. Many of the sentences are long and string clauses together with conjunctions. The sentences mimic speech patterns (lines 2–15).f. Angelou often begins her sentences with conjunctions, which gives the piece an informal, conversational style (lines 6, 10, 12).

**12.** Responses will vary. Students may suggest that Angelou's tone becomes more serious as the selection progresses. Throughout the selection, Angelou's tone is humorous, frustrated, serious, thoughtful, condemning, reflective, and frank. Students may suggest that Angelou changes her tone throughout the selection to become more persuasive at the end when she gives advice to the reader. Students may use the following examples to support their responses: a. In lines 1–13, Angelou's tone is somewhat lighthearted and humorous as she describes the colorful "'getups'" she enjoyed putting together. Angelou uses this tone in the beginning to engage the reader. b. Angelou's tone becomes vexed or frustrated in lines 14–24 as she describes her son's embarrassment about her clothing. She describes herself responding "huffily" to her son. This frustrated tone appeals to readers who have experienced similar situations. c. In lines 25–28, Angelou's tone shifts again to become serious and reflective as she shares what she learned through her experience with her son. This shift in tone gives Angelou credibility with the reader. d. In lines 45–55, Angelou's tone is condemning of those who try to make fashion decisions for others and those who judge people according to whether they meet the latest fashion trends. This condemning tone helps persuade readers to agree with Angelou. e. In lines 56–63, Angelou's tone is serious, thoughtful, and frank as she gives readers advice on how to be themselves. Angelou's serious tone at the end makes her argument more persuasive.

**Vocabulary**

1. C
2. A
3. D
4. A
5. C
6. D
7. D
8. B

**Writing and Grammar**

1. B
2. A
3. A
4. C
5. A
6. D
7. C
8. A
9. B
10. B
11. A
12. D

**Writing**

Rubric: Interpretive Essay

Includes a thesis statement that identifies the key points the writer will discuss
Supports key points with evidence—details, examples, or quotations from the text
Identifies the author and title of the work in an interesting introduction
Provides plot details as needed to help the reader understand the interpretation
Summarizes the interpretation in a conclusion and tells why the story is interesting or important
Has an appropriate tone for the audience and purpose
Uses precise language to examine and explain the work
Varies sentence structures
Uses correct grammar, spelling, and punctuation

## Unit 5, Test A

**Comprehension**

1. A
2. B
3. C
4. B
5. A
6. A

**Comprehension**

7. B
8. C
9. D
10. A
11. C
12. A
13. C

**Comprehension**

14. B

**15.** C

**16.** A

**Written Response**

**Short Response**

**17.** Responses will vary. Students may identify one of the following examples of imagery: a. In line 2, the speaker appeals to the sense of sight by describing the flower on which the butterfly sits. b. In line 5, the speaker appeals to the senses of sight and touch by comparing the butterfly's motionlessness to that of "frozen seas." c. In lines 7–9, the speaker appeals to the senses of sight, touch, and hearing by describing the breeze moving through the trees and "calling" the butterfly.

**18.** Responses will vary. Students may provide two of the following examples from stanza 1: a. The word "hour" in line 1 rhymes with "flower" in line 2. b. The word "indeed" in line 3 rhymes with "feed" in line 4. c. The word "seas" in line 5 rhymes with "breeze" in line 7 and "trees" in line 8. d. The word "then" in line 6 rhymes with "again" in line 9.

**Extended Response**

**19.** Responses will vary. Students may suggest moods such as joyful, respectful, peaceful, nostalgic, and affectionate. Students should recognize that figurative language helps create the mood in the poem. Students may support their answers with three of the following examples: a. The personification of the breeze in line 1 of the first poem creates a joyful, playful mood. It helps you imagine the breeze dancing through the trees and encouraging the butterfly to take flight. b. The figurative language in lines 12–19 of the first poem helps create a respectful, sweet mood. The speaker invites the butterfly to rest near him and share happy childhood memories. c. The metaphor in line 4 of the second poem creates a pleasant, nostalgic mood. The butterfly reminds the speaker of the carefree joy of his childhood. d. The figurative language in lines 14–18 of the second poem creates an energetic, youthful mood. The speaker remembers himself running outdoors, "hunting" the butterfly and never catching it.

**Comprehension**

**20.** C

**21.** B

**22.** A

**23.** D

**Written Response**

**Short Response**

**24.** Responses will vary. Students may use the following examples to support the inference: a. The author stands motionless under the tree to gain the owls' trust (lines 5–8). b. The author shows patience and respect when he takes an owl and places it on his shoulder for a few minutes. He returns each owl safely to the branch (lines 10–12). c. The author puts all of the owls on his arm and carries them gently out of the forest (lines 12–19). d. The owls live in the author's attic. He prepares a branch for them and gives them food. He also leaves the window open for them to come and go as they please (lines 17–22).

**25.** Responses will vary. Students may provide one of the following examples: a. The author describes how the owls perched on his arm (lines 17–19). This example appeals to the sense of touch. b. The author describes how he walked out of the forest (lines 17–19). This example appeals to the sense of sight. c. The author describes what he put in the attic for the owls (lines 17–19). This appeals to the sense of sight. d. The author describes how he sets out food for the owls (lines 17–19). This example appeals to the sense of taste. e. The author describes the size of the farm that he moved to in New Hope (lines 22–24).

This appeals to the sense of sight.

**Extended Response**

**26.** Responses will vary. Students may infer that the owls feel comfortable and safe around the author. Students may use the following examples to support the inference: a. The owls stay on the branch when the author stands motionless under the tree (lines 5–8). b. The baby owl allows the author to pick it up and place it on his shoulder (lines 10–12). c. The author puts all of the owls on his arm and carries them out of the forest (lines 12–19). d. The owls live in the author's attic. They are able to leave through an open window, but they always come back (lines 17–22).

**Vocabulary**

**1.** C
**2.** D
**3.** C
**4.** C

**1.** D
**2.** A
**3.** C
**4.** B
**5.** D
**6.** A
**7.** B
**8.** D
**9.** C
**10.** A
**11.** C
**12.** D

**Writing**

Rubric: Personal Response to a Poem
1. Clearly presents an overall response to the work
2. Supports key points with details and quotations
3. Identifies the title and author of the work in the introduction
4. Gives enough information about the work for readers to understand the response
5. Includes transitional words and phrases
6. Summarizes the response in a conclusion
7. Tone is honest and engaging
8. Uses literary terms when describing the work
9. Varies sentence beginnings
10. Uses correct grammar, spelling, and punctuation

## Unit 5, Test B/C

**Comprehension**

**1.** D
**2.** A
**3.** D
**4.** C
**5.** C
**6.** B

**Comprehension**

**7.** A
**8.** C
**9.** D
**10.** B
**11.** A
**12.** C
**13.** A

**Comprehension**

**14.** B
**15.** C
**16.** A

**Written Response**

**Short Response**

**17.** Responses will vary. Students may use one of the following examples of figurative language: "To a Butterfly" a. Line 9 of the first poem, "And calls you forth again," is an example of personification. b. Line 13 of the first poem, "And rest as in a sanctuary," is an example of a simile. c. Line 4 of the second poem, "Historian of my Infancy," is an example of a metaphor. "Starlings in Winter" d. Line 5, "they are acrobats," is a metaphor. e. Line 10, "they float like one stippled star," is a simile. f. Line 21, "this wheel of many parts," is a metaphor. g. Line 24, "Ah, world, what lessons you prepare for us," is an example of personification.

**18.** Responses will vary. "Starlings in Winter" is written in free verse. Students may use the following examples to support the answer: a. The lengths of the lines vary. For example, line 2 is much longer than line 4. b. There is no rhyme scheme. For example, none of the lines in stanza 2 end with a rhyme. c. There is no set pattern of rhythm. For example, the rhythm in lines 14–18 does not match the rhythm in lines 29–32.

**Extended Response**

**19.** Responses will vary. Students should recognize that the speaker most likely had a pleasant childhood that he now remembers with affection. Students might use the following examples as support: a. In lines 1–6 of the first poem, the speaker patiently watches the butterfly with childlike awe and wonder. He is amazed that the butterfly can be so still. b. In lines 16–19 of the first poem, the speaker invites the butterfly to rest and "talk" of happy summer days. He describes his childhood as "sweet" and carefree. c. In lines 1–9 of the second poem, the speaker pleads with the butterfly to stay with him. The butterfly has awakened the speaker's childhood memories, and the speaker wants to prolong the happiness of the moment. d. In lines 10–13 of the second poem, the speaker happily recalls the "pleasant" days when he would chase butterflies with his sister. e. The second poem ends with the image of the speaker chasing the butterfly as a happy, energetic youth, concerned with nothing more than capturing his "prey" (lines 14–16).

**20.** Responses will vary. Students may suggest any of the following: a. The imagery in lines 1–6 of the first poem suggests the peacefulness of the situation and the elegance and delicacy of the butterfly. The speaker watches in awe the complete stillness of the butterfly. b. The imagery in lines 7–9 of the first poem suggests playfulness and innocence. The breeze "finds" the still butterfly and encourages it to take flight. c. The imagery in lines 10–15 of the first poem suggests rest and safety. The speaker is comfortable surrounded by his sister's flowers, and he invites the butterfly to peacefully rest near him. d. The imagery in lines 16–19 of the first poem suggests joy and innocence. It is a beautiful day, and the speaker fondly remembers happy summer days as a child. e. The imagery in line 4 of the second poem suggests feelings of nostalgia. The butterfly reminds the speaker of his childhood. f. The imagery in lines 10–18 of the second poem suggests the affectionate, fond memories of childhood. It also conveys the idea that the butterfly is as fragile as it is beautiful.

**Comprehension**

**21.** C
**22.** B
**23.** A
**24.** A

**Written Response**

**Short Response**

**25.** What inference could you make about the author's personality? Give one example from the selection to support your inference.
25. Responses will vary. Students may infer that the author is patient, intelligent, or sensitive. Students may use the following examples to support their inferences: a. The author stands motionless under the tree for fifteen minutes or half an hour. He does this for several weeks (lines 6–10). This supports the inference that the author is patient. b. The author lifts each owl and places it on his arm. Then after a few minutes, he returns the owl to the branch. He does this for several weeks (lines 10–14). This supports the inference that the author is patient. c. The author walks slowly out of the woods with all the owls perched on his arm (lines 17–19). his supports the inference that the author is patient. d. The author knows that he must not disturb the owls because they will fly away (lines 4–5). This supports the inference that the author is intelligent and sensitive to the feelings of the owls. e. The author comes up with a plan to make the owls comfortable with him (lines 6–12). This

supports the inference that the author is intelligent.
f. The author was smart enough to prepare for the owls' arrival. He has a branch set out for them and some food (lines 17–19). This supports the inference that the author is intelligent and sensitive to the needs of the owls.

**26.** Responses will vary. Students may infer that author cares for and respects the owls. Students may provide the following details: a. The author shows his respect for the owls when he takes time to make the owls comfortable with his presence (lines 4–10). b. The author shows respect and care for the owls when he takes them from their branch and places them on his arm for several minutes at a time (lines 10–14) . c. The author shows care for the owls when he walks slowly out of the woods (lines 17–19). d. The author shows care for the owls when he provides them with a branch and food in his attic (lines 17–19). e. The author shows respect for the owls when he leaves the window open in the attic. This allows the owls to come and go as they please (lines 19–22).

## Extended Response

**27.** Responses will vary. Students should explain that the imagery in the selection depicts nature as mysterious and delicate. Students may support their answers with the following examples: a. The images of the deep woods and skittish owls create a mysterious picture of nature (lines 1–3). b. The image of the author carefully approaching and observing the owls indicates that nature is delicate (lines 4–8). c. The images of the author's gentle interaction with the owls suggest that the owls could flee at any time. This shows the delicateness of nature (lines 9–16). d. The images of the owls living within the author's house are unexpected and further reinforce the idea that nature is mysterious (lines 17–22).

**28.** Responses will vary. Students should recognize that Kunitz wants to feel at home in his new country environment and hopes to accomplish this by establishing a bond with nature. He becomes part of the owls' world and makes them a part of his world. Students may support their answers with the following examples: a. The author is determined. He vows to befriend the owls and makes a plan to carry out this vow (lines 4–8). b. The author is respectful. He carefully approaches the owls and shows them consideration. (lines 9–16). c. The author is creative. He sets up a new home for the owls in his attic (lines 17–22). d. The author is reflective. He describes his experiences with the owls in detail and recognizes the importance of the experiences (lines 1–24).

## Vocabulary

**1.** D
**2.** B
**3.** C
**4.** D

## Writing and Grammar

**1.** A
**2.** A
**3.** D
**4.** B
**5.** C
**6.** D
**7.** B
**8.** C
**9.** D
**10.** C
**11.** A
**12.** D

## Writing

Rubric: Personal Response to a Poem
1. Clearly presents an overall response to the work
2. Supports key points with details and quotations
3. Identifies the title and author of the work in the introduction
4. Gives enough information about the work for readers to understand the response
5. Includes transitional words and phrases
6. Summarizes the response in a conclusion

7. Tone is honest and engaging
8. Uses literary terms when describing the work
9. Varies sentence beginnings
10. Uses correct grammar, spelling, and punctuation

## Unit 6, Test A

### Comprehension

**1.** D
**2.** A
**3.** A
**4.** B
**5.** A
**6.** D
**7.** B
**8.** C
**9.** D
**10.** D
**11.** A

### Comprehension

**12.** C
**13.** B
**14.** A
**15.** C
**16.** A
**17.** B
**18.** D

### Comprehension

**19.** A
**20.** B

### Written Response

#### Short Response

**21.** Responses will vary. Students may give a summary such as the following: When the group stops walking, Uitziton proves that his decision to keep the sticks was wise. He uses the sticks to create a fire, and the formerly cold group is now grateful and warm.

**22.** Responses will vary. Students may recognize that the ancient Greeks valued subtlety, practicality, humility, simplicity, or wisdom. Students may provide one of the following examples: a. Athene's subtle, simple gift will provide more to the new city than Poseidon's grand gift (lines 44–53). b. Humble Athene is chosen as the city's patron over proud Poseidon (lines 54–55). c. Athene's gift will give the Athenians practical benefits such as food and increased trade. Poseidon's gift is more for show than practicality (lines 22–53). d. Athene shows wisdom and foresight in her gift, and Poseidon shows pride and strength in his gift (lines 22–53).

### Extended Response

**23.** Responses will vary. Students should recognize that Poseidon shows bad behavior and Athene shows good behavior. Students may support their answers with two of the following examples: a. Poseidon's gift is obvious and showy. He is more concerned about showing off his power and strength than about providing the city with a thoughtful, beneficial gift (lines 22–28). b. Poseidon's response to Athene's gift is rude and arrogant. He laughs at her small gift, assuming that his gift is better (lines 37–42). c. Athene's gift is subtle, simple, and practical. She focuses on giving the city a thoughtful, beneficial gift (lines 31–36, 44–53). d. Athene approaches the gods with humility. She does not try to show off her powers (lines 31–36,44–53).

### Vocabulary

**1.** C
**2.** A
**3.** B
**4.** D
**5.** D
**6.** B
**7.** B
**8.** A

### Writing and Grammar

**1.** B
**2.** C
**3.** D
**4.** A
**5.** B
**6.** A
**7.** B
**8.** D
**9.** D
**10.** C
**11.** B
**12.** D

### Writing

Rubric: Cause-and-Effect Essay
Identifies a true cause-and-effect relationship
Presents a thesis statement that explains the connection between causes and effects

Includes facts, examples, and other details to support each cause and effect
Presents causes and effects in a sensible order
Shows the relationship between causes and effects by using transitions
Has an interesting introduction and a conclusion that summarizes the cause-and-effect relationship
Has a tone that is appropriate for the audience and purpose
Explains each cause and effect with precise language
Varies sentence lengths to add interest and sophistication
Uses correct grammar, spelling, and punctuation

## Unit 6, Test B/C

**Comprehension**

**1.** A
**2.** D
**3.** B
**4.** D
**5.** B
**6.** A
**7.** B
**8.** B
**9.** D
**10.** D
**11.** A

**Comprehension**

**12.** C
**13.** B
**14.** A
**15.** C
**16.** A
**17.** B
**18.** D

**Comprehension**

**19.** A
**20.** C

**Written Response**

**Short Response**

**21.** Responses will vary. Students may give a summary such as the following: Someone opens the first bundle and reveals that it holds a valuable emerald. The people begin to fight over the jewel. Uitziton quiets the people and opens the second bundle, revealing that it holds two sticks.

**22.** Responses will vary. Students should note that Athene's gift reveals the value of practicality. Athene offers a simple, practical gift that will provide more to the new city than will Poseidon's grand gift. The judges appreciate the practical nature of the olive shrub, choosing it over a gift that, at first glance, seems much more impressive (lines 31–36,44–53).

**Extended Response**

**23.** Responses will vary. Students may support their answers with the following examples: a. Myths often explain how natural elements were created. This story tells how the natural elements of the salt spring and the olive tree came to be (lines 22–25,31–36). The story also tells how the city of Athens came to be (lines 54–55. b. Myths show the consequences of both good and bad behavior. In this story, Athene is rewarded for her good behavior (humbleness, simplicity, practicality) by being made the patron of the new city. Poseidon is punished for his bad behavior (arrogance, rudeness) by losing the contest (lines 54–59). c. Myths feature gods who have supernatural powers. This story's main characters are two gods who exhibit amazing strength (Poseidon) and wisdom (Athene) (lines 22–28,44–53). d. Sometimes the gods featured in myths are flawed. In this story, Poseidon is portrayed as showy and arrogant. These two flaws cost him the contest (lines 22–28,37–43).

**24.** Responses will vary. Students may recognize that the Aztecs valued the qualities of respect for religion and religious practices, bravery, cleverness, peace, foresight, practicality, and virtuosity. For whichever value a student chooses, the student should compare and contrast the importance of the value in Aztec society to the importance of the value today in the United States. Students should give real-life examples of the role of the value today in the United States. Students may support their answers with any of the following details from the legend: a. Uitziton waits for a sign from the heavens before deciding to move from Aztlan (lines 1–6) b. Uitziton, the hero of the story, is described as being "brave" and "clever" (line 4). c. Uitziton tells his people to stop fighting, and they listen to him (lines 33–36). d. Uitziton has the foresight and wisdom to realize that the common sticks will be more valuable and practical than the exotic emerald (lines 40–42). e. As one of the group's chiefs, Uitziton looks out for his people's best interests and helps ensure their well-being (lines 43–48).

**Vocabulary**

**1.** C
**2.** A
**3.** C
**4.** B
**5.** D
**6.** B
**7.** B
**8.** A

**Writing and Grammar**

**1.** B
**2.** C
**3.** D
**4.** A
**5.** B
**6.** A
**7.** B
**8.** D
**9.** D
**10.** B
**11.** C
**12.** D

**Writing**

Rubric: Cause-and-Effect Essay
Identifies a true cause-and-effect relationship
Identifies a true cause-and-effect relationship
Includes facts, examples, and other details to support each cause and effect
Presents causes and effects in a sensible order
Shows the relationship between causes and effects by using transitions
Shows the relationship between causes and effects by using transitions
Has a tone that is appropriate for the audience and purpose
Explains each cause and effect with precise language
Varies sentence lengths to add interest and sophistication
Uses correct grammar, spelling, and punctuation

## Unit 7, Test A

**Comprehension**

**1.** B
**2.** B
**3.** C
**4.** D

**Comprehension**

**5.** D
**6.** C
**7.** A
**8.** A

**Comprehension**

**9.** B
**10.** D

**Written Response**

**Short Response**

**11.** Responses will vary. Students may offer a summary such as the following: Goodall was shaken up by the chimpanzees' threatening behavior, but she was excited that it made them less afraid of her.

**12.** Responses will vary. Students may support the conclusion with one of the following examples from each excerpt: a. As a child, Goodall watched the ducks and dragonflies in London's parks and the animals in the London Zoo (*Jane Goodall: Pioneer Researcher*, lines 1–7). b. Goodall hid in a henhouse to watch how eggs were laid (*Jane Goodall: Pioneer Researcher*, lines 13–16). c. Goodall observed chimpanzee behavior in the rain (*In the Shadow of Man*, lines 1–4). d. Goodall observed the antics of Flo and her children during a heavy storm (*In the Shadow of Man*, lines 4–12).

**Extended Response**

**13.** Responses will vary. Students may conclude that Goodall respected the chimpanzees but was sometimes put in danger by them. Students may use three of the following details as support: a. Goodall wanted to learn about Africa's animals, not harm them (*Jane Goodall: Pioneer Researcher*, lines 44–45). b. Goodall wanted to observe the chimpanzees up close, and she sat through heavy storms to do so (*In the Shadow of Man*, lines 1–16). c. When Goliath confronted Goodall, she respectfully looked away so her stare was not seen as a threat (*In the Shadow of Man*, lines 27–29). d. Goodall was threatened by a group of chimpanzees, but she reacted appropriately and did not allow the incident to stop her research (*In the Shadow of Man*, lines 33–46). e. Goodall viewed the near-attack in a positive light; it made the chimpanzees less afraid of her (*In the Shadow of Man*, lines 44–46).

**Comprehension**

**14.** C
**15.** C
**16.** C
**17.** A
**18.** B
**19.** A

**Written Response**

**Short Response**

**20.** Responses will vary. Students may say that two topics of this excerpt are the dangers of Goodall's work and the behaviors of the chimpanzees at the park.

**21.** Responses will vary. Students may offer a summary such as the following: Now in her early sixties, Goodall continues to work on behalf of chimpanzees, although direct contact with them can sometimes be dangerous.

**Extended Response**

**22.** Responses will vary. Students should recognize that Goodall is considered important because of her love and respect for chimpanzees, her findings on chimpanzee behavior, her courage in dangerous situations, and her tireless efforts to improve the lives of chimpanzees. Students may use the following details as support: a. Goodall shows respect for the chimpanzees (*In the Shadow of Man*, lines 21–29) ; ("Crusading for Chimps and Humans," lines 15–16). b. Goodall encounters several dangerous situations involving chimpanzees, but she does not let fear stop her work (*In the Shadow of Man*, lines 33–46) ; ( "Crusading for Chimps and Humans," (lines 17–30.) d. Goodall seems to be just as passionate about chimpanzees in her sixties as she was as a child (*Jane Goodall: Pioneer Researcher, lines 15–16*) ; ("Crusading for Chimps and Humans," lines 44–45). c. Goodall promotes conservation and makes numerous efforts to improve chimpanzees' lives ("Crusading for Chimps and Humans," ( lines 1–6).

**Vocabulary**

**1.** C
**2.** A
**3.** C
**4.** A

**5.** A
**6.** A
**7.** D
**8.** B

**1.** B
**2.** C
**3.** A
**4.** D
**5.** A
**6.** C
**7.** A
**8.** A
**9.** B
**10.** A
**11.** B
**12.** D

**Writing**

1. Focuses on a single experience
2. Re-creates the event with descriptive details and dialogue
3. Gets the reader's attention with an interesting introduction
4. Makes the order of events clear by using transitional words and phrases
5. Concludes by summarizing the significance of the event
6. Uses the active voice
7. Brings the event alive for the reader by using sensory language

8. Uses a variety of sentence types (statements, questions, commands, and exclamations)
9. Uses correct grammar, spelling, and punctuation

## Unit 7, Test B/C

### Comprehension

**1.** B
**2.** B
**3.** D
**4.** D

### Comprehension

**5.** C
**6.** A
**7.** D
**8.** D

### Comprehension

**9.** B
**10.** A

### Written Response

### Short Response

**11.** Responses will vary. Students may give one of the following examples from each excerpt: a. As a child, Goodall hid by herself for five hours in the henhouse (*Jane Goodall: Pioneer Researcher*, lines 13–16). b. Goodall moved from England to Kenya to pursue her dream of working with African wildlife (*Jane Goodall: Pioneer Researcher*, lines 26–32). c. Goodall faced an attack by chimpanzees in Gombe, Tanzania (*In the Shadow of Man*, lines 21–46). d. Goodall remained calm during the attack and did not let the frightening experience hinder her work (*In the Shadow of Man*, lines 36–46).

**12.** Responses will vary. Students should recognize that the excerpt would not be as personal. It would tell the events from another person's point of view or from multiple sources. This style could provide a more objective view of the events, but it might fail to convey Goodall's thoughts and feelings. Students may also mention that, if written by someone else, the excerpt could contain the author's bias about Goodall.

### Extended Response

**13.** Responses will vary. Students may summarize the excerpt in the following way: Jane Goodall was born in London, England in 1934. As a small child, she enjoyed watching animals and insects in London's parks and zoos. Jane was so interested in animals that she carried a toy chimpanzee with her everywhere and once hid in a henhouse for five hours in order to see how eggs were laid. The Goodall family eventually moved to Bournemouth, a coastal town where Goodall could explore the countryside surrounding her home., At a young age, Goodall dreamed about traveling to Africa to see the animals there. After she finished school, she was invited to visit the continent and eventually saved enough money for the trip. Jane didn't want to leave Africa, a diverse land rich in culture, natural resources, and animals. Jane was able to stay in Africa after taking a job with Dr. Louis Leakey, the curator of the National Museum of Natural History.

**14.** Responses will vary. Students should recognize that Goodall's love of and respect for the natural world started when she was young and continued throughout her adult life. The determination, courage, and compassion that enabled her to achieve her goals were evident from her childhood on. Students may use the following examples from the excerpts: a. As a child, Goodall was intrigued by the animals in London's parks and zoo, and she was especially fond of her toy chimpanzee (*Jane Goodall Pioneer Researcher*, lines 1–12). Goodall's interest in animals continued into her adulthood and inspired her to travel to Africa to study chimpanzees. b. Even as a child, Goodall wanted to know the secrets of the animal world. She waited for hours in a henhouse to see how eggs were laid (*Jane Goodall: Pioneer Researcher*, lines 13–16).

As an adult in Tanzania, Goodall patiently waited out a chimpanzee threat, even though her instincts told her to run (*In the Shadow of Man*, lines 36–38). c. As a child, Goodall did not want to see even the smallest creature harmed (*Jane Goodall: Pioneer Researcher*, lines 3–7). As a young adult, Goodall wanted to learn about Africa's animals, not harm them (*Jane Goodall: Pioneer Researcher*, lines 43–44). In Tanzania, Goodall persistently observed chimpanzees in the rain to learn about their behaviors (*In the Shadow of Man*, lines 1–14). d. Goodall courageously traveled to Africa as a young adult and interviewed with Dr. Leakey (*Jane Goodall: Pioneer Researcher*, lines 30–32; 47–56). She displayed her courage later when the chimpanzees nearly attacked her in the forest. She reacted calmly and did not let the incident stop her from continuing her work (*In the Shadow of Man*, lines 33–46).

**Comprehension**

**15.** A

**16.** B

**17.** A

**18.** B

**19.** D

**20.** A

**Written Response**

**Short Response**

**21.** Responses will vary. Students may provide the following details to support their answers: a. Goodall returns to Gombe to see the chimpanzees (line 13). b. Goodall creates safe places for chimpanzees through conservation (line 15). c. Goodall tries to improve the chimpanzees environment (line 16 ).

**22.** Students may offer a summary such as the following: Goodall returns to Gombe after being gone for six months. She no longer conducts field research, but she remains active in improving the lives of chimpanzees. Several chimpanzees are in the camp when Goodall arrives.

**Extended Response**

**23.** Responses will vary. Students may respond with the following: a. The article's topic is Jane Goodall. Specifically, Miller describes Goodall's return to the camp in Gombe and her encounter with the chimpanzee family living there (lines 1–40). b. The purpose of this article is to inform the reader about Goodall's work and to describe the relationship she had with the chimpanzees in Gombe. Miller describes Goodall's conservation work and her attempt to improve conditions in which chimpanzees live (lines 14–16). c. The tone of this article is serious and anxious. Miller describes Goodall's return to Gombe and work matter-of-factly. He creates a feeling of suspense as the group encounters the chimpanzees. The experience with Frodo was clearly frightening to Miller. He seems to regard Goodall's work with the chimpanzees as important but extremely dangerous (lines 14–16).

**24.** Responses will vary. Students may say that the treatment of the subject and the scope of the article are effective. Students may note the following details in their response: a. The article's personal tone is effective because it communicates the danger that Goodall sometimes experiences as well as the lighthearted aspects of her relationship with the chimpanzees. b. The purpose to inform would be more effective if Miller had included detailed information about Goodall's current work. It would also be more effective if Miller had described typical male chimpanzee behavior. The reader does not know whether Frodo's behavior is unusual or common among male chimpanzees. c. The article might also have been more effective if Miller had described Goodall's other dangerous encounters with Frodo or if he had balanced Frodo's attack with a positive account of Frodo's relationship with Goodall.

**Vocabulary**

**1.** A
**2.** C
**3.** C
**4.** D
**5.** A
**6.** D
**7.** B
**8.** A

**1.** B
**2.** C
**3.** D
**4.** C
**5.** A
**6.** A
**7.** D
**8.** B
**9.** A
**10.** C
**11.** A
**12.** D

**Writing**

Rubric: Personal Narrative
1. Focuses on a single experience
2. Re-creates the event with descriptive details and dialogue
3. Gets the reader's attention with an interesting introduction
4. Makes the order of events clear by using transitional words and phrases
5. Concludes by summarizing the significance of the event
6. Uses the active voice
7. Brings the event alive for the reader by using sensory language
8. Uses a variety of sentence types (statements, questions, commands, and exclamations)
9. Uses correct grammar, spelling, and punctuation

## Unit 8, Test A

**Comprehension**

**1.** D
**2.** C
**3.** A
**4.** B
**5.** C
**6.** B
**7.** A
**8.** C

**Comprehension**

**9.** B
**10.** C
**11.** C
**12.** A
**13.** D
**14.** A
**15.** C
**16.** A
**17.** A
**18.** D
**19.** C
**20.** A

**Comprehension**

**21.** B
**22.** A

**Written Response**

**Short Response**

**23.** Responses will vary. Students may use one of the following opinions: a. "I'm an incurable optimist." (line 44) b. "You might think of this as a labor of love." (line 45) c. "And maybe that would encourage you to love me in return." (line 48) d. "It is possible for all of us to work on this—at home, in our schools, at our jobs." (line 49) e. "It is possible to work on human relationships in every area of our lives." (lines 49–50)

**24.** Responses will vary. Students may provide one of the following pieces of information: a. Jordan was born in Houston, Texas on February 21, 1936 (line 7). b. Jordan's parents were Benjamin and Arlyne Jordan (lines 7–8). c. Jordan's father was a warehouse clerk and a Baptist preacher (lines 8–9). d. Jordan's family lived in the Fifth Ward (line 9). e. Jordan spent time with her grandfather working at his junkyard business (lines 11–12) f. Jordan recited poems and stories at church (line 16).

**Extended Response**

**25.** Responses will vary. Students should suggest that the main idea is that people, especially parents, need to work to build a tolerant society. Students may suggest the following examples of persuasive techniques that support the main idea: a. The author explains that American race relations have had a "rocky history" (line 8). The author uses an appeal by association because she expects the readers to be part of American society. This persuasive technique supports the main idea that people need to build a tolerant society b. The author says that "the nation seems to be suffering from compassion fatigue" (lines 18–19). Her emotional appeal supports the main idea that work is needed to build a tolerant society. c. The author uses an appeal to logic when she mentions the situation in Bosnia (lines 21–22). She wants people to logically see that a tolerant society is necessary to prevent negative situations. d. The author uses emotional appeals when she describes the innocence of children (lines 33–37). This persuasive technique supports the main idea that parents need to help build a tolerant society. e. The author uses an emotional appeal when she explains that her goal is to bring people together (lines 44–48). This persuasive technique supports the main idea that people need to work toward a tolerant society.

### Vocabulary

1. D
2. A
3. D
4. B
5. A
6. D

### Writing and Grammar

1. B
2. C
3. C
4. B
5. B
6. C
7. A
8. C
9. B
10. C
11. D
12. B

### Writing

Rubric: Persuasive Essay
Presents a thesis statement taking a position on a clearly identified issue
Uses convincing details to support the position
Answers opposing arguments and counterclaims
Explains the issue in a memorable introduction
Uses transitions to create a consistent organizational pattern
Concludes by summarizing the position and issuing a call to action
Reflects the writer's commitment to his or her ideas
Uses persuasive language effectively
Varies sentence lengths and structures
Uses correct grammar, spelling, and punctuation

## Unit 8, Test B/C

### Comprehension

1. D
2. A
3. D
4. B
5. B
6. C
7. C
8. A
9. B

### Comprehension

10. C
11. A
12. B
13. B
14. C
15. D
16. B
17. A
18. A
19. B
20. C

### Comprehension

21. B
22. A

### Written Response

### Short Response

23. Responses will vary. Students should recognize that Jordan is appealing to common sense by saying that a more diverse society is obviously going to force people to learn to live together. People will have no choice other than to

learn how to deal with each other.

**24.** Responses will vary. Students may provide two of the following facts: a. Jordan received "an Honorary Doctorate from Harvard University" (lines 82–83). b. In 1990, Jordan was "named to the Texas Women's Hall of Fame" (line 83). c. She received the Eleanor Roosevelt Val-Kill Medal in 1992 (lines 84–85). d. Jordan received the "Springarn Medal from the National Association for the Advancement of Colored People" (lines 85–87). e. Jordan received the Presidential Medal of Freedom in 1994 (line 87).

**Extended Response**

**25.** Responses will vary. Students should suggest that the loaded language in the selection reveals that the author has biases in favor of Barbara Jordan and her work. Students may provide the following examples of loaded language: a. The author says that Jordan "worked to improve the lives of the poor and the working class" (lines 2–4). This loaded language reveals a bias in favor of Jordan's gifts to humanity. b. The author says that Jordan lived in "one of Houston's long-standing communities of African-Americans" (lines 9–10). The loaded language in this example reveals the author's bias that Jordan came from a stable, respected community. c. Lines 13–15 contain loaded language that reveals the author's bias that Jordan was an extremely determined person who beat many odds. d. The author says that Jordan "had a strong voice, and a lively manner of speaking" (lines 16–18). This description contains loaded language that shows a bias in favor of Jordan's speaking abilities. e. The author says that Jordan "easily became a winner in various contests" (lines 24–25). This loaded language reveals a bias in favor of Jordan's speaking skills. f. The author says that Jordan learned to "defend her ideas by speaking more clearly and sharpening her thinking" (lines 31–32). This loaded language reveals the author's bias that Jordan could quickly develop her skills. g. The author says that Jordan "became nationally known for her persuasive speaking skills, particularly after giving a compelling speech in favor of the impeachment of President Nixon" (lines 62–64). This loaded language reveals the author's bias that Jordan was an excellent public speaker.

**26.** Responses will vary. Students may suggest that Jordan's childhood, education, and political activities influenced her thoughts about race relations. Students may use the following examples as support: a. In "Barbara Jordan: Congresswoman," you learn that Jordan grew up in a poor family in an African-American community (lines 7–10). Her childhood most likely influenced her bias in "All Together Now" that race relations "have had a rocky history" (line 8). b. In "Barbara Jordan: Congresswoman," you learn that Jordan's grandfather encouraged her not to let people's prejudices stop her from succeeding (lines 11–15). Her grandfather's encouragement most likely influenced her strong bias in "All Together Now" that it is extremely important to create a tolerant society (lines 20–21). He may also have affected her belief that children learn their attitudes from parents and teachers (lines 35–37). c. In "Barbara Jordan: Congresswoman," you learn that Jordan complete[illegible] high school, college, and law school (lines 24–35). Her determination to bette[illegible] herself and her situation most likely affected her bia[illegible] in "All Together Now" tha[illegible] people should help better the lives of others (lines 44–48). d. In "Barbara Jordan: Congresswoman," you learn that Jordan was the first African-American woman elected to the Texas Senate and the first African American from the South elected to the U.S. House of Representatives (lines 45–47; 57–59). Jordan's achievements as an African American most likely affected her bias in "All Together Now" that people need to work toward improving race relations (lines 49–50). Her time in politics may have also affected her bias that it is people who need to better race relations, not government (lines 3–6).

**Vocabulary**

1. B
2. C
3. B
4. B
5. A
6. D

**Writing and Grammar**

1. B
2. C
3. C
4. C
5. B
6. A
7. A
8. C
9. A
10. B
11. C
2. A

**Writing**

Rubric: Persuasive Essay
Presents a thesis statement taking a position on a clearly identified issue
Uses convincing details to support the position
Answers opposing arguments and counterclaims
Uses transitions to create a consistent organizational pattern
Concludes by summarizing the position and issuing a call to action
Reflects the writer's commitment to his or her ideas
Uses persuasive language effectively
Varies sentence lengths and structures
Uses correct grammar, spelling, and punctuation

## Unit 9, Test A

**Using the Internet**

1. D
2. C
3. A

**Using the Library and Reference Sources; Evaluating Sources and Sites**

4. B
5. A
6. A
7. C
8. C

**Written Response**

**Short Response**

9. Responses will vary. Students may give two of the following items: a. Publication date—shows when the source was published or updated. b. Author's background—tells the author's qualifications for writing. c. Author's sources—shows how well-researched and reliable the source is. d. Preface or introduction—introduces the source and may describe the author's purpose.

**Identifying Primary and secondary sources; collecting data**

10. A
11. C
12. D
13. A
14. B
15. A

**Paraphrasing, Summarizing, and Plagiarizing**

16. C
17. A
18. B
19. D
20. A

**Written Response**

**Written Response**

**Short Response**

21. Students may present a summary such as the following: During the Qin dynasty, many convicted criminals labored on the wall as well as on other projects.

**Prewriting and Researching**

22. B
23. A
24. C
25. D
26. C
27. B

**28.** B
**29.** A
**30.** C
**31.** D
**32.** C
**33.** C

**Written Response**

**Written Response**

**Short Response**

**34.** Students should respond that "Ellis Island History—A Brief Look" by the National Park Service is a government Web site.

**Drafting, Revising, and Editing**

**35.** B
**36.** D
**37.** C
**38.** B
**39.** B
**40.** C
**41.** A
**42.** A
**43.** C
**44.** A
**45.** B
**46.** D
**47.** C
**48.** A
**49.** C
**50.** D

## Unit 9, Test B/C

**Using the Internet**

**1.** C
**2.** D
**3.** A

**Using the Library and Reference Sources; Evaluating sources and Sites**

**4.** D
**5.** C
**6.** B
**7.** A
**8.** C

**Written Response**

**Short Response**

**9.** Responses will vary. Students may suggest two of the following items: a. The publication date tells you whether the source is outdated. b. The author's background information tells you whether he or she is qualified to relay the material. c. The author's sources show how well-researched and reliable the source is. d. The preface or introduction introduces the source and may describe the author's purpose.

**Identifying primary and secondary sources; collecting data**

**10.** A
**11.** C
**12.** D
**13.** A
**14.** B
**15.** B

**Paraphrasing, Summarizing, and Plagiarizing**

**16.** C
**17.** B
**18.** A
**19.** D
**20.** A

**Written Response**

**21.** Students may present a summary such as the following: The emperor stated that any male over four feet tall could be forced to work, so even boys were taken away to build the Great Wall.

**Prewriting and Researchi**

**22.** B
**23.** A
**24.** B
**25.** C
**26.** C
**27.** D
**28.** C
**29.** A
**30.** B
**31.** A
**32.** C
**33.** D
**34.** C

**Drafting, Revising, and editing**

**35.** B
**36.** D
**37.** C
**38.** B
**39.** B
**40.** B
**41.** A
**42.** A
**43.** D
**44.** C
**45.** C

**Written Response**

**46.** Students should write the following Works Cited entry: Shapiro, Mary J. Gateway to Liberty. New York: Random House, 1986.

**47.** Students should write the following Works Cited entry: Evans, Humphrey. The Mystery of the Pyramids. New York: Thomas Y. Crowell Publishers, 1979.

**48.** Students should note that the supporting detail is that temples and other buildings surrounded the Pyramids.

**49.** Students should note that the supporting detail is that Ellis Island remains open as a historical site.

**50.** Students should note that the supporting detail is that thousands of immigrants went through Ellis Island each day.

## Benchmark Test 1

### Comprehension

**51.** B
**52.** A
**53.** D
**54.** A
**55.** C
**56.** B
**57.** B
**58.** C
**59.** D
**60.** A
**61.** B
**62.** A
**63.** D

### Written Response

### Short Response

**64.** Responses will vary. Students may cite one of the following internal conflicts: a. The narrator wants to show off his good report card, but he does not want to make Clyde feel bad (lines 9–10). b. The narrator wants to offer to help Clyde, but he does not want to appear to be bragging (lines 117–118).

**65.** Responses will vary. Students should recognize that the resolution of the story occurs when Clyde realizes that he shares his father's determination and refusal to fail. This resolution is explicit when Sam says "you are just like your father" (line 114) The conflict is resolved as Clyde discovers that his father, too, has experienced failure and that the best course of action is to stay in the academic program and work hard.

### Extended Response

**66.** Responses will vary. Students should recognize that Clyde and his father both encounter failure and that they both demonstrate persistence or dedication. Students may respond with the following explanations: a. Clyde experiences failure when he gets his report card and learns that he is failing math (lines 13–14) Similarly, his father encounters failure when he buys the trombone but is unable to play it at first (lines 84–85) Clyde demonstrates persistence or dedication when he decides to continue with the academic course (line 52) just as his father demonstrates persistence or dedication when he continues to practice the trombone (line 92) b. Clyde's adviser recommends that he drop the academic course because his grades are low (lines 22–23) Similarly, a neighbor complains and tells Clyde's father that he can't play the trombone well (lines 90–91) Clyde admits that when others doubt him, he is inspired to try harder (lines 111–112) Similarly, Mrs. Jones says that Clyde's father practiced harder after the neighbor complained and told him he couldn't play well (lines 93–94)

### Comprehension

**67.** A
**68.** D
**69.** C
**70.** C
**71.** A
**72.** A
**73.** D
**74.** A
**75.** C
**76.** B
**77.** A

### Written Response

### Short Response

**78.** Responses will vary. Students may identify one of the following conflicts: a. King Minos keeps Daedalus and Icarus imprisoned in a tower because they are the only ones who know how to escape the labyrinth (lines 65–74) Their imprisonment is an external conflict. b. Daedalus warns Icarus not to fly too close to the sun, but Icarus either forgets or is too curious to heed the advice (lines 82–89) Icarus' conflict is an internal one.

c. Icarus flies too close to the sun and his wings melt, causing him to fall into the ocean (lines 83–85) Icarus' conflict is an external one.

**79.** Responses will vary. Students may predict that James would disagree with Sammy, claiming that Icarus should have listened to his father. Students may argue that because James is a practical person, he would probably fail to see Sammy's point about wanting to fly as high as possible and instead claim that Icarus should have been more careful.

**Extended Response**

**80.** Responses will vary. Students should recognize that Voigt uses James's thoughts, speech, and actions, Sammy's thoughts and speech, and the narrator's comments to characterize James. Students may support their responses with two of the following examples: a. When Sammy says that he wants to be an astronaut and a tennis player, James tells him to be practical (lines 18–19) Voigt uses James's comment to show that he is a sensible, realistic person. b. James says that he thinks he'd be good at international banking law (lines 36–37) Voigt uses James's comment to show that he is interested in professions that are grounded in facts rather than imagination. c. James sputters when Sammy says that he wouldn't want to have a job in which "you didn't do anything" (lines 38–39) Voigt uses James's actions (i.e., sputtering) to show that he is dismissive of Sammy's comment and therefore slightly conceited. d. James reminds himself that Sammy is "just a kid" (line 43) e. James thinks to himself that Sammy doesn't understand the importance of grades (lines 46–47) Voigt uses James's thoughts to characterize him as pompous and self-important. f. The narrator says that James used to know how hot the sun burns, but that he has forgotten (line 59) Voigt uses the narrator's comment to show that James is forgetful or that he doesn't care much about science. g. Sammy thinks to himself that James could never tell a story the way it should be told (lines 85–87) Voigt uses Sammy's thoughts to characterize James as unimaginative.

**Comprehension**

**1.** B
**2.** B
**3.** A
**4.** D
**5.** D
**6.** B
**7.** A
**8.** D

**Comprehension**

**9.** A
**10.** B
**11.** C
**12.** B

**Comprehension**

**13.** A
**14.** B
**15.** B

**Written Response**

**Short Response**

**16.** Responses will vary. Students may cite the following details: a. The writer of "Lifesaver" says that Mack saw a patch of calm water while waves were lapping nearby (lines 14–15) According to "Rip Current Safety," a "break in the incoming wave pattern" (line 35) is one of the telltale signs of a rip current. b. In "Lifesaver," the writer says that Mack saw a boy being dragged out to sea (line 30) According to "Rip Current Safety," rip currents can sweep even strong swimmers out to sea (lines 10–11)

**17.** Responses will vary. Students should recognize that the writer believes that rip currents are deadly or extremely dangerous. Students may support their responses with the following details: a. The writer of "Lifesaver" says that rip currents cause more deaths than shark attacks, tornadoes, lightning, or hurricanes (lines 24–25)

This detail emphasizes the writer's position that rip currents are deadly or extremely dangerous. b. The writer of "Lifesaver" says that 80 percent of beach rescues are rescues from rip currents and that more than 100 people die each year as a result of rip currents (lines 25–28) This detail emphasizes the writer's position that rip currents are deadly or extremely dangerous.

**Extended Response**

**18.** Responses will vary. Students should acknowledge that Mack acted appropriately. Students may support their answers with the following details: a. According to "Rip Current Safety," you should remain calm to preserve energy and think clearly if you are caught in a rip current (line 47) In "Lifesaver," the writer says that Mack tried to calm the boy (line 33) Mack's attempt to calm the boy shows that he followed the rules for surviving rip currents. b. According to "Rip Current Safety," you should float or calmly tread water if you are unable to swim out of a rip current (line 50) In "Lifesaver," the writer says that Mack began to tread water when he first reached the boy (line 37) and that he kept treading forward when he realized that the current was too strong to swim (lines 48–49) The fact that Mack waited while treading water shows that he followed the rules for surviving rip currents. c. According to "Rip Current Safety," you should draw attention to yourself if you are unable to reach the shore (lines 52–53 ) In "Lifesaver," the writer says that Mack waved and called and waved his right arm when he saw a lifeguard Jeep on the shore (lines 54–55) Mack's calling and waving show that he followed the rules for surviving rip currents.

**Vocabulary**

**1.** A
**2.** B
**3.** D
**4.** B
**5.** C
**6.** A
**7.** B
**8.** D
**9.** C
**10.** A
**11.** D
**12.** C
**13.** B
**14.** C
**15.** D
**16.** A
**1.** C
**2.** A
**3.** B
**4.** D
**5.** C
**6.** A
**7.** B
**8.** D
**9.** B
**10.** D
**11.** A
**12.** A
**13.** B
**14.** C
**15.** A
**16.** C
**17.** D
**18.** C
**19.** B
**20.** A

**Writing**

Rubric: Comparison-Contrast Essay

Identifies the characters or subjects being compared and/or contrasted
Includes a thesis statement that identifies similarities and/or differences
Supports key ideas with examples
Includes a strong introduction and a satisfying conclusion
Follows a clear organizational pattern
Connects ideas with transitions
Uses language that is appropriate for the audience and purpose
Uses precise words to explain similarities and differences
Varies sentence beginnings
Uses correct grammar, spelling, and punctuation

# Benchmark Test 2

**Comprehension**

**1.** D
**2.** C
**3.** C

**4.** C
**5.** B
**6.** A
**7.** D
**8.** B
**9.** C
**10.** A
**11.** C
**12.** B
**13.** C
**14.** C
**15.** A
**16.** B
**17.** D
**18.** C
**19.** D
**20.** A
**21.** D
**22.** B
**23.** A

## Written Response

### Short Response

**24.** Responses will vary. Students should recognize that the author's style is formal and serious. Students may point out that the author's style is very detailed and descriptive. Also, students may note that sentence structures change when the author begins to describe what happened to Earth. Students may include two of the following details: a. Lines 1–4 are a single long sentence that includes such words as "echoing corridors," "uppermost levels," and "swiftly growing vegetation." The lengthy sentence and formal diction are an example of the author's serious style. b. In lines 39–44, the author includes such details as "domes and radio towers," "curiously shaped structures," and "a squat smokestack." The rich details of these sentences are an example of the author's descriptive style. c. In lines 81–83, the author includes such phrases as "the faint whisper of the oxygen feed" and "an occasional metallic crepitation." The technical diction is an example of the author's very formal style. d. Lines 113–115 contain one complicated sentence that includes four clauses and six prepositional phrases. The structure of this sentence is an example of the almost mythological style the author uses to describe the end of life on Earth.

**25.** Responses will vary. Students should recognize that the narrator shows that Marvin shares the feelings of the people who lived in the Colony when Armageddon came to Earth, even though he did not share the experience. Marvin's response to the story shows both his exceptional empathy and his yearning for Earth. Students may support their responses with one of the following details: a. In lines 108–109, the narrator says that Marvin could not "picture the glowing, multicolored pattern of life on the planet he had never seen." This detail emphasizes that Marvin never experienced life on Earth, making his empathy all the more remarkable. b. In lines 110–111, the narrator states that Marvin "could share the agony of those final days." This detail shows that Marvin shares the feelings of the survivors of the Armageddon in the Colony, even though he did not share the experience.

### Extended Response

**26.** Responses will vary. Students may suggest that the story's topic is a boy's journey to view the world his parents came from. Students may also suggest that the story's theme is that Earth is precious and that our actions today can affect the future. Students may support their responses with some of the following details: a. In line 13, the narrator says of Marvin, "For the first time in his life, he was going Outside." This detail shows that the topic of the story is a boy's important journey. b. In line 22, the narrator describes the terrain ahead of Marvin as "the land which he had never yet entered." This detail suggests that the topic of the story is a boy's important journey. c. In line 90, the narrator says that Earth "called" to Marvin's "heart across the abyss of space" , showing that Earth has great meaning for Marvin, even though he has never been there. This detail suggests that the theme of the story is "Earth is precious." d. In line 102, the narrator describes the ruins of Earth as "a perennial reminder of the ruinous past", suggesting that humanity's past actions have been ruinous. This detail supports the story's theme that our actions today can affect the future. e. In line 106, the narrator indicates that the story of Earth's destruction "until this moment had meant no more" to Marvin than "the fairy tales he had once been told." This detail shows that Marvin has never seen Earth before, a fact indicating that the topic of the story is a boy's important journey. f. In line 124, the narrator states that one day Marvin's "children's children would return to claim their heritage" showing that Earth has now become Marvin's goal for the future. This detail suggests that the story's theme is that Earth is precious and that our actions today can affect the future.

**Comprehension**

**27.** D
**28.** A
**29.** D
**30.** C
**31.** D
**32.** B
**33.** C
**34.** D
**35.** A
**36.** D

**Comprehension**

**37.** B
**38.** D
**39.** D
**40.** A
**41.** B
**42.** A
**43.** C
**44.** D
**45.** B

**Comprehension**

**46.** C
**47.** A

**Written Response**

**Short Response**

**48.** Responses will vary. Students may include two of the following stages: a. In lines 11–12, the author says, "A young puppy (two to four months) is socially similar to a child aged four to seven years." his detail shows that like young children, very young dogs are highly impressionable. b. In line 33, the author says, "A puppy from five to six months of age is similar to a preadolescent child." This detail shows that puppies will show some bad behavior at this age. c. In line 38, the author says that from six to seven months is a puppy's "most difficult developmental period." This detail shows that puppies at this age show the same behavioral challenges as human teenagers. d. In line 45, the author says that when a puppy is from eight to ten months old, owners will "see a slow decrease in the difficult behavior." This detail shows that puppies begin to mature toward the end of the first year. e. In lines 47–48, the author writes, "By the time your pet reaches ten months," it "will behave properly most of the time." This detail shows that a dog nearing its first birthday is as developed as a human nearing his or her twenty-first birthday.

**49.** Responses will vary. Students may suggest that dogs misbehave because they see themselves as dominant within the family pack. Students may support their responses with two of the following details: a. In lines 23–24 of the excerpt from *Cesar's Way*, the author says, "If you don't become your dog's pack leader, he will assume that role and try to dominate you." This detail shows that not knowing its proper role will cause a dog to behave in unwanted ways. b. In lines 25–26 of the excerpt from *Dog Training Basics*, the author says that a puppy is "driven, through instinct, to work his way up the hierarchical ladder, testing other pack members." This detail shows that instinct can cause a puppy to misbehave. c. In line 41 of the excerpt from *Dog Training Basics*, the author says that a puppy at six to seven months old is driven by hormones to do "things that he knows are incorrect." This detail shows that hormones can cause dogs to misbehave.

**Extended Response**

**50.** Responses will vary. Students should understand that both selections identify the pack as a central factor in the way dogs behave. Both authors claim that understanding the pack's role lies at the heart of dog training. Students may support their responses with some of the following details: a. In line 19 of the excerpt from *Cesar's Way*, the author says, "The key to my method is what I call 'the power of the pack.'" This detail shows that the pack is very important in dog behavior and training. b. In line 22 of the excerpt from *Cesar's Way*, the author says, "The concept of a 'pack' is ingrained in your dog's DNA." This detail shows that the pack mentality is a key part of dog behavior. c. In lines 22–23 of the excerpt from *Cesar's Way*, the author says, "In the pack, there are only two roles: the role of leader and the role of follower." This detail shows that a dog's submissive or dominant behavior stems from the idea of the pack. d. In line 24 of the excerpt from *Dog Training Basics*, the author says that "puppies learn which dogs are dominant or submissive" from the pack. This detail shows that the pack provides dogs with a model for behavior. e. In line 29 of the excerpt from *Dog Training Basics*, the author says, "the puppy learns social behaviors from his dog pack." This detail shows that the pack teaches young dogs the correct way to behave.

**Vocabulary**

**1.** D
**2.** A
**3.** C
**4.** B
**5.** B
**6.** D
**7.** C
**8.** A
**9.** C
**10.** A
**11.** B
**12.** D
**13.** D
**14.** A
**15.** C
**16.** B

**1.** B
**2.** C
**3.** A
**4.** B
**5.** D
**6.** C
**7.** C
**8.** A
**9.** B
**10.** D
**11.** B
**12.** A
**13.** A
**14.** B
**15.** D
**16.** D
**17.** A
**18.** B
**19.** D
**20.** C

**Writing**

Rubric: Interpretive Essay

1. Includes a thesis statement that identifies the key points the writer will discuss
2. Supports key points with evidence—details, examples, or quotations from the text
3. Identifies the author and title of the work in an interesting introduction
4. Provides plot details as needed to help the reader understand the interpretation
5. Summarizes the interpretation in a conclusion and tells why the story is interesting or important
6. Has an appropriate tone for the audience and purpose
7. Uses precise language to examine and explain the work
8. Varies sentence structures

9. Uses correct grammar, spelling, and punctuation

## Benchmark Test 3

**Comprehension**

**1.** B
**2.** C
**3.** A
**4.** B
**5.** B
**6.** D

**Comprehension**

**7.** A
**8.** C
**9.** D
**10.** C
**11.** B
**12.** A

**Comprehension**

**13.** C
**14.** D

**Written Response**

**Short Response**

**15.** Responses will vary. Students may say that the two selections emphasize hospitality, love, and compassion as cultural values. Students may support their responses with two of the following details: a. In the myth, Baucis and Philemon show hospitality when they welcome the strangers "warmly" (line 9 In "Pirate Grace," the narrator says that "it was the custom for all Gaelic chieftains to offer hospitality to any member of another friendly clan" (line 14) Later, Pirate Grace asks the Lord of Howth's servant, "Has he forgotten the rule of hospitality?" (line 51) and in the end, Pirate Grace makes the Lord of Howth vow always to hold a place at his dining table for visitors (line 100) These details support the idea that both stories emphasize hospitality as a cultural value. b. In describing Baucis and Philemon's marriage, the narrator says that "their love for each other remained as strong as it had been on their wedding day" (lines 3–4) In "Pirate Grace," the Lord of Howth is "beside himself with fear" when he loses his son, and the narrator refers to the Lord's son as "his beloved son" (lines 75–76) These details support the idea that both stories emphasize love as a cultural value. c. In the myth, the narrator says that Baucis and Philemon wept when they saw their neighbors' homes destroyed (line 20) In the legend, when the Lord of Howth comes to Grace's castle to rescue his son, the narrator says that Grace "felt sorry for the man, and for his child" (lines 92–93) Furthermore, in the end Grace shows mercy and returns the Lord's son. These details support the idea that both stories emphasize compassion as a cultural value.

**16.** Responses will vary. Students may identify and explain one of the following conflicts: a. At the beginning of the legend, a wet and hungry Grace appears at the Lord of Howth's castle. However, the Lord does not allow her to enter the castle or join him at dinner (lines 21–57) This is an external conflict because it occurs between two characters. b. When the Lord of Howth discovers that his son has been kidnapped, he must reconcile his fear of Grace with his desire to rescue his son (lines 80–85) This is an internal conflict because it takes place within the Lord of Howth's mind. c. After declaring that he isn't afraid of Grace, the Lord of Howth must face her and beg her forgiveness so that he can get his son back (lines 74–76) The conflict between the two characters is external, but the conflict within the Lord of Howth's mind is internal.

**Extended Response**

**17.** Responses will vary. Students should recognize that both selections share the universal theme that generosity, hospitality, and kindness are admirable qualities and that selfishness and unkindness are destructive qualities. Students may support their responses with some the following details: a. Baucis and Philemon demonstrate generosity and hospitality when they welcome the strangers into their cottage and prepare a meal for them (lines 8–16 In turn, the gods reward the couple by sparing them and honoring their wishes (lines 22–23) The fact that Baucis and Philemon are rewarded demonstrates the universal theme that generosity and hospitality are admirable qualities. b. In "Baucis and Philemon," most of the Phrygians refuse to give the strangers shelter (lines 6–7) Later, the Phrygians are punished for their behavior (lines 16–20) The fact that the Phrygians are punished demonstrates the universal theme that selfishness and unkindness are destructive qualities. c. In "Pirate Grace," the Lord of Howth refuses to let Grace and her men into his castle to eat (lines 30–40) Later, the Lord is punished when Grace kidnaps his son to teach him a lesson (lines 56–70) The fact that the Lord of Howth is punished demonstrates the universal theme that selfishness and unkindness are destructive qualities. d. In "Pirate Grace," Grace's reason for kidnapping the son of the Lord of Howth is to teach the father a lesson about hospitality. In the end, she returns his son and offers the Lord of Howth a meal at her table (lines 102–104) The Lord of Howth also vows always to leave an open seat at his dinner table (lines 99–101) The story's ending demonstrates the universal themes that generosity and hospitality are admirable qualities and that selfishness and unkindness are destructive qualities.

**Comprehension**

**1.** C
**2.** A
**3.** D
**4.** B

**Comprehension**

**5.** A
**6.** B
**7.** D
**8.** B
**9.** C
**10.** B
**11.** D
**12.** D

**Comprehension**

**13.** C
**14.** B

**Written Response**

**Short Response**

**15.** Responses will vary. Students should understand that the number of times the dog thumps its tail is based on how well the farmer knows the person who is passing by. Students may support their responses with one or two of the following details: a. According to line 15, the dog thumps its tail more than four times if the person passing by is a good friend. b. According to lines 18–19, the dog thumps its tail "with all its might," suggesting that the people passing by are very good friends. The farmer can assume from the dog's thumping that the people outside are Sam Rogers and Dave Merryman. c. In line 20, the dog cannot stop thumping its tail "for delight." The dog's joy tells the farmer that Sam Rogers and Dave Merryman—both of whom are good friends—are passing by outside.

**16.** Responses will vary. Students may suggest that the speaker's feelings change from indifference to respect and compassion. Students may support their responses with one or two of the following details: a. The speaker says "You wouldn't have looked twice at her" (line 9), suggesting that the speaker has no strong feelings one way or the other about the dog before the action of the poem takes place. b. The speaker notes that "It was clear she loved the man" (line 14), suggesting that the speaker has a kind of detached respect for the dog. c. The speaker begins to worry about the man and his dog (lines 41–42), suggesting that the speaker develops feelings of compassion for the dog when she disappears. d. The villagers search all morning for the man and his dog, lining up and calling to one another (lines 43–45). The speaker's dedication to searching for the dog reveals a concern for the animal's safety. e. The speaker joins the other villagers in praising the dog, giving her milk, and calling her by her name when everyone realizes that she saved the man's life (lines 64–66). This kindness suggests that the speaker respects the dog for her loyalty. f. In line 72, the speaker expresses disapproval at the man's selling the dog. This disapproval suggests that the speaker feels compassion for the dog because of her loyalty to her owner.

**Extended Response**

**17.** Responses will vary. Students may suggest that the imagery in "Hound on the Church Porch" reveals that the farmer and his dog have a fond relationship. Students may support their responses with some of the following details: a. The farmer's dog makes a "pleasant sound" with its tail every time a friend goes by (line 9). The dog's pleasant demeanor suggests that it loves and respects the farmer and the farmer's friends. b. The farmer listens closely every time his dog thumps its tail (line 12). By listening closely, the farmer shows that he trusts and respects his dog. c. The farmer "glowed all through" (line 21) at the sound of his hound's thumping tail. His glowing appearance suggests that he and his dog have a fond relationship. d. The narrator says that "every inch of him filled out with pride" (line 25) contemplating the friendships he has with those walking by outside. The farmer's pride stems from his appreciation and respect for his hound. Students may suggest that the imagery in "A Man in Our Village" reveals that the dog loves her owner but that the owner's feelings toward his dog are mixed. Students may support their responses with the following details: a. The dog's coat is "unkempt" (line 7) and she is described as "small and thin" (line 8). The dog's appearance suggests that her owner does not take good care of her. b. The dog frequently stays "behind the man / watching his every step, staying / close to his heels, watching him" (lines 11–13). The dog's attentiveness, coupled with the repetition of "watching," suggests that the dog is devoted to the man and his safety. c. The narrator says that "nobody patted her or fondled her ears" (line 19), which suggests that even the dog's owner does not give her affection. d. The narrator describes the dog as being "as frail . . . as his winter shadow" (lines 33–34). The dog's frailty suggests that she is malnourished and that she is not adequately cared for. e. When the villagers find the man and his dog, she has "crept and curled herself" over the man's heart (line 60). Her position on the man's chest suggests that she has kept him alive with the warmth of her body, thus revealing her devotion to her owner.

**Comprehension**

**1.** A
**2.** C
**3.** C
**4.** D
**5.** A

**Comprehension**

**6.** D
**7.** B
**8.** B
**9.** C
**10.** B

**Comprehension**

**11.** D
**12.** B

**Written Response**

**Short Response**

**13.** Responses will vary. Students may cite two of the following details: a. According to the review, *The Prairie Builders* is exciting and begins with a suspenseful scene (lines 1–2) The fact that the book begins in an exciting, suspenseful way supports the reviewer's claim that the book is written for children. b. According to the review, Collard uses colorful narrative, vivid description, and gorgeous photographs (lines 7–8 The inclusion of vivid descriptions and colorful photographs supports the reviewer's claim that *The Prairie Builders* is written for children. c. According to the review, Collard uses clear and simple terms to convey scientific information (line 12) The fact that Collard simplifies complicated information supports the reviewer's claim that *The Prairie Builders* is written for children. d. According to the review, Collard shows children working as volunteers (lines 17–19) and children enjoy reading about interesting things other children are doing. The inclusion of this detail about children supports the reviewer's claim that *The Prairie Builders* is written for children.

**14.** Responses will vary. Students may say that the fire crew is careful, experienced, and well prepared. Students may cite one or two of the following details to support their responses: a. According to the excerpt, the crew starts the fire on day when the conditions are ideal (lines 2–3) he ideal conditions suggest that the crew is experienced. b. According to the excerpt, Drobney wants to double-check everything before proceeding (line 4) Her thoroughness suggests that she and her crew are careful and experienced. c. According to the excerpt, the crew members carry special tools to extinguish stray embers (lines 14–16) The fact that they carry such tools suggests that the crew members are careful, experienced, and well prepared. d. According to the excerpt, fire engines and crews are standing by in case the fire gets out of control (lines 16–17) The presence of fire engines and crews suggests that the fire starters are experienced and well prepared.

**Extended Response**

**15.** Responses will vary. Some students may suggest that the reviewer exaggerates the strengths of Collard's book, but most will agree that it is a fair assessment. Students may cite some of the following details to support their responses: a. The reviewer claims that Collard "condenses years of complicated history" (line 11) In lines 36–37 of the excerpt, Collard condenses the European settlers' first contact with the prairie into one sentence: "Amazingly, when Europeans first saw the prairie, they . . . called it "The Great American desert" In line 51 of the excerpt, Collard condenses six decades into one sentence: "And for almost a century, no one seemed to miss them" Both examples support the reviewer's claim that Collard condenses years of complicated history. b. The reviewer claims that Collard "conveys scientific information in clear and simple terms" (line 12). In lines 26–35 of the excerpt, Collard explains what an ecosystem is by describing how the prairie looked long ago Later, Collard uses an analogy of a eight-by-seven-foot parcel of a football field to demonstrate one-tenth of one percent of the original 36 million acres of Iowa prairie that remained in the early 1900s (lines 46–49) Collard's straightforward description of the tallgrass prairie ecosystem and analogy of the football field support the reviewer's claim that Collard conveys scientific information in clear and simple terms. c. The reviewer claims that Collard "makes the narrative personal, using relevant dialogue and letting the participants speak for themselves" (lines 14–15) In the first section of the excerpt from *The Prairie Builders,* Collard focuses on Pauline Drobney, using personal and relevant dialogue: "'How's it look?' she asks. 'Everyone ready? The wind staying in check?'" (line 5) Later, in lines 66–71, Collard quotes Congressman Neal Smith at length, using Smith's words to tell the story of how he found the land for the Wildlife Preserve Collard's focus on Drobney and the quote from Smith support the reviewer's claim that Collard makes the narrative personal, uses relevant dialogue, and lets the participants speak for themselves.

**Vocabulary**

**1.** B
**2.** D
**3.** A
**4.** C
**5.** B
**6.** A
**7.** C
**8.** D
**9.** B
**10.** C
**11.** A
**12.** D
**13.** C
**14.** D
**15.** A
**16.** B

**1.** D
**2.** B
**3.** C
**4.** C
**5.** A
**6.** D
**7.** C
**8.** C
**9.** D
**10.** A
**11.** D
**12.** A
**13.** C
**14.** B
**15.** A
**16.** C
**17.** B
**18.** C
**19.** B
**20.** A

**Writing and Grammar**

Rubric: Personal Response to a Poem
Clearly presents an overall response to the work
Supports key points with details and quotations
Identifies the title and author of the work in the introduction
Gives enough information about the work for readers to understand the response
Includes transitional words and phrases
Summarizes the response in a conclusion
Tone is honest and engaging
Uses literary terms when describing the work
Varies sentence beginnings
Uses correct grammar, spelling, and punctuation

## Benchmark Test 4

**Comprehension**

**1.** D
**2.** A
**3.** C
**4.** B
**5.** B
**6.** D
**7.** C
**8.** B

**Written Response**

**Short Response**

**9.** Responses will vary. Students may suggest that Pierre is a kind, gentle person. Students may also suggest that Pierre is a religious person or that he has an extraordinary connection with animals. Students may support their responses with one of the following details: a. In line 14, Pierre says that Joseph is "kind," "gentle," and "faithful" These words, which also describe Pierre's own character, suggest that Pierre is a kind, gentle soul because he recognizes these qualities in Joseph. These observations also suggest that Pierre has a strong connection with animals. b. In line 15, Pierre says Joseph has "a beautiful spirit" This observation also suggests that Pierre is a kind, gentle soul because he sees Joseph's beautiful spirit. His observation also suggests that Pierre has a strong connection with animals. c. Pierre's decision to name the horse Joseph after the saint suggests that he is a religious person.

**10.** Responses will vary. Students should recognize that Pierre's internal conflict is between his advancing age and his desire to keep working with Joseph or his dependence on Joseph for survival. This conflict is resolved when Joseph dies and Pierre follows because he cannot survive without his friend. Students may support their responses with one or two of the following details: a. Pierre is "panic-stricken at the thought of not driving Joseph every day" (lines 76–77) Pierre's panic reveals the main conflict that he must reconcile his growing age with his desire to keep working with Joseph or his dependence on Joseph for survival. b. Pierre cannot express his grief when Joseph dies, saying "No . . . no . . . you don't understand, Jacques" (lines 97–98) . Pierre's inability to express his grief reveals the main conflict that he must reconcile his growing age with his desire to work with Joseph or his dependence on the horse for survival. c. After learning of Joseph's death, Pierre is so distraught that he does not hear the oncoming truck (lines 111–113) . Pierre's death resolves the conflict because he cannot live without Joseph.

**Extended Response**

**11.** Responses will vary. Students may suggest that the theme of the story is that trust and commitment lie at the heart of true friendship, and that the trust and commitment Pierre and Joseph share exemplify true friendship. Students may support their responses with some of the following details: a. According to the narrator, Pierre "used to boast that he didn't need reins—he never touched them" (18–19) to guide Joseph, showing the depth of his trust in his horse. This trust supports the theme that trust and commitment lie at the heart of true friendship. b. According to the narrator, Joseph seemed to smile at Pierre (lines 22–23) , suggesting the horse's commitment to his human friend. This commitment supports the theme that trust and commitment lie at the heart of true friendship. c. In lines 36–37, Pierre says that "a blind man" could work with Joseph , foreshadowing the degree to which he will come to depend on his friend. This dependence supports the theme that trust and commitment lie at the heart of true friendship. d. Jacques tells the president that Pierre and Joseph "share a secret," (line 69) , revealing the depth and trust in their relationship. This secretive quality supports the theme that trust and commitment lie at the heart of true friendship. e. According to the narrator, when Pierre learns of Joseph's death, "It was as though his heart and soul had died" (lines 106–107) . Pierre's response to Joseph's death reveals the degree to which the two characters trusted each other and were committed to each other, which supports the theme that trust and commitment lie at the heart of true friendship.

**Comprehension**

**12.** B
**13.** C
**14.** D
**15.** A
**16.** B
**17.** C
**18.** B
**19.** A
**20.** B
**21.** D
**22.** B
**23.** A

**Written Response**

**Short Response**

**24.** Responses will vary. Students should recognize that the author's main claim is that over-scheduling is harmful for children. Students may recognize that the author states her claim explicitly in the following sentence: "All work and no play could make for some very messed-up kids" (line 31)

**25.** Responses will vary. Students may cite two of the following examples:

a. In lines 6–7, the author says that Steven Guzman will "squeeze in" time with friends "if he's lucky" . These examples of loaded language reveal the author's bias about Steven's—and children like him—having too little free time. b. In line 32, the author simplifies the conclusions of child experts by saying that "fun is good" . This example of loaded language reveals that the author is biased in favor of allowing children more free time. c. In line 39, the author says that children's free time is "rapidly diminishing". This example of loaded language reveals that the author is biased against how little free time children have.

**Extended Response**

**26.** Responses will vary. Some students may suggest that the author uses appeals to authority more frequently than other types of appeals. Other students may suggest that the author uses a variety of persuasive techniques and that she does not use one type more than the others. Students may support their responses with some of the following examples: a. In lines 7–8, the author uses a testimonial from Steven Guzman to support her argument that children are overscheduled: "Sometimes I think, like, since I'm a kid, I need to enjoy my life . . . . But I don't have time for that" . This example of testimonial indicates that the author uses a variety of persuasive techniques to support her argument. b. In lines 10–13, the author uses appeal to authority by citing a survey conducted by researchers at the University of Michigan's Institute for Social Research . This example, when considered with other persuasive techniques, may indicate that the author uses appeal to authority most often to support her argument. c. In lines 25–27, the author uses appeal to authority by citing sociologist Sandra Hofferth . This example, when considered with other persuasive techniques, may indicate that the author uses appeal to authority most often to support her argument. d. In line 31, the author uses appeal to fear by stating that "All work and no play could make for some very messed-up kids" . This example of emotional appeal indicates that the author uses a variety of persuasive techniques to support her argument. e. In line 32, the author uses logical appeal by stating that "fun is good" . This example of logical appeal indicates that the author uses a variety of persuasive techniques to support her argument. f. In lines 32–35, the author uses appeal to authority by citing T. Berry Brazelton, a Harvard pediatrician who has written several books on parenting.. This example, when considered with other persuasive techniques, may indicate that the author uses appeal to authority most often to support her argument. g. In lines 37–38, the author uses appeal to authority and appeal to fear by citing Brazelton's warning that "If we don't pay attention to this, we're going to create obsessive-compulsive people". This emotional appeal indicates that the author uses a variety of persuasive techniques to support her argument, while the expert quotation suggests that the author uses appeal to authority most often.

**Comprehension**

**27.** A
**28.** B
**29.** D
**30.** C
**31.** D
**32.** A
**33.** B
**34.** C

**Comprehension**

**35.** B
**36.** B
**37.** D
**38.** A
**39.** C
**40.** D
**41.** A

**42.** B
**43.** A
**44.** A

**Written Response**

**Short Response**

**45.** Responses will vary. Students may say that the main idea of the excerpt from *Now Is Your Time!* is that Latimer used his extraordinary intelligence and skill to achieve goals that were beyond the reach of most African Americans of his time. Students may support their responses with two of the following details: a. In the excerpt from *Now Is Your Time!* Myers writes that Latimer "believed in himself and in his own mental capacities" (lines 3–4) . This sentence supports the main idea that Latimer used his intelligence and skills to achieve his goals. b. Myers points out that Latimer rose to great success as an inventor despite being the "son of a man held in bondage" (line 36) . This detail supports the main idea that Latimer achieved goals that were beyond the reach of most African Americans of his time. c. Myers writes that "Latimer's ability outweighed all other factors" (lines 41–42) , including his race. This detail supports the main idea that Latimer used his intelligence and skills to achieve goals that were beyond the reach of most African Americans of his time.

**46.** Responses will vary. Students may include two of the following details: a. In "Lighting," the author notes that Edison created a system for distributing electricity to homes (text box). This detail supports the idea that electric lighting changed the way people live today. b. In the final section of "Lighting," the author lists many modern uses for artificial lighting (lines 51–55) , demonstrating how electric lighting has changed the way people live today. c. In the excerpt from *Now Is Your Time!* Myers points out that incandescent lighting was "safer, cleaner, and much more convenient" than gas lighting (lines 25–26) , showing that electric lighting has changed the way people live today. d. Myers lists several cities where Latimer helped install electric lighting systems (lines 31–33) , showing the widespread effects of electric lighting and how it changed the way people live.

**Extended Response**

**47.** Responses will vary. Students should note that while he was not the only inventor who helped develop electric lighting, Edison invented the first practical incandescent lightbulb, pumping air out of a glass bulb so the filament would not burn out quickly. Students should also note that Edison helped build a system for delivering electric lighting to homes and worked with a group of experts that included Lewis Latimer. Students may support their responses with some of the following details: a. According to "Lighting," Edison built "the first practical electric light" (text box). Myers verifies this fact: "In 1879 Thomas Alva Edison invented the incandescent light bulb" (line 11) . Edison's invention of the lightbulb proves that he was a leader in the development of electric lighting. b. In "Lighting," the author explains that Edison encased the filament in a lightbulb so that it didn't burn away too quickly (line 33) , showing that his idea helped bring about modern lighting. c. The author of "Lighting" notes that "other inventors were working on lightbulbs" (text box) and suggests that Edison's real achievement was "to demonstrate the first practical electric light." d. The author of "Lighting" notes that Edison "devised a system to make electricity and distribute it to many homes" and "set up a company to mass-produce his lightbulbs" (text box). These details show that Edison helped popularize electric lighting. e. In the excerpt from *Now Is Your Time!* Myers writes that Edison, along with fellow inventors, "changed the way we now live in cities" (line 30) by popularizing electric lighting.

**Vocabulary**

**1.** C
**2.** D
**3.** C
**4.** A
**5.** D
**6.** C
**7.** B
**8.** A
**9.** B
**10.** D
**11.** C
**12.** A
**13.** C
**14.** D
**15.** B
**16.** B

**Writing and Grammar**

**1.** A
**2.** D
**3.** D
**4.** B
**5.** A
**6.** B
**7.** C
**8.** A
**9.** C
**10.** A
**11.** D
**12.** D
**13.** A
**14.** B
**15.** A
**16.** B
**17.** C
**18.** C
**19.** A
**20.** B

**Writing**

Rubric: Persuasive Essay
1. Presents a thesis statement taking a position on a clearly identified issue
2. Uses convincing details to support the position
3. Answers opposing arguments and counterclaims
4. Explains the issue in a memorable introduction
5. Uses transitions to create a consistent organizational pattern 6. Concludes by summarizing the position and issuing a call to action
7. Reflects the writer's commitment to his or her ideas
8. Uses persuasive language effectively
9. Varies sentence lengths and structures
10. Uses correct grammar, spelling, and punctuation

**Grade 7 Unit 1 Unit Test**
**Reading Comprehension Item Analysis**

| | Test A | Test B/C |
|---|---|---|
| 1 Plot stages: | | 22, 23 |
| • exposition, | 22 | 17 |
| • conflict (internal and external), | 4, 19 | 4, 20 |
| • rising action, | 22 | 13 |
| • climax, | 9, 22 | 9 |
| • falling action, | 16, 22 | 21 |
| • resolution | 22 | 21 |
| 2 Setting (in fiction and in nonfiction) | 1, 6, 14, 20 | 1, 13, 18, 22 |
| 3 Sequence, identify | 8, 10, 12 | 8, 11, 15 |
| 4 Cause and effect, recognize | 7, 11, 15 | 7, 10, 14, 16 |
| 5 Make inferences | 2, 5, 17, 21 | 2, 5, 19 |
| 6 Use chronological order | 3, 13, 18 | 3, 6, 12 |

**Grade 7 Unit 1 Unit Test**
**Vocabulary Item Analysis**

| | Test A | Test B/C |
|---|---|---|
| 1 Latin roots | 1, 2, 3 | 1, 2, 3 |
| 2 Prefixes & Suffixes | 4, 5, 6 | 4, 5, 6 |
| 3 Analogies | 7, 8, 9 | 7, 8, 9 |

**Grade 7 Unit 1 Unit Test**
**Writing and Grammar Item Analysis**

| | Test A | Test B/C |
|---|---|---|
| 1 Avoids run-on sentences | 3, 4 | 3, 4 |
| 2 Punctuates possessives correctly | 7, 9 | 7, 9 |
| 3 Maintains pronoun-antecedent agreement | 6, 11 | 6, 11 |
| 4 Uses correct pronoun case | 10, 12 | 10, 12 |
| 5 Introduction: | | |
| • Identifies the topic | 1 | 1 |
| • Explains why the topic is significant | 2 | 2 |
| 6 Uses sensory details to show the reader what the person or place is like | 5, 8 | 5, 8 |

## Grade 7 Unit 2 Unit Test
## Reading Comprehension Item Analysis

| | Test A | Test B/C |
|---|---|---|
| 1 Character traits | 1, 9, 12, 13, 19, 23 | 1, 9, 13, 19 |
| 2 Characterization | 5, 6, 8, 15, 23 | 3, 7, 16, 21 |
| 3 Point of view (first person, limited, omniscient) | 2, 10, 11 | 2, 5, 11 |
| 4 Make inferences | 5, 6, 12, 23 | 3, 9, 15, 21 |
| 5 Visualize | 3, 14, 21 | 4, 12, 15 |
| 6 Draw conclusions | 17, 18, 20, 22 | 10, 14, 18, 20, 22 |
| 7 Predict | 4, 7, 16 | 6, 8, 17 |

## Grade 7 Unit 2 Unit Test
## Vocabulary Item Analysis

| | Test A | Test B/C |
|---|---|---|
| 1 Idioms | 1, 2, 3, 4 | 1, 2, 3, 4 |
| 2 Similes | 5, 6, 7, 8 | 5, 6, 7, 8 |

## Grade 7 Unit 2 Unit Test
## Writing and Grammar Item Analysis

| | Test A | Test B/C |
|---|---|---|
| 1 Uses correct verb tense | 6, 7 | 7, 8 |
| 2 Compares correctly (comparative, superlative) | 5, 10 | 4, 11 |
| 3 Avoids misplaced modifiers | 3, 9 | 3, 10 |
| 4 Introduction | | |
| • Identifies the characters or subjects being compared and/or contrasted | 1 | 1 |
| • Includes a thesis statement that identifies similarities and/or differences | 2 | 2 |
| 5 Organization | | |
| • Includes a strong introduction and a satisfying conclusion | 12 | 12 |
| • Follows a clear organizational pattern | 11 | 6 |
| 6 Connects ideas with transitions | 4, 8 | 5, 9 |

**Grade 7 Unit 3 Unit Test**
**Reading Comprehension Item Analysis**

| | Test A | Test B/C |
|---|---|---|
| 1 Comparison and contrast | 3, 14, 15, 19, 20, 21 | 14, 19, 20 |
| 2 Theme (and character) | 9, 11, 23 | 6, 10, 21 |
| 3 Symbol | 8, 10, 22 | 3, 9, 22 |
| 4 Make inferences | 2, 7, 12, 16 | 2, 7, 13, 16 |
| 5 Cause and effect | 4, 5, 13,17 | 5, 8, 11, 12, 15, 17 |
| 6 Identify author's perspective | 1, 6, 18 | 1, 4, 18 |

**Grade 7 Unit 3 Unit Test**
**Vocabulary Item Analysis**

| | Test A | Test B/C |
|---|---|---|
| 1 Connotation and denotation | 1, 2, 3, 4 | 1, 2, 3, 4 |
| 2 Context clues | 5, 6, 7, 8 | 5, 6, 7, 8 |

**Grade 7 Unit 3 Unit Test**
**Vocabulary Item Analysis**

| | Test A | Test B/C |
|---|---|---|
| 1 Punctuates dialogue correctly | 4, 11 | 3, 10 |
| 2 Combines sentences (coordinating conjunctions) | 2, 6 | 2, 5 |
| 3 Combines clauses: independent and dependent | 7, 12 | 7, 11 |
| 4 Ideas: | | |
| • Develops and resolves a central conflict | 5 | 4 |
| • Includes descriptive details that reveal the setting and characters | 9 | 8 |
| 5 Organization: | | |
| • Introduces the characters, setting, or action in a way that gets a reader's attention | 1 | 1 |
| • Follows a clear sequence of events | 8 | 6 |
| 6 Uses sensory language to show what fictional characters and places are like | 3, 10 | 9, 12 |

## Grade 7 Unit 4 Unit Test
## Reading Comprehension Item Analysis

| | Test A | | Test B/C | |
|---|---|---|---|---|
| | *After 20 Years* | *Getups* | *After 20 Years* | *Getups* |
| 1 Mood | 2, 6 | 9 | 2, 6, 11 | 5 |
| 2 Style | | 11 | 12 | 8, 11 |
| • Word choice | 4 | 2 | | |
| • Sentence Structure | 3 | | | |
| 3 Tone | 3, 8 | 5, 8 | 3, 5 | 3, 12 |
| 4 Summarize | 1, 5, 11 | | 1, 8, 10 | |
| 5 Understand dialogue | 4, 7, 9 | | 4, 7, 9 | |
| 6 Distinguish fact from opinion | | 1, 7, 10 | 4, 7, 9 | |
| 7 Monitor (use clarify to monitor) | 10 | 2, 6 | | 1, 6, 10 |

## Grade 7 Unit 4 Unit Test
## Vocabulary Item Analysis

| | Test A | Test B/C |
|---|---|---|
| 1 Synonyms | 1, 2, 3, 4 | 1, 2, 3, 4 |
| 2 Literal and Figurative Meanings | 5, 6, 7, 8 | 5, 6, 7, 8 |

## Grade 7 Unit 4 Unit Test
## Writing and Grammar Item Analysis

| | Test A | Test B/C |
|---|---|---|
| 1 Maintains subject-verb agreement: agree in number | 4, 10 | 4, 10 |
| 2 Maintains subject-verb agreement: with compound subject | 5, 6 | 5, 6 |
| 3 Introduction: | | |
| • Includes a thesis statement that identifies the key points the writer will discuss | 3 | 3 |
| • Identifies the author and title of the work in an interesting introduction | 2 | 2 |
| 4 Body: | | |
| • Supports key points with evidence—details, examples, or quotations from the text | 7 | 7 |
| • Provides plot details as needed to help the reader understand the interpretation | 9 | 9 |
| 5 Has an appropriate tone for the audience and purpose | 1, 12 | 1, 12 |
| 6 Uses precise language to examine and explain the work | 8, 11 | 8, 11 |

## Grade 7 Unit 5 Unit Test
## Reading Comprehension Item Analysis

| | Test A | Test B/C |
|---|---|---|
| 1 Imagery | 7, 9, 14, 17, 20, 22, 23, 25 | 7, 12, 21, 22, 23, 27 |
| 2 Figurative language<br>• Figurative language and mood (metaphor, personification) | 2, 8, 11<br>19 | 8, 15, 17<br>1 |
| 3 Make inferences | 4, 14, 15, 21, 24, 26 | 6, 14, 24, 25, 26, 28 |
| 4 Sound devices (rhyme/rhyme scheme, analysis of rhyme, repetition, onomatopoeia, alliteration, rhythm and meter) | 1, 3, 5, 10, 18 | 2, 5, 11, 16 |
| 5 Lyric Poetry (narrative, haiku, humorous, reading a narrative poem) | 6, 13, 16 | 3, 10, 13 |
| 6 Poetic form: line and stanza<br>(free verse) | 5, 12, 18<br>12 | 4, 9, 13<br>18 |
| 7 Speaker, understand | 4, 14, 15, 16 | 3, 6, 10, 14 |

## Grade 7 Unit 5 Unit Test
## Vocabulary Skills Item Analysis

| | Test A | Test B/C |
|---|---|---|
| Connotation | 1, 2, 3, 4 | 1, 2, 3, 4 |

## Grade 7 Unit 5 Unit Test
## Writing and Grammar Item Analysis

| | Test A | Test B/C |
|---|---|---|
| 1 Uses correct sentence type (declarative, interrogative, imperative, exclamatory) | 1, 7 | 1, 8 |
| 2 Uses the active voice | 8, 12 | 9, 12 |
| 3 Introduction<br>• Presents overall response to the work<br>• Identifies the title and author of the work in the introduction | <br>4<br>3 | <br>4<br>3 |
| 4 Supports key points with details and quotations | 9, 11 | 6, 10 |
| Includes transitional words and phrases | 2, 10 | 2, 11 |
| Uses literary terms when describing the work | 5, 6 | 5, 7 |

## Grade 7 Unit 6 Unit Test
## Reading Comprehension Item Analysis

| | Test A | Test B/C |
|---|---|---|
| 1 Characteristics of myths and legends | 1, 12, 16, 19, 23 | 2, 12, 16, 20 |
| 2 Cultural values (in myths, legends)<br>• Universal and recurring theme | 6, 9, 22<br>20 | 4, 9, 22<br>19 |
| 3 Cause and effect | 2, 10, 13 | 1, 10, 13 |
| 4 Chronological order | 3, 5, 7, 14, 17 | 3, 6, 8, 14, 17 |
| 5 Monitoring | 4, 8, 15, 18 | 5, 7, 15, 18 |
| 6 Summarize | 4, 11, 21 | 5, 11, 21 |

## Grade 7 Unit 6 Unit Test
## Vocabulary Item Analysis

| | Test A | Test B/C |
|---|---|---|
| 1 Compound words | 1, 2, 3, 4 | 1, 2, 3, 4 |
| 2 Homographs | 5, 6, 7, 8 | 5, 6, 7, 8 |

## Grade 7 Unit 6 Unit Test
## Writing and Grammar Item Analysis

| | Test A | Test B/C |
|---|---|---|
| 1 Uses correct sentence structure: independent clause in simple sentence/compound sentence | 5, 8 | 5, 8 |
| 2 Uses correct sentence structure: complex sentences | 1, 3 | 1, 3 |
| 3 Ideas<br>• Identifies a true cause-and-effect relationship<br>• Presents a thesis statement that explains the connection between causes and effects<br>• Includes facts, examples, and other details to support each cause and effect | <br>7<br>2<br>4 | <br>2, 7<br>2<br>4 |
| 4 Organization<br>• Presents causes and effects in a sensible order<br>• Shows the relationship between causes and effects by using transitions<br>• Has an interesting introduction and a conclusion that summarizes the cause-and-effect relationship | <br>9<br>6<br>10 | <br>9<br>6<br>10 |
| 5 Has a tone that is appropriate for the audience and purpose | 11, 12 | 11, 12 |

**Grade 7 Unit 7 Unit Test**
**Reading Comprehension Item Analysis**

| | Test A | Test B/C |
|---|---|---|
| 1 Biography and Autobiography | 1, 5, 9 | 1, 8, 10, 12 |
| 2 Chronological order | 3, 6, 7, 18 | 4, 6, 7, 20 |
| 3 Make inferences | 2, 4, 8, 10 | 2, 3, 9, 21 |
| 4 Summarize | 11, 13, 21, 22 | 5, 13, 22, 23, 24 |
| 5 Synthesize | 10, 12, 13, 22 | 9, 11, 14 |
| 6 Identify treatment and scope of article | 14, 15, 16, 20 | 16, 18, 23, 24 |
| 7 Evaluate texts for usefulness | 15, 17, 19 | 15, 17,19 |

**Grade 7 Unit 7 Unit Test**
**Vocabulary Item Analysis**

| | Test A | Test B/C |
|---|---|---|
| 1 Latin words and roots | 1, 2, 3, 4 | 1, 2, 3, 4 |
| 2 Base words | 5, 6, 7, 8 | 5, 6, 7, 8 |

**Grade 7 Unit 7 Unit Test**
**Writing and Grammar Item Analysis**

| | Test A | Test B/C |
|---|---|---|
| 1 Capitalizes correctly: proper nouns | 4, 6 | 3, 7 |
| 2 Punctuates Titles Correctly: quotation marks, italics | 3, 8 | 2, 10 |
| Description: | | |
| • Focuses on a single experience | 12 | 12 |
| • Re-creates the event with descriptive details and dialogue | 9 | 11 |
| • Gets the reader's attention with an interesting introduction | 1 | 1 |
| • Brings the event alive for the reader by using sensory language | 2 | 5 |
| 3 Makes the order of events clear by using transitional words and phrases | 5, 7 | 6, 9 |
| 4 Uses a variety of sentence types (statements, questions, commands, and exclamations) | 10, 11 | 4, 8 |

## Grade 7 Unit 8 Unit Test
## Reading Comprehension Item Analysis

| | Test A | Test B/C |
|---|---|---|
| 1 Text features | 2, 6, 8, 24 | 1, 2, 4, 6, 7, 9, 24 |
| 2 Fact and opinion | 3, 11, 16, 17, 23 | 5, 10, 24 |
| 3 Elements of argument: claim, support, counterargument | 10, 14, 20 | 11, 13, 19 |
| 4 Main idea and supporting details | 9, 21, 25 | 17, 18, 21 |
| 5 Author's bias (Loaded Language) | 5, 15, 19 | 8, 14, 16, 25, 26 |
| 6 Patterns of organization: cause and effect, chronological order | 1, 4, 7, 18, 22 | 2, 3, 15, 22 |
| 7 Persuasive techniques | 12, 13, 25 | 12, 19, 20, 23 |

## Grade 7 Unit 8 Unit Test
## Vocabulary Item Analysis

| | Test A | Test B/C |
|---|---|---|
| 1 Idioms | 1, 2, 3 | 1, 2, 3 |
| 2 Prefixes and Latin roots and words | 4, 5, 6 | 4, 5, 6 |

## Grade 7 Unit 8 Unit Test
## Writing and Grammar Item Analysis

| | Test A | Test B/C |
|---|---|---|
| 1 Uses commas correctly: appositive phrases | 1, 9 | 1, 9 |
| 2 Uses commas correctly: introductory words and phrases, items in a series | 2, 3 | 2, 3 |
| 3 Uses colons correctly: lists, formal greeting, between numerals in the time | 4, 10 | 4, 10 |
| 4 Ideas | | |
| • Presents a thesis statement taking a position on a clearly identified issue | 5 | 5 |
| • Uses convincing details to support the position | 6 | 6 |
| 5 Organization | | |
| • Uses transitions to create a consistent organizational pattern | 7 | 7 |
| • Concludes by summarizing the position and issuing a call to action | 11 | 11 |
| 6 Uses persuasive language effectively | 8, 12 | 8, 12 |

## Grade 7 Unit 9 Unit Test
## Research Unit Item Analysis

| | | Test A | Test B/C |
|---|---|---|---|
| 1 | Using the Internet | 1, 2, 3 | 1, 2, 3, 4 |
| 2 | Using the Library and Reference Sources | 4, 5, 7 | 2, 4, 5, 6 |
| 3 | Evaluating Sources | 6, 8, 9 | 7, 8, 9 |
| 4 | Primary and Secondary Sources | 10, 11, 12 | 10, 11, 12 |
| 5 | Collecting Data | 13, 14, 15 | 13, 14, 15 |
| 6 | Paraphrasing | 17, 20 | 18, 19, 32 |
| 7 | Summarizing | 19, 21 | 16, 21 |
| 8 | Plagiarizing | 16, 18 | 17, 20 |
| 9 | Prewriting: Topic | 22, 23 | 22, 23 |
| 10 | Prewriting: Research Questions | 24, 25 | 26, 27 |
| 11 | Prewriting: Evaluate Sources | 26, 27, 34 | 24, 28, 29 |
| 12 | Researching: Source cards | 28, 29 | 30, 31 |
| 13 | Researching: Take notes | 30, 31 | 32, 33 |
| 14 | Researching: Organize, outline | 32, 33 | 25, 34 |
| 15 | Drafting: Introduction (facts to include) | 35, 36 | 35, 36 |
| 16 | Drafting: Conclusion (facts to include) | 37, 38 | 37, 39 |
| 17 | Drafting: Works Cited List | 39, 40, 41 | 40, 46, 47 |
| 18 | Revising: Introductions | 42, 43, 44 | 38, 41, 42 |
| 19 | Revising: Connected Ideas/Transitions | 45, 46, 47 | 43, 44, 45 |
| 20 | Revising: Supporting Ideas | 48, 49, 50 | 48, 49, 50 |

**Item Analysis**
**Grade 7, Benchmark Test 1**

| Skill | Passage 1 (singlet) *from* Fast Sam, Cool Clyde, and Stuff | Passage 2 (singlet) *from* Sons from Afar | Passage 3 (doublet) Lifesaver | Passage 4 (doublet) Rip Current Safety | Passage 3 and 4 Passage 3 and 4 Connecting Questions |
|---|---|---|---|---|---|
| **Reading Comprehension** | | | | | |
| Character<br>• major<br>• minor<br>• traits | 4, 16 | | | | |
| Characterization | | 21, 25, 30 | | | |
| Conflict<br>• internal/external | 8, 14 | 28 | | | |
| Plot<br>• plot stages and development<br>• flashback<br>• foreshadowing | 1, 2, 11, 12, 15 | 17 | | | |
| Point of view | 7 | 20, 23 | | | |
| Setting | 3 | 18, 19 | | | |
| Draw conclusions | | | 35 | 40 | 45 |
| Make inferences | 6, 10 | 22 | | | |
| Predict | 13 | 29 | 38 | | |
| Visualize | 5 | 24 | 31 | | |
| Sequence | 9 | 26, 27 | | | |
| Analyze writer's position | | | 37, 47 | 41 | |
| Chronological order (time and transition words) | | 34, 36 | 42 | | |
| Synthesize | | | | | 43, 44, 46, 48 |
| Cause and Effect | | | 32, 33 | 39 | |

## em Analysis
## rade 7, Benchmark Test 1

| Vocabulary Skills | Item Numbers |
| --- | --- |
| Prefixes and Suffixes | 1, 2, 3, 4 |
| Context Clues | 5, 6, 7, 8 |
| Multiple-Meaning Words | 9, 10, 11, 12 |
| Synonyms and Antonyms | 13, 14, 15, 16 |

| Writing and Grammar Skills | Item Numbers |
| --- | --- |
| Organization | 1, 20 |
| Word Choice | 3, 8, 9 |
| Transitions | 7, 19 |
| Sentence Fluency | 11, 17 |
| Complete Sentences | 4, 5 |
| Punctuation | 6, 12 |
| Pronouns | 13, 16, 18 |
| Modifiers | 10, 14 |
| Verbs | 2, 15 |

**Item Analysis**
**Grade 7, Benchmark Test 2**

| Skill | Passage 1 (singlet)<br>If I Forget Thee, Oh Earth. . . | Passage 2 (doublet)<br>*from* Cesar' Way | Passage 3 (doublet)<br>*from* Dog Training Basics | Passage 2 and 3<br>Passage 2 and 3 Connecting Questions |
|---|---|---|---|---|
| **Reading Comprehension** | | | | |
| Mood | 3, 11, 14 | | | |
| Style<br>• diction<br>• sentence structure | 9, 16, 17, 24 | | | |
| Symbol | 13, 19, 23 | | | |
| Theme<br>• identify theme<br>• topic vs. theme | 22, 26 | | | |
| Character | 6, 20, 25 | | | |
| Plot and conflict | 6, 18, 21 | | | |
| Setting | 1, 7, 12 | | | |
| Cause and effect | | 33 | 37, 41 | 49 |
| Comparison and contrast | | 29 | 38 | 46 |
| Make inferences | 5 | 27 | 39, 44 | |
| Monitor | 4 | 28, 31 | 40 | |
| Summarize plot | 2, 10, 15 | | | |
| Fact and opinion | | 30, 34, 35 | | |
| Chronological order | | | 42, 43, 48 | |
| Writer's position | | 32, 36 | 45 | |
| Synthesize | | | | 47, 50 |

**em Analysis**
**rade 7, Benchmark Test 2**

| Vocabulary Skills | Item Numbers |
|---|---|
| Thesaurus, Dictionary, Synonyms | 1, 2, 3, 4 |
| Denotation and Connotation | 5, 6, 7, 8 |
| Literal and Figurative Meanings | 9, 10, 11, 12 |
| Latin roots | 13, 14, 15, 16 |

| Writing and Grammar Skills | Item Numbers |
|---|---|
| Plot and Sequence | 7, 14, 17 |
| Characters | 1, 12, 16 |
| Resolution and Conclusion | 19, 20 |
| Word Choice | 3, 10 |
| Sentence Fluency | 8, 13 |
| Punctuation | 11, 18 |
| Combining Sentences | 2, 9 |
| Clauses | 5, 15 |
| Subject-Verb Agreement | 4, 6 |

**Item Analysis**
**Grade 7, Benchmark Test 3**

| | **Passage 1 (doublet)** | **Passage 2 (doublet)** | **Passages 1 and 2** | **Passage 3 (doublet)** |
|---|---|---|---|---|
| **Skill** | Baucis and Philemon | Pirate Grace | Passages 1 and 2 Connecting Questions | Hound on the Church Porch |
| **Reading Comprehension** | | | | |
| Cultural values from myths and legends | 3 | | 13, 15 | |
| Theme, universal | | 12 | 17 | |
| Poetic structure (3 of 5)<br>• line<br>• stanza<br>• rhyme<br>• rhythm<br>• meter | | | | 18, 19 |
| Figurative language & imagery (hit all 4)<br>• simile<br>• metaphor<br>• personification<br>• imagery | | | | 21 |
| Sound devices<br>• onomatopoeia<br>• alliteration<br>• repetition | | | | 20 |
| Speaker | | | | |
| Character | | 8, 9 | | |
| Plot and conflict | 4 | 7, 16 | | |
| Setting/Mood | 1, 2 | | | |
| Monitor | | 11 | | 32 |
| Cause and effect | 6 | | 14 | |
| Chronological order | | 10 | | |
| Visualize | 5 | | | |
| Identify opinions/ Writer's position | | | | |
| Conclusions | | | | |
| Synthesize | | | | |

| **Passage 4 (doublet)** | **Passages 3 and 4** | **Passage 5 (doublet)** | **Passage 6 (doublet)** | **Passages 5 and 6** |
|---|---|---|---|---|
| A Man in Our Village | Passages 3 and 4 Connecting Questions | Book Review of The Prairie Builders | *from* The Prairie Builders | Passages 5 and 6 Connecting Questions |
| | | | | |
| | | | | |
| | | | | |
| 22 | 30 | | | |
| 24, 28 | 34 | | | |
| 23, 27 | | | | |
| 29, 33 | | | | |
| | 31 | | | |
| | | | | |
| | 26 | | | |
| | | 36 | | |
| | | | 41, 43 | |
| | | | 42, 44 | |
| | 25 | 37 | 40 | |
| | | 35, 39, 47 | | 45 |
| | | 38 | 48 | 45 |
| | | | | 46, 49 |

## Item Analysis
## Grade 7, Benchmark Test 3

| Vocabulary Skills | Item Numbers |
| --- | --- |
| Easily Confused Words and Homographs | 1, 2, 3, 4 |
| Dictionary Use | 5, 6, 7, 8 |
| Context Clues | 9, 10, 11, 12 |
| Compound words | 13, 14, 15, 16 |

| Writing and Grammar Skills | Item Numbers |
| --- | --- |
| Organization | 10, 15 |
| Word Choice | 6, 14, 17 |
| Introduction/Conclusion | 1, 8 |
| Supporting Details | 13, 16 |
| Tone | 4, 12 |
| Sentence Types | 3, 20 |
| Active Voice | 9, 19 |
| Modifiers and Fragments | 7, 11 |
| Sentence Structure | 2, 5, 18 |

| Skill | Passage 1 (singlet) A Scent for Two | Passage 2 (singlet) Burning Out at Nine? | Passage 3 (doublet) Lighting | Passage 4 (doublet) *from* Now is Your Time! | Passages 3 and 4 Passages 3 and 4 Connecting Questions |
|---|---|---|---|---|---|
| **Reading Comprehension** | | | | | |
| Character | 5, 6, 9 | | | | |
| Plot and conflict | 2, 7, 10 | | | | |
| Setting/Mood | 1, 3, 4 | | | | |
| Theme | 8, 11 | | | | |
| Elements of an argument | | 16, 18, 24 | | | |
| Fact and opinion | | 15, 17, 23 | | | |
| Persuasive techniques | | 12, 20, 26 | | | |
| Bias | | 13, 21, 25 | | | |
| Text features | | | 28, 31, 34 | | |
| Characteristics of an autobiography/biography | | | | 36, 41, 43 | |
| Main idea and supporting details • outlining, topic sentence, take notes | | | 27, 30 | 35, 39 | 44, 45, 46 |
| Paraphrase | | 22 | 29 | 40 | |
| Synthesize and Summarize | | 14 | | | 47 |
| Patterns of organization | | | 33 | 37, 38 | |
| Avoid plagiarism | | 19 | 32 | 42 | |

**Item Analysis**
**Grade 7, Benchmark Test 4**

| Vocabulary Skills | Item Numbers |
| --- | --- |
| Denotation and Connotation | 1, 2, 3, 4 |
| Idioms | 5, 6, 7, 8 |
| Content-Area Words and Specialized Vocabulary | 9, 10, 11, 12 |
| Latin Roots/Recognizing Base Words | 13, 14, 15, 16 |

| Writing and Grammar Skills | Item Numbers |
| --- | --- |
| Thesis | 3, 6 |
| Tone | 5, 18, 19 |
| Narrow a Topic | 2, 20 |
| Develop Research Questions | 1, 9 |
| Locate Informational Sources | 12, 15 |
| Evaluate Informational Sources | 16, 17 |
| Punctuation and Capitalization | 4, 10 |
| Commas | 8, 11, 13 |
| Colons | 7, 14 |

## ART CREDITS

**Cover** Photograph by Sharon Hoogstraten.

*fluorescent and incandescent light bulbs* Illustrations by Dan Stuckenschneider (Uhl Studios); Screen shot from *World Book Online Reference Center* © 2007 World Book, Inc. By permission of the publisher. www.worldbook.com.